Lecture Notes in Computer Science 5493

Commenced Publication in 1973
Founding and Former Series Editors:
Gerhard Goos, Juris Hartmanis, and Jan van Leeuwen

Lecture Notes in Computer Science

Sølvi Ystad   Richard Kronland-Martinet
Kristoffer Jensen (Eds.)

Computer Music Modeling and Retrieval

Genesis of Meaning in Sound and Music

5th International Symposium, CMMR 2008
Copenhagen, Denmark, May 19-23, 2008
Revised Papers

 Springer

Volume Editors

Sølvi Ystad
Richard Kronland-Martinet
CNRS, Laboratoire de Mécanique et d'Acoustique (LMA)
31 chemin Joseph Aiguier, 13402 Marseille CEDEX 20, France
E-mail: {ystad, kronland}@lma.cnrs-mrs.fr

Kristoffer Jensen
Aalborg University Esbjerg
Niels Bohr Vej 8, 6700 Esbjerg, Denmark
E-mail: krist@aaue.dk

Library of Congress Control Number: 2009929553

CR Subject Classification (1998): J.5, H.5, C.3, H.5.5, G.3, I.5

LNCS Sublibrary: SL 3 – Information Systems and Application, incl. Internet/Web and HCI

ISSN   0302-9743
ISBN-10   3-642-02517-X Springer Berlin Heidelberg New York
ISBN-13   978-3-642-02517-4 Springer Berlin Heidelberg New York

springer.com

© Springer-Verlag Berlin Heidelberg 2009
Printed in Germany

Typesetting: Camera-ready by author, data conversion by Scientific Publishing Services, Chennai, India
Printed on acid-free paper   SPIN: 12696697   06/3180   5 4 3 2 1 0

Preface

CMMR is an annual event focusing on important aspects of computer music. CMMR 2008 was the fifth event in this series and was co-organized by Aalborg University Esbjerg, Denmark (http://www.aaue.dk), the Laboratoire de Mécanique et d'Acoustique, CNRS in Marseille, France (http:/www.lma.cnrs-mrs.fr) and the Network for Cross-Disciplinary Studies of Music and Meaning, University of Southern Denmark (http://www.ntsmb.dk/). The conference was held in Copenhagen, May 19–23, 2008.

The four previous editions of CMMR gathered a large number of noteworthy papers by researchers from the field of computer music. The proceedings of these conferences were published in the *Lecture Notes in Computer Science* series (LNCS 2771, LNCS 3310, LNCS 3902 and LNCS 4969). The present edition follows the lineage of the previous ones, including a collection of 21 papers specially reviewed and corrected for this proceedings volume.

The field of computer music embraces a large number of research areas that span from information retrieval, programming, artificial intelligence to acoustics, signal processing and sound modeling. In the last CMMR gatherings an increased emphasis was placed on the role of human interaction at all levels of musical practice, as well as perceptual and cognitive aspects in order to establish relations between the structure of sounds and their impact on human beings. The identification of perceptually relevant sound structures is linked to the notion of the sense of sounds, which was the title of the CMMR 2007 conference.

CMMR 2008 further expanded the "Sense of Sounds" concept by taking into account the musical structure as a whole by proposing the theme "Genesis of Meaning in Sound and Music". The purpose was to establish rigorous research alliances between computer and engineering sciences (information retrieval, programming, acoustics, signal processing) and areas within the humanities (in particular perception, cognition, musicology, philosophy), and to globally address the notion of sound meaning and its implications in music, modeling and retrieval. As a step in this direction, NTSMB, the Network for Cross-Disciplinary Studies of Music and Meaning as well as *JMM: The Journal of Music and Meaning* participated in CMMR 2008. The conference was partly supported by the French National Agency (ANR) within the project senSons (http://www.sensons.cnrs-mrs.fr).

The current book is divided into two main chapters, one that concerns retrieval of meaning and another that concerns generation of meaning. The first part of the retrieval chapter deals with perceptual and cognitive aspects spanning from EEG analysis to social interaction analysis through movement capture, while the second part addresses more traditional music information retrieval issues linked to synchronization, labeling, music query and classification. The generation chapter presents music performance strategies and experiences as well as tools for score analyses and representation.

We would like to thank the Program Committee members for their valuable paper reports and thank all the participants who made CMMR 2008 Genesis of Meaning in Sounds and Music a stimulating and unique event. Finally, we would like to thank Springer for accepting to publish the CMMR 2008 proceedings in their LNCS series.

March 2009   Sølvi Ystad
Richard Kronland-Martinet
Kristoffer Jensen

Organization

CMMR 2009 "Genesis of Meaning in Sound and Music" was jointly organized by Aalborg University Denmark, Laboratoire de Mécanique et d'Acoustique - CNRS, Marseille, France and the Network for Cross-Disciplinary Studies of Music and Meaning, Denmark, University of Southern Denmark.

Symposium Chairs

General Chair

Kristoffer Jensen   Aalborg University Esbjerg, Denmark

Digital Art Chair

Lars Graugaard   Aalborg University Esbjerg, Denmark

Program Committee

Conference Chair

Kristoffer Jensen   Aalborg University Esbjerg, Denmark

Program Chairs

Cynthia M. Grund	University of Southern Denmark, Denmark
Richard Kronland-Martinet	Laboratoire de Mécanique et d'Acoustique - CNRS, Marseille, France

Paper Chair

Sølvi Ystad	Laboratoire de Mécanique et d'Acoustique - CNRS, Marseille, France

Members

Mitsuko Aramaki	CNRS-INCM, Marseille, France
Gérard Assayag	IRCAM, Paris, France
Antonio Camurri	University of Genoa, Italy
Ole Kuhl	Aalborg University Esbjerg, Denmark
Laurent Daudet	Université Pierre et Marie Curie, Paris, France
Barry Eaglestone	University of Sheffield, UK
Anders Friberg	Royal Institute of Technology, Sweden
Ichiro Fujinaga	McGill University, Canada
Bruno Giordano	McGill University, Canada

Cynthia M. Grund   University of Odense, Denmark
Goffredo Haus   Laboratory for Computer Application in
                            Music, Milan, Italy
Kristoffer Jensen   Aalborg University Esbjerg, Denmark
Anssi Klapuri   Institute of Signl Processing, Tampere
                            University of Technology, Finland

Richard
  Kronland Martinet   CNRS, Marseille, France
Marc Leman   University of Ghent, Belgium
Francois Pachet   SONY CSL - Paris, France
Davide Rochesso   University of Verona, Italy
Leonello Tarabella   University of Pisa, Italy
Vesa Valimaki   Helsinki University of Technology, Finland
Thierry Voinier   CNRS-LMA, Marseille, France
Gerhard Widmer   University of Vienna, Austria

Sponsoring Institutions

Aalborg University Esbjerg, Denmark
CNRS, Laboratoire de Mécanique et d'Acoustique, Marseille France.
French National Research Agency (ANR, JC05-41996, "senSons")
Re-New - Digital Arts Forum, Denmark

Table of Contents

2   Generating the Meaning: Tools and Performance

Timbre Perception of Sounds from Impacted Materials: Behavioral, Electrophysiological and Acoustic Approaches

Mitsuko Aramaki[1,2], Mireille Besson[1,2], Richard Kronland-Martinet[3], and Sølvi Ystad[3]

[1] CNRS - Institut de Neurosciences Cognitives de la Méditerranée,
31, chemin Joseph Aiguier 13402 Marseille Cedex 20, France
{aramaki,besson}@incm.cnrs-mrs.fr
[2] Aix-Marseille - Université,
58, Bd Charles Livon 13284 Marseille Cedex 07, France
[3] CNRS - Laboratoire de Mécanique et d'Acoustique,
31, chemin Joseph Aiguier 13402 Marseille Cedex 20, France
{kronland,ystad}@lma.cnrs-mrs.fr

Abstract. In this paper, timbre perception of sounds from 3 different impacted materials (Wood, Metal and Glass) was examined using a categorization task. Natural sounds were recorded, analyzed and resynthesized and a sound morphing process was applied to construct sound continua between different materials. Participants were asked to categorize the sounds as Wood, Metal or Glass. Typical sounds for each category were defined on the basis of the behavioral data. The temporal dynamics of the neural processes involved in the categorization task were then examined for typical sounds by measuring the changes in brain electrical activity (Event-Related brain Potentials, ERPs). Analysis of the ERP data revealed that the processing of Metal sounds differed significantly from Glass and Wood sounds as early as 150 ms and up to 700 ms. The association of behavioral, electrophysiological and acoustic data allowed us to investigate material categorization: the importance of damping was confirmed and additionally, the relevancy of spectral content of sounds was discussed.

1 Introduction

Natural sounds carry a large amount of acoustic information that can be extracted by classical signal analysis techniques such as spectral analysis or time-frequency decompositions. Nevertheless, such techniques do not aim at explaining how the brain captures the information that allows us to identify different aspects of the sound source, such as its size, shape or material. The current study focuses on the perception of sounds produced by impacted materials, i.e., Wood, Metal and Glass. We aim at identifying the perceptual properties of these sounds (which are related to the concept of "invariants"

S. Ystad, R. Kronland-Martinet, and K. Jensen (Eds.): CMMR 2008, LNCS 5493, pp. 1–17, 2009.

in ecological acoustics [1]), that characterize material categories, without considering the mechanical correlates of the sound source[1].

Results of acoustic analysis are considered together with the results of behavioral and electrophysiological analyses. In particular, we examine the agreement between the acoustic relevancy of sound descriptors with respect to sound categorization as revealed by statistical analysis and their perceptual/cognitive relevancy as revealed by the objective measures of the electrical brain activity. As a first approach to the identification of these invariants for material perception, we investigate the sound descriptors that are known to be relevant for timbre perception and for material identification.

Previous studies on the perception of sound categories (of musical instruments or human voices) have mainly been based on the notion of timbre. Timbre is a perceptual and subjective attribute of sounds that is not well understood and is often defined by what it is not: "an indispensable key feature for the appreciation of sound quality other than pitch, loudness, duration and spatial location" (American National Standards Institute, 1973). Timbre is a complex feature of sounds that requires a multidimensional representation. Several authors [2,3,4,5] have used dissimilarity ratings to characterize the sounds of musical instruments and to identify timbre spaces based on the perceptual distances between sounds. The dimensions of these timbre spaces are correlated with various descriptors such as attack time (the way the energy rises at the sound onset), spectral bandwidth (spectrum spread), spectral center of gravity or spectral centroid (correlated to the brightness of sound) and spectral flux (the way the spectrum varies with time). Another important dimension of timbre, introduced by [6], is the roughness (distribution of interacting frequency components within the limits of a critical band). In a musical context, the roughness is closely linked to the concept of consonance/dissonance [7,8].

Regarding the perception of impact sounds, previous acoustic studies have examined the perception of the physical characteristics of the sound source, that are the properties of the actions and objects. Regarding perception of objects, [9] has shown that the perceived hardness of a mallet striking a metallic object is predictable from the characteristics of attack time. Further, strong correlations have been found between the perceived size of objects and the pitch of the generated sounds [10,11,12,13,14] and between the perceived shape of objects and the distribution of spectral components [15,16]. Finally, perception of material seems mainly to correlate with the damping of spectral components [17,18,19]. Damping also remains a robust acoustic descriptor to identify macro-categories (i.e., wood-plexiglass and steel-glass categories) across variations in the size of objects [20]. From a physical point of view, the damping is due to various mechanisms of loss and differs as a function of materials [21,22]. The quality of percussive sounds is highly correlated to the frequency-dependency of the damping: high frequency components being generally more heavily damped than low frequency ones. Consequently, different damping for high and for low frequency components involve

---

[1] Had the aim been to study the perceptual influence of the mechanical properties of the object (material, geometry), we would have studied structures and material independently. From a mechanical point of view, the respective contribution of object and material properties to sound perception is difficult to determine since identical sounds can be obtained by manipulating the characteristics of one or of the other.

intrinsic timbre modifications. Nevertheless, a global characterization of the damping can be given by the sound decay which measures the decrease of the sound energy as a function of time. Since damping is known to be important for material identification, we investigated the relevancy of sound decay for sound categorization in addition to previously presented timbre descriptors.

We used the flexibility of synthesis processes to construct the stimuli by extending the concept of analysis by synthesis [23]. Thus, we recorded, analyzed and resynthesized sounds from everyday life objects made of different materials (i.e., impacted wooden beams, metallic plates and various glass bowls). Further, we generated realistic sounds unambiguously evoking each material category. In practice, we used an additive synthesis model so that sounds were reconstructed as the sum of a number of frequency components controlled separately in amplitude, frequency and temporal evolution. Then, we created continuous transitions between sounds from different materials (i.e., {Wood-Metal}, {Wood-Glass} and {Glass-Metal}) through a morphing process based upon an interpolation between the values of the parameters of the sounds at the extremes of a continuum. Sounds from these continua were used in a categorization task so as to be sorted as Wood, Metal or Glass. In this way, the limits of the categories on each continuum and consequently, a set of unambiguous, "typical" sounds for each category could be identified.

We analyzed both the percentage of responses in each category and Reaction Times (RTs), as RTs are known to provide a good measure of the chronometry of mental processes [24,25]. Then, we examined the temporal dynamics of the brain processes associated with the perception and categorization of these sounds. In practice, we recorded Event Related Potentials (ERPs) time-locked to the sounds to analyze the different stages of information processing as they unfold in real time. The ERPs elicited by a stimulus (a sound, a light, etc ...) are characterized by a succession of positive (P) and negative (N) deflections relative to a baseline (usually measured within the 100 ms or 200 ms that precedes stimulus onset). These deflections (called components) are characterized not only by their polarity but also by their latency of maximum amplitude (relative to stimulus onset), their distribution across different electrodes located at standard positions on the scalp and by their functional significance. Typically, the first positive-negative-positive components following stimulus presentation, the P100, N100 and P200, reflect the sensory and perceptual stages of information processing, and are obligatory responses to the stimulation [26,27]. Depending upon the characteristics of the stimulation, this N100/P200 complex presents differences. Then, depending of the experimental design and of the task at hand, different late ERP components are elicited (N200, P300, N400 ...).

Results from studies based on the analysis of the ERPs have provided interesting information regarding the time course of timbre processing. For instance, the Mismatch Negativity (MMN; [28]) is considered as a good index of pre-attentive discrimination between tones with different acoustic, perceptual, cognitive and/or emotional attributes (see [29] and [30] for a review). [31] have shown that a MMN is elicited by infrequent pure tones presented among frequent harmonically rich tones. Moreover, recent results have shown increased MMN amplitude and latency with changes in spectral centroid [32,33], roughness [34], attack time and spectrum fine structure (even harmonic attenuation; [33]. These results thus suggest that such timbre descriptors are processed pre-attentively. Otherwise, in a discrimination task, [35] found increased N100 and P200 amplitude as a function of spectro-temporal complexity (see also [36,37]). Moreover, the use of a source estimation method (LORETA, [38]) allowed them to uncover possible generators of the N100 and P200 components: N100 resulting from activity in the right posterior Sylvian and inferior parietal regions and P200 from left and right regions of the posterior Sylvian fissure in the vicinity of the secondary auditory cortex. Finally, the late positive component, with maximum amplitude around 300 ms, the P300, is thought to reflect the categorization of task relevant events [39,40]. For instance, [29] showed that P300 latency was longest for emotion deviants, intermediate for timbre deviants and shortest for pitch deviants.

In the present experiment, regarding the ERPs, since Metal sounds show richer spectra than Wood or Glass sounds, we predicted that Metal sounds would elicit larger P200 amplitude [37]. Indeed, the spectrum of sounds generated from impacted structures with a given geometry is generally richer for Metal than for Wood or Glass. This can be explained by physical and signal processing considerations because the spectral density of energy integrates the energy of each frequency component over the entire duration of the sound. Due to differences in mechanisms of loss between materials, Metal is associated to less damped vibrations than Wood and Glass [21]. Consequently, the spectral energy of each mode is higher for Metal sounds, particularly in the high frequency range where modes are rapidly damped for Wood and Glass sounds. This general spectral behavior is in line with the results of the acoustic analyses of the sounds used in the present experiment. Sounds also differed from each other on several acoustic parameters: the number of spectral components (higher for Metal than for Wood or Glass), the damping (lower for Metal than for Wood and Glass) and the spectral distribution (quasi-harmonic for Glass, non harmonic for Metal and Wood) and these differences may also influence the ERP components. Note that since we used an explicit categorization task, we also expected N200-P300 components to be generated [41] and their amplitude and/or latency should reflect the characteristics of the categorization processes (i.e., shorter latency and larger amplitude for the sounds that are easier to categorize).

2   Methods

2.1   Participants and Stimuli

Twenty-two participants (11 women and 11 men), 19 to 35 years-old, were tested in this experiment. They were all right-handed, non-musicians (no formal musical training), had normal audition and no known neurological disorders. They all gave written consent to participate in the experiment and they were paid for their participation.

To design the stimuli, we first recorded impact sounds from everyday life objects made of different materials (i.e. impacted wooden beams, metallic plates and various glass bowls) to insure the generation of realistic sounds. Then, we used a simplified version of the analysis-synthesis model described in [42], based on an additive synthesis technique to resynthesize these recorded sounds (at 44.1 kHz sampling frequency):

$$s(t) = \theta(t) \sum_{m=1}^{M} A_m \sin(\omega_m t) e^{-\alpha_m t} \tag{1}$$

where $\theta(t)$ is the Heaviside function, M the number of components, and the parameters A_m, α_m and ω_m are respectively the amplitude, damping coefficient and frequency of the mth component.

To minimize timbre variations induced by pitch changes, all resynthesized sounds were tuned to the same chroma (note C): Wood sounds to the pitch C4, Metal sounds to C4 and C5 and Glass sounds to C6 and C7. The specific properties of the different materials did not, however, allow us to tune all sounds to the same octave. For instance, Glass sounds can not be transposed to low pitches as they will no longer be recognized as Glass sounds. Nevertheless, based on [43], we considered that the octave differences between sounds should not influence sound categorization. When the pitch was changed, the new value of the damping coefficient of each tuned frequency component was evaluated according to a damping law measured on the original sound [44]. Sounds were also equalized in loudness by gain adjustments. These sounds were called *reference* sounds of each material categories.

Finally, we built 15 continua (5 for each transition: {Wood-Metal}, {Wood-Glass} and {Glass-Metal}) composed of 20 hybrid sounds that simulate a progressive transition between different materials. By using a morphing process, the interpolation was computed both on the amplitudes of the spectral components and on their damping parameters. Sound examples are available at http://www.lma.cnrs-mrs.fr/~kronland/Categorization/sounds.html.

2.2 Procedure and Recording ERPs

Participants were asked to categorize sounds pseudo-randomly presented through one loudspeaker, as Wood, Metal or Glass, as fast as possible, by pressing one response button out of three. The association between response buttons and material categories was balanced across participants. Brain electrical activity (Electroencephalogram, EEG) was recorded continuously from 32 Biosemi Pin-type active electrodes (Amsterdam University) mounted on an elastic headcap and located at standard left and right hemisphere positions over frontal, central, parietal, occipital and temporal areas (International extended 10/20 system sites [45]: Fz, Cz, Pz, Oz, Fp1, Fp2, AF3, AF4, F7, F8, F3, F4, Fc5, Fc6, Fc1, Fc2, T7, T8, C3, C4, Cp1, Cp2, Cp5, Cp6, P3, P4, PO3, PO4, P7, P8, O1, O2). Moreover, to detect horizontal eye movements and blinks, the electrooculogram (EOG) was recorded from Flat-type active electrodes placed 1 cm to the left and right of the external canthi, and from an electrode beneath the right eye. Two additional electrodes were placed on the left and right mastoids. EEG was recorded at a sampling rate of 512 Hz using Biosemi amplifier. The EEG was re-referenced off-line to the algebric average of the left and right mastoids and filtered with a lowpass of 40 Hz. Data were analyzed using routines of Matlab EEGLAB toolbox [46]. Data were segmented in single trials of 2500 ms, starting 200 ms before the onset of the sound.

3   Sound Descriptors

To characterize sounds from an acoustic point of view, we considered the following sound descriptors: attack time AT, spectral centroid SC, spectral bandwidth SB, spectral flux SF, roughness R and normalized sound decay α.

The attack time AT is a temporal timbre descriptor which characterizes signal onset. It is defined by the time necessary for the signal energy to raise from 10% to 90% of the maximum amplitude of the signal.

The spectral centroid SCG is a spectral timbre descriptor which is commonly associated to the brightness of the sound and is defined by [47]:

$$SC = \frac{1}{2\pi} \frac{\sum_k \omega(k) \, | \, \hat{s}(k) \, |}{\sum_k | \, \hat{s}(k) \, |} \tag{2}$$

while the spectral bandwidth SB, commonly associated to the spectrum spread is defined by [48]:

$$SB = \frac{1}{2\pi} \sqrt{\frac{\sum_k | \, \hat{s}(k) \, | \, (\omega(k) - 2\pi \times SC)^2}{\sum_k | \, \hat{s}(k) \, |}} \tag{3}$$

where ω and $\hat{s}$ represent the frequency and the Fourier transform of the signal, respectively.

The spectral flux SF is a spectro-temporal timbre descriptor quantifying the time evolution of the spectrum and is defined by [49]:

$$SF = \frac{1}{C} \sum_{c=1}^{C} | \, p_{n,n-1} \, | \tag{4}$$

where C represents the number of local spectra (frames) and $p_{n,n-1}$ the Pearson product moment correlation coefficient between the local spectra at the discrete times n and $n-1$.

Based on the [50] and [51] models, the roughness R of a sound, commonly associated to the presence of several frequency components within the limits of a critical band, can be computed by summing up the partial roughness r_{ij} for all pairs of frequency components (i,j) contained in the sound [52]:

$$r_{ij} = 0.5 \times (A_i A_j)^{0.1} \times \left(\frac{2 \min(A_i, A_j)}{A_i + A_j} \right)^{3.11} \times (e^{-3.5s|\omega_i - \omega_j|} - e^{-5.75s|\omega_i - \omega_j|}) \tag{5}$$

where

$$s = \frac{0.24}{0.0207 \times \min(\omega_i, \omega_j) + 2\pi \times 18.96} \tag{6}$$

and where A_i and A_j, ω_i and ω_j are respectively the amplitudes and frequencies of a pair of frequency components (i,j).

Finally, sound decay quantifies the global amplitude decrease of the temporal signal. Since the sounds consist of the sum of exponentially damped sine waves (Equation (1)), the sound decay is directly estimated by the slope of the logarithm of the envelope of the temporal signal. Nevertheless, since the damping is frequency dependent, this decrease depends on the spectral content of the sound. Consequently, we chose to consider a normalized sound decay α with respect to a reference that takes into account the spectral localization of the energy. Then, we defined α as the ratio of the sound decay to the SC value.

4 Results

4.1 Behavioral Data

Participants' responses and RTs were collected for each sound. Sounds were considered as *typical* if they were classified in one category (i.e., Wood, Metal or Glass) by more than 70% of the participants. This threshold value was determined using a statistical approach based on hierarchical cluster analysis (see [53] for details).

Data were averaged as a function of participants' responses in each category (Table 1). Results were analyzed using repeated-measures Analysis of Variance (ANOVAs) including Material (Wood, Metal and Glass) as a within-subject factor. For this and following analyses, effects were considered significant if the p-value was less than .05. When interactions between 2 or more factors were significant, post-hoc comparisons (Tukey tests) were computed. Clearly, participants more often categorized sounds as Metal than as Wood or Glass [$F(2,42)=25.31$, $p<.001$] and RTs were slower for Glass sounds [$F(2,42)=29.1$, $p<.001$] than for Wood and Metal sounds.

Table 1. Percentages of responses (N) in each material category (W=Wood, M=Metal, G=Glass), of responses N_{typ} associated to typical sounds of each category (i.e., sounds classified in the category by more than 70% of the participants), and of responses N_{nontyp} associated to non typical sounds (i.e., sounds classified by less than 70% of the participants). Mean RTs for each category are also indicated in milliseconds. The data are reported with their respective standard deviation ($\pm$SD) across participants.

	N	RT	N_{typ}	RT	N_{nontyp}	RT
W	31($\pm$7)	936($\pm$195)	17($\pm$2)	829($\pm$185)	14($\pm$5)	1080($\pm$250)
M	42($\pm$5)	1028($\pm$275)	29($\pm$1)	964($\pm$254)	13($\pm$3)	1170($\pm$323)
G	27($\pm$5)	1152($\pm$247)	9($\pm$1)	1010($\pm$211)	18($\pm$3)	1203($\pm$263)

4.2 Electrophysiological Data

To examine the time course of the perception of typical sounds, as defined from the results of the behavioral data, as well as potential differences between the 3 sound categories, ERPs data were averaged separately for the typical sounds of each material category (Wood, Metal and Glass). Based upon visual inspection of the ERP traces, the following time windows were chosen for statistical analysis to focus on specific ERP components: 0-50 ms, 50-80 ms (P100), 80-150 ms (N100), 150-230 ms (P200), 230-330 ms (N280), 400-550 ms and 550-700 ms (Negative Slow Wave, NSW and P550).

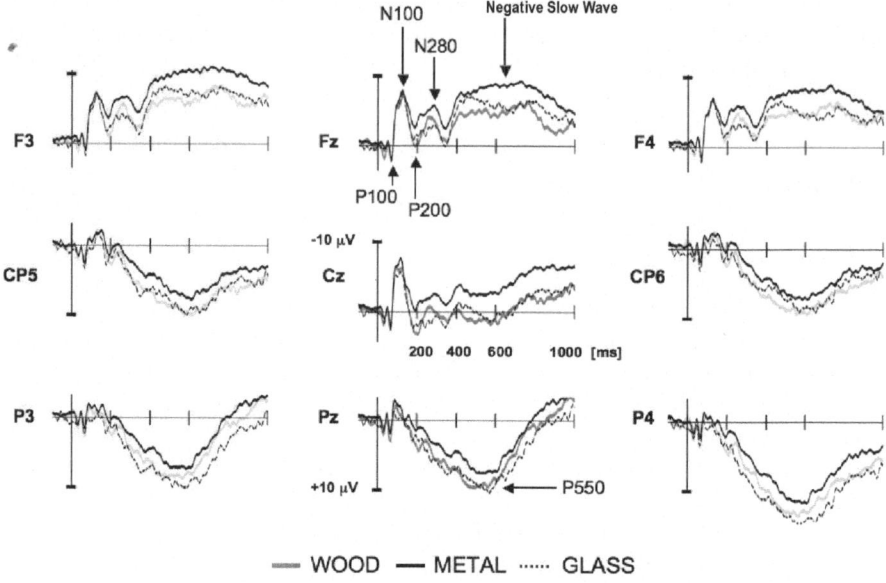

Fig. 1. Event-Related Potentials (ERPs) to typical sounds of Wood (grey solid trace), Metal (black solid trace) and Glass (dotted trace) at midline (Fz, Cz, Pz) and at lateral electrodes ({F3, CP5, P3} / {F4, CP6, P4}). The amplitude (in microvolt μV) is represented on the ordinate and negativity is up. The time from sound onset is on the abscissa (in millisecond, ms).

Separate repeated-measures ANOVAs were conducted for midline and lateral electrodes. Factors were Material (Wood, Metal and Glass) and Electrodes (Fz, Cz, Pz) for midline analyses. Factors were Material, Hemispheres (left vs. right), Regions of Interest (3 ROIs: fronto-central, centro-temporal and centro-parietal) and Electrodes (3 for each ROI: {AF3, F3, FC5} / {AF4, F4, FC6}; {T7, C3, CP5} / {T8, C4, CP6}; {CP1, P7, P3} / {CP2, P8, P4}) for lateral analyses. Effects were considered significant if the p-value was less than 0.05. Results are reported in Table 2.

Figure 1 shows the ERPs recorded at midline electrodes and at one lateral electrode per ROI (selected as the most representative of the ROI). Typical sounds from each category elicited small positive components, with maximum amplitude around 65 ms post-sound onset (P100), large negative components peaking around 100 ms (N100) followed by relatively positive (P200) and negative (N280 and NSW) components at fronto-central sites or large positive components (P550) at parietal sites. Results of ANOVAs revealed no main effect of Material on P100 amplitude (Midlines, p=.76; Lateral, p=.69) or on N100 amplitude (Midlines, p=.07; Lateral, p=.22) either at midline or at lateral electrodes. By contrast, at both midline and lateral electrodes, Metal sounds elicited smaller P200 and larger N280 and NSW components than Wood and Glass sounds that did not differ from each other (Table 3). Moreover, Metal sounds elicited smaller P550 component than Wood sounds (Table 2). This effect was largest over fronto-central and centro-temporal regions in the 400-550 ms latency range and over fronto-central region in the 550-700 ms latency range (see Table 4).

Table 2. F statistics and mean amplitude values (in μV) for the main effect of the Material factor (W = Wood, M = Metal, G = Glass) in the latency windows in which the effects were significant. Amplitude differences (W-M, M-G and W-G in μV) are indicated only when significant. For this and following tables, the level of significance is given by * (p<.05), ** (p<.01), *** (p<.001). $^{(a)}$ indicates a marginally significant effect at p=.059.

	150-230 ms		230-330 ms		400-550 ms		550-700 ms	
	P200 comp.		N280 comp.		NSW and P550 comp.			
	Mid.	Lat.	Mid.	Lat.	Mid.	Lat.	Mid.	Lat.
F(2,42)	5.26**	4.11*	4.99*	4.88*	4.00*	4.08*	4.00*	3.18*
W	0.92	0.46	0.47	0.96	1.63	3.65	0.99	4.00
M	-1.57	-1.35	-1.30	-0.78	-1.39	1.05	-1.97	1.56
G	0.48	0.13	1.35	1.32	0.51	2.25	0.78	3.13
W-M	2.49*	1.81*	–	1.74*	3.02*	2.6*	2.96*	2.44*
M-G	-2.05*	–	-2.65**	-2.10*	–	–	-2.75$^{(a)}$	–
W-G	–	–	–	–	–	–	–	–

Table 3. F statistics, mean amplitude values (in μV) for Material (W = Wood, M = Metal, G = Glass) by Electrode (Fz, Cz, Pz) interaction in the latency windows in which the effects were significant. Amplitude differences (W-M, M-G and W-G in μV) are indicated only when significant.

	150-230 ms			230-330 ms			400-550 ms			550-700 ms		
	P200 component			N280 component			NSW and P550 components					
	$F_{(4,84)}=3.63^{**}$			$F_{(4,84)}=2.83^{*}$			$F_{(4,84)}=3.99^{**}$			$F_{(4,84)}=7.06^{***}$		
	Fz	Cz	Pz	Fz	Cz	Pz	Fz	Cz	Pz	Fz	Cz	Pz
W	-1.25	1.57	2.44	-2.63	0.06	3.98	-4.21	0.99	8.12	-4.45	0.75	6.67
M	-3.93	-1.43	0.65	-4.77	-2.00	2.86	-7.75	-2.82	6.39	-8.71	-3.20	6.00
G	-1.49	1.09	1.83	-1.56	1.20	4.42	-5.05	-0.15	6.74	-4.61	0.32	6.65
W-M	2.68***	3.00***	1.79***	2.14***	2.06***	–	3.54***	3.81***	1.73*	4.26***	2.45***	–
M-G	-2.44***	-2.52***	-1.18**	-3.21***	-3.20***	-1.56**	-2.7***	-2.67***	–	-4.1***	-3.52***	–
W-G	–	–	–	–	–	–	–	–	–	–	–	–

4.3 Acoustic Data

A set of sound descriptors (as defined in Section 3) were calculated for the typical sounds from each material category: attack time AT, spectral centroid SCG, spectral bandwidth SB, spectral flux SF, roughness R and normalized sound decay α. An acoustic analysis was conducted to determine whether each sound descriptor explains sound categorization.

Table 4. F statistics, mean amplitude values (in μV) for Material (W = Wood, M = Metal, G = Glass) by Region (R1 = Fronto-central, R2 = Centro-temporal, R3 = Centro-parietal) interaction in the latency windows in which the effects were significant. Amplitude differences (W-M, M-G and W-G in μV) are indicated only when significant.

	400-550 ms $F(4,84)=3.9^{**}$			550-700 ms $F(4,84)=4.59^{**}$		
	R1	R2	R3	R1	R2	R3
W	-2.18	4.84	8.28	-1.76	5.55	8.23
M	-6.28	2.53	6.91	-6.23	3.53	7.39
G	-3.68	3.03	7.41	-2.87	4.17	8.10
W-M	4.1^{***}	2.31^{***}	1.37^{*}	4.47^{***}	–	–
M-G	-2.6^{***}	-0.5^{***}	–	-3.36^{***}	–	–
W-G	–	–	–	–	–	–

Table 5. Statistics (χ^2) and mean values (reported with their respective standard deviation, $\pm$SD) for the Material factor (Wood, Metal, Glass) corresponding to AT (in ms), SCG (in Hz), SF, R (in asper) and α (in dB). The level of significance of post-hoc comparisons are indicated next to the mean values.

	AT	SCG	SF	R	α
$\chi^2(2,198)=$	20.08^{***}	33.55^{***}	97.21^{***}	71.71^{***}	159.81^{***}
Wood	$0.24(\pm0.47)$	$2573^{*}(\pm597)$	$105^{*}(\pm69)$	$0.4(\pm0.32)$	$-0.088^{*}(\pm0.033)$
Metal	$0.11^{*}(\pm0.63)$	$3536(\pm1154)$	$655(\pm719)$	$1.71^{*}(\pm1.24)$	$-0.013^{*}(\pm0.006)$
Glass	$0.37(\pm0.48)$	$3426(\pm891)$	$550(\pm403)$	$0.58(\pm0.45)$	$-0.037^{*}(\pm0.016)$

A Kruskal-Wallis test was computed for each sound descriptor including Material (Wood, Metal and Glass) as a factor. Results are presented in Table 5. Except for SB, all descriptors explained the differentiation of at least one category from the other 2. Specifically, AT and R were relevant to discriminate Metal from both Wood and Glass; SCG and SF to discriminate Wood from both Metal and Glass and α to discriminate the 3 categories.

5   Discussion

Behavioral data allowed us to define which of the 20 sounds from each continuum were most typical of each material category (i.e., the sounds that were categorized as Wood, Metal or Glass by more than 70% of the participants). The ERPs to these typical sounds were then analyzed to examine the time course of sound perception. Acoustic analysis of these typical sounds revealed the relevancy of sound descriptors to explain sound categorization. Results of these analyses allowed us to discuss sound descriptors that are most relevant for material perception.

Results of the acoustic analysis showed that the normalized sound decay α alone allowed the discrimination of the 3 material categories. Since in our case, the normalized sound decay characterizes the damping, the relevancy of α is in line with previous results showing that damping is an important cue in the perception of sounds from impacted materials [17,18,19,20]. However, while damping may be of particular importance for sound perception, results of several studies have shown that it is not sufficient for a complete discrimination between different materials. For instance, [19] concluded that the length of bars influenced the perception of material with glass and wood being associated with shorter bars (i.e., higher frequencies) than rubber and steel. Similarly, [15] also found frequency effects on material perception: glass and rubber were associated with higher pitches than wood and steel. Finally, [20] concluded that within a macro-category, material identification is based on plate size (i.e., signal frequency) so that steel and plastic were identified more often from larger plates than wood and glass.

Consequently, our perception of material seems to be guided by additional cues other than damping that most likely are linked to the spectral content of sounds. To directly test for the influence of damping and spectral complexity on the perception of the sounds used here, we constructed 9 stimuli by independently combining the spectra of typical sounds (of Wood, Metal or Glass) with the damping characteristics of these sounds. The experimental design is detailed in[2]. The percentage of responses obtained for the 9 hybrid sounds is presented in Table 6. Results confirmed that typical sounds (with spectrum and damping within the same category) were associated with the highest percentage of responses in their respective category. Moreover, results revealed that sounds with Metal damping and spectrum of Wood or Glass, were categorized as Metal, thereby showing that damping remains a robust descriptor to characterize the Metal category. For sounds with Wood damping, the one with Metal spectrum was still categorized as Wood while the one with Glass spectrum was categorized as Glass so that damping did not entirely characterize the Wood category. Finally, sounds with Glass

---

[2] **Experimental protocol: Participants:** 10 participants (3 women, 7 men) were tested in this experiment. They were all non-musicians and had normal audition. **Stimuli:** one reference sound (Section 2.1) of each material category (Wood, Metal and Glass) was selected. From the 3 reference sounds, 9 hybrid sounds were created using the additive synthesis model defined in Equation (1). The sounds were constructed by independently combining each spectrum (A_m and ω_m values) with the damping law characteristic of each material categorie (measured on the original sound). Thus, these sounds correspond to the 9 possible combinations between the 3 spectra and the 3 damping law characteristics of each material category. The sounds are available at http://www.lma.cnrs-mrs.fr/~kronland/Categorization/sounds.html. **Procedure:** sounds were presented through headphones (Stax SR-202 with amplifier SRM-310). As a training, participants first listened passively to 2 typical sounds of each material category (different to the typical sounds used for the construction of the stimuli). Then, they listened passively to the 9 hybrid sounds presented randomly. Finally, they were asked to categorize these 9 sounds as Wood, Metal or Glass by using a computer keyboard. Participants could listen to the sounds as often as they wanted before answering. The responses for the 9 sounds were collected.

damping combined with either Wood or Metal spectrum lost their Glass specificity: they were mostly categorized as Metal. Thus, damping is not sufficient to characterize the Wood and Glass categories. Clearly, this experiment further showed that both damping and the spectral content of sounds are relevant cues for material categorization. Therefore, at least, one descriptor other than the normalized sound decay α (that robustly characterizes the damping of each material category since the 3 values of α for a given material damping have close values across different spectra, see Table 6) needs to be considered for an accurate sound categorization of materials.

Table 6. Percentage of responses in each material category (W, M and G) and normalized sound decay values (α) for the 9 sounds constructed by combination of Wood, Metal and Glass spectrum with Wood, Metal and Glass damping. The highest percentage obtained by each sound among the 3 categories is highlighted in bold.

	Wood damp.				Metal damp.				Glass damp.			
	W	M	G	α	W	M	G	α	W	M	G	α
Wood spec.	**80**	20	0	-0.033	0	**90**	10	-0.001	10	**70**	20	-0.012
Metal spec.	**60**	20	20	-0.047	0	**100**	0	-0.002	20	**70**	10	-0.020
Glass spec.	40	0	**60**	-0.047	0	**60**	40	-0.001	0	20	**80**	-0.013

Regarding the ERPs, the analysis revealed no significant differences on the amplitude of the N100 component that is notably influenced by variations in sound onset parameters [54]. This is not surprising insofar as the AT differences between sound categories were approximately 0.1 ms (see values in Table 5) and were therefore below the temporal resolution of hearing [55]. Then, typical Metal sounds elicited brain activity that differed from the other 2 typical sound categories starting around 150 ms after sound onset and lasting until the end of the recording period at some scalp sites. In particular, Metal sounds elicited smaller P200 and P550 components, and larger N280 and NSW components than Wood and Glass sounds. Results from previous experiments have shown that the P200 component, that typically reflects sensory and perceptual processing, is sensitive to spectral complexity [37,56]. In particular, [35] found larger P200 amplitude, and an additional effect on N100 amplitude, for instrumental tones (complex spectra) relative to sine wave tones. It should be noted, however, that while increased spectral complexity enhanced the amplitude of the N100 and/or P200 components in previous studies [37,35], the present results showed decreased P200 amplitude and increased N280 amplitude to Metal sounds. Two factors may account for these differences. First, the present task and experimental design differed from previous experiments because we used an explicit sound categorization task. Such tasks are known to elicit N200-P300 components that are thought to reflect the categorization and decision processes [41,39]. Thus, the occurrence of the N280 and P550 (P300-like component) is likely to be task-dependent. Note that since N280 amplitude was larger for Metal sounds, the reduction in P200 amplitude may result from an overlap effect. Second, the present sounds differed from those used in previous studies. In the experiments by [35] and [37], stimuli differed in spectral complexity but were equated in pitch (F4/B4 and C4, respectively) and in duration (400 and 500 ms, respectively). By contrast, our stimuli differed both in pitch (the chroma was the same, i.e., C, but the octaves sometimes differed) and in duration (mean values of normalized sound decay[3] for each category in Table 5). However, differences in pitch are not likely to explain the large ERPs differences between Metal sounds and the other 2 sound categories because the largest pitch differences are found between Glass sounds (notes C6 and C7) and the other 2 sound categories (Wood: note C4 and Metal: notes C4 and C5). By contrast, [57] have shown that increasing sound duration from 200 to 300 ms significantly increased N200 amplitude. Consequently, the N280 enhancement for Metal sounds can reflect a sound duration effect because of the longer duration of Metal sounds. Finally, a long-lasting NSW larger for Metal sounds than the other 2 sound categories developed over frontal regions. Based on previous studies, NSW may reflect processes related to the maintenance of stimuli in working memory, expectancy since a row of XXXX followed sound offset [58], attention [59] and also sound duration (as the "sustained potential" reported by [60]).

To summarize, the analysis of the electrophysiological data revealed that spectral complexity and sound duration seem to be relevant cues to explain the differentiation of the ERPs to Metal sounds compared to the ERPs to Glass and Wood sounds. Note that the occurrence of an N280 component is most likely driven by the categorization task but the increased amplitude of this component to Metal sounds is most likely linked to the longer duration of Metal compared to Wood and Glass sounds. The relevance of sound descriptors investigated in Section 4.3 can be compared with results from ERPs. In particular, we can support that descriptors reflecting the spectral content of sounds (i.e., SB, SCG, SF and R) and sound duration (which is related to α) may be relevant from a perceptual point of view. Note that the roughness R seems to be the most relevant descriptor to account for electrophysiological data since it allowed the distinction of Metal sounds from the other 2 categories. Moreover, from a perceptual point of view, the roughness R most accurately describes the typical dissonance of Metal sounds. By contrast, AT (characterizing sound onset) revealed as relevant descriptor by acoustic analysis to discriminate Metal sounds from both Wood and Glass sounds was not considered as a relevant descriptor from a perceptual point of view since no differences on N100 components were found in the ERPs results.

6 Conclusion

The aim of the current experiment was to investigate the perception of sounds from different impacted materials. For that purpose, we collected behavioral and electrophysiological data from a categorization experiment and we conducted acoustic analysis of typical sounds by investigating sound descriptors known to be relevant for timbre

---

[3] In our case, the normalized sound decay is related to sound duration. We chose to investigate sound decay instead of sound duration since the perceptual correlate of sound duration is not well defined. Actually, its estimation still is an open issue for rapidly damped signals since the perceived duration differs from the actual duration of the signals.

and material perception. Synthesis allowed the generation of perfectly controlled stimuli and the construction of sound continua through a morphing process. From the behavioral data, we were able to define typical sounds for each material category. ERPs results allowing the investigation of the brain dynamics processes supported the assumption that our perception of impact sounds from material categories is based on the damping (characterized by normalized sound decay) together with spectral content (characterized by spectral descriptors). Further, these relevant descriptors should allow us to address the problem of identifying acoustic invariants of sound categories. Future studies will aim at defining these invariants, assumed to be based on a combination of the relevant descriptors.

Acknowledgments

This research was supported by a grant from the Human Frontier Science Program (HSFP #RGP0053) to Mireille Besson and a grant from the French National Research Agency (ANR, JC05-41996, "senSons") to Sølvi Ystad. Mitsuko Aramaki was supported by a post-doctoral grant from the HFSP and the ANR.

References

1. Michaels, C.F., Carello, C.: Direct perception. Prentice-Hall, Englewood Cliffs (1981)
2. Grey, J.M.: Multidimensional perceptual scaling of musical timbres. Journal of the Acoustical Society of America 61(5), 1270–1277 (1977)
3. Krumhansl, C.L.: Why is musical timbre so hard to understand. In: Structure and perception of electroacoustic sound and music. Elsevier, Amsterdam (1989)
4. Krimphoff, J., McAdams, S., Winsberg, S.: Caractérisation du timbre des sons complexes. ii: Analyses acoustiques et quantification psychophysique. Journal de Physique 4(C5), 625–628 (1994)
5. McAdams, S., Winsberg, S., Donnadieu, S., De Soete, G., Krimphoff, J.: Perceptual scaling of synthesized musical timbres: common dimensions, specificities, and latent subject classes. Psychological Research 58, 177–192 (1995)
6. von Helmholtz, H.L.F.: On the sensations of tone as the physiological basis for the theory of music, 2nd edn (1877)
7. Sethares, W.A.: Local consonance and the relationship between timbre and scale. Journal of the Acoustical Society of America 94(3), 1218–1228 (1993)
8. Vassilakis, P.N.: Selected Reports in Ethnomusicology (Perspectives in Systematic Musicology). In: Auditory roughness as a means of musical expression, Department of Ethnomusicology, University of California, vol. 12, pp. 119–144 (2005)
9. Freed, D.J.: Auditory correlates of perceived mallet hardness for a set of recorded percussive events. Journal of the Acoustical Society America 87(1), 311–322 (1990)
10. Tucker, S., Brown, G.J.: Investigating the perception of the size, shape and material of damped and free vibrating plates. Technical Report CS-02-10, Université de Sheffield, Department of Computer Science (2002)
11. van den Doel, K., Pai, D.K.: The sounds of physical shapes. Presence 7(4), 382–395 (1998)
12. Kunkler-Peck, A.J., Turvey, M.T.: Hearing shape. J. of Experimental Psychology: Human Perception and Performance 26(1), 279–294 (2000)

13. Carello, C., Anderson, K.L., Kunkler-Peck, A.J.: Perception of object length by sound. Psychological Science 9(3), 211–214 (1998)
14. Lutfi, R.A., Oh, E.L.: Auditory discrimination of material changes in a struck-clamped bar. Journal of the Acoustical Society of America 102(6), 3647–3656 (1997)
15. Rocchesso, D., Fontana, F.: The sounding object (2003)
16. Lakatos, S., McAdams, S., Caussé, R.: The representation of auditory source characteristics: simple geometric form. Perception & Psychophysics 59, 1180–1190 (1997)
17. Wildes, R.P., Richards, W.A.: Recovering material properties from sound. In: Richards, W.A. (ed.), ch. 25, pp. 356–363. MIT Press, Cambridge (1988)
18. Gaver, W.W.: How do we hear in the world? explorations of ecological acoustics. Ecological Psychology 5(4), 285–313 (1993)
19. Klatzky, R.L., Pai, D.K., Krotkov, E.P.: Perception of material from contact sounds. Presence: Teleoperators and Virtual Environments 9(4), 399–410 (2000)
20. Giordano, B.L., McAdams, S.: Material identification of real impact sounds: Effects of size variation in steel, wood, and plexiglass plates. Journal of the Acoustical Society of America 119(2), 1171–1181 (2006)
21. Chaigne, A., Lambourg, C.: Time-domain simulation of damped impacted plates: I. theory and experiments. Journal of the Acoustical Society of America 109(4), 1422–1432 (2001)
22. Valette, C., Cuesta, C.: Mécanique de la corde vibrante (Mechanics of vibrating string). Traité des Nouvelles Technologies, série Mécanique. Hermès (1993)
23. Risset, J.-C., Wessel, D.L.: Exploration of timbre by analysis and synthesis. In: The psychology of music, 2nd edn. Cognition and Perception, pp. 113–169. Academic Press, London (1999)
24. Donders, F.C.: On the speed of mental processes. Acta Psychol. 30, 412–431 (1969)
25. Sternberg, S.: Memory-scanning: mental processes revealed by reaction-time experiments. American Scientist 57(4), 421–457 (1969)
26. Rugg, M.D., Coles, M.G.H.: The ERP and Cognitive Psychology: Conceptual issues. In: Electrophysiology of mind. Event-related brain potentials and cognition. Oxford Psychology, vol. 25, pp. 27–39. Oxford University Press, Oxford (1995)
27. Eggermont, J.J., Ponton, C.W.: The neurophysiology of auditory perception: from single-units to evoked potentials. Audiology & Neuro-Otology 7, 71–99 (2002)
28. Näätänen, R.: Attention and brain function. Erlbaum, Hillsdale, NJ (1992)
29. Goydke, K.N., Altenmuller, E., Moller, J., Munte, J.: Changes in emotional tones and instrumental timbre are reflected by the mismatch negativity. Cognitive Brain Research 21, 351–359 (2004)
30. Tervaniemi, M.: Musical sound processing in the human brain: evidence from electric and magnetic recordings. Annals of the New York Academy of Sciences 930, 259–272 (2001)
31. Tervaniemi, M., Winkler, I., Näätänen, R.: Pre-attentive categorization of sounds by timbre as revealed by event-related potentials. NeuroReport 8, 2571–2574 (1997)
32. Toiviainen, P., Tervaniemi, M., Louhivuori, J., Saher, M., Huotilainen, M., Näätänen, R.: Timbre similarity: convergence of neural, behavioral, and computational approaches. Music Perception 16, 223–241 (1998)
33. Caclin, A., Brattico, E., Tervaniemi, M., Näätänen, R., Morlet, D., Giard, M.-H., McAdams, S.: Separate neural processing of timbre dimensions in auditory sensory memory. Journal of Cognitive Neuroscience 18(12), 1959–1972 (2006)
34. De Baene, W., Vandierendonck, A., Leman, M., Widmann, A., Tervaniemi, M.: Roughness perception in sounds: behavioral and erp evidence. Biological Psychology 67, 319–330 (2004)
35. Meyer, M., Baumann, S., Jancke, L.: Electrical brain imaging reveals spatio-temporal dynamics of timbre perception in humans. NeuroImage 32, 1510–1523 (2006)

36. Shahin, A., Bosnyak, D.J., Trainor, L.J., Roberts, L.E.: Enhancement of neuroplastic p2 and n1c auditory evoked potentials in musicians. The Journal of Neuroscience 23(12), 5545–5552 (2003)
37. Shahin, A., Roberts, L.E., Pantev, C., Trainor, L.J., Ross, B.: Modulation of p2 auditory-evoked responses by the spectral complexity of musical sounds. NeuroReport 16(16), 1781–1785 (2005)
38. Pascual-Marqui, R.D., Michel, C.M., Lehmann, D.: Low resolution electromagnetic tomography: a new method for localizing electrical activity in the brain. International Journal of Psychophysiology 18, 49–65 (1994)
39. Sutton, S., Braren, M., Zubin, J., John, E.R.: Evoked potential correlates of stimulus uncertainty. Science 150, 1187–1188 (1965)
40. Donchin, E., Coles, M.G.H.: Is the p300 component a manifestation of context updating? Behavioral and Brain Sciences 11, 357–374 (1988)
41. Ritter, W., Simson, R., Vaughan, H.G.: Event-related potential correlates of two stages of information processing in physical and semantic discrimination tasks. Psychophysiology 20, 168–179 (1983)
42. Aramaki, M., Kronland-Martinet, R.: Analysis-synthesis of impact sounds by real-time dynamic filtering. IEEE Transactions on Audio, Speech, and Language Processing 14(2), 695–705 (2006)
43. Parncutt, R.: Harmony - A Psychoacoustical Approach. Springer, Heidelberg (1989)
44. Aramaki, M., Baillères, H., Brancheriau, L., Kronland-Martinet, R., Ystad, S.: Sound quality assessment of wood for xylophone bars. Journal of the Acoustical Society of America 121(4), 2407–2420 (2007)
45. Jasper, H.H.: The ten-twenty electrode system of the international federation. Electroencephalography and Clinical Neurophysiology 10, 371–375 (1958)
46. Delorme, A., Makeig, S.: Eeglab: an open source toolbox for analysis of single-trial eeg dynamics. Journal of Neuroscience Methods 134, 9–21 (2004)
47. Beauchamp, J.W.: Synthesis by spectral amplitude and "brightness" matching of analyzed musical instrument tones. Journal of the Audio Engineering Society 30(6), 396–406 (1982)
48. Marozeau, J., de Cheveigné, A., McAdams, S., Winsberg, S.: The dependency of timbre on fundamental frequency. Journal of the Acoustical Society of America 114, 2946–2957 (2003)
49. McAdams, S.: Perspectives on the contribution of timbre to musical structure. Computer Music Journal 23(3), 85–102 (1999)
50. Plomp, R., Levelt, W.J.M.: Tonal consonance and critical bandwidth. Journal of the Acoustical Society of America 38, 548–560 (1965)
51. Terhardt, E.: On the perception of periodic sound fluctuations (roughness). Acustica 30(4), 201–213 (1974)
52. Vassilakis, P.N.: Sra: A web-based research tool for spectral and roughness analysis of sound signals. In: Proceedings of the 4th Sound and Music Computing (SMC) Conference, pp. 319–325 (2007)
53. Aramaki, M., Brancheriau, L., Kronland-Martinet, R., Ystad, S.: Perception of impacted materials: sound retrieval and synthesis control perspectives. In: Ystad, S., Kronland-Martinet, R., Jensen, K. (eds.) Computer Music Modeling and Retrieval - Genesis of Meaning of Sound and Music. LNCS, vol. 5493, pp. 134–146. Springer, Heidelberg (2009)
54. Hyde, M.: The n1 response and its applications. Audiology & Neuro-Otology 2, 281–307 (1997)
55. Gordon, J.W.: The perceptual attack time of musical tones. Journal of Acoustical Society of America 82(1), 88–105 (1987)
56. Kuriki, S., Kanda, S., Hirata, Y.: Effects of musical experience on different components of meg responses elicited by sequential piano-tones and chords. The Journal of Neuroscience 26(15), 4046–4053 (2006)

57. Kushnerenko, E., Ceponiene, R., Fellman, V., Huotilainen, M., Winkler, I.: Event-related potential correlates of sound duration: similar pattern from birth to adulthood. NeuroReport 12(17), 3777–3781 (2001)
58. Walter, W.G., Cooper, R., Aldridge, V.J., McCallum, W.C., Winter, A.L.: Contingent negative variation: an electrical sign of sensorimotor association and expectancy in the human brain. Nature 230, 380–384 (1964)
59. King, J., Kutas, M.: Who did what and when? using word- and clause-level erps to monitor working memory usage in reading. Journal of Cognitive Neuroscience 7(3), 376–395 (1995)
60. Alain, C., Schuler, B.M., McDonald, K.L.: Neural activity associated with distinguishing concurrent auditory objects. Journal of Acoustical Society of America 111(2), 990–995 (2002)

Perception of Harmonic and Inharmonic Sounds: Results from Ear Models

Albrecht Schneider and Klaus Frieler

Institute for Musicology, University of Hamburg, Germany
{aschneid,klaus.frieler}@uni-hamburg.de

Abstract. We report on experiments in which musically relevant harmonic and inharmonic sounds have been fed into computer-based ear models (or into modules which at least simulate parts of the peripheral auditory system) working either in the frequency or in the time domain. For a major chord in just intonation, all algorithms produced reliable and interpretable output, which explains mechanisms of pitch perception. One model also yields data suited to demonstrate how sensory consonance and 'fusion' are contained in the ACF of the neural activity pattern.

With musical sounds from instruments (carillon, *gamelan*) which represent different degrees of inharmonicity, the performance of the modules reflects difficulties in finding correct spectral and/or virtual pitch(es) known also from behavioral experiments. Our measurements corroborate findings from neurophysiology according to which much of the neural processing relevant for perception of pitch and consonance is achieved subcortically.

1 Introduction

During the past decades, a vast amount of research in sensation and perception of sounds has been undertaken in both sensory physiology and psychophysics, respectively (e.g., Popper & Fay 1992, Ehret & Romand 1997, Terhardt 1998, Zwicker & Fastl 1999, Plack et al. 2005). At the same time, the field of music perception gained new impetus due to approaches influenced by cognitive psychology (e.g., Sloboda 1985, Krumhansl 1990, Bregman 1990), or by cognitive science in general (e.g., Balaban et al. 1992). There have been efforts to bring together facts and models from both fields (e.g., Handel 1989, Bregman 1990, McAdams & Bigand 1993, Leman 1995), however, many problems still wait to be investigated.

In the following, we shall deal with the perception of inharmonic sounds as they are found in a number of music cultures. One reason to do so is that most of the experiments in hearing, and in sound perception in general, have been conducted with periodic sounds having harmonic spectra, or with inharmonic sounds which have little if any relevance for music (e.g., white or pink noise).

S. Ystad, R. Kronland-Martinet, and K. Jensen (Eds.): CMMR 2008, LNCS 5493, pp. 18–44, 2009.

Another reason is that perception of inharmonic sounds can be simulated with computer-based ear models in a bottom-up approach whereby certain mechanisms as well as limits of perceptual analysis might become evident. These, in turn, could have implications for music cognition. As will be demonstrated in this chapter by experimental data obtained from measurements done with computer ear models, our auditory system constrains perception of sound stimuli and thereby also influences cognition.

2   Perception of Harmonic Sounds

Empirical research in auditory perception almost always has a focus on pitch since it is a fundamental property of sounds (Houtsma 1995, Terhardt 1998, Plack & Oxenham 2005), which may be used in various systems of human communication including speech and music. Typically, explorations of pitch stem from periodic time signals such as sinusoids or complex tones comprising a number of harmonics in addition to a fundamental frequency. It has been found in many experiments that the pitch perceived from such periodic signals corresponds closely to the fundamental frequency of a complex harmonic tone, or to the frequency with which a complex waveshape composed of harmonics lacking a fundamental repeats per time unit. Different from abbreviations common in psychoacoustics, we will label the fundamental f_1 (since it is the lowest partial of a harmonic spectrum), and the repetition frequency of a harmonic complex lacking a fundamental, f_0. Fig. 1 shows the time function $y(t)$ of a harmonic complex tone (10 partials) with f_1 at 100 Hz, and partial amplitudes $A_n = 1/n$ (n = harmonic number 1, 2, 3,...). The length of the period according to $T = 1/f$ is 10 ms. Fig. 2 shows the same signal of which partials 1-3 have been removed while f_0 has been added to the graph as an extra (sinusoidal) component ($f_0 = 100\,\text{Hz}, A = 1$) to indicate that the two signals are likely to yield the same pitch in subjects. This model implies that our system of hearing includes a mechanism for periodicity extraction from sound signals such as speech and music. Periodicity extraction has been a major issue in hearing theory since long (cf. de Hesse 1972, de Boer 1976, Lyon & Shamma 1996, Schneider 1997a/b, 2000a, de Cheveigné 2005, Langner 2007).

The steep wavecrests at the onset of each vibration period as obvious from Fig. 1 (and also Fig. 2), in accordance with the 'volley principle' of Wever and Bray (Wever 1949, chs. 8, 9) have been regarded as triggering synchronized trains of neural spikes, which are suited to elicit a stable pitch percept. The same pitch, though is heard if the phase relations between signal components are changed so that no strong peaks are found at the onset of each period yet a certain periodicity of the signal is retained (Schneider 1997b, 123-135). The change of phase relations can affect the salience of pitch, and will often result in a change of the timbral quality of a given sound.

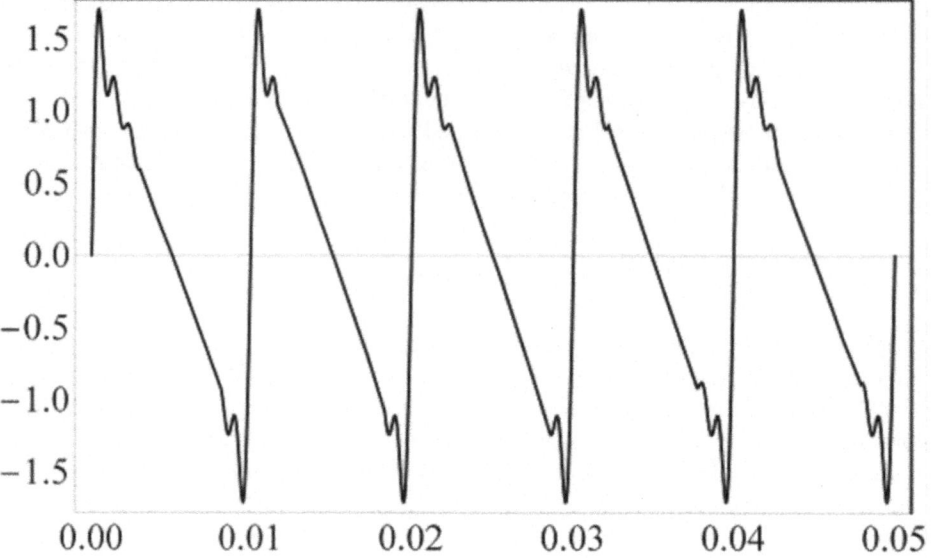

Fig. 1. Harmonic complex tone, 10 partials, $f_1 = 100$ Hz, $A_n = 1/n$

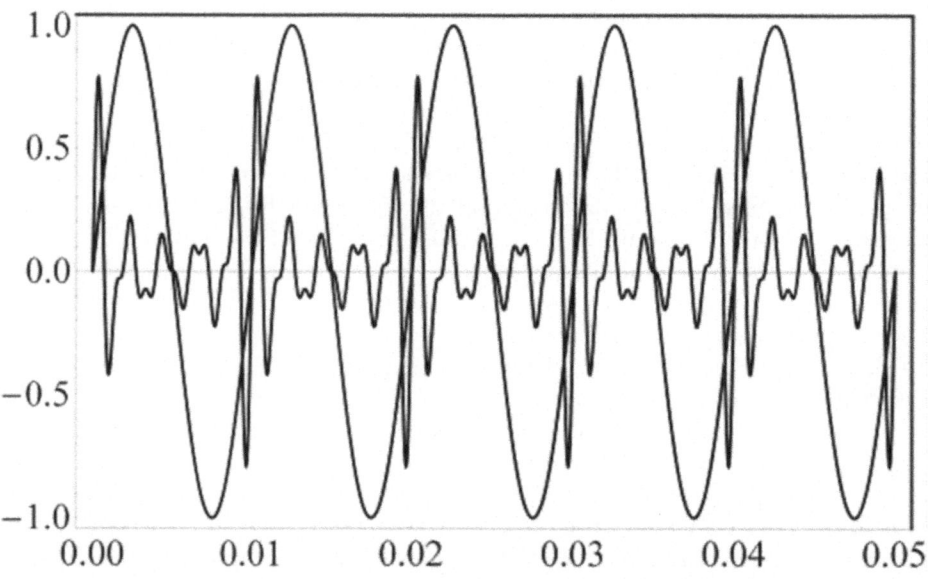

Fig. 2. Harmonic complex tone, partials 4-10, plus repetition frequency of complex waveshape $f_0 = 100$ Hz, $A = 1$ of the periodic signal

3   Harmonicity, Consonance and Fusion (*Verschmelzung*)

It is possible to construct very stable chords from complex tones which have a number of harmonics being phase-locked. For example, if one builds a chord from three complex tones having fundamental frequencies $\{300\,\text{Hz}, 400\,\text{Hz}, 500\,\text{Hz}\}$ and seven harmonics each with amplitudes defined by $A = 1/n$ ($n = 1, 2, \ldots$), the resulting sound represents a major chord in just intonation (Schneider 1997a, Fig. 1). Such chords which in real instruments are available from organ mixture stops, had been used by the psychologist Carl Stumpf to study the phenomenon of *Verschmelzung*, which can be regarded as a perceptual and cognitive quality experienced when listening attentively to chords such as the example given here. Due to the strict periodicity of the waveshape of the respective sound as well as to the likewise perfect harmonicity of the spectral components making up the complex tones, the sound offers an optimum of 'fusion', on the one hand, and still allows identification of many partials, on the other. Moreover, due to the strict periodicity of the sound, one perceives a low pitch at 100 Hz, which corresponds to the f_0. One can regard the f_0 as a virtual *basse fondamentale* whose function as the base note of major chords was explained in Rameau's theory of harmony (Rameau 1722, 1737). The output of the SPINET model (Cohen et al. 1995) centered in the frequency domain alternates between 100 Hz (the repetition frequency of the complex waveshape) and 300 Hz (the lowest spectral component). With a pitch extraction algorithm operating in the time domain on a normalized autocorrelation function (ACF; Boersma 1993), the pitch assigned to the overall major chord is 100 Hz. If fed into a model of the auditory periphery (AMS; Meddis & O'Mard 1997, 2003; see below), the output is a sum ACF (SACF, Fig. 3), which aggregates periodicities found in the neural activity patterns (NAP) within the channels defined by basilar membrane (BM) filters. The aggregation across channels for the pure major chord yields strong peaks at the time lags τ (ms) listed in Tab. 1 together with the relative height of peaks expressing the AC coefficient $r_{xx'}$, and the frequencies corresponding to a certain lag ($f = 1/\tau$). The SACF was calculated for 100 ms and is displayed in Fig. 3.

In the first column, the period T of the complex waveshape as well as its multiples are found; consequent to $f_0 = 1/T$, $f_0 = 100$ Hz is determined by the strongest peaks marking each period. Since the periods repeat identically, and $f_n = 1/n\tau$, the respective frequency values must be subharmonics $(1/2, 1/3, 1/4, \ldots)$ of f_0.

In column 4 of Tab. 1, a period corresponding to $2f_0$ as well as the fundamental frequencies of the three harmonic tones making up the major chord appear. Neglecting small numerical deviations from ideal frequency ratios, a complete harmonic series 1:2:3:4:5 (plus some periodicities representing divisions or multiples of either spectral or virtual pitches) is embedded in each period of $T = 10$ ms. Thereby a very high degree of harmonicity is encoded in the SACF, which (provided the model is valid in regard to physiological functions) will evoke strong sensations of consonance in subjects. Moreover, sounds as that used in this experiment will also give rise to difference and combination tones if presented with sufficient SPL.

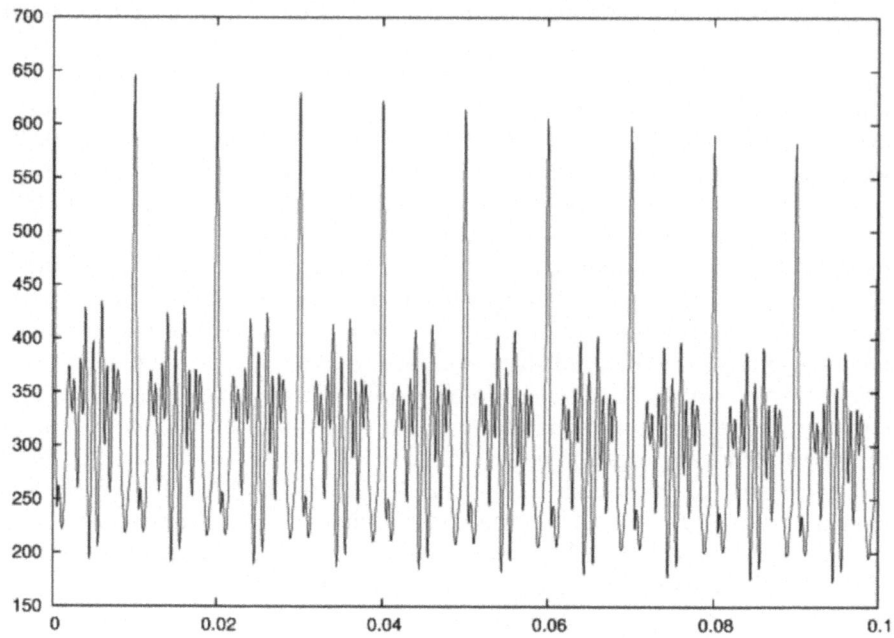

Fig. 3. SACF (100 ms), pure major chord

Table 1. Pure major chord, SACF; lags τ (ms), relative amplitudes of the ACF $r_{xx'}$, frequencies

τ (ms)	$r_{xx'}$	f (Hz)	τ (ms)	$r_{xx'}$	f (Hz)
10	646.63	100.00	6.02	434.76	166.09
20	638.52	50.00	3.98	428.54	251.31
30	630.44	33.33	4.98	397.72	200.84
40	622.46	25.00	3.35	380.90	298.14
50	614.49	20.00	7.46	375.83	134.08
60	606.52	16.66	6.67	374.22	150.00
70	598.62	14.29	1.98	374.01	505.26
80	590.77	12.50	8.00	370.46	125.00
90	582.94	11.11	2.54	361.11	393.44

One can take sounds such as that analyzed here as a paradigm for Stumpf's concept of consonance, which comprises both 'fusion' (*Verschmelzung*) and apperception of tonal relations (Schneider 1997a, 2008, 30-33). A musically trained listener (as was Stumpf himself), exposed to a complex harmonic chord audible for a sufficient time (> 2 seconds), can be expected to switching back and forth between a more holistic and integrative mode of hearing as well as a more analytical one; whereas the former will support the experience of 'fusion' as a Gestalt phenomenon, the latter is needed to apprehend the tonal relations between complex tones as well as between their constituents (Stumpf 1926, ch. 11).

Stumpf (1890, 1926) had already assumed a neural basis for the sensation of fusion. Since then a range of experimental data and hypotheses has been brought forward in favour of a neural basis of sensory consonance (e.g., Hesse 1972, Keidel 1989, 1992, Tramo et al. 2001, Langner 2007). Most of the approaches are based in the time domain and operate on periodicity detection in one way or another (e.g., coincidence detection of spike trains which form harmonic ratios). Some models include both temporal and spectral features.

4   Perception of Inharmonic Sounds

Investigation of inharmonic sounds in psychoacoustics often has been pursued by either adding a constant frequency value k to all harmonic frequencies, thereby turning them into an inharmonic series, like, for example, $230, 430, 630, 830, \ldots,$ 1630 Hz (with the original $f_1 = 200$ Hz, and $k = 30$ Hz), or by a modulation technique which yields inharmonic signals where no fundamental is present (e.g., 1230, 1430, 1630, 1830 Hz, $\ldots$; see de Boer 1976). In both cases, the degree of inharmonicity can be varied continuously according to the size of the constant, k. Further, a 'pseudo-fundamental' can be fitted to an incomplete series of detuned partials as long as the degree of inharmonicity is rather small (see Schneider 2000a). Such a 'pseudo-fundamental' again represents the quasi-periodicity of the signal, and hence equals f_0. With increasing inharmonicity of the spectrum, the periodicity of the signal decreases. A proven method to measure the periodicity of whatever time function $y(t)$ is the ACF. It was originally applied to the analysis of continuous movements within turbulent media as well as to the detection of periodicities in brain waves from which then a Fourier spectrum could be derived (Wiener 1961). Consequent to the Wiener-Khintchine theorem (Hartmann 1998, ch. 14), which relates the Fourier transform of the ACF of a signal to its energy spectral density, one can expect the ACF to degenerate in proportion to increasing spectral inharmonicity of a time signal $y(t)$. That is, the ACF will be the more irregular (with rather small and diminishing peaks and no clear periodicity) the more the spectral composition of the signal is shifting into inharmonicity.

Whereas the ACF of a perfectly periodic signal mirrors the periodicity $y(t) = y(t+T)$, (T = period length in samples or ms) inherent in the signal by marking prominent peaks (the correlation coefficient $r_{xx'}$ is unity at these points), the ACF of sounds recorded from idiophones such as Western swinging or carillon bells is not just as regular. For example, the sound recorded from the bass clock of the famous carillon of Brugge (built in 1742-48 by Joris Du Mery) yields the ACF shown in Fig. 4. Though the spectrum of this bell sound contains a considerable number of quasi-harmonic components (Schneider & Leman 2002,

Tab. 2 and Fig. 2), they do not all correspond to a single harmonic series in which harmonic frequencies f_n are defined by $f_n = n f_1$. Furthermore, there are quite many spectral components with inharmonic frequency ratios relative to the hum note, which in this bell is ∼97.3 Hz. Consequently, the ACF of this sound, though still containing a number of peaks at certain lag points, does not exhibit a clear periodicity which could be interpreted as corresponding to the f_0 of the signal. The leftmost strong peak after onset (for which $r_{xx'} = 1$) occurs after a lag of τ ∼1350 samples, which, for a sampling frequency of 44.1 kHz, corresponds to ∼30 ms and yields a frequency of, roughly, 33.3 Hz, which is about 1/3 of the lowest spectal component contained in the bell sound.

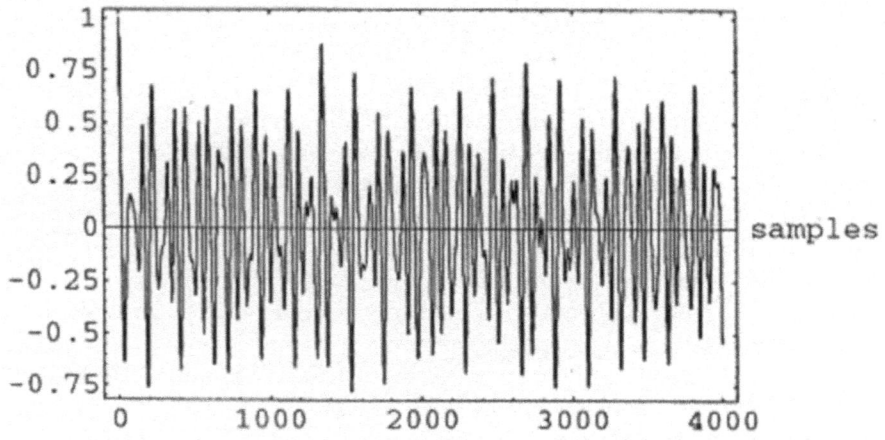

Fig. 4. ACF, bass clock (bell no. 1), Brugge carillon

Sounds from many other idiophones such as gong chimes found in Javanese and Balinese *gamelan*, respectively, are much more inharmonic in spectral composition than is the carillon bell we have refered to (for examples and detailed analyses, see Schneider 1997b). In extreme cases such as shallow gongs like the Chinese *tam-tam*, the spectrum is very inharmonic, and also very dense with spectral components which interact, giving rise to amplitude modulation (AM). In addition, due to certain nonlinearities in the pattern of vibration, modal frequencies can be quite unstable so that the whole sound becomes transitory and fluctuating. In the *tam-tam*, the ACF drops to $r_{xx'}$ ∼0.5 or less immediately after onset of the sound, and then goes down to $r_{xx'}$ ∼0.25 (Schneider & Bader 2003, Figs. 5 and 6), which indicates that there is very little temporal and spectral coherence in the sound. As a result of both the complex pattern of vibration, and the likewise complex inharmonic spectrum, no definite pitch can be assigned to such a sound.

In regard to sounds and the pitch they may evoke, one can distinguish two extremes which may be considered as marking the two poles of dimensions suited to classify sounds in regard to pitch perception and pitch salience (see below):

1. A sinusoidal of given frequency and amplitude, which, as a stationary signal, yields one stable pitch percept corresponding to the frequency of the signal $y(t) = A\sin(2\pi f t)$.

2. A complex inharmonic sound which comprises many spectral components irregularly spaced along the frequency axis, and which undergoes AM (as well as some FM since modal frequencies can be unstable). The *tam-tam* is a clear example of this type of sounds which lack periodicity and do not yield any clear pitch percept. Rather, such sounds have a sound colour or timbral quality (in this case, a metallic, clangy and swirling sound quality) which may indicate a certain pitch area on a broad scale from low to high, yet do not give rise to any definite pitch. As is known from experiments with filtered noise bands, even these can be arranged to form a rough sequence of 'pitches' or, rather, different degrees of brightness (Hesse 1982), which, due to the interaction of the variables of tone height and tonal brightness, *appear* as 'pitches'.

The dimensions (quasi-continua) can be arranged according to the degree of periodicity of the time signal as well as the harmonicity of the corresponding spectrum; in addition, the psychoacoustic attributes of pitch and pitch salience (cf. Terhardt 1998, ch. 11) can be matched to the other features. Without going into details of signals and systems theory (Bachmann 1992, Terhardt 1998, Hartmann 1998), and allowing for some simplifications, we can establish the following bipartite scheme:

Signal:	completely/predominantly stationary	_ predominantly transient
Periodicity:	clear ――――――――――――――――――――――――――――――	uncertain
Spectrum:	harmonic ――――――――――――――――――――――――――	inharmonic
Frequencies:	stable ―――――――――――――――――――――――――――――	fluctuating
Pitch:	clear and salient ―――――――――――――――――	ambiguity of pitch(es)
Typical:	sensation of a single/dominant pitch	several pitches/no clear pitch

Most sounds produced from musical instruments can be ordered along these dimensions. Sounds from aerophones and chordophones thereby fall on the left side, sounds from membranophones and, in particular, idiophones predominantly on the right. Of course, the plucking of a string in a chordophone such as a harpsichord or guitar also results in a transitory and often quite inharmonic onset of a sound (Keiler et al. 2003, Bader 2005) before a quasi-stationary state in the vibrating system as well as in the sound radiated from such systems is reached. In idiophones (xylophones, metallophones; e.g., gongs and gong chimes, bells) many of which are set to vibration by an impulse there is no quasi-stationary regime in the vibrating system since the transitory onset is immediately followed by an often rapid decay of modes of vibration due to friction forces in the material set to motions as is obvious in many African and Asian xylophone types yet also in some metallophones (Schneider 1997b). Ambiguity of pitch perception increases with increasing inharmonicity of the sounds produced by idiophones such as found in the Javanese and Balinese *gamelan* (Schneider 1997b, 2000a/b, 2001). Perception is complicated by the fact that many sounds radiated from xylophones and metallophones (e.g., gong chimes of the Javanese *bonang* or Balinese *trompong* type) are quite short in duration, which means that pitch perception of complex inharmonic sounds must be achieved within a time span of, in many cases, 100-250 ms from onset.

In what follows, sounds recorded from certain idiophones will be analyzed by means of different software tools which in turn represent different models of peripheral auditory signal processing. In particular, an algorithm developed by Hermes (1988) based on the subharmonic matching process as proposed by Terhardt (1979, 1998) as well as an algorithm close to the concept of the harmonic sieve (Cohen et al. 1995) will be employed. Both models consider spectral properties of sounds and hence operate in the frequency domain. In contrast, the auditory model of Meddis and Hewitt (1991a/b) developed further by Meddis and O'Mard (1997, 2003) is based in the time domain. In several respects, it is similar to the Auditory Image Model (AIM) developed by Patterson et al. (1995) as well as to some other temporal approaches (de Cheveigné 2005). In the present study, the Auditory Modelling System (AMS, Meddis & O'Mard 2003) is used.

The analyses for the subharmonic estimation of pitch as well as for the estimations based on the harmonic sieve as implemented in the spatial pitch network model (SPINET; Cohen et al. 1995) have been performed by using routines included in the Praat environment (Version 5.0.38; Boersma & Weenink 2008). Though this software was designed for experimental phonetics, it can handle a broad range of musical sounds. As a first step of analysis, our sound examples have been processed in the frequency domain by means of a filter bank which simulates the excitation pattern on the BM, and which yields a cochleagram (scaled in Bark) as output. This type of analysis is useful for finding strong spectral components, which can be regarded as pitch candidates. If a cochleagram contains several such strong components (marked by dark lines in graphics based on greyscales), it is very likely that these will be perceived as separate spectral pitches, or that they interact in forming virtual pitches (cf. Terhardt 1979, 1998, Schneider 1997b, 2000a/b).

Let us begin with the cochleagram obtained from the sounds of four of the bells (nos. 1-4) of the Du Mery carillon of Brugge (Fig. 5). For the analysis, all sounds recorded close to the bells located on top of the belfry of Brugge[1] have been cut to segments of 0.6-1 s duration from the onset, and all selections have been normalized at -3 dB level. The cochleagram of the four sound segments represent a bell scale comprising the musical notes of *g, a, bb, c'*, whereby the prime (that is, the second partial of a typical minor-third bell; Schneider & Leman 2002) is taken as the decisive spectral component with regard to tuning and pitch.

---

[1] The equipment included two Neumann U 67, two TAB V72a preamps (fixed gain +32dB), one Telefunken V76 (variable gain 3-76dB), and a Panasonic SV 3800 DAT (48kHz/16 bit).

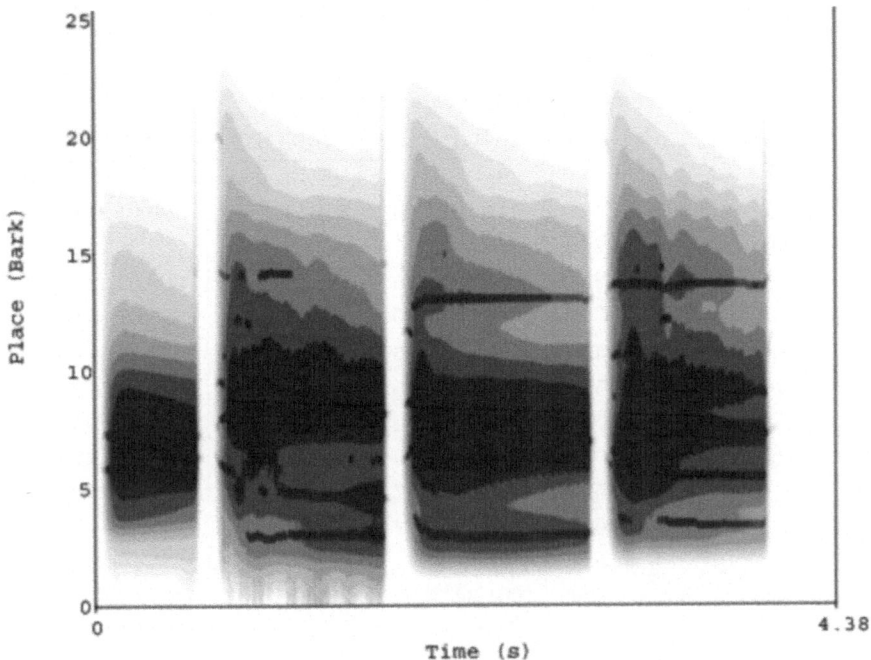

Fig. 5. Cochleagram of four bell sounds from the Brugge Carillon (Bells no. 1 - 4)

In Tab. 2 the relevant modal frequencies determined by spectrographic analysis (amplitude levels omitted) for the strong partials of the four bell sounds in question are shown up to the double octave (a theoretical frequency ratio of 8:1 to the hum).

In Tab. 2, components a/b denote degenerate pairs of eigenmodes. The strong spectral components listed here as well as many more present in each sound radiated from one of the bells form the acoustical input to a bank of filters which produces the cochleagram as output. The excitation patterns (1-4) reflect that there are several strong components in each sound which could function as spectral pitches, and which might also contribute to the formation of virtual pitches.

The estimation of a single (low and/or dominant) pitch per bell sound with the Praat algorithm based on the SPINET model yields no interpretable result. The respective graph is empty for most of the duration of the four sound segments, and erratic for the remainder. This result may be surprising, or even disappointing because all four bell sounds contain a considerable number of quasi-harmonic components besides the inharmonic ones. One has to remember though that the spatial pitch network constitutes a weighted harmonic sieve, which yields a pitch estimate best if the spectral components of a stimulus correspond to a single harmonic series. In this respect, it closely resembles other spectral pattern matching (or harmonic template) models which can deal with

Table 2. Eigenfrequencies and frequency ratios with respect to the hum of bells no. 1-4 from the Brugge carillon

Partial Name		No. 1 (g) f_n (Hz) f_1/f_n		No. 2 (a) f_n (Hz) f_1/f_n		No. 3 (bb) f_n (Hz) f_1/f_n		No. 4 (c') f_n (Hz) f_1/f_n	
0						65.13	0.50		
1	Hum	97.43	1.00	111.10	1.00	121.43	1.00	129.01	1.00
2	Prime	195.84	2.01	218.50	1.97	243.80	2.01	262.36	2.03
3	Tierce	233.81	2.40	261.60	2.35	292.77	2.41	309.62	2.40
4	Quint	294.51	3.02	328.57	2.96	361.88	2.98	393.61	3.05
5	Nominal	391.04	4.01	438.40	3.95	492.84	4.06	521.39	4.04
6a	10th	488.39	5.01	550.08	4.95	607.46	5.00	642.82	4.98
6b		492.86	5.05	569.38	5.12	627.23	5.16	666.34	5.16
7	11th	514.99	5.28	577.04	5.19	642.07	5.28	688.21	5.33
8		525.22	5.39	630.31	5.67			696.39	5.40
9a		573.35	5.88						
9b		576.26	5.91						
10	12th	589.41	6.05	661.34	5.95	741.58	6.01	763.68	5.92
								729.01	6.13
11	13th	627.59	6.44	755.07	6.32			847.23	6.57
12		683.73	7.01	701.85	6.80			923.12	7.15
13		712.67	7.31						
14		746.30	7.66					988.71	7.66
15a	Double	818.46	8.40	918.04	8.26	1027.05	8.46	1098.69	8.51
15b	Octave	824.06	8.46						

harmonic spectra, and fail to assign a low (virtual) pitch to complex tones as inharmonicity increases to a point where the spectral components no longer fit well to one template or sieve. With increasing spectral inharmonicity, the error term calculated from the frequency deviations of the components relative to the center frequencies of a template or harmonic sieve surpasses a certain limit.

This implies that the probability for a certain spectral component to match a template or sieve decreases with increasing detuning of harmonic partials towards inharmonicity. For truly inharmonic sounds such as produced by *gamelan* instruments, the harmonic sieve model seems inappropriate for analysis because the distribution of spectral components along the frequency axis in such sounds usually is too complex, and too irregular to be matched to a harmonic series of frequencies (see below).

Applying the subharmonic matching model as devised by Hermes (1988) to the same four bell sound segments yields a much clearer result. The algorithm indeed produces one low pitch per sound (plus some artefacts, see Fig. 6), which in this case apparently represents the prime (2nd partial) of each sound.

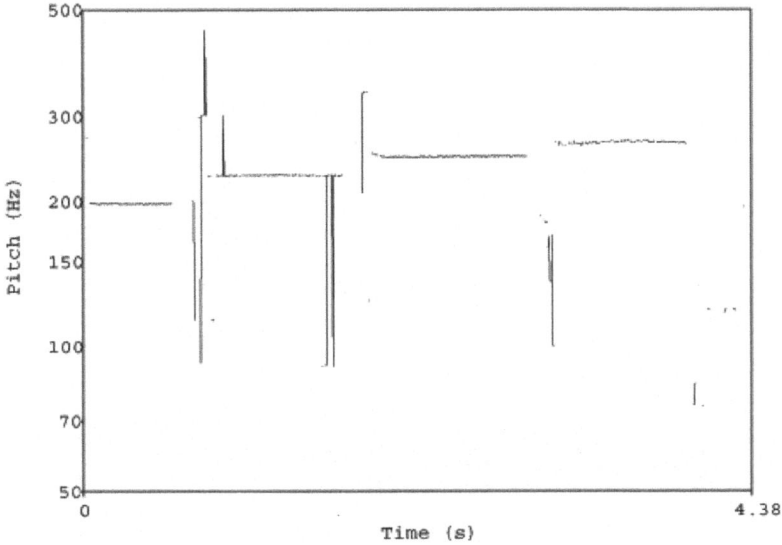

Fig. 6. Pitch of four bell sounds from the Brugge carillon, bell no. 1 - 4); Subharmonic matching

The result of this analysis conforms to behavioral data which consistently demonstrate that many (if not most) subjects judge the main pitch of a bell to be equal to the so-called strike tone or strike note (German: *Schlagton*; Dutch: *Slagtoon*). The strike note is a virtual pitch typically located at or close to the frequency of either the second or the first partial of the bell spectrum (Terhardt & Seewann 1984). Since these two partials are an octave apart, yet equivalent as to their chroma, the results provided by the subharmonic matching model seem reasonable.

In a second trial, more complex sounds recorded in Bali by Rolf Bader from a *gendér wayang* (see Schneider 2001b) were fed into the SPINET as well as into the subharmonic matching model, respectively. Before that, the basic cochlea-gram analysis was carried out. The *gendér* used in this analysis is a metallophon that consists of ten bronze plates. A bamboo resonator is attached to each plate and is usually tuned so as to match a low spectral component of the plate. The gendér instruments are played in pairs labelled *pengumbang* and *pengisep* with regard to their tuning. The lowest mode of each plate on the *pengumbang* is tuned 20-50 cents low relative to the respective plate and mode frequency on the *pengisep*. Since the two instruments are played so as to produce many intervals in parallel, this results in complex inharmonic sounds, which undergo AM permanently (for details, see Schneider 1997b, 2000a, 2001b). For the present analysis, the sounds recorded from plates no. 3, 4, 5 of the *pengumbang* played by a local musician in Bali have been used, which respresent part of a scale. The segments of these sounds subjected to analysis last about three seconds each. All sounds have been normalized at -6dB.

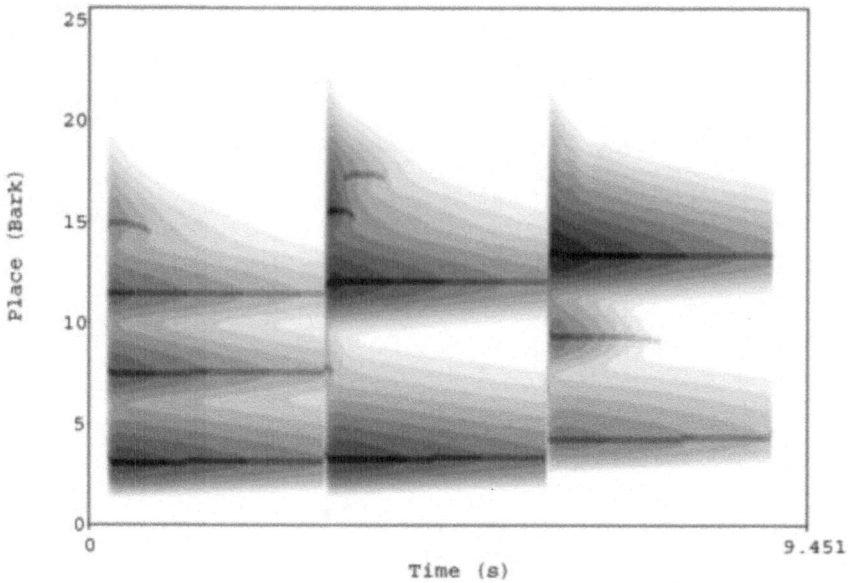

Fig. 7. Cochleagram of three sound segments recorded from a *gendér* (Bali)

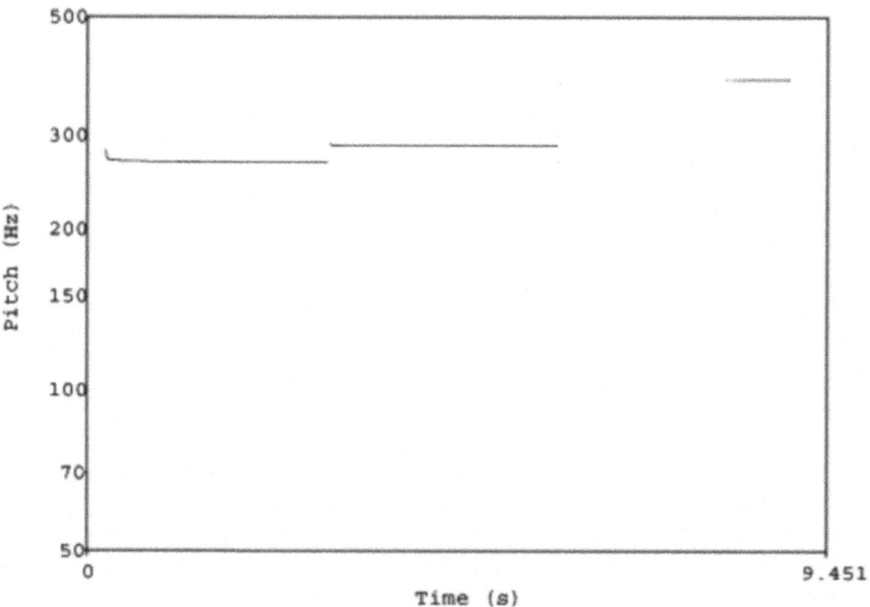

Fig. 8. Pitch estimates, 3 *gendér* sounds, subharmonic matching model

The cochleagram reveals that there are different zones of BM excitation, and that each sound segment offers several strong components which function as pitch candidates. In fact, at least two pitches can be identified by listeners in such sounds, namely a low pitch of a sinusoidal quality and a high pitch of metallic timbre. Depending on the strength of playing (Balinese music culture distinguishes between soft and strong styles of playing), the number of modes excited in each plate of course differs considerably, and so does the number of spectral and virtual pitches which are elicited. An analysis of the three sound segments with the SPINET model fails altogether. The subharmonic matching model yields the graph in Fig. 8 as output; frequency in this plot ranges from 50 Hz to 500 Hz (ordinate gives log frequency).

From Fig. 8 it is evident that the algorithm produces a single pitch estimate for each sound segment. In this case, these estimates do *not* correspond to low spectral components of the three sounds, which would have been found at 212.44 Hz, 247.7 Hz, and 286.6 Hz, respectively. Instead, the model yields three frequencies which seem to indicate virtual pitches. For the third sound segment, this frequency appears only towards the end of decay when spectral complexity is already reduced compared to the onset.

To check the performance of a model based in the time domain, we used the sound of a *bonang* kettle gong from West Java (Sunda; see Schneider 1997b), the sound from bell no. 1 of the Brugge carillon (Schneider & Leman 2002) as well as one of the *gendér* sounds as acoustic input. Processing of sound stimuli in the AMS (Meddis & O'Mard 1997, 2003) functionally includes the following basic steps: 1) peripheral excitation and BM filtering, 2) inner hair cell (IHC) model, half-wave rectifier, low-pass filtering, 3) extraction of periodicities within each channel by means of ACF, 4) aggregation of periodicities across channels with a summary ACF (SACF), which allows to find the pitch estimate of sounds. Since the AMS tries to emulate the auditory pathway as close as possible, it includes modules such as an outer/middle ear filter, conversion to stapes velocity, IHC/auditory nerve (AN) synapse, receptor potential, refractory period within a nerve fiber, etc. The model has been refined and expanded over the years to include a nonlinear BM (Lopez-Poveda & Meddis 2001) as well as other new features (see Meddis 2006). It is of importance to notice that the AMS model (after BM filtering and IHC transduction) operates on patterns of AN spike probabilities. Hence, the within-channel ACF as well as the SACF is not obtained from the waveshape of the sound yet from the neural activity patterns consequent to peripheral auditory stimulation.

The main components of the spectrum of the *bonang* gong are listed in Tab. 3. The measurements were obtained with the 'Frequency at peak'-option (parabolic interpolation) of Spectro 3.01 (G. Scavone, P. Cook) running on a NeXT. The amplitudes are calculated relative to 0 dBfs; in an undistorted signal, all amplitudes must be ≤ 0 dBfs.

The spectrum of the *bonang* sound is shown in Fig. 9. The spectal envelope is indicated as a dash-dotted line, and contours of equal loudness as dashed lines. Peaks with amplitudes which can be expected to evoke a loudness sensation equal

Table 3. Spectrum of *bonang* gong (Sunda); main spectral components (no. 1-16)

No.	f (Hz)	Rel. Ampl. (dB)	Bark (z)	Pitch Candidate
1	318.27	-27.7	3	X
2	638.30	-49.7	6	
3	1289.15	-42.5	10	
4	1401.48	-29.7	10	X
5	1448.85	-39.6	10	
6	1511.84	-42.8	11	
7	1599.07	-54.7	11	
8	1627.26	-52.5	11	
9	1719.67	-59.4	11	
10	1885.08	-47.7	12	
11	2304.28	-46.5	13	
12	2378.47	-49.2	14	
13	2408.19	-35.2	14	X
14	2507.20	-37.5	14	X
15	2583.97	-58.6	14	
16	2637.69	-47.7	14	X

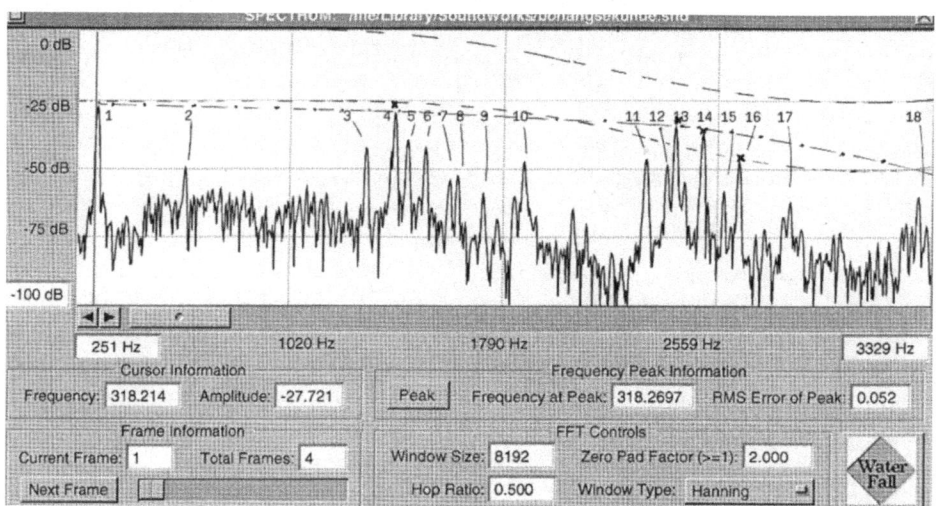

Fig. 9. Spectrum of a *bonang* sound

to, or greater than that of the lowest strong component at 318.3 Hz are marked
with an 'x'. There are four relevant components (nos. 4, 13, 14, 16) in addition
to the lowest one, which can be considered as candidates possibly giving rise to

spectral pitches and/or contributing to a virtual pitch. This feature accounts for most of the ambiguity this sound brings about in regard to pitch perception. Another factor is that groups of narrowly spaced spectral components fall into the same critical band (CB). The respective CBs have been indicated in Tab. 3 according to data given in Zwicker & Fastl (1999, 159; Tab. 6.1). Groups of inharmonic spectral components falling into the same CB have two perceptual effects: first, they cause AM and roughness sensation; second, they further increase the pitch ambiguity of this peculiar sound. One has to remember that the *bonang* is a gong chime (usually comprising ten kettle gongs tuned to a scale; cf. Schneider 1997b) in the *gamelan* of Java which is often used to render the so-called nuclear theme, that is, a basic melodic pattern.

The *bonang* sound in question yields no interpretable result with the SPINET. Evidently, harmonic template or sieve models are unsuited to deal with such complex inharmonic spectra. Because of the spectral composition of this *bonang* sound, its time function cannot be expected to be sufficiently periodic to facilitate detection of a common period, T. The ACF calculated directly from the sound input indeed reveals no obvious period or regular fine structure.

Compared to a standard ACF, the AMS operates differently in that the signal is split into BM filter channels first[2], then undergoes transduction by means of an IHC and low pass filtering module before the within-channel periodicity, and finally the SACF is calculated. It could be that, nothwithstanding the CB problem obvious from the data in Tab. 3, such a stepwise processing might improve the result of each within-channel ACF, and thereby also the final SACF. The image obtained from the output of all within-channel ACFs indeed shows that for components which can be resolved individually by the peripheral filter bank, a period is found corresponding to the frequency of the component by $T_n = 1/f_n$. The image is difficult to analyse, though, for channels which contain the ACF calcaluted from several inharmonic components falling into the same filter band. A peak-picking algorithm applied to the SACF data finds major peaks at lags corresponding to 158.94, 350.36, 105.49, 108.11, 705.88, 470.59, 128.69, 205.13, and 237.62 Hz, respectively. The frequencies, which are ordered according to peak height expressing $r_{xx'}$, do not correspond to spectral components (though 350.36 Hz is relatively close to the lowest modal frequency of the *bonang*). One could hypothesize that a peak around 9.4 ms (~106 Hz) is representing a near-periodicity, which can be established from subharmonic matching of several of the spectral components of the *bonang* (in particular, nos. 1-3; cf. Tab. 3). Since there are peaks in the SACF at 105.5 and 108.1 Hz, respectively, a quasi-period of ~106 Hz, which (as a common denominator) fits to a number of spectral components, seems feasable. Fig. 10 shows the SACF of the *bonang* sound for 100 ms.

---

[2] For the present analysis, a gammatone filter bank (with CF from 100 to 4000 Hz) has been used because of the moderate signal level of the sounds (carillon bell, *bonang*, *gendér*). Otherwise, the nonlinear BM model (Lopez-Poveda & Meddis 2001) available in the AMS would have been employed.

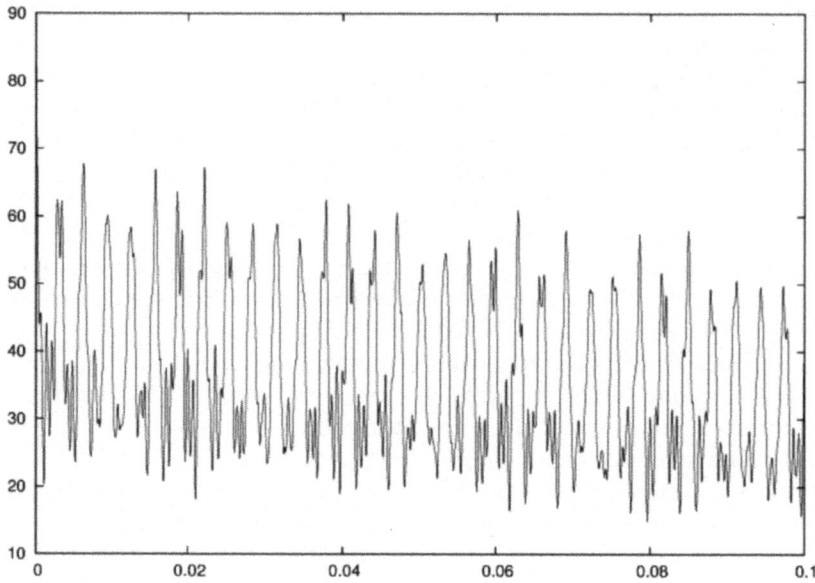

Fig. 10. SACF (100 ms), *bonang* sound

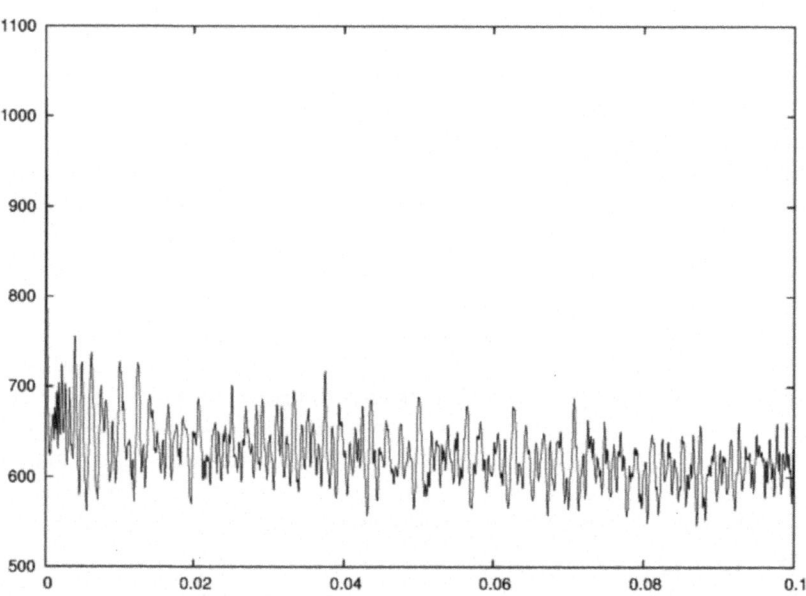

Fig. 11. SACF (100 ms), sound from carillon bell no. 1, Brugge

For the first of the carillon bells, the same analysis in the time domain was carried out. Due to the much less inharmonic, in parts quasi-harmonic spectral structure of the bell sound (see Tab. 2), the resulting SACF contains a number of small yet distinct peaks (Fig. 11).

A peak-picking algorithm applied to the SACF data detects the time point for each of the smaller peaks. Those listed in the following table have been ordered with respect to their relative height (expressing the degree of correlation $r_{xx'}$) and the time lag (τ). In addition, the frequency corresponding to the lag due to $f = 1/\tau$ for each peak is given.

Table 4. Peaks found in the SACF of the bell sound ordered according to height

No.	Rel. Height	τ (ms)	f (Hz)
1	755.88	4.02	248.70
2	737.85	6.25	160.00
3	727.17	10.10	99.38
4	727.05	4.98	200.80
5	726.38	12.50	80.13
6	724.86	2.20	452.83
7	717.55	37.50	26.68
8	714.90	10.30	97.56

Some of the data can be interpreted (at least hypothetically) thus: peaks 3 and 8 are very close to the frequency of the hum note of this bell, that is, they might indicate the period corresponding to the lowest spectral component of the bell. Peak no. 4 comes close to the period and frequency of the prime. The strongest peak (no. 1 at 4.02 ms) might indicate some period as well since there are peaks also at near-multiples of its lag, that is, at 8.19, 12.5, 16.6, 20.7, 25.1, and 29.2 ms.

If the peaks are ordered according to the time lags $\tau < 12.5$ ms (which means $f > 80$ Hz), leaving aside the values for the peak height, the following frequencies are found: 80.13, 84.66, 87.91, 89.55, 94.5, 97.56, 99.38, 109.84, 122.14, 132.6, 160, 200.84, 248.7, 280.7, 303.8, 369.23, 452.83, 558.14, 666.66, 800, 1021.28,and 1920 Hz. Of these frequency values (which fit an exponential function $e^{0.33f}$ fairly well), those which are in the range of ca. 85-100 Hz seem to indicate that there is a periodicity of the partly harmonic, partly inharmonic signal which roughly corresponds to the lowest spectral component.

Finally, one of the *gendér* sounds (plate/scale step no. 3) was subjected to the same type of analysis. The SACF (Fig. 12) in this case is particularly complex due to the dense inharmonic spectrum, which contains strong peaks from 212 Hz up to 6.6 kHz, and moreover exhibits two maxima in the spectral envelope at ca. 2.6 and 6.6 kHz, respectively (cf. Schneider 2001b, Fig. 4).

A peak-picking algorithm applied to the SACF data finds the strongest peak at a lag of 5.02 ms which corresponds to 199.17 Hz. This is not too far away from the

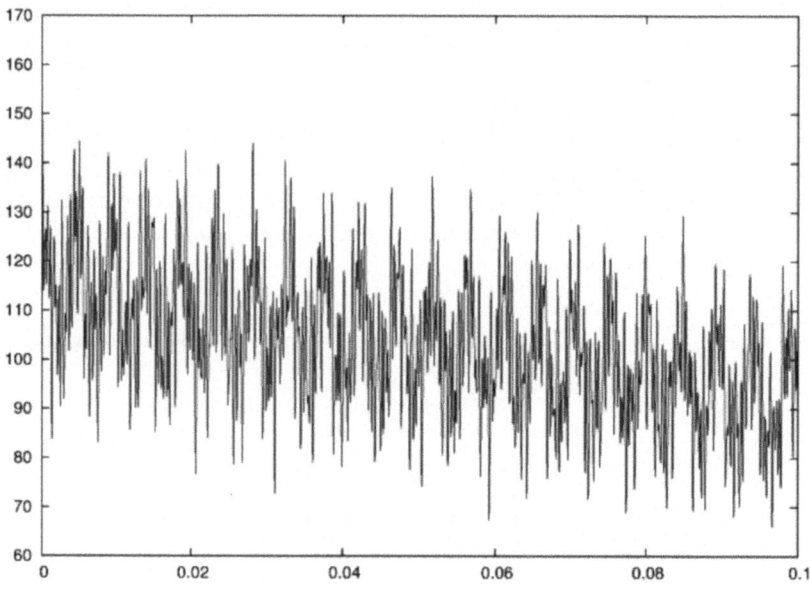

Fig. 12. SACF (100 ms), sound of *gendér* plate no. 3

base mode frequency of the plate (∼212.5 Hz), however, a multitude of relatively strong peaks in the SACF makes it unlikely that a common period could be extracted (a cluster analysis applied to the SACF data did not help much to clear the picture). Due to their spectral and temporal structure, *gendér* sounds are ambiguous in pitch. Typically, one can assign (for example, by attuning a tone generator or simply by singing a syllable such as "la") a main (low) pitch to each *gendér* sound; in experiments, subjects try to match the frequency of a sine tone (or the fundamental of the syllables they sing) to that spectral component of the *gendér* sound which represents the base mode of the transversal bending waves of the vibrating plate. Detecting this low component is possible if it can be resolved by peripheral filtering (a condition which applies to our example), and probably processed individually after mechano-electrical transduction (as the output from within-channel periodicity extraction in the AMS module indicates).

Perceiving a low pitch, though, in most *gendér* (and, similarly, *bonang* and *trompong*) sounds goes along with perceiving from one to three additional components in higher frequency regions. If such components result from a single strong spectral peak unhampered by neighbours, they can mostly be interpreted as 'side pitches' complementing a 'main' (low) pitch. Because of the inharmonic composition of the spectrum, main pitch and side pitches do not fuse, that is, they are perceived as being more or less unrelated. In this respect, the perceptual situation is much different from a complex harmonic sound (see above, section 3). If groups of inharmonic spectral components fall into the same CB in frequency regions much higher than the base frequency, they may not give rise to a clear side pitch yet, rather, to a sensation of a cluster-like band of frequencies. This sensation often interferes with the percept of the low pitch, which thereby appears less salient. Together, low pitch plus side pitches, or low pitch plus spectral disturbances (plus some FM as well as a considerable degree of AM) make up a situation where perceptual ambiguity is almost inevitable.

One of the reasons why the *gendér* sounds are so awkward with regard to pitch perception, seems to be the geometry of the plates, which have a trapezoid cross section. Wave dispersion within this geometry allows for more complex patterns of reflections at boundaries, which in turn result in rich inharmonic sounds in particular during the transient portion (Bader 2004 and personal communication). Since the plates are hit with mallets, and the number of notes played per time unit in the *gong kebyar* style often is high, listeners are confronted with fast sequences of transient inharmonic sounds, to the effect that pitch perception for each short sound segment as well as for sonorities formed from several sounds produced simultaneously will be ambiguous.

5 Discussion

Comparing the results from the two models operating in the frequency domain to the AMS operating in the time domain, it seems reasonable to state that all can handle periodic signals where they detect f_0 and/or spectral components of the actual sound input. In regard to inharmonic sounds, both the subharmonic matching model and the AMS based on the ACF approach can analyze signals which are not strictly periodic, and which have a partly harmonic, partly inharmonic spectrum like, for example, carillon bells such as found at Brugge. To be sure, these bells are excellent specimen which have been carefully tuned both with regard to their spectral composition as well as constituting a musical scale when played one after another.

The results obtained from computer-based ear models are in line with many observations and experiments which demonstrate that with increasing spectral inharmonicity and the periodicity of the signal decreasing correspondingly, the pitch or, rather, pitches assigned by listeners to such sounds as produced by bells, gong chimes etc., typically become ambiguous (Terhardt, Stoll & Seewann 1982b, Terhardt & Seewann 1984, Schneider 1997b, 2000a/b, 2001a/b).

In one experiment, in which we employed samples from bell no. 2 of the Brugge carillon for the reproduction of a chorale (*Ich bin's, ich sollte büßen...*, J. S. Bach; four voice transcript for piano or organ), apperception even for skilled listeners was difficult. Even though the fundamental frequencies of all notes realized with the bell sounds were identical with the fundamental frequencies as defined by the notation of the given piece, the spectral inharmonicity of the bell led to severe problems in analyzing the musical structure, which consists of chords played one after another. With each chord comprising four bells sounds (one for each voice), the resulting spectral inharmonicity is considerable, and evidently hampers detection of the pitches, which is necessary for listeners to be able to follow the motion of the four voices, on the one hand, and to understand the tonal functions of the simultaneous chords, on the other. In regard of variables related to perception (such as consonance, roughness, etc.), the bell version of the chorale differs significantly from one played with a (synthesized) pipe organ (Schneider 2001a).

It is quite obvious that perceptual and cognitive processing of complex inharmonic sounds, and music played with such sounds is more difficult and demanding than is perception of harmonic complex tones as well as listening to music based on such. As has been observed in experiments with evoked potentials, several parameters (such as the latencies for P1 and N1) change significantly when inharmonic instead of harmonic sounds are used as stimuli (cf. Sinex 2005, 380-81).

The ambiguity of pitch experienced in complex inharmonic sounds such as radiated from bells and gongs can be attributed to both the spectral composition and the temporal structure of such stimuli. Though spectral and temporal structure interacts in may ways, they should be examined separately. For example, many sounds from carillons and *gamelan* instruments, due to the inharmonicity and density of spectral components (for examples, see Schneider 1997b, 2000a/b, 2001a/b, Schneider & Leman 2002) mean an increased workload of spectral processing by the auditory system. Even though in many stimuli some of the strong components can be resolved (according to CB filter bands), and may thus serve as spectral cues for pitch perception, they often form arbitrary frequency ratios, and hence give rise to separate spectral pitches. Also, one finds inharmonic sounds in which some of the strong spectral components are closely spaced in frequency, and thereby interact both as spectral pitch candidates as well as producing AM.

Given such a spectral structure, the corresponding time function cannot be periodic, and the auditory system in such cases fails to extract a basic periodicity corresponding to f_0 as temporal information relevant for pitch perception. If several inharmonic sounds are played simultaneously (as is the case in *gamelan* music and also in music played on a carillon), ambiguity increases as a function of the resulting spectral inharmonicity and density, which hampers identification of musically relevant objects (e.g., motives, themes, phrases) within each voice as well as separation of voices in chords and sonorities.

It is not possible, at this point, to discuss the physiological relevance and validity of various auditory models as well as objections which have been raised against approaches centered either in the frequency or in the time domain (see de Boer 1976, Lyon & Shamma 1996, Terhardt 1998, Lopez-Poveda 2005, Plack & Oxenham 2005, de Cheveigné 2005). In regard to spectral models, the neglect of information available from the temporal envelope and its fine structure has often been critized. On the other hand, objections against a purely temporal approach to pitch and interval perception repeatedly have pointed to the weak neuroanatomical and neurophysiological foundations of, in particular ACF-based models. Empirical evidence for the validity of the ACF-approach has been sought in interspike-interval codes recorded from the AN where data allow to regard so-called all-order interspike interval histograms (ISIH), in particular, if pooled from a sample of AN fibers, as being "autocorrelation-like neural representations of the stimulus" (Cariani & Delgutte 1996a, 1712). Basically the same approach has been used more recently to show that the ISIH obtained in experiments on AN fibers of the cat for consonant musical intervals, namely the perfect fifth (ratio of the two fundamental frequencies 660 Hz : 440 Hz = 3:2) and the perfect fourth (4:3) entails perfect periodicity (Tramo et al. 2001). For the more dissonant interval of the tritone (45:32), the ISIH is less clear in regard to periodicity, and for the minor second (469 Hz : 440 Hz $\approx$ 16:15), periodicity is more difficult to extract from the ISIH because the first strong peak occurs only after a lag τ ~35 ms.

The fact that a periodic sound stimulus such as a vowel can trigger a periodic spike response synchronized to the phase of a tone has been known for decades. Also, it was shown that the spectrum of the input signal can be reconstructed from the neural discharge pattern in AN fibers. There have been a number of observations with regard to nuclei and mechanisms along the auditory pathway, where neural periodicity coding and analysis might be performed (cf. Keidel 1992, Ehret 1997, de Ribaupierre 1997, Schneider 1997b, 84-95, 104-109, 135-142; 2000a). Further, it has been argued that stimulus periodicity is mapped in the auditory cortex (AI; see Schulze et al. 2002). Recently, observations as well as hypothetical interpretations have been condensed into a temporal model of pitch and timbre perception as well as the neural basis of harmonicity detection (Langner 2007).

The concept of periodicity is so fundamental to natural processes such as vibration and sound that it would be a surprise if the sense of hearing in mammals would not be capable to detect such periodicities, and to use them as temporal cues for pitch and interval perception (see also Keidel 1989, Yost 2004). From the empirical evidence available, it can be inferred that most if not all of the neural processing necessary to determine the low pitch of signals as well as to perceive basic musical intervals, is achieved in subcortical networks (mainly of the brainstem and thalamus).

The inharmonic variety of sounds, which no doubt is also a natural phenomenon as evident from many environmental sounds, can be viewed as a deviation from the basic, periodic as well as harmonic situation. In experiments, deviations of periodicity and harmonicity of sounds can be realized sytematically and continuously in order to study the perceptual effects of, for example, mistuning of individual partials, or of regular spaced yet inharmonic partials etc. (cf. Roberts 2005). With respect to musical instruments and their sounds viewed from a transcultural perspective, one finds many degrees of inharmonicity as well as sounds with weak spectral and temporal coherence. Ambiguity of pitch and timbre, which in such sounds is a natural consequence to their temporal and/or spectral organization, in many musical cultures however is a feature that apparently is wanted. For examples, one might point to the *gong kebyar* style of Balinese *gamelan* music with a multitude of inharmonic sonorities as well as to plenty of AM resulting from the difference in tuning between *pengumbang* and *pengisep* metallophones mentioned above[3]. With carillon music, the degree of overall inharmonicity perhaps is smaller compared to a *gamelan gong kebyar* performance, however, the ambiguity of pitches produced by each single bell as well as by sequences of bell sounds in principle is the same as is with metallophones from Java or Bali. With carillons, a particularly difficult task is to derive the tonal meaning of chords or even rapid chord progressions played on such instruments[4]. Even a single major chord played on a carillon, due to the spectral composition of so-called minor-third bells, which are still predominant in European carillons, often appears indifferent with respect to tonality (that is, somewhere in between major and minor). This situation in which the acoustic sound structure is not identical with the musical structure of many of the pieces played on such carillons causes kind of 'friction' as well as perceptual ambiguity, which, to be sure, poses problems to analytical listening and music cognition. However, such a sound structure can also be appreciated as an enrichment of our perceptual and cognitive experience.

Whereas musically trained listeners in general will succeed in perceiving and categorizing major or minor chords played on conventional chordophones, for example a piano, they mostly have difficulties performing such tasks when the stimuli come from a (real or sampled) carillon. Judging the size of intervals or the structure of chords played simultaneously for such stimuli is demanding due to fact that bell sounds rarely give rise to simple and unambiguous pitch percepts. Rather, one has to deal with two or more (spectral and/or virtual) pitches per bell sound (Terhardt & Seewann 1984, Terhardt 1998). Listening analytically to carillon music therefore always includes the task of reducing the complex acoustical input (which implies high dimensionality in regard to perception and cognition) to a simpler, musically relevant representation reduced in dimensionality. This task is complicated if pieces are played in fast tempo, and in a virtuos performing style, which makes it difficult if not impossible to perform analytical listening in quasi-real time. Of course, training will improve the performance of listeners who try to analyze musical structures from pieces played on a carillon. Also, there are Gestalt effects in that well-known melodies will be identified acccording to their basic melodic and rhythmic patterns notwithstanding the unusual sound quality of bells.[5]

---

[3] An illustrative and easily available example is found on the CD *Music from the morning of the world*, rec. by David Lewiston in Bali (Elektra/Asylum/Nonesuch Records 1988), no. 2 (*gamelan gong kebyar: baris; gambang betjak*). Also, *The Music of Bali*, rec. by David and Kay Parsons (celestial harmonies 1997), offers good examples (e.g., *Kebyar trompong, Ujan Mas*).

[4] Good examples are found on the CD *Torenmuziek Dordrecht. Beiaardmuziek van Staf Nees. Carillon-recital Grote Kerk Dordrecht.* Henry Groen & Boudewijn Zwart (TMD 2001).

[5] Very instructive examples from *Lili Marleen*, and Turlough O'Carolan's *Lord Inchiquin*, to familiar Christmas charols can be found on the CD *Folk songs and popular music on European carillons* (Various artists, Eurocarillon 2000).

6   Conclusion

In the present study, algorithms which model parts of the auditory system have been tested on harmonic and inharmonic sounds in order to demonstrate that perceptual qualities such as salience or ambiguity of pitch, sensation of harmonicity and consonance as well as roughness and dissonance, are established on a relatively low level of auditory processing. Though we by no means underestimate the role of top-down processing (which employs natural or learned categories, schemas, memory etc.), we want to emphasize biological foundations of hearing, which govern perceptual processes up to the point of generating musical meaning. In music, meaning basically rests in specific sound structures as well as in relations sounds form among each other. Listening to music, from an ecological point of view, is not just a matter of cognitive activity leading to some mental representations of abstract musical structures (see also Clarke 2005, ch. 1); rather, one has to see that much of the neural processing in particular of musical sound and speech which are carrying information is achieved subcortically, and that musicians even seem to dispose of enhanced subcortical processing capabilities (cf. Musacchia et al. 2007). Of course, listening to music, in particular in an attentive mode, requires cognitive analysis and awareness. However, perception of inharmonic sounds, and of music composed of such sounds, clearly demonstrates that even for musically trained subjects analytical skills cannot easily overcome the constraints imposed by acoustic and psychoacoustic parameters.

Acknowledgements

We would like to thank Aimé Lombaert (Brugge) and Marc Leman (Ghent) for support in recording the bells at Brugge used in this analysis, and Rolf Bader (Hamburg) for providing some of his field recordings from North Bali.

References

1. Bachmann, W.: Signalanalyse. Grundlagen und mathematische Verfahren. Vieweg, Braunschweig (1992)
2. Bader, R.: Additional modes in transients of a Balinese gender dasa plate. Journal of the Acoust. Soc. of America 116, 2621 (2004) (abstract)
3. Bader, R.: Computational Mechanics of the classical guitar. Springer, Berlin (2005)
4. Balaban, M., Ebcioglu, K., Laske, O.: Understanding Music with AI: Perspectives on Music cognition. The AAAI Pr./MIT Pr., Menlo Park/Cambridge (1992)
5. Boersma, P.: Accurate short-term analysis of the fundamental frequency and the harmonics-to-noise-ratio of sampled sound. Proc. of the Inst. of Phonetic Sciences 17, 97–110 (1993)
6. Boersma, P., Weenink, D.: Praat: doing phonetics by computer. Version 5.038 (2008)
7. Bregman, A.: Auditory Scene Analysis. In: The perceptual organization of sound. MIT Pr., Cambridge (1990)

8. Cariani, P., Delgutte, B.: Neural Correlates of the pitch of complex tones. I: Pitch and pitch salience. Journal of Neurophysiology 76, 1698–1716 (1996)
9. Cariani, P., Delgutte, B.: Neural Correlates of the pitch of complex tones. II: Pitch shift, pitch ambiguity, phase invariance, pitch circularity, and the dominance region for pitch. Journal of Neurophysiology 76, 1717–1734 (1996)
10. Clarke, E.: Ways of Listening. A ecological approach to the perception of musical meaning. Oxford U. Pr., London (2005)
11. Cohen, M., Grossberg, S., Wyse, L.: A spectral network model of pitch perception. Journal of the Acoust. Soc. of America 98, 862–879 (1995)
12. de Boer, E.: On the "Residue" and auditory pitch perception. In: Keidel, W.D., Neff, W.D. (eds.) Handbook of Sensory physiology, ch. 13, vol. V, 3. Springer, Berlin (1976)
13. de Cheveigné, A.: Pitch perception models. In: Plack, C., et al. (eds.) Pitch. Neural coding and perception, pp. 169–233 (2005)
14. de Ribaupierre, F.: Acoustical information processing in the auditory thalamus and cerebral cortex. In: Ehret, G., Romand, R. (eds.) The Central Auditory System, ch. 5, pp. 317–388. Oxford U. Pr., Oxford (1997)
15. Ehret, G.: The auditory midbrain, a "shunting yard" of acoustical information processing. In: Ehret, G., Romand, R. (eds.) The Central Auditory System, ch. 4, pp. 259–316. Oxford U. Pr., Oxford (1997)
16. Handel, S.: Listening. An Introduction to the perception of auditory events. MIT Pr., Cambridge (1989)
17. Hartmann, W.: Signals, Sound, and Sensation. Springer, New York (1998)
18. Hermes, D.: Measurement of pitch by subharmonic matching. Journal of the Acoust. Soc. of America 83, 257–264 (1988)
19. Hesse, H.-P.: Die Wahrnehmung von Tonhöhe und Klangfarbe als Problem der Hörtheorie. A. Volk, Köln (1972)
20. Hesse, H.-P.: The Judgment of musical intervals. In: Clynes, M. (ed.) Music, mind and brain, pp. 217–225. Plenum Pr., New York (1982)
21. Houtsma, A.: Pitch perception. In: Moore, B. (ed.) Hearing, 2nd edn., pp. 267–295. Academic Pr., London (1995)
22. Keidel, W.-D.: Biokybernetik des Menschen. Wiss. Buchges, Darmstadt (1989)
23. Keidel, W.-D.: Das Phänomen des Hörens. Ein interdisziplinärer Diskurs. Naturwissenschaften 79, 300–310, 347–357 (1992)
24. Keiler, F., Karadogan, C., Zölzer, U., Schneider, A.: Analysis of transient musical sounds by auto-regressive modeling. In: Proc. 6th Intern. Conf. on Digital Audio Effects DAFx 2003, pp. 301–304. Queen Mary, Univ. of London, London (2003)
25. Krumhansl, C.: Cognitive Foundations of musical Pitch. Oxford U. Pr., Oxford (1998)
26. Langner, G.: Die zeitliche Verarbeitung periodischer Signale im Hörsystem: Neuronale Repräsentation von Tonhöhe, Klang und Harmonizität. Zeitschrift für Audiologie 46, 8–21 (2007)
27. Leman, M.: Music and Schema theory. Cognitive foundations of systematic musicology. Springer, Berlin (1995)
28. Lopez-Poveda, E.: Spectral processing by the peripheral auditory system: facts and models. Intern. Rev. of Neurobiology 70, 7–48 (2005)
29. Lopez-Poveda, E., Meddis, R.: A human nonlinear cochlear filterbank. Journal of the Acoust. Soc. of America 110, 3107–3118 (2001)
30. Lyon, R., Shamma, S.: Auditory representations of timbre and pitch. In: Hawkins, H., McMullen, T., Popper, A., Fay, R. (eds.) Auditory Computation, ch. 6, pp. 221–270. Springer, New York (1996)

31. McAdams, S., Bigand, E. (eds.): Thinking in Sound. The Cognitive psychology of human audition. Clarendon Pr., Oxford (1993)
32. Meddis, R., Hewitt, M.: Virtual pitch and phase sensitivity of a computer model of the auditory periphery. I: Pitch identification. Journal of the Acoust. Soc. of America 89, 2866–2882 (1991a)
33. Meddis, R., Hewitt, M.: Virtual pitch and phase sensitivity of a computer model of the auditory periphery. II: Phase sensitivity. Journal of the Acoust. Soc. of America 89, 2883–2894 (1991b)
34. Meddis, R., O'Mard, L.: A unitary model of pitch perception. Journal of the Acoust. Soc. of America 102, 1811–1820 (1997)
35. Meddis, R., O'Mard, L.: AMS Tutorial (Version 2.3). Univ. of Essex, Dept. of Psychol., Colchester (2003)
36. Meddis, R.: Auditory-nerve first-spike latency and auditory absolute threshold: a computer model. Journal of the Acoust. Soc. of America 119, 406–417 (2006)
37. Musacchia, G., Sams, M., Skoe, E., Kraus, N.: Musicians have enhanced subcortical auditory and audiovisual processing of speech and music. Proc. Nat. Acad. Science 104(40), 15894–15898 (2007)
38. Patterson, R., Allerhand, M., Giguère, C.: Time-domain modeling of peripheral auditory processing: a modular architecture and a software platform. Journal of the Acoust. Soc. of America 98, 1890–1894 (1995)
39. Plack, C., Oxenham, A.: The Psychophysics of pitch. In: Plack, C., et al. (eds.) Pitch. Neural coding and perception, pp. 7–55. Springer, New York (2005)
40. Plack, C., Oxenham, A., Fay, R., Popper, A. (eds.): Pitch. Neural Coding and Perception. Springer, New York (2005)
41. Popper, A., Fay, R. (eds.): The Mammalian Auditory Pathway: Neurophysiology. Springer, Berlin (1992)
42. Rameau, J.-P.: Traité de l'harmonie. Ballard, Paris (1722)
43. Rameau, J.-P.: Génération harmonique ou traité de musique théorique et pratique. Prault fils, Paris (1737)
44. Roberts, B.: Spectral pattern, grouping, and the pitches of complex tones and their components. Acta Acustica united with Acustica 91, 945–957 (2005)
45. Schneider, A.: *Verschmelzung*, tonal fusion, and consonance: Carl Stumpf revisited. In: Leman, M. (ed.) Music, Gestalt, and Computing. Studies in Cognitive and Systematic Musicology, pp. 117–143. Springer, Berlin (1997a)
46. Schneider, A.: Tonhöhe - Skala - Klang. Akustische, tonometrische und psychoakustische Studien auf vergleichender Grundlage. Orpheus-Verlag, Bonn (1997b)
47. Schneider, A.: Inharmonic Sounds: implications as to 'Pitch', 'Timbre' and 'Consonance'. Journal of New Music Research 29, 275–301 (2000a)
48. Schneider, A.: Virtual Pitch and musical instrument acoustics: the case of idiophones. In: Enders, B., Stange-Elbe, J. (eds.) Musik im virtuellen Raum. KlangArt-Kongreß, pp. 397–417. Rasch, Osnabrück (2000b)
49. Schneider, A.: Complex inharmonic sounds, perceptual ambiguity, and musical imagery. In: Godøy, R.I., Jørgensen, H. (eds.) Musical Imagery, pp. 95–116. Swets & Zeitlinger, Lisse, Abingdon (2001a)
50. Schneider, A.: Sound, Pitch, and Scale: From "Tone measurements" to sonological analysis in ethnomusicology. Ethnomusicology 45, 489–519 (2001b)
51. Schneider, A.: Foundations of Systematic Musicology: a study in history and theory. In: Schneider, A. (ed.) Systematic and Comparative Musicology: Concepts, methods, findings, pp. 11–61. P. Lang, Frankfurt/M. (2008)

52. Schneider, A., Leman, M.: Sonological and psychoacoustic Characteristics of carillon bells. In: Leman, M. (ed.) The quality of bells. Brugge Eurocarillon 2002 (=Proc. Of the 16th Meeting of the FWO Research Soc. on Foundations of Music research). IPEM, Univ. of Ghent, Ghent (2002)
53. Schneider, A., Bader, R.: Akustische Grundlagen musikalischer Klänge. In: Mitteilungen der Math. Ges. in Hamburg Bd XXII, pp. 27–44 (2003)
54. Schulze, H., Neubauer, H., Ohl, F., Hess, A., Scheich, H.: Representation of stimulus periodicity in the auditory cortex: recent findings and new perspectives. Acta Acustica united with Acustica 88, 399–407 (2002)
55. Sinex, D.: Spectral processing and sound source determination. International Review of Neurobiology 70, 371–398 (2005)
56. Sloboda, J.: The musical Mind. The Cognitive Psychology of Music. Clarendon Pr., Oxford (1985)
57. Stumpf, C.: Tonpsychologie, Bd 2. J. Barth, Leipzig (1890)
58. Stumpf, C.: Die Sprachlaute. J. Springer, Berlin (1926)
59. Terhardt, E.: Calculating virtual pitch. Hearing Research 1, 155–182 (1989)
60. Terhardt, E.: Akustische Kommunikation. Springer, Berlin (1998)
61. Terhardt, E., Seewann, M.: Pitch of complex signals according to virtual-pitch theory: tests, examples, and predictions. Journal of the Acoust. Soc. of America 71, 671–678 (1982a)
62. Terhardt, E., Seewann, M.: Algorithm for extraction of pitch salience from complex tonal signals. Journal of the Acoust. Soc. of America 71, 679–688 (1982b)
63. Terhardt, E., Seewann, M.: Auditive und objektive Bestimmung der Schlagtonhöhe von historischen Kirchenglocken. Acustica 54, 129–144 (1984)
64. Tramo, M., Cariani, P., Delgutte, B., Braida, L.: Neurobiological Foundations for the theory of harmony in Western tonal music. In: Zatorre, R., Peretz, I. (eds.) The Biological Foundations of music (=Annals of the N.Y. Acad. of Sciences), vol. 930, pp. 92–116. New York Acad. of Sciences, New York (2001)
65. Wever, E.: Theory of hearing. Wiley, New York (1949)
66. Wiener, N.: Cybernetics or control and communication in the animal and in the machine, 2nd edn. MIT Pr., New York (1961)
67. Yost, W.: Determining an auditory scene. In: Gazzaniga, M. (ed.) The Cognitive Neurosciences, 3rd edn., ch. 28, pp. 385–396. MIT PR., Cambridge (2004)
68. Zwicker, E., Fastl, H.: Psychophysics. In: Facts and Models, 2nd edn. Springer, Berlin (1999)

Semantic Contours in Tracks
Based on Emotional Tags

Michael Kai Petersen, Lars Kai Hansen, and Andrius Butkus

Technical University of Denmark, DTU Informatics,
Building 321, DK.2800, Kgs.Lyngby, Denmark
{mkp,lkh,ab}@imm.dtu.dk
http://www.imm.dtu.dk

Abstract. Outlining a high level cognitive approach to how we select media based on affective user preferences, we model the latent semantics of lyrics as patterns of emotional components. Using a selection of affective *last.fm* tags as top-down emotional buoys, we apply LSA latent semantic analysis to bottom-up represent the correlation of terms and song lyrics in a vector space that reflects the emotional context. Analyzing the resulting patterns of affective components, by comparing them against *last.fm* tag clouds describing the corresponding songs, we propose that it might be feasible to automatically generate affective user preferences based on song lyrics.

Keywords: Pattern recognition, emotions, text processing.

1   Introduction

Both words and music move in time, and as T.S. Elliot phrased it "only by the form, the pattern, can words or music reach". A panoply of sensations and emotions are elicited when we listen to a song, which in turn reflect cognitive aspects of the underlying structure in both sound and lyrics. Over the past half century these aspects of musical affect have been the focus of a wide field of research ranging from how emotions arise based on the underlying harmonic and rhythmical structures forming our expectations [1-3], to how we consciously experience these patterns empathetically as contours of tensions and release [4]. Basic feelings of happiness, being sad or getting angry are not just perceived but materialize as changes in heart rate, skin conductance, respiration or blood pressure, as has been documented in numerous cognitive studies of music and emotions [5]. Applying biosensors to measure the features that underlie the various affective states, the resulting patterns appear sufficiently consistent to determine what emotions are being triggered based on the physiological changes alone [6]. But listening to songs involves not only basic elements of affect, but also higher level structures reflected in the lyrics which provide the basis for a song. To a large extent language allows us to share and describe distinct affective aspects that we extract from the continuous affective ebb and flow of emotions shaping our frame of mind. Despite the often idiosyncratic character of tags defined by

S. Ystad, R. Kronland-Martinet, and K. Jensen (Eds.): CMMR 2008, LNCS 5493, pp. 45–66, 2009.

hundred thousands of users in social networks like *last.fm*, a number of studies within the music information retrieval community indicate that users often tend to agree on the affective terms they attach to music, which can be interpreted as a simplified mood ground-truth reflecting the perceived emotional context of the music [7-8].

During the past decade advances in neuroimaging technologies enabling studies of brain activity have established that musical structure to a larger extent than previously thought is being processed in "language" areas of the brain [9], and specifically related to lyrical music some fundamental aspects appear essentially identical to those of language [10]. Neural resources between music and language appear to be shared both in syntactic sequencing and also semantic processing of patterns reflecting tension and resolution [11-13], adding support for findings of linguistic and melodic components of songs being processed in interaction [14]. Similarly there appears to be an overlap between language regions in the brain and so-called mirror neurons, which transfer sensory information of what we perceive by re-enacting them on a motor level. Mediating the inputs across audiovisual modalities, the resulting sensory-motor integrations are represented in a similar form, whether they originate from actions we observe in others, only imagine or actually enact ourselves [15-16]. This has led to the suggestion that our empathetic comprehension of underlying intentions behind actions, or the emotional states reflected in sentences and melodic phrases, are based on an imitative re-enactment of the perceived motion [17].

So if both low-level features of media and our emotional responses can be encoded in words, we hypothesize that this might allow us to define a high level cognitive model emulating how we select media based on affective user preferences. In such a model the bottom-up part would resemble cognitive component analysis [18]. Coined as a term to describe aspects of unsupervised clustering of data, the underlying algorithms approximate how our brain discovers self-organizing patterns when assembling images from lines and edges of visual objects [19], reconstructs words from the statistical regularities of phonemes in speech [20] or learn the meaning of words based on their co-occurrence within multiple contexts [21-23]. But equally important: cognitive processes involve a large amount of top-down feedback which sculpts the receptive responses of neurons on every level and vastly outnumbers the sensory inputs [24-26]. That is, the brain applies an analysis-by-synthesis approach, which combines a top-down capability to infer structure from bottom-up processing of statistical regularities in what we perceive. Our emotions are in this sense essential for maintaining a balance between cognition and perception, as core affect is an integral element in what attracts us to objects and turn what we sense into meaningful representations that can be categorized in words [27-29].

A way to emulate this approach of the human brain in relation to search of media, could be to apply unsupervised learning of features based on latent semantics, extracted from lyrics associated with songs. And combine the bottom-up extracted representation with top-down aspects of attention reflecting preferred emotional structures, similar to the combinations of user generated affective terms found in tag clouds in social networks like last.fm. Selecting a number of frequently used emotional *last.fm* tags as buoys to define a semantic plane of psychological valence and arousal dimensions, we project a number of song lyrics into this space and apply LSA latent semantic analysis [21-23], to model the correlation of texts and affective terms as vectors reflecting the emotional context of the songs. We outline in the following sections: the affective plane used for modeling emotional structure, the extraction of latent semantics from texts associated with media, an analysis of the emotional patterns, followed by a discussion of the potential in combining latent semantics and emotional components to enable personalized search of media.

2   Affective Plane

Drawing on standard psychological parameters for emotional assessment, affective terms are often mapped out along the two psychological dimensions of valence and arousal [30-32]. Within this 2D emotional plane the dimension of valence describes how pleasant something is along an axis going from positive to negative associated with words like happy or sad, whereas arousal captures the amount of involvement ranging from passive states like mellow and sad to active aspects of excitation as reflected in terms like angry or happy. This approach to represent emotions within an affective space framed by valence and arousal dimensions goes beyond earlier attempts to define distinct categories like Hevner's circle of adjectives (1935). Based on responses from participants listening to musical excerpts, clusters of words were grouped into eight segments of similar adjectives covering emotions like happy, lyrical, calm, dreamy, sad, serious, tragic, angry and exciting [33]. How many different parameters are required to capture the various components in an affective space has since then been the subject of a number of studies. The results indicate that a model which provides a good fit to how people describe emotional states, can be defined based on five underlying latent variables: anger, sadness, disgust, fear and happiness [34]. In such a model these factors are not necessarily correlated with whether they are perceived as pleasant or unpleasant, as opposing aspects might often occur together even if they represent contrasting positive and negative aspects of valence. Empirical results for rating of emotional words, also indicate that certain terms e.g. synonyms for happy or anger seem to be based on one category only and are defined as either positive or negative along a single dimension. Whereas other affective terms appear more complex and appear to be combinations of more emotional categories, like despair being perceived as a mixture of sadness and anxiety, or excitement involving aspects of both happiness and surprise [35]. In any linguistic description we perceive not only the lexical meaning of words but infuse them with feelings of positive or negative valence [30], which might serve to filter what is essential and determine what becomes part of our memories [28]. Experiments using MDS multidimesional scaling to group musical excerpts according to similarity instead of word categories, indicated that the model which provides the best fit to the emotional responses seems again to be based on the two psychological dimensions of valence and arousal, but here combined with an additional third dimension capturing aspects of shape related to the degree of melodic continuity or rhythmical fragmentation in the music [36]. In a further cluster analysis of the data, the participants were found to separate the responses into two segments along the arousal dimension, meaning how energetic or laid back the music was perceived as being. The similarity judgements of musical excerpts within the two clusters in turn appeared to be divided along the fault lines of valence, essentially separating the emotional reactions into an affective plane consisting of happy, mellow, angry and sad quadrants.

If we attempt to model top-down cognitive attentional aspects reflecting affective structure, tag-clouds in music social networks like *last.fm* provide an interesting case. The affective terms which are frequently chosen as tags by users to describe music seem to form clusters around primary moods like mellow, sad, or more agitated feelings like angry and happy. This correlation between social network tags and the specific music tracks they are associated with, has been used in the music information retrieval community to define a simplified mood ground-truth, reflecting not just the words people frequently use when describing the perceived emotional context, but also which tracks they agree on attaching these tags to [7-8]. Selecting twelve of these frequently used tags:

happy, funny, sexy, romantic
soft, mellow, cool
angry, aggressive
dark, melancholy, sad

makes it possible to define an affective plane reflecting the above cognitive models of emotional responses to music, as a basis for extracting latent semantics.

3   Semantic Space

To generate the bottom-up part of how we cognitively extract meaning from strings of texts, LSA latent semantic analysis models comprehension from word occurrences in multiple contexts, analogous to human language acquisition [21-23]. Words rarely come shrink-wrapped with a definitive meaning but are continuously modified by the context in which they are set. No matter how many examples of word usage for a verb are listed in a dictionary they remain just that: case stories which illustrate how a predicate will map onto a certain value given a specific argument. Replacing any of the surrounding words in the sentence will create yet another instantiation of the proposition, which we might again interpret differently depending on what phrases come before or after in the text. Instead of attempting to define the specific meaning of a word based on how it fits within a particular grammatical phrase structure, LSA latent semantic analysis, models the plethora of meanings a word might have by concatenating all the situations in which it appears and represent them as a single vector within in a high dimensional semantic space. Squeezing as many of the syntactic relations and senses of word usage into a single vector, makes it possible to extract statistical properties based on how often a term appears in a large number of paragraphs. And subsequently condense this representation into meaningful semantic relations constructed from an average of the different contexts in which the word is used.

Initially a text corpus is constructed which allows for modeling terms as linear combinations of the multiple paragraphs and the sentences in which they occur, assembled from tens of thousands of pages of literature, poetry, wikipedia and news articles. The underlying text corpora can be thought of as resembling human memory where numerous episodes combined with lexical knowledge are encoded into strings of text. Spanned by rows of words and columns of documents, the cells of this huge term-document matrix sum up how frequently each word appears in a corresponding paragraph of text. However in a simple co-occurrence matrix any similarities between words like car and vehicle will be lost as each individual term appears only within its own horizontal row. Nor will it be obvious that a word like rock might mean something completely different depending on which of the contextual columns it appears in. The raw matrix counts of how many times a word occurs in different contexts does therefore not by itself provide a model of comprehension, as we would normally expect texts that describe the same topic to share many of the terms that are used, or imagine that words that resemble each other are also applied in a similar fashion. Most of these relations remain hidden within the matrix, because there are tens of thousands of redundant variables in the original term-document matrix obscuring the underlying semantic structure. Reducing the dimensionality of the original matrix using SVD singular value decomposition [28], the number of parameters can be diminished so we can fit synonymous words or group similar documents into a much smaller number of factors that can be represented within a semantic space.

Geometrically speaking, the terms and documents in the condensed matrix derived from the SVD dimensionality reduction, can be interpreted as points in a k dimensional subspace, which enables us to calculate the degree of similarity between texts based on the dot product of their corresponding vectors. But before comparing terms or documents, the entries in the cells of the matrix need to be adjusted so they reflect how we cognitively perceive associative processes. First by replacing the raw count of how often a word appears in a text by the logarithm of that number. This will smooth the word frequency so it resembles the shape of learning curves typically found in empirical psychological conditioning experiments. Likewise the degree of association of two words both occurring in two documents will be higher than if they each appear twice separately in a text. Here a local weighting function defines how salient the word occurrence is in the corresponding document, and a global weighting function how significant its appearance is among all the contexts [37]. As a next step the word count is divided by the entropy of the term, to ensure that the term frequency will be modified by how much information the word actually adds about the context it appears in. This log-entropy weighting significantly improves the results when compared to a raw word frequency count [23]. Another way to interpret the relations between words forming a semantic neighborhood would be to think of them as nodes constituting a neural network. In such a network of nodes, resembling populations of neurons in our brains, LSA could model the strength of the links connecting one word to another. When we come across a word like 'sad' in a phrase, it will create a node in our short term episodic memory, which will in turn trigger neighboring nodes representing words or events that invoke similar connotations in our past memories. The strength of the connections initially based on word co-occurrence are gradually transformed into semantic relations as the links between nodes are being constrained by the limitations of our memory. As a result only those nodes which remain sufficiently activated when our attention shifts towards the next phrase will be integrated into the patterns forming our working memory. And whether these connections grow sufficiently strong for the nodes to reach a threshold level of activation necessary for being integrated in working memory, can be seen as a function of the cosine between the word vectors [38].

When we compare two terms in the LSA semantic space based on the the cosine of the angle between their vectors, values in-between 0.05 and 1 will indicate increasingly significant degrees of similarity between the words, while a negative or low value around 0 will indicate a random lack of correlation. If we for instance select the affective term sad and calculate the cosine between the angle of its vector representation and any other word in the text corpus, we can determine which other term vectors are semantically close, and in decreasing order list to what degree they share aspects reflecting the meaning of that word:

1.00 sad
0.74 grief
0.73 sorrow
0.63 mourn
0.62 sigh
0.58 weep
0.53 tear
0.51 griev
0.50 piti
0.49 ala

Looking at these nearest neighbors it would seem that instead of interpreting sad isolated as a single vector made from the various documents in which it appears, we might rather think of the meaning of that word as a semantic neighborhood of vectors. In this part of our LSA semantic space these nearest neighbors form a network of nodes, where each word add different aspects to the meaning depending on the strength of their associative links to sad. So if we imagine text comprehension as a process that combines the words which shape a sentence with the associations they trigger we can model this as a bottom-up spreading activation process. In this network the strength of links between nodes will be defined by their weights and consequently the connections among all nodes can be mapped out in a connectivity matrix. Being exposed to an incoming word the stimulus will spread from the node generated in episodic memory, to its semantically nearest neighbors stored in long term working memory. How many of these connections grow sufficiently strong for the nodes to be integrated in long term working memory, determines whether our comprehension is reduced to an assembly line where separate words are merely glued together based on the incoming text alone. Or it will instead provide a blueprint for reconstructing a situation model, resembling an animated pin-ball machine where the associations triggered by the words bounce off walls forming an intricate maze of memories. And once reality kicks in, in terms of the constraints posed by the limited capacity of our working memory, what nodes will remain activated could be understood as proportional to the LSA cosine similarity of vectors, triggered by the words being parsed and their nearest neighbors already residing in our memories [38].

4 Results

In the next subsections we outline the structure of the LSA patterns in regards to the distribution of emotional components, compare the LSA analyses of lyrics against their corresponding last.fm tag clouds, and finally explore correlations between LSA patterns and the underlying musical structure of the songs.

4.1 Distribution of LSA Components

Projecting the lyrics of twenty-four songs selected from the weekly top track charts at last.fm, we compute the correlation between lyrics and the previously selected twelve affective tags used as markers in the LSA space, while discarding cosine values below a threshold of 0.09. Whereas the user-defined tags at last.fm describe a song as a whole, we aim to model the shifting contours of tension and release which evoke emotions, and therefore project each of the individual lines of the lyrics into the semantic space. Analyzing individual lines on a timescale of seconds also reflects the cognitive temporal constraints applied by our brains in general when we bind successive events into perceptual units [39]. We perceive words as successive phonemes and vowels on a scale of roughly 30 milliseconds, which are in turn integrated into larger segments with a length of approximately 3 seconds. We thus assume that lines of lyrics consisting of a few words each correspond to one of these high level perceptual units.

The outputs are matrixes consisting of columns of LSA values triggered by each line in the lyrics in response to the twelve emotional tags making up the rows. Similar to an emotional space, the columns of the matrix reflect a vertical span from positive to negative valence. The upper rows in the columns correspond to active positive emotions like happy and funny followed by more passive aspects like mellow and cool towards the center of the columns. Further down the values in the columns correspond to active negative aspects like angry while the bottom rows in the matrix reflect passive negative emotions such as melancholic and sad. When the individual lines of lyrics are projected against the selected *last.fm* tags, it results in twelve dimensional vector values signifying affective components that are activated simultaneously rather than discrete emotions. Initially adding up the LSA values in the matrices along each row, we can plot the activation of each emotional component over the entire lyrics. Analyzing a small sample of twenty-four songs, the summed up values of LSA correlation between the individual and the *last.fm* affective terms appears to divide the lyrics into roughly three groups:

Balanced distribution of emotions where the lyrics simultaneously trigger affective components from the outer extremes of both happy and sad. Combined with more passive positive aspects like soft it results in types of patterns as found in the songs: "21 Things i want in a lover" (Alanis Morissette), "Bleeding love" (Leona Lewis), "The Scientist" (Coldplay), "Mad world" (Gary Jules), "Nothing else matters" (Metallica), "Starlight" (Muse) and "Come away with me" (Norah Jones). (Fig.1).
- or alternatively the patterns juxtapose active positive and negative elements of happy and versus angry against each other, with relatively less contribution from passive positive aspects like soft, as in the songs: "Everybody hurts" (R.E.M), "Iris" (Goo Goo Dolls), "Wonderwall" (Oasis), "Time to pretend" "Rehab" (Amy Winehouse). (Fig.2).

Centered distribution of emotional components emphasizing passive positive aspects like soft mellow or cool combined with passive negative emotions close to sad, with relatively less significant contributions from active positive affective components such as happy as in the songs: "Now at last" (Feist), "My immortal" (Evanescence), "Creep" (Radiohead) and "Colorblind" (Counting Crows). (Fig.3).

Uniform distribution of emotional components activated across the entire affective spectrum of valence and arousal as in the songs: "Always where i need to be" (The Kooks), "San Quentin" (Johnny Cash), "Clocks" (Coldplay), "What I've done" (Linkin Park), "Falling slowly" (Glenn Hansard), "Stairway to heaven" (Led Zeppelin), "Smells like teen spirit" (Nirvana) and "Such great heights" (The Postal Service)(Fig.4).

4.2   LSA Emotions Versus last.fm Tags

The tag clouds at *last.fm* describe a song as a whole, so in order to assess to what degree the retrieved LSA correlation values of lyrics and affective terms approximate the user-defined tags, we use the accumulated LSA values summed up over the entire lyrics as outlined in previous section. To facilitate a comparison between lyrics and the tag clouds, which my only contain a few of the selected *last.fm* affective terms used in the LSA analysis, we subsequently group the LSA values of closely related tags into an emotional space consisting of four segments of emotions framed by the dimensions of valence and arousal:

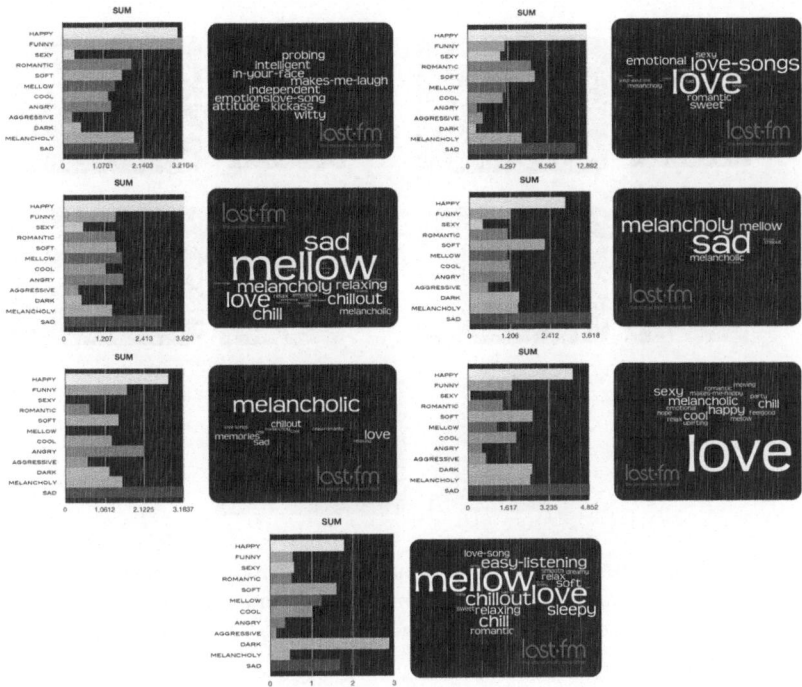

Fig. 1. Accumulated LSA values of emotional components triggered by the lyrics and their corresponding *last.fm* tag clouds - from top left and across: "21 Things i want in a lover" (Alanis Morissette), "Bleeding love" (Leona Lewis), "The Scientist" (Coldplay), "Mad world" (Gary Jules), "Nothing else matters" (Metallica), "Starlight" (Muse) and "Come away with me" (Norah Jones)

active positive - happy, funny, sexy, romantic
passive positive - soft, mellow, cool
active negative - angry, aggressive
passive negative - dark, melancholy, sad

Within the tag-clouds a number of more idiosyncratic expressions like "kickass" or "makes-me-laugh" will similarly have to be mapped onto one of the above four affective groups, in this case defined as active positive. Terms referring to complex emotions like "love" has similarly been assigned to this segment based on user-rated valence and arousal values [32] . To simplify the comparison against the tags, the emotional segment with the highest accumulated LSA values has been highlighted for each of the songs below:

"21 Things i want in a lover" (Alanis Morissette)
last.fm tags include: "attitude, in-your-face, kickass, makes-me-laugh" (Fig.1)
LSA values summed in groups: **active positive: 8,4** passive positive: 4,2 active negative: 1,5 passive negative: 4,4

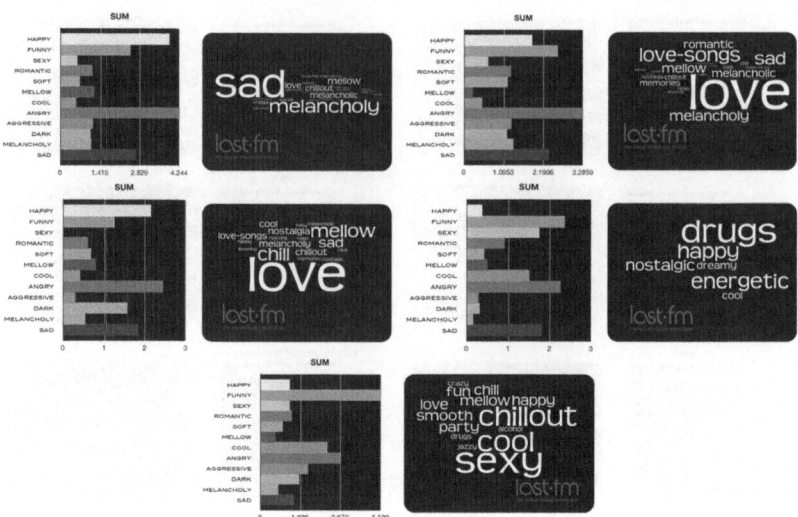

Fig. 2. Accumulated LSA values of emotional components triggered by the lyrics and their corresponding *last.fm* tag clouds - from top left and across: "Everybody hurts" (R.E.M), "Iris" (Goo Goo Dolls), "Wonderwall" (Oasis), "Time to pretend" "Rehab" (Amy Winehouse)

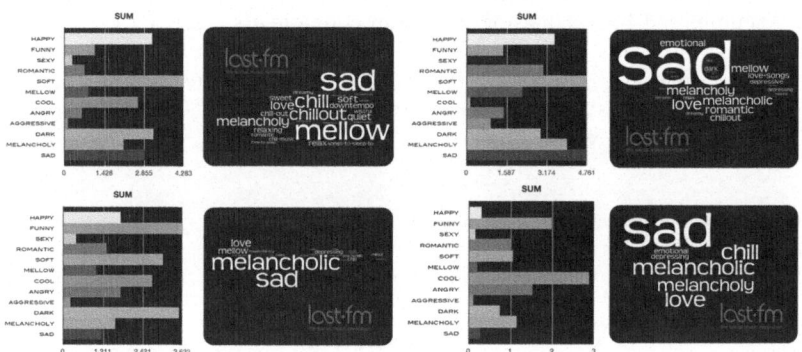

Fig. 3. Accumulated LSA values of emotional components triggered by the lyrics and their corresponding *last.fm* tag clouds - from top left and across: "Now at last" (Feist), "My immortal" (Evanescence), "Creep" (Radiohead) and "Colorblind" (Counting Crows)

"Bleeding love" (Leona Lewis)
last.fm tags include: " love, romantic, sweet, sexy, melancholy, sad" (Fig.1)
LSA values summed in groups: **active positive: 25,3** passive positive: 15,2 active negative: 2,6 passive negative: 18,2

"The Scientist" (Coldplay)
last.fm tags include: "mellow, sad, love, chill, melancholy" (Fig.1)

Fig. 4. Accumulated LSA values of emotional components triggered by the lyrics and their corresponding *last.fm* tag clouds - from top left and across: "Always where i need to be" (The Kooks), "San Quentin" (Johnny Cash), "Clocks" (Coldplay), "What I've done" (Linkin Park), "Falling slowly" (Glenn Hansard), "Stairway to heaven" (Led Zeppelin), "Smells like teen spirit" (Nirvana) and "Such great heights" (The Postal Service)

LSA: **active positive: 7,2** passive positive: 4,5 active negative: 2,2 passive negative: 4,9

"Mad world" (Gary Jules)
last.fm tags include: "sad, melancholy, mellow" (Fig.1)
LSA values summed in groups: active positive: 5.6 passive positive: 4,6 active negative: 1,8 **passive negative: 6,5**

"Nothing else matters" (Metallica)
last.fm tags include: "melancholic, love, chillout, sad" (Fig.1)
LSA values summed in groups: active positive: 5,2 passive positive 2,7: active negative: 2,7 **passive negative: 5,9**

"Starlight" (Muse)
last.fm tags include: "love, cool, chill, happy, melancholic, sexy" (Fig.1)
LSA values summed in groups: active positive: 7,4 passive positive: 5,6 active negative: 1,2 **passive negative: 10,0**

"Come away with me" (Norah Jones)
last.fm tags include: "mellow, love, chillout, sleepy" (Fig.1)
LSA values summed in groups: active positive: 3,4 passive positive: 3,8 active negative: 0,5 **passive negative: 5,1**

"Everybody hurts" (R.E.M)
last.fm tags include: "sad, melancholy, mellow, chillout" (Fig.2)
LSA values summed in groups: **active positive: 8,1** passive positive: 2,5 active negative: 5,4 passive negative: 4,9)

"Iris" (Goo Goo Dolls)
last.fm tags include: "love, sad, mellow, romantic, melancholy" (Fig.2)
LSA values summed in groups: **active positive: 6,5** passive positive: 1,9 active negative: 4,6 passive negative: 4,9

"Wonderwall" (Oasis)
last.fm tags include: "love, chill, mellow, sad" (Fig.2)
LSA values summed in groups: **active positive: 4,1** passive positive: 1,9 active negative: 2,7 passive negative: 3,9)

"Time to pretend" (MGMT)
last.fm tags include: "drugs, happy, energetic, nostalgic" (Fig.2)
LSA values summed in groups: **active positive: 5,4** passive positive: 2,4 active negative: 2,6 passive negative: 2,3

"Rehab" (Amy Winehouse)
last.fm tags include: "sexy, cool, chillout, fun, happy, party, smooth" (Fig.2)
LSA values summed in groups: **active positive: 9,6** passive positive: 4,8 active negative: 5,9 passive negative: 4,2

"Now at last" (Feist)
last.fm tags include: "sad, mellow, chill" (Fig.3)
LSA values summed in groups: active positive: 5,2 passive positive: 7,7 active negative: 0,7 **passive negative: 8,2**

"My immortal" (Evanescence)
last.fm tags include: "sad, love, melancholy" (Fig.3)
LSA values summed in groups: active positive: 8,0 passive positive: 7,1 active negative: 2,4 **passive negative: 11,6**

"Creep" (Radiohead)
last.fm tags include: "melancholic, sad, love, mellow" (Fig.3)
LSA values summed in groups: **active positive: 7,0** passive positive: 6,7 active negative: 1,9 passive negative: 6,3

"Colorblind" (Counting Crows)
last.fm tags include: "sad, chill, melancholic, love" (Fig.3)
LSA values summed in groups: active positive: 3,5 **passive positive: 4,2** active negative: 1,6 passive negative: 2,1

"Always where i need to be" (The Kooks)
last.fm tags include: "makes-me-happy, sounds-like-summer, party, cool" (Fig.4)
LSA values summed in groups: active positive: 2,6 passive positive: 1,6 active negative: 1,3 **passive negative: 2,9**

"San Quentin" (Johnny Cash)
last.fm tags include: "prison, angry, black, cynical" (Fig.4)
LSA values summed in groups: **active positive: 3,6** passive positive: 1,1 active negative: 1,9 passive negative: 1,7

"Clocks" (Coldplay)
last.fm tags include: "chill, mellow, cool" (Fig.4)
LSA values summed in groups: **active positive: 5,5** passive positive: 3,1 active negative: 2,5 passive negative: 2,6

"What I've done" (Linkin Park)
last.fm tags include: "love, energetic, intense, memories" (Fig.4)
LSA values summed in groups: active positive: 4,4 passive positive: 3,4 active negative: 1,1 **passive negative: 5,8**

"Falling slowly" (Glenn Hansard)
last.fm tags include: "mellow, love, feel-good, sad" (Fig.4)
LSA values summed in groups: **active positive: 6,6** passive positive: 4,3 active negative: 3,5 passive negative: 3,3

"Stairway to heaven" (Led Zeppelin)
last.fm tags include: "melancholic, cool, mellow, sad" (Fig.4)
LSA values summed in groups: active positive: 7,3 passive positive: 6,5 active negative: 4,7 **passive negative: 7,7**

"Smells like teen spirit" (Nirvana)
last.fm tags include: "love, cool, energetic, kick-ass, melancholic" (Fig.4)
LSA values summed in groups: **active positive: 8,4** passive positive: 4,6 active negative: 2,5 passive negative: 7,7

"Such great heights" (The Postal Service)
last.fm tags include: "love, chill, mellow, happy" (Fig.4)
LSA values summed in groups: **active positive: 8,2** passive positive: 7,6 active negative: 3,5 passive negative: 5,7

To summarize, in order to assess to what degree the retrieved LSA correlation values of lyrics and affective terms approximate the user-defined *last.fm* tags describing the songs, we compared the maximum accumulated LSA values against the twenty-four tag clouds. Mapping the highest accumulated LSA values onto one of the four generalized groups of emotions we retrieved the following results:

Thirteen lyrics were correctly identified to represent emotions related to active positive aspects of valence: "21 Things i want in a lover" (Alanis Morissette), "Bleeding love" (Leona Lewis), "Iris" (Goo Goo Dolls), "Wonderwall" (Oasis), "Time to pretend" (MGMT), "Rehab" (Amy Winehouse), "Smells like teen spirit" (Nirvana), "Such great heights" (The Postal Service), - or passive negative aspects of valence as in the songs: "Mad world" (Gary Jules), "Nothing else matters" (Metallica), "Now at last" (Feist), "My immortal" (Evanescence), "Stairway to heaven" (Led Zeppelin).

Five songs were wrongly identified to represent active positive aspects of valence instead of passive positive: "The Scientist" (Coldplay), "Clocks" (Coldplay), "Falling slowly" (Glenn Hansard) - or passive negative: "Everybody hurts" (R.E.M), "Creep" (Radiohead).

Three songs were wrongly identified to represent passive negative aspects of valence instead of active positive: "Starlight" (Muse), "Always where i need to be" (The Kooks), "What I've done" (Linkin Park)

One song was wrongly identified as active positive aspects of valence instead of active negative: "San Quentin" (Johnny Cash). One song was wrongly identified as representing passive positive aspects of valence instead of passive negative: "Colorblind" (Counting Crows). One song was wrongly identified as passive negative instead of passive positive: "Come away with me" (Norah Jones)

4.3   LSA Emotions Mapped over Time

While the accumulated LSA values facilitate characterizing the patterns in terms of their distribution of emotional components, and simplify a comparison against the corresponding *last.fm* tag clouds, mapping eight examples of the retrieved LSA matrices over time, allows us to explore to what extent the triggered emotions reflect the underlying musical structure of the songs. The grayscale plots define the range of emotions that are triggered by each line in the lyrics over time. A third dimension is indicated by the amount of saturation, where black signifies higher cosine correlation between the affective terms and the lyrics. Separating the grayscale plots into sections corresponding to the structure of the song, makes it possible to compare the patterns of emotions against the formal divisions of the song. Adding up the LSA values for each line in the lyrics, provides an alternative view of the accumulated emotional peaks and valleys, plotted over time in colors based on the values from the greyscale matrices.

Taking as an example the Metallica song "Nothing else matters", LSA peak values of happy and sad are triggered simultaneously by the lyrics "Couldn't be much more from the heart" in line 2, 17 and 37 marking the beginning of the 1'st and 2'nd section, as well as the final lines of the coda. The persistent pattern of juxtaposed angry, cool and funny components is caused by lines of

"Nothing else matters", interspersed between clusters of dark, melancholy and sad elements resulting from the "Never cared for .." sections in the lyrics. The three happy-sad peaks partition the overall structure of the song. In between these peaks, the texture consists of the pointed angry-cool-funny structures, connected to the declining slopes made out of the contrasting clusters. (Fig.5).

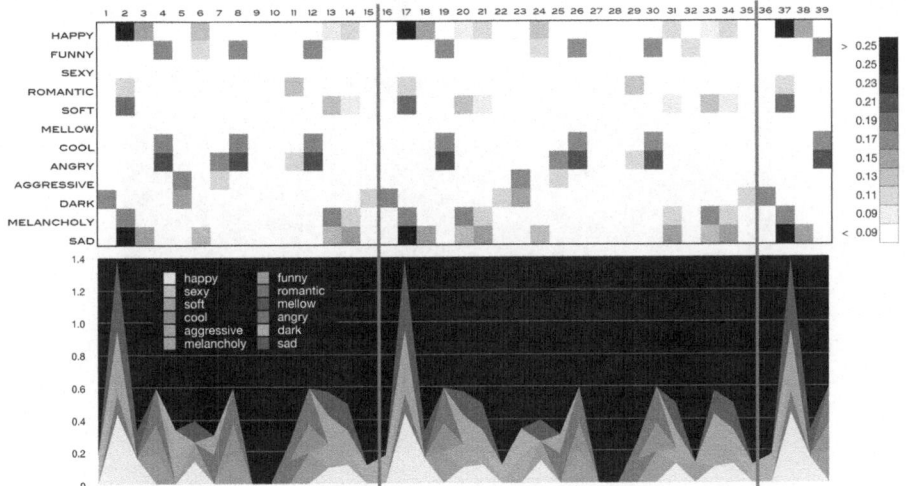

Fig. 5. Nothing else matters (Metallica): LSA patterns of emotions triggered by the lyrics, separated into sections corresponding to the musical structure of the song (top). Accumulated LSA values for each line of the lyrics (bottom).

The ABAB musical structure of the Coldplay song "The scientist" is marked by the vertical LSA columns triggering almost every emotion at line 3 and 24 followed by scattered activation of mellow and soft emotions., reflecting the lines "You don't know how lovely you are" and "Tell me you love me", in the beginning and middle of the two A sections respectively. In contrast the subsequent two B sections, commencing at line 13 and 30, are characterized by a sustained juxtaposition of happy and sad aspects largely devoid of more central soft and romantic components. Two affective peaks dominate the beginning of the first A section and the middle of the second A section. Following the peaks, the remaining parts of the A sections are characterized by scattered aspects of more central emotions, that lead into the shorter B sections with simultaneous balanced activation of happy and sad components (Fig.6).

The layout of the song "Iris" by Goo Goo Dolls is marked by the LSA saturated clusters in the intro culminating in line 6 "And all i can breathe is your life" and a less strong activation in the second verse at line 15 "When everything feels like the movies", which are in both cases generated by simultaneous happy and sad elements combined with romantic and soft aspects. This is contrasted with the pattern concluding both the first and second verse, triggered by funny and alternating angry and aggressive elements in the lines "Cause I don't think

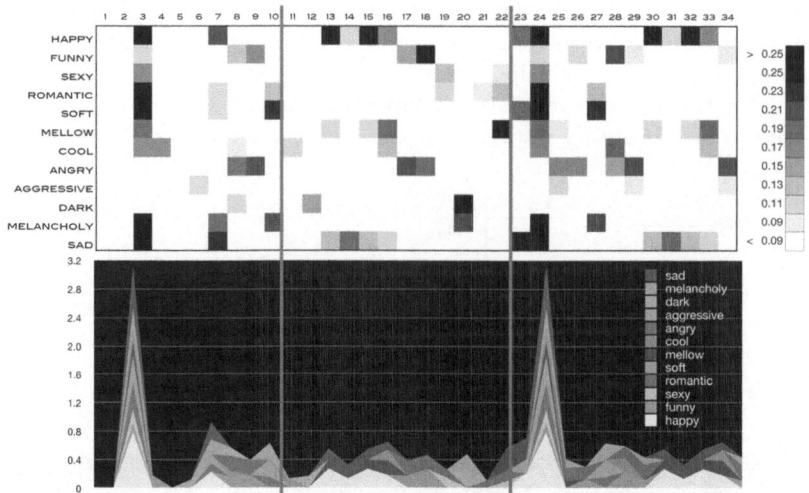

Fig. 6. The Scientist (Coldplay): LSA patterns of emotions triggered by the lyrics, separated into sections corresponding to the musical structure of the song (top). Accumulated LSA values for each line of the lyrics (bottom).

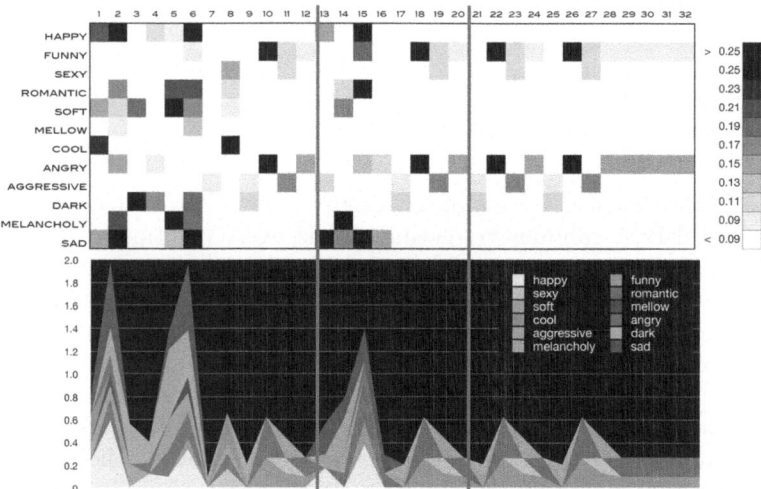

Fig. 7. Iris (Goo Goo Dolls): LSA patterns of emotions triggered by the lyrics, separated into sections corresponding to the musical structure of the song (top). Accumulated LSA values for each line of the lyrics (bottom).

that they'd understand" and "When everything's made to be broken", similarly sustained throughout the refrain "I just want you to know who I am" that brings the song to an end. Two connected peaks are generated from simultaneous happy and sad elements combined with romantic and soft aspects, culminating in the

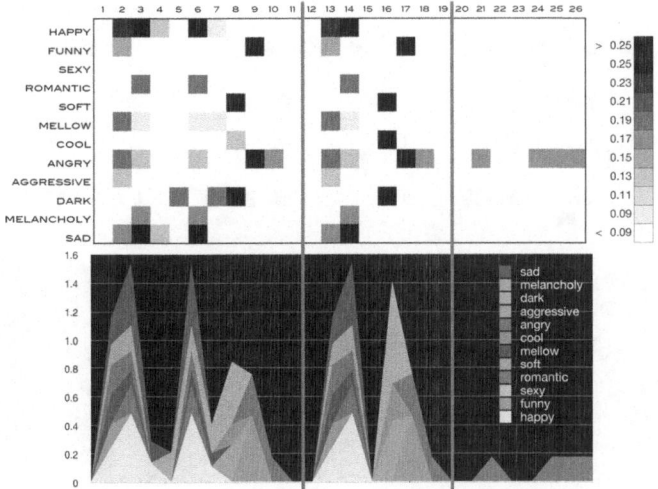

Fig. 8. Wonderwall (Oasis):LSA patterns of emotions triggered by the lyrics, separated into sections corresponding to the musical structure of the song (top). Accumulated LSA values for each line of the lyrics (bottom).

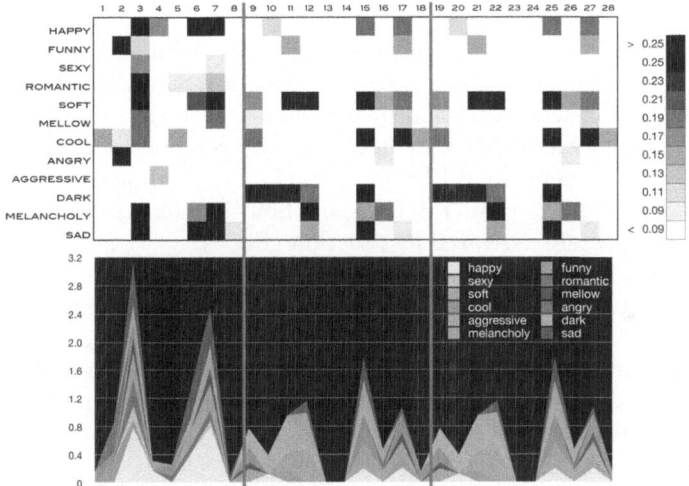

Fig. 9. Now at last (Feist): LSA patterns of emotions triggered by the lyrics, separated into sections corresponding to the musical structure of the song (top). Accumulated LSA values for each line of the lyrics (bottom).

beginning of the first verse followed by a slightly lower peak in the beginning of the second verse. In between a balanced texture is activated by funny and alternating angry and aggressive elements (Fig.7).

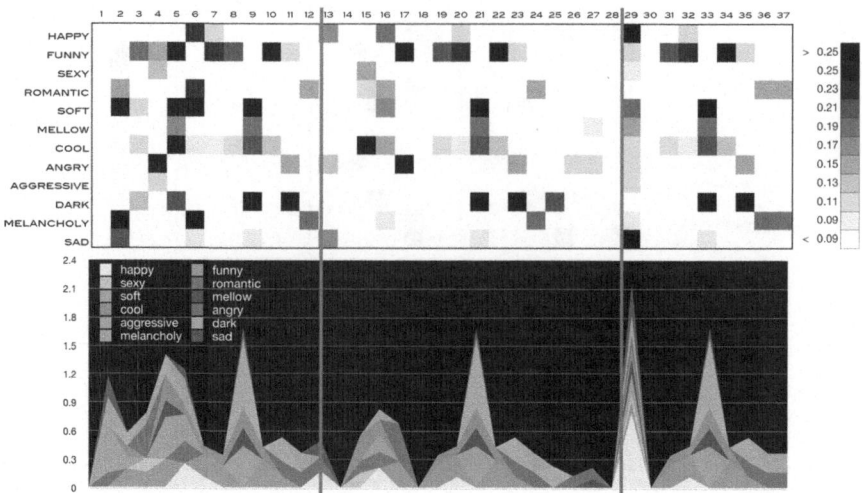

Fig. 10. Creep (Radiohead): LSA patterns of emotions triggered by the lyrics, separated into sections corresponding to the musical structure of the song (top). Accumulated LSA values for each line of the lyrics (bottom).

A simultaneous activation of happy and sad elements in line 3, 6 and 14 characterize the first two sections of the Oasis song 'Wonderwall" corresponding to the lyrics "I don't believe that anybody feels the way I do about you now". It is followed in the second section by soft cool and dark components triggered by line 16 "And all the lights that light the way are blinding" contrasted with elements of anger , here caused by line 9 and 17 "There are many things that I would like to say to you but I don't know how", which are sustained through the end of the sparsely activated last section (Fig.8).

The very beginning of Feist's "Now at last" is marked by the cluster generated by the lyrics "For I've lost the last last love" in line 3 eliciting a wide range of emotions followed by a smaller peak emphasizing the soft aspects triggered by line 7 "To the joys before me", that make up the two following sections with the added aspect of cool caused by line 15 and 25 "When the spring is cold" (Fig.9).

Apart from the isolated spike in line 29 "Whatever makes you happy" marking the beginning of the third section in Radiohead's "Creep" in a centered distribution of emotional components, the song is throughout reflecting the pointed cool soft dark textured peaks caused by the text "But I'm a creep" in line 9, 21 and 33 of the lyrics. (Fig. 10).

The lyrics of Led Zeppelin's "Stairway to heaven" trigger components uniformly distributed across a range of emotions resulting in a coherent texture even though only a few lines are repeated, as in the text "makes me wonder" in lines 10-11, 16-17 and 26. A number of sad peaks establish the melancholy atmosphere at the end of the first section line 9 "Sometimes all of our thoughts

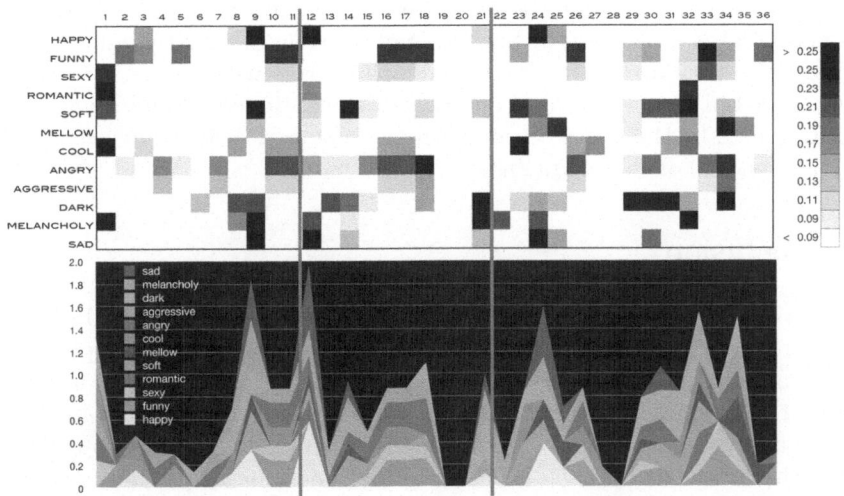

Fig. 11. Stairway to heaven (Led Zeppelin): LSA patterns of emotions triggered by the lyrics, separated into sections corresponding to the musical structure of the song (top). Accumulated LSA values for each line of the lyrics (bottom).

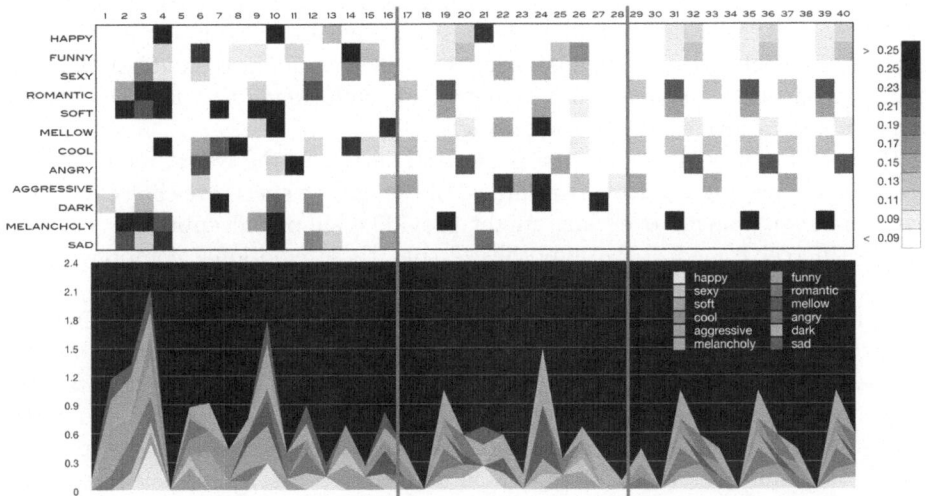

Fig. 12. Such great heights (The Postal Service): LSA patterns of emotions triggered by the lyrics, separated into sections corresponding to the musical structure of the song (top). Accumulated LSA values for each line of the lyrics (bottom).

are misgiven" as well as the beginnings of the second section in line12 "There's a feeling I get when i look to the west" as well as the section in line 24 "Yes there are two paths you can go by but in the long run". (Fig. 11).

The generally light atmosphere of "Such great heights" by The Postal Service, is generated from the very beginning of the song culminating in line 4 "And when we kiss they are perfectly aligned", that leads into the second and third sections marked by the repeated patterns of romantic happy and funny components triggered by the text "But everything looks perfect from far away" in line 19, 31, 35 and 39 of the song.(Fig.12).

5   Conclusion

While we have here only analyzed twenty-four songs our first results indicate that it is possible to describe the emotional context of songs by applying LSA latent semantic analysis to extract latent semantics from the lyrics using a selection of *last.fm* affective tags. Summing up the retrieved emotional values in the LSA analyses along each row, the matrices can be divided into roughly three groups characterized by a balanced, centered or uniform distribution of emotional components.

Assessing to what degree the summed up LSA correlation values of lyrics and affective terms approximate the user-defined *last.fm* tags within a choice of four emotional segments, thirteen of the lyrics were correctly identified. Three of the eleven lyrics that were wrongly identified due to LSA failing to distinguish more subtle differences between happy versus mellow, might be improved by adjusting the weights in the additive model which is initially simply summing up al values equally. Similarly other lyrics mistakenly identified as sad instead of happy or the other way around, could be due to a few peaks influencing the balance between positive and negative valence too strongly.

Considering how the emotional peaks and valleys of the lyrics, seem to align with the underlying musical structure of the songs, we speculate that extracting emotional components over time might provide a simplified approach to model how we perceive media. We hypothesize that these emotional components reflect compositional forms perceived as patterns of tension and release, which form the dramatic undercurrents of an unfolding structure. As exemplified in the plots of song lyrics each matrix column corresponds to a time window of a few seconds, which is also the approximate length of the high level units from which we mentally construct our perception of continuity within time. Interpreted in that context we suggest that the LSA analysis of textual components within a similar size of time window is able to capture a high level representation of the shifting emotions triggered when we listen to a song. Or from a cognitive perspective the dimensionality reduction enforced by LSA might be interpreted as a simplified model of how mental concepts are constrained by the strengths of links connecting nodes in our working memory. It seems that even if we turn off the sound, the emotional context as well as the overall formal structural elements can still be extracted from media based on latent semantics.

References

1. Meyer, L.B.: Meaning in music and information theory. Journal of Aesthetics and Art Criticism 15, 412–424 (1957)
2. Temperley, D.: Music and probability. MIT Press, Cambridge (2007)
3. Huron, D.: Sweet anticipation: Music and the psychology of expectation. MIT Press, Cambridge (2006)
4. Jackendoff, R., Lerdahl, F.: The capacity for music: what is it, and what's special about it? Cognition, 33–72 (2006)
5. Krumhansl, C.L.: Music: A link between cognition and emotion. Current Directions in Psychological Science, 35–55 (2002)
6. Jongwha, K., André, E.: Emotion recognition based on physiological changes in music listening. IEEE Transactions on pattern anlysis and machine intelligence 12, 2067–2083 (2008)
7. Levy, M., Sandler, M.: A semantic space for music derived from social tags. In: Proceedings of the 8th International Conference on Music Information Retrieval, pp. 411–416 (2007)
8. Hu, X., Bay, M., Downie, S.J.: Creating a simplifed music mood classification ground-truth set. In: Proceedings of the 8th International Conference on Music Information Retrieval, pp. 309–310 (2007)
9. Levitin, D.J., Menod, V.: Musical structure is processed in "language" areas of the brain: a possible role for Brodmann Area 47 in temporal coherence. NeuroImage 20(4), 2142–2152 (2003)
10. Calln, C., Tsytsarev, V., Hanakawa, T., Calln, A., Katsuhara, M., Fukuyama, H., Turner, R.: Song and speech: Brain regions involved with perception and covert production. NeuroImage 31(3), 1327–1342 (2006)
11. Koelsch, S., Siebel, W.A.: Towards a neural basis of music perception. Trends in Cognitive Sciences 9(12), 578–584 (2005)
12. Steinbeis, N., Koelsch, S.: Shared neural resources between music and language indicate semantic processing of musical tension-resolution patterns. Cerebral Cortex 18(5), 1169–1178 (2008)
13. Slevc, L.R., Rosenberg, J.C., Patel, A.D.: Language, music and modularity, Evidence for shared processing of linguistic and musical syntax. In: Proceedings of the 10th International Conference on Music Perception & Cognition (2008)
14. Schön, D., Gordon, R.L., Besson, M.: Musical and linguistic processing in song perception. Annals of the New York Academy of Sciences 1060, 71–81 (2005)
15. Gallese, V.: Embodied simulation: From neurons to phenomenal experience. Phenomenology and the Cognitive Sciences 4, 23–48 (2005)
16. Gallese, V., Lakoff, G.: The brain's concepts: the role of the sensory motor system in conceptual knowledge. Cognitive Neuropsychology 22, 455–479 (2005)
17. Molnar-Szakacs, I., Overie, K.: Music and mirror neurons: from motion to 'e' motion. Social cognitive and affective neuroscience 1(33), 235–241 (2006)
18. Hansen, L.K., Feng, L.: Cogito componentiter - ergo sum. In: Rocha, J., et al. (eds.) Independent Component Analysis and Blind Signal Separation. LNCS, vol. 3886, pp. 446–453. Springer, Heidelberg (2006)
19. Bell, A.J., Sejnowski, T.T.: The independent components of natural scenes are edge filters. Vision Research 37(23), 3327–3338 (1997)
20. Feng, L., Hansen, L.K.: On phonemes as cognitive components of speech. In: Proceedings of IAPR workshop on cognitive information processing (2008)

21. Furnas, G.W., Deerwester, S., Dumais, S.T., Landauer, T.K., Harshman, R., Streeter, L.A., Lochbaum, K.E.: Information retrieval using a singular value decomposition model of latent semantic structure. In: 11th annual international SIGIR conference, pp. 465–480 (1988)
22. Deerwester, S., Dumais, S.T., Furnas, G.W., George, W., Landauer, T., Harshman, R.: Indexing by latent semantic analysis. Journal of the American Society for Information Science 41(6), 391–407 (1990)
23. Landauer, L.K., Dumais, S.T.: A solution to Plato's problem: The latent semantic analysis theory of acquisition, induction, and representation of knowledge. Psychological Review, 211–240 (1997)
24. Cudeiro, J., Sillito, A.M.: Looking back: corticothalamic feedback and early visual processing. Trends in Neurosciences 29(6), 298–306 (2006)
25. Sillito, A.M., Cudeiro, J., Jones, H.E.: Always returning: feedback and sensory processing in visual cortex and thalamus. Trends in Neurosciences 29(6), 307–316 (2006)
26. Maunsell, J.H.R., Treue, S.: Feature-based attention in visual cortex. Trends in Neurosciences 29(6), 317–322 (2006)
27. Storbeck, J., Clore, G.L.: On the interdependence of cognition and emotion. Cognition & Emotion 21(6), 1212–1237 (2007)
28. Duncan, S., Barret, L.F.: Affect is a form of cognition: a neurobiological analysis. Cognition & Emotion 21(6), 1184–1211 (2007)
29. Barret, L.F.: Solving the emotion paradox: categorization and the experience of emotion. Personality and social psychology review 10(1), 20–46 (2006)
30. Osgood, C.E., Suci, G.J., Tannenbaum, P.H.: The measurement of meaning. University of Illinois Press, Urbana (1957)
31. Russel, J.A.: A circumplex model of affect. Journal of personality and social psychology 39(6), 1161–1178 (1980)
32. Bradley, M.M., Lang, P.J.: Affective norms for English words (ANEW), Stimuli, instruction manual and affective ratings, The Center for Research in Psychophysiology, University of Florida (1999)
33. Schubert, E.: Update of the Hevner adjective checklist. Perceptual and Motor Skills (96), 1117–1122 (2003)
34. Power, M.J.: The structure of emotion: an empirical comparison of six models. Cognition & Emotion 20(5), 694–713 (2006)
35. Strauss, G.P., Allen, D.N.: Emotional intensity and categorisation ratings for emotional nonemotional words. Cognition & Emotion 22(1), 114–133 (2008)
36. Bigand, E., Vieillard, S., Madurell, F., Marozeau, J., Dacquet, A.: Multidimensional scaling of emotional responses to music: the effect of musical expertise and of the duration of the excerpts. Cognition & Emotion 19(8) (2005)
37. Martin, D.I., Berry, M.W.: Mathematical foundations behind latent semantic analysis. In: Handbook of latent semantic analysis. Erlbaum, Mahwah (2007)
38. Kintsch, W.: Comprehension - a paradigm for cognition. Cambridge University Press, Cambridge (1998)
39. Pöppel, E.: A hierarchical model of temporal perception. Trends in Cognitive Sciences 1(2), 56–61 (1997)

Chunking Sound for Musical Analysis

Rolf Inge Godøy

Department of Musicology, University of Oslo, P.B. 1017 Blindern, N-0315
Oslo, Norway
r.i.godoy@imv.uio.no

Abstract. One intriguing issue in music analysis is that of segmentation, or parsing, of continuous auditory streams into some kinds of meaningful and analytically convenient units, a process that can be denoted as *chunking*. The purpose of this paper is to present a theory of chunking in musical analysis based on perceptual features of sound and on our own research on musical gestures, suggesting that music-related actions are essential in the process of chunking.

Keywords: Chunking, musical analysis, timescales, action-units, coarticulation.

1 Introduction

One crucial question in musical analysis is that of different timescales in our experience of music: Is our experience of music most dependent on local, moment-by-moment features of musical sound, or is it more dependent on longer stretches such as whole tunes, movements, or even whole works, or perhaps rather on a combination of different timescales? In other words: How long stretches of music do we have to listen to in order to have meaningful perceptions of style, mood, type of melodic, harmonic, rhythmical, textural, timbral, etc. qualities? Unfortunately, such questions, as well as a number of related questions regarding feature focus in musical experience, has not been so well addressed in mainstream music analysis literature. But also in the face of recent developments within the domain of music information retrieval, be that based on sound files or on symbolic input (conventional western music notation), as well as from a general music perception perspective, I believe the question of timescales in musical experience is more relevant than ever. In this paper, I shall argue that we may distinguish basically thee different timescales in musical experience: The *micro-level* of continuous sound, the *meso-level* of what we could call *chunks*, and the *macro-level* of more large-scale contexts such as tunes, movements, or whole works. Of these three timescales, I shall argue that the meso-level is the most significant, hence the focus in this chapter on *chunking sound for musical analysis*.

The idea of meso-level chunks as the most significant timescale in musical experience raises some issues about the epistemology, or knowledge aims, of musical analysis, issues that I shall briefly discuss in the next section (section 2). This leads to a discussion of timescales in music (section 3), and a discussion of some principles of chunking (section 4), and of how chunking relates to body action units (section 5), and specifically to the principle of coarticulation, meaning the fusion of micro-level

S. Ystad, R. Kronland-Martinet, and K. Jensen (Eds.): CMMR 2008, LNCS 5493, pp. 67–80, 2009.

sound and body actions into meso-level chunks (section 6). This will lastly be followed by some concluding remarks on the macro-level contextual effects emerging
from sequences of chunks (section 7).

2 Epistemology of Musical Analysis

Musical analysis is a large and heterogeneous field including a multitude of approaches, methods, and theories (see [1] for an overview). On the one hand, musical
analysis has come to include as analytic tools various elements that are really rules for
how to generate music within a certain style, i.e. how to construct a suitable progression of chords, have good voice-leading and/or handling of dissonance, be that in ren-
aissance, baroque, classical, or romantic music, or in jazz, or how to use series of
pitches in twelve tone music, or how to make Xenakis-style distributions of tones in
large masses of sound, for that matter. On the other hand, there are instances of musical analysis that aim at extracting various 'deeper' or 'hidden' features that are
thought to be essential for the music, such as in the Schenkerian approach of finding
the underlying structures of melodic and harmonic progressions, or in various pitch-
class set theory approaches trying to demonstrate hidden relationships between various pitch constellations.

Common to very many instances of musical analysis is that they are based on notation, i.e. see the discrete symbols of the score as the object of analysis, often having
little, if any, regard for the rich set of emergent features of continuous sound such as
timbre, texture and expressivity, as well as not being well equipped for dealing with
non-notated music from various oral and/or improvisation based musical cultures. The
focus on the note symbols of the score has also encouraged focus on features that are
perceptually problematic such as the various hidden structures mentioned above. On
this background, there is clearly a need for an epistemology of musical analysis in the
sense of an evaluation of what features are focused on and what features are ignored,
as well as an evaluation of the perceptual significance of the various features that are
focused on in musical analysis (see [2] for an extensive discussion of this).

With the advent of technologies and methods for studying musical sound, such as
various models of signal processing, signal representations, and perceptual modeling,
we have of course been given vastly better means for accessing perceptually significant features of musical sound, and are no longer restricted to the note symbol para-
digms of past musical analysis. However, these new means for studying musical
sound also raises questions of what features of musical sound we now should focus on
as well as how to represent these features in musical analysis.

One strategy for a perceptual feature based approach to musical sound was presented more than 40 years ago in the work of Pierre Schaeffer and his associates at the
Groupe de Recherches Musicales in Paris [3, 4]. Briefly stated, the strategy of
Schaeffer was that of taking the listener's subjective experience of sound features as
the point of departure, i.e. taking the seemingly simple question of "what do we hear
now?" as the basis for a very extensive differentiation of perceptually significant features of musical sound. This feature differentiation proceeds in a top-down manner in
the sense of going from depictions of the overall dynamical, timbral, and tonal/pitch-
related shapes of the sound, down to various sub-features of these shapes, ending up

with the most minute details in the sound (for an English language summary of this strategy see [2] and [5]). The scope of this strategy is universal in the sense of being applicable to any kind of musical sound, be that instrumental, vocal, electronic, or environmental, and to any kind of music, notated or non-notated (does not distinguish between 'score' and 'performance'), and any features in the sound that we may think of.

The basic rationale of this strategy is to think of features as dimensions, hence, ending up with a multi-dimensional modeling of sound features summarized in what is called the *typology* and *morphology* of sonic objects. *Sonic objects* are fragments of musical sound, typically in the 0,5 to 5 seconds range, holistically perceived as somehow meaningful units, as what I here call *chunks*. The *typology* of sonic objects is concerned with the overall shape of the sonic object, i.e. the mentioned dynamical, timbral, and pitch-related contours or envelopes, and the *morphology* is concerned with the various internal features of the sonic object such as its fluctuations in intensity, timbre, and pitch. The focus on sonic objects is based on the idea that perceptually significant features are actually local features, i.e. that features such as dynamical, timbral, and tonal/pitch-related shapes and all possible sub-features of these, are manifest within the temporal confines of sonic objects, and that focusing on more large-scale stretches of musical sound will make explorations of such local features impossible. This local vs. global issue is actually crucial for musical analysis as a whole, so we shall now have a look at various timescales involved in musical analysis.

3 Timescales

Considering this issue of local vs. global in music, listeners obviously enjoy long stretches of music such as whole tunes, movements, and extended works, sometimes lasting several hours. But how large-scale forms of music are perceived by listeners is not a well-researched topic. What musical analysis tells us about large-scale forms, e.g. Schenkerian ideas of *Urlinie* stretching through an entire Beethoven symphony, are based on score analysis and assumptions that these features actually are important for the listener. The few perception studies that have been made of the efficacy of large-scale forms in western classical music do cast doubt about the importance of large-scale forms in musical experience, i.e. it seems that listeners may enjoy as much, and/or find musically just as acceptable, re-edited versions of music where the chunks have been put together in new sequences [6, 7]. This suggests that for the listener, macro-scale forms may be less important than meso-level chunks, hence that musical analysis would find more perceptually important features in a meso-level chunk focus.

If we consider the timescales involved in music, ranging form fractions of milliseconds up to hours, we know that we perceive different features at different timescales, e.g. that we have a range for pitch and timbre perception in the 20 to 20000 Hz range, and that below the approximately 20 Hz limit we can perceive various rhythmical, textural, melodic, modal, etc. features (see [8] for a schematic overview). In the sub-20 Hz range we also have what is called usable tempos in the approximately 30 to 240 bpm (beats per minute) range, and we have so-called phase transitions if we go beyond these limits, i.e. at tempos slower than 30 bpm we need to subdivide pulses in order to keep track of time and at tempos faster than approximately 240 bpm we tend to fuse pulses into groups such as to have slower pulses.

In addition to these *event-density ranges*, we also have *minimal duration thresholds* for perceiving various features such as pitch, timbre, simultaneity of events, order of events, etc [9]. On the other hand, I shall also ague that we have *maximum duration thresholds* for when something is no longer perceived as a chunk, i.e. is perceived as consisting of two or more chunks in a sequence. The general point here is that we have different features at different levels of temporal resolution, and that we also have duration thresholds for the manifestation of perceptually significant features, however these thresholds may be context-dependent and hence also flexible.

With the duration·thresholds in the approximately 0,5 to 5 seconds range for what I here call chunks, we can see that chunks represent the convergence of several significant features in the perception and cognition of musical sound, summarized in the following:

- *Rhythmical-textural features* including various motion patterns such as waltz, tango, reggae, etc. and all kinds of textures such as homophonic, heterophonic, polyphonic, etc. and all kinds of ornaments such as trills, mordents, turns, double turns, etc.
- *Expressivity features* such as various fluctuations in tempo, dynamics, and pitch
- *Dynamical and timbral shapes* such as crescendo and diminuendo and the associated timbral changes, or the opening and closing of mutes, shifting of bowing position, etc.
- *Melodic shapes* ranging from small melodic motives to more extended melodic shapes
- *Modal-tonal features* of all kinds that require a minimum of tones in succession in order to be established and recognized
- *Harmonic progressions* needing a minimum of chords in succession in order to be established and recognized
- *Stylistic idioms*, meaning various short textural-melodic-modal fragments typical of various styles, e.g. what is called 'signatures' in [10]

These elements could be called 'music immanent' in that they are simply based on how much time it takes for any feature to manifest itself, cf. the abovementioned minimum and maximum duration thresholds for feature focus. But such seemingly obvious observations of timescales are however non-trivial and epistemologically significant for musical analysis, because these timescales constrain our focus in analytic work, i.e. determine what features it is possible to study. For Schaeffer and his co-workers, the focus on sonic objects, i.e. on meso-level chunks, was initially a product of pragmatic work with sound fragments in the early days of the *musique concrète*. Before the advent of the tape recorder, mixing of sounds in compositions was done by having sound fragments recorded in loops (called *sillon fermé*) on 78 rpm phonograms and having a team of assistants putting down and lifting up the pickups as needed in the course of the mix. But the experience of listening to these innumerable repetitions of looped sound fragments lead to an acute awareness of the feature richness of the sonic objects, which in turn led to the abovementioned typological and morphological ordering of these features and the conclusion that the most important timescale for music research was that of the sonic object.

As for the selection of sonic objects in the first place, it was of course possible to just make an arbitrary cut in any recording and to study this cut as a sonic object. Such arbitrary cutting could lead to interesting insights, but the problem was that the artifact of the arbitrary cutting itself would lead to different perceptions of the sonic object as each new object would establish its own internal context, i.e. have its own "head, body, and tail" [4]. As an alternative, Schaeffer suggested more non-arbitrary cutting by looking for what we would call naturally occurring qualitative discontinuities in the sound. Schaeffer found this in what he called stress-articulation (*articulation-appui*) where 'articulation' was defined by Schaeffer as 'breaking up the sonorous continuum by successive distinct energetic events' ([3]: 396), and 'stress' as the prolongation of the sound, similar to vowels in speech ([3]: 366). This then lead to the typological categories of *sustained*, *impulsive*, and *iterative* sonic objects, categories we shall see in section 6 below also reflect basic categories of body actions.

4 Chunking Principles

Knowing very well that sound is an ephemeral, temporal phenomenon, it may seem strange to talk about 'sonic objects' or 'chunks of sound' as if they were solid things that we can look at and hold in our hands. Obviously, the terms 'object' and 'chunk' here are metaphors referring to mental images of what we have heard, just like we refer to other time-dependent events as if they were something solid. As for choice of words, we may in various contexts see 'parsing', 'segmentation', 'punctuation', and 'chunking' used more or less synonymously to refer to the cutting up of continuous streams of sensory information. We have in our research chosen the term 'chunking' because it in addition to this cutting up of continuous streams also has the connotation of something solid, i.e. has a dual meaning that is well in accordance with what we have in mind here. Our use of the word 'chunking' owes much to the work of G. A. Miller on mental re-coding of sensory information into more compact, solid, and tractable entities in our minds [11]. However, transformations of time-dependent sensory information to more solid images in our minds has been one of the main topics of phenomenological philosophy, and we have also seen a convergence of different disciplines in that chunking is an integral and absolutely indispensible element in our minds.

To begin with, we find various notions of chunking in western music theory in what is often referred to as principles of form, or *Formenlehre*, e.g. as in [12], and we see extensions of this line of thinking in more recent music cognition works, e.g. as in [13], and computational implementations, e.g. as in [14]. The notions of chunking we find in these and similar theoretical works are basically founded on notation as well as on conventions of style within so-called common practice music.

But if we are looking for more universal and notation-independent principles of chunking, we should look for more general principles in the continuous auditory signal of musical sound. In the now large domain of music information retrieval as well as within the domain of auditory scene analysis [15], we find a number of signal-based, bottom-up approaches to chunking where the leading principle is that of trying to detect qualitative discontinuities of various kinds. Often, we find modular approaches that include analysis of the signal in view of detecting onsets, beats, and other features that may serve as cues for chunking the continuous signal into some-how perceptually meaningful chunks [16].

Both notation-based and signal-based approaches to chunking are mostly *exogenous* in the sense of looking for chunking cues in the signal, in many ways in accordance with classical Gestalt principles [15]. However some of these projects also include elements that take into account top-down or schema-based elements in chunk-ing, what could be called *endogenous* elements in chunking (see [17] for a discussion of this). The point is that there may be conflicting chunking cues in the signal in cases where there are many qualitative discontinuities in rapid succession, e.g. as in textur-ally dense passages, or there may be few or none qualitative discontinuities as in passages of protracted and/or only slowly evolving sounds. In such cases, we may use top-down projections of chunking schemas on the sound so as to order the various sound-events into somehow coherent chunks. Well-known examples of this are the emergence of sensations of meter in cases of missing beats [18] or projection of meter onto a series of regular pulses [19]. In view of a more general theory of chunking, it seems reasonable then to assume that chunking in most cases will be a combination of exogenous (or bottom-up) and endogenous (or top-down) elements.

Endogenous elements for chunking seem to a large extent to be based on prior learning, e.g. on that people in music and other domains such as language have ac-quired expertise for detecting chunks and chunk boundaries that non-experts do not have. But we would also be interested in trying to find more universal principles of chunking. A project in this vein is the phenomenological investigations of temporal awareness as presented in various writings by Husserl in the period from 1893 to 1917 [20]. By an introspective but lucid analysis of temporal consciousness, Husserl arrived at the conclusion that there has to be an intermittent interruption of the con-tinuous stream of sensations in order to perceive meaning. This implies that we some-how have to break up the continuous stream of sound, vision, action, etc. and make what we could call more a-temporal chunks out of what we sense, otherwise we would just have a stream of amorphous sensations and not be able to find any mean-ing. Husserl stated that perception thus has a discontinuous element, that it proceed by a series of 'now-points', and that each such now-point also includes memories of the recent past, what he called *retentions*, as well as anticipations for the future, what he called *protentions*. In other words, Husserl claimed that perception and cognition ba-sically proceeds by a series of chunks containing stretches of past, present, and ex-pected future sensations.

Husserl's idea of perception and cognition by a series of discontinuous 'now-points' may seem paradoxical when we consider musical sound (and other sensory informa-tion) as temporally continuous signals, i.e. we seem to have a conflict of *discontinuity* and *continuity* here. Yet if we think of the abovementioned principles of different time-scales involved in music perception, Husserl's ideas make a lot of sense because meso-level chunk features are typically manifest only as features of a certain stretch of time and have to be perceived and remembered holistically as a cumulative image of such stretches of time, hence can be seen as an instance of discontinuous perceptual aware-ness of continuous sound. Similar notions of discontinuity in perception and cognition seem also to be supported by some recent neurocognitive research [21, 22, 23].

In the domain of motor control, there has been a more than one century long debate on discontinuity vs. continuity, between the adherents of motor programs (i.e. pre-programming of actions) and the adherents of continuous feedback in the execution of actions [24]. There seems now to be a consensus that motor control will variably have both continuous and discontinuous elements, however for many tasks, there can be no doubt that there must be a high degree of pre-planning or anticipatory behavior [25, 26], something that we believe will be of particular importance for understanding chunking of music-related actions. Interestingly, it has also been shown that mean durations of human actions tend to be in approximately the same range as the above-mentioned range for the sonic objects, i.e. centered around approximately 2,5 seconds and rarely shorter than approximately 0,5 seconds or rarely longer than approximately 5 seconds [27]. Since the duration of actions and of sonic objects seem to be approximately in the same range, we should also have a look at various music-related actions that may contribute to chunking of musical sound.

5 Action Units

There are many and obvious links between musical sound and body movement, and there are good reasons for claiming that the perception of musical sound also evokes sensations of body movement when listening to music even when not seeing musicians perform or other people move or dance to the music [28, 29, 30]. This body-related understanding of music perception and cognition is founded on the general idea of embodied cognition [31] and more specifically on what can be called the motor theory of perception [32, 33] as well as several other recent findings on the links between sound and action (see [17] for an overview). There are different variants of the motor theory of perception, but the essential point is understanding perception and cognition as dependent on mental simulation of actions that we believe are at the cause of what we hear or see. In the case of music, this means having some kind of motor sensation of sound-producing actions when we hear or merely imagine music, e.g. when we hear ferocious drumming we have some sensations of the effort of energetic drumming gestures, or when we hear calm, slow music, we have some sensations of slow, protracted movement.

We can divide sound-related gestures into the two main categories of sound-producing and sound-accompanying, and these in turn have several sub-categories. From listeners point of view, musical sound will thus have quite rich gestural affordances, i.e. may evoke many variant images of actions in the minds of the listeners, but there are still some action categories that are quite fundamental and also general in the sense that they reflect basic body motion schemas with the associated biomechanical and motor control constraints. With the principle of motor equivalence [34], variants of sound-producing actions may be seen as similar, e.g. hitting a drum with a mallet, without a mallet, hitting a piano key, etc., all belong to the category of impulsive actions. Also, these basic action categories fit well with the abovementioned typological categories for sonic objects:

- *Sustained actions* such as protracted bowing or blowing
- *Impulsive actions* such as hitting and plucking
- *Iterative actions* where there are many and fast repetitions such as in tremolo or trills

It should be noted that we may have so-called phase transitions [35] between these categories in the sense of shifts from one category to another with changes in speed, e.g. a rapid iterative sound gradually slowing down may become an impulsive sound, and conversely, impulsive sounds may become iterative sounds if the rate of onsets is speeded up. Also, we may have combinations of different speeds, e.g. fast finger actions combined with the slower hand/arm/shoulder movement in the performance of a rapid passage on the piano. This last mentioned phenomenon is actually related to what we call *coarticulation*, meaning that local action-events and sound-events are subsumed into higher-level action-events and sound-events, causing a contextual smearing as we shall see in the next section.

The individual action units can in many cases be understood as centered around what we call *goal-points*, meaning salient points in the music such as downbeats and other accents or melodic peaks that function as goals for the movement trajectories [17], similar to the idea of *key-frames* in animation, a concept that may be extended to motor control in general [26]. In our case, we see the trajectories to these goal-points as *prefixes*, and the trajectories from these goal-points as *suffixes* [17], equivalent to the so-called *interframes* in animation and human motor control, i.e. the continuous movement trajectories between keyframes [26]. The idea of prefixes and suffixes, besides describing often seen action trajectories in music, also addresses the problem of sometimes unclear boundaries between the chunks as prefixes and suffixes may very well overlap. As suggested in [17], modeling sound-related actions as a series of prefix-goal-point-suffix can accommodate both clearly disjunct actions and seemingly continuous, as well as the undulating types of actions that can be seen in figure 2 below.

One essential element with sound-related actions is that the element of pre-planning, what can be called *anticipatory cognition*, may shed light on the enigmatic issue of compressed overview images of musical sound, an issue that is one of the central features of chunking in music and was one of the main points of Husserl's investigations. The sound-related action unit can be envisaged anticipatorily in a 'now-point', both in terms of its kinematics, i.e. its visual trajectory, and in terms of its effort. In other words: The anticipatory image of an action can be seen as corresponding to Husserl's now-point, something that can be better understood when we look at the phenomenon of coarticulation.

6 Coarticulation

Coarticulation can here be defined as the fusion of otherwise separate action units into more superordinate action units. Coarticulation can be found in most cases of human action and has been extensively studied in linguistics [36], as well as to a certain extent in other domains such as human movement science, robotics, sign language, however in music we have so far just seen a few studies of coarticulation. Let's consider one example in speech:

> 'Look into a mirror and say (rather deliberately) the word *tulip*. If you look closely, you will notice that your lips round before you say "t", Speech scientists call this phenomenon *anticipatory lip round-ing*.'...'anticipatory lip rounding suggests that a plan for the entire word is available before the word is produced. If "tulip" were produced in a

piece-meal fashion, with each sound planned only after the preceding sound was produced, the rounding of the lips required of "u" would only occur *after* "t" was uttered.' ([37]: 14) And: 'Anticipatory lip rounding illustrates a general tendency that any theory of serial ordering must account for–the tendency of effectors to coarticulate.' (ibid: 15)

The reference to 'serial ordering' in this quote concerns the abovementioned problem posed by Lashley and his suggested solution of anticipatory behavior. This means that also on the control side, coarticulation has the effect of chunking prospective actions, similar to Husserl's idea of perceiving a chunk in a 'now-point' that includes a segment of the past as well as a segment of the future.

One remarkable feature of coarticulation is that is affects both sound-producing actions and sound perception, and does so both on a memory level and on a more acoustic level. In terms of acoustics, multiple excitations without intermittent damping, e.g. the repeated striking of a bell, a drum, or piano keys with the sustain pedal depressed, or in similar cases for other instruments where there is incomplete damping between the tone-events, we have cases of coarticulation understood as a contextual smearing due to the mass-spring phenomenon of excitation followed by energy dissipation. But we may also think of coarticulation on a more purely perceptual level in the form of contextual inclusion of sound-events in higher order chunks, e.g. the inclusion of the different segments of tone envelopes in a holistic perception of tones. Perceptual effects of coarticulation can to a certain extent be simulated with diphone synthesis where one may create a smearing effect in the transitions between the tones, or with physical model synthesis that simulates non-damped resonance of multiple excitations.

As for sound-producing gestures, we have seen a few studies of coarticulation in music, such as in piano playing [38], in sting instrument performance [39], on wind instruments [40], and in drumming [41], but there is clearly a need for more research here.

What coarticulation demonstrates is that sound-events on traditional musical instruments (and of the human voice as well) are always included in some kind of action trajectory. This is an element that may be lost in western note-centered musical analysis, but in our perspective, chunking is very closely linked with the sound-producing actions. We are presently in the process of making systematic studies of chunking in music by coarticulation, and as an example, we can have a look at an excerpt from the last movement of Beethoven's *Tempest Sonata* for piano (Sonata nr. 17, Op. 31 no. 2, in d-minor).

As we can see from the notation in figure 1, this music will call for the pianist to move his/her hands so as to position them in the optimal position in order for the fingers to play the notes, i.e. we would expect this to become a clear case of coarticulation, something that can be seen in the motiongram in figure 2 (i.e. an image generated by the compression of each frame of the video to just one horizontal line, and aligning these lines in succession so as to give a rough indication of the movement (see [42] for details) of the DVD recording of this passage [43].

Fig. 1. The opening of the last movement of Beethoven's Piano Sonata nr. 17 Op. 31 no. 2 in d-minor

In our lab, we have had a different pianist play this passage, using a setup with electromagnetic trackers recording the wrist movements of the pianist and the MIDI note data simultaneously on a Disklavier, as can be seen in figure 3. A plot of the wrist movements in relation to the note onsets of a short excerpt of this passage can be seen in figure 4, and it seems that this pianist moved the right hand less than François René Duchable [43].

Although we still have a long way to go in our studies of coarticulation, we believe that coarticulation concerns most features in the chunking of musical sound, and in particular features such as textures and ornaments, melodic figures and timbral contours, features we can see are clearly manifest on the meso-level timescale of musical sound, cf. section 3 above. In sum, we believe we have reasonable grounds for understanding coarticulation in music as a gateway to better understanding of chunking of musical sound, as well as a way to better understanding the co-existence of continuity and discontinuity in music.

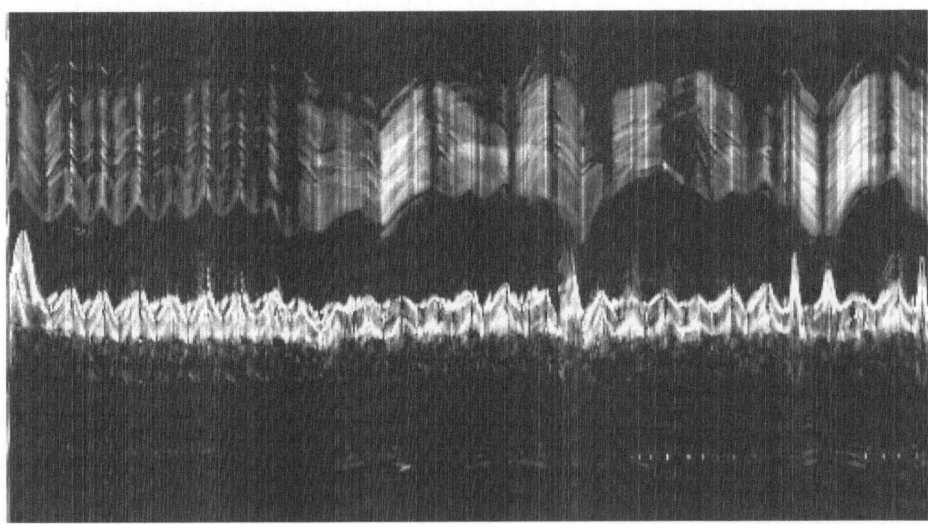

Fig. 2. Motiongram (bottom part of the picture) combined with a spectrogram (upper part of the picture) of François René Duchable's performance of the opening of the last movement of Beethoven Piano Sonata nr. 17 Op. 31 no. 2 in d-minor. We can clearly see the trajectories of the circular hand motions the pianist makes in the performance.

Fig. 3. Setup for recording wrist movements in relation to tone onsets on a Disklavier

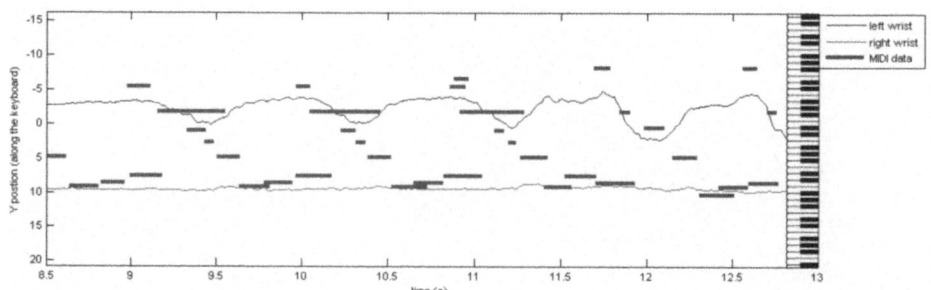

Fig. 4. Plotting of the wrist movements in relation to the note onsets in an excerpt from the opening passage of the last movement of Beethoven Piano Sonata nr. 17 Op. 31 no. 2 in d-minor.

7 Conclusion

Although there is good reason to claim that music perception and cognition (including motor control in musical performance) proceeds by a series of chunks, we obviously still have sensations of continuity in music. If we consider each chunk as consisting of a goal-point preceded by a prefix and succeeded by a suffix as mentioned in section 5 earlier, we can see that there may be overlap of successive prefixes and suffixes thereby creating a sensation of continuity. But we could also assume that there is a kind of 'recency' memory, a kind of 'lingering' or 'resonance' of just heard chunks, so as to create a sensation of continuity. Based on this, we could suggest a model with three parallel layers in musical analysis:

- *Sub-chunk level* of continuous sound
- *Chunk level* of based on perception and cognition by 'now-points'
- *Supra-chunk level* based on succession of concatenated and/or partially overlapping chunks

With this model, we can see the coexistence of chunks and more continuous experience. We may intentionally zoom in or out to different levels of resolution according to the knowledge goals that we may have in musical analysis. With different features at different levels of resolution, the important point in musical analysis is to be aware of what we are gaining and what we are missing when we shift our level of zoom. Having tried to give an overview of the main elements of meso-level chunks of musical sound, what is now clearly needed is more research of the effects of various concatenations on the supra-chunk level. In other words, we need better theories of montage in music.

References

1. Bent, I.D., Pople, A.: "Analysis". Grove Music Online,
   http://www.oxfordmusiconline.com/subscriber/article/grove/
   music/41862 (accessed November 26, 2008)
2. Godøy, R.I.: Formalization and Epistemology. Scandinavian University Press, Oslo (1997)

3. Schaeffer, P.: Traité des objets musicaux. Éditions du Seuil, Paris (1966)
4. Schaeffer, P. (with sound examples by Reibel, G., Ferreyra, B.): Solfège de l'objet sonore. INA/GRM, Paris (1998) (first published in 1967)
5. Godøy, R.I.: Gestural-Sonorous Objects: embodied extensions of Schaeffer's conceptual apparatus. Organised Sound 11(2), 149–157 (2006)
6. Karno, M., Koneçni, V.J.: The effects of structural interventions in the first movement of Mozart's symphony in G minor, K.550, on aesthetic preference. Music Perception 10, 63–72 (1992)
7. Eitan, Z., Granot, R.Y.: Growing oranges on Mozart's apple tree: "Inner form" and aesthetic judgment. In: Baroni, M., Addessi, A.R., Caterina, R., Costa, M. (eds.) Proceedings of the 9th International Conference on Music Perception & Cognition (ICMPC9), Bologna/Italy, August 22-26, pp. 1020–1027 (2006)
8. Snyder, B.: Music and Memory: An Introduction. The MIT Press, Cambridge (2000)
9. Moore, B.C.J. (ed.): Hearing. Academic Press, San Diego (1995)
10. Cope, D.: Computers and Musical Style. A-R Editions, Inc., Madison (1991)
11. Miller, G.A.: The magic number seven, plus or minus two: Some limits on our capacity for processing information. Psychological Review 63, 81–97 (1956)
12. Schönberg, A.: Fundamentals of Musical Composition. Faber and Faber, London & Boston (1967)
13. Lerdahl, F., Jackendoff, R.: A Generative Theory of Tonal Music. The MIT Press, Cambridge (1983)
14. Cambouropoulos, E.: Musical Parallelism and Melodic Segmentation: A Computational Approach. Music Perception 23(3), 249–269 (2006)
15. Bregman, A.: Auditory Scene Analysis. The MIT Press, Cambridge (1990)
16. Jehan, T.: Creating Music by Listening. Ph.D thesis, Massachusetts Institute of Technology (2005),
http://web.media.mit.edu/~tristan/phd/pdf/
Tristan_PhD_MIT.pdf
17. Godøy, R.I.: Reflections on chunking in music. In: Schneider, A. (ed.) Systematic and Comparative Musicology: Concepts, Methods, Findings. Hamburger Jahrbuch für Musikwissenschaft, Band 24, pp. 117–132. Peter Lang, Vienna (2008)
18. Large, E.W.: On Synchronizing Movement to Music. Human Movement Science 19, 527–566 (2000)
19. Fraisse, P.: Rhythm and Tempo. In: Deutsch, D. (ed.) The Psychology of Music, 1st edn., pp. 149–180. Academic Press, New York (1982)
20. Husserl, E.: On the phenomenology of the consciousness of internal time (1893-1917). Translated by Brough, J.B. Kluwer Academic Publishers, Dordrecht (1991)
21. Pöppel, E.: A Hierarchical model of time perception. Trends in Cognitive Science 1(2), 56–61 (1997)
22. Varela, F.: The specious present: The neurophenomenology of time consciousness. In: Petitot, J., Varela, F.J., Pachoud, B., Roy, J.M. (eds.) Naturalizing Phenomenology, pp. 266–314. Stanford University Press (1999)
23. Engel, A.K., Fries, P., Singer, W.: Dynamic predictions: oscillations and synchrony in top-down processing. Nat. Rev. Neurosci. 2(10), 704–716 (2001)
24. Elliott, D., Helsen, W., Chua, R.: A Century Later: Woodworth's (1899) Two-Component Model of Goal-Directed Aiming. Psychological Bulletin 127(3), 342–357 (2001)
25. Lashley, K.S.: The problem of serial order in behavior. In: Jeffress, L.A. (ed.) Cerebral mechanisms in behavior, pp. 112–131. Wiley, New York (1951)

26. Rosenbaum, D., Cohen, R.G., Jax, S.A., Weiss, D.J., van der Wel, R.: The problem of se-rial order in behavior: Lashley's legacy. Human Movement Science 26(4), 525–554 (2007)
27. Schleidt, M., Kien, J.: Segmentation in behavior and what it can tell us about brain func-tion. Human Nature 8(1), 77–111 (1997)
28. Godøy, R.I.: Motor-mimetic Music Cognition. Leonardo 36(4), 317–319 (2003)
29. Godøy, R.I., Haga, E., Jensenius, A.: Playing 'Air Instruments': mimicry of sound-producing gestures by novices and experts. In: Gibet, S., Courty, N., Kamp, J.-F. (eds.) GW 2005. LNCS (LNAI), vol. 3881, pp. 256–267. Springer, Heidelberg (2006)
30. Haga, E.: Correspondences between Music and Body Movement. University of Oslo, Oslo (2008) (unpublished doctoral dissertation)
31. Gallese, V., Metzinger, T.: Motor ontology: The Representational Reality Of Goals, Ac-tions And Selves. Philosophical Psychology 16(3), 365–338 (2003)
32. Liberman, A.M., Mattingly, I.G.: The Motor Theory of Speech Perception Revised. Cogni-tion 21, 1–36 (1985)
33. Galantucci, B., Fowler, C.A., Turvey, M.T.: The motor theory of speech perception re-viewed. Psychonomic Bulletin & Review 13(3), 361–377 (2006)
34. Kelso, J.A.S., Fuchs, A., Lancaster, R., Holroyd, T., Cheyne, D., Weinberg, H.: Dynamic cortical activity in the human brain reveals motor equivalence. Nature 392(23), 814–818 (1998); Large, E. W.: On Synchronizing Movement to Music. Human Movement Science 19, 527–566 (2000)
35. Haken, H., Kelso, J.A.S., Bunz, H.: A theoretical model of phase transitions in human hand movements. Biological cybernetics 51(5), 347–356 (1985)
36. Hardcastle, W., Hewlett, N. (eds.): Coarticulation: theory, data and techniques. Cambridge University Press, Cambridge (1999)
37. Rosenbaum, D.A.: Human Motor Control. Academic Press, Inc., San Diego (1991)
38. Engel, K.C., Flanders, M., Soechting, J.F.: Anticipatory and sequential motor control in piano playing. Experimental Brain Research 113, 189–199 (1997)
39. Wiesendanger, M., Baader, A., Kazennikov, O.: Fingering and Bowing in Violinists: A Motor Control Approach. In: Altenmüller, E., Wiesendanger, M., Kesselring, J. (eds.) Music, Motor Control and the Brain, pp. 109–123. Oxford University Press, Oxford (2006)
40. Jerde, T.E., Santello, M., Flanders, M., Soechting, J.F.: Hand Move-ments and Musical Performance. In: Altenmüller, E., Wiesendanger, M., Kes-selring, J. (eds.) Music, Motor Control and the Brain, pp. 79–90. Oxford University Press, Oxford (2006)
41. Dahl, S.: Movements and analysis of drumming. In: Altenmüller, E., Wiesen-danger, M., Kesselring, J. (eds.) Music, Motor Control and the Brain, pp. 125–138. Oxford University Press, Oxford (2006)
42. Jensenius, A.R.: Action - Sound: Developing Methods and Tools to Study Music-related Body Movement. Ph.D thesis, University of Oslo (2007)
43. Duchable, F.-R.: Francois-Rene Duchable playing Beethoven Piano Sonata nr. 17 Op. 31 no. 2 in d-minor, last movement, Allegretto. On Ludwig Van Beetho-ven: Les Concertos pour piano n°1 & 3. A la decouverte des Concertos. Francois-Rene Duchable, piano, John Nelson, conductor, Ensemble Orchestral de Paris [DVD]. Harmonia Mundi (2003)

Towards a Model of Musical Chunks

Kristoffer Jensen and Ole Kühl

Aalborg University Esbjerg, Niels Bohr Vej 8,
6700 Esbjerg, Denmark
{ok,krist}@aaue.dk

Abstract. The 'chunk' phenomenon has attracted some attention lately. In the auditory domain a chunk is seen as a segment of sound. This work first investigates theories of chunks from cognitive science and musicology. We define the chunk as a closed entity of a certain size and with a dynamic structure containing a peak. The perceptual analysis of three songs leads to a collection of chunks, classified according to their internal structure. Common signal processing methods are then used to extract loudness, pitch and brightness of the chunks. The features are modeled in a simple chunk model, consisting of height, slope, peak and peak position, and the values of the model are furthermore estimated for each chunk. Histogram plots are used to give values for the probability of each chunk type. The model parameters from the features are finally compared to the parameters found by listening and determining the *shape* of each chunk.

Keywords: Music retrieval, cognition, chunking, feature extraction, temporal perception.

1 Introduction

The art of phrasing is essential for expressiveness in music. The impact of a musical phrase is dependent on how it is shaped by the individual performer, who, even in notated music, often will have considerable freedom in structuring the perceptual surface of the musical auditory stream. At the level of the individual phrase, there are infinite possibilities for variation of the so-called expressive devices in music, such as timing and dynamic shape. In spite of the importance of phrasing in musical communication, musicology has very little to say about phrases. The Oxford Dictionary of Music, for instance, states that "The art of phrasing by a performer is often instinctive and is one of the features by which a supreme artist may be distinguished from one of lesser inspiration, whether conductor, singer, or instrumentalist." [1] And the Grove Music Online points out that phrases "are important to the analysis of music", but adds: "Yet phrasing theory is a relative newcomer to music theory, and still occupies a somewhat peripheral and problematic position within it." [2] The fact of the matter is that there has been very little systematic investigation of this crucial area.

This paper explores the idea, introduced in an earlier paper [3], that musical expression at the phrase level is organized in units of a certain size, sometimes called gestalts or chunks. Following a brief introduction to the history of "the chunking

S. Ystad, R. Kronland-Martinet, and K. Jensen (Eds.): CMMR 2008, LNCS 5493, pp. 81–92, 2009.
© Springer-Verlag Berlin Heidelberg 2009

theory of temporal perception", we discuss how this phenomenon emerges at the auditory level, and how chunking is an important element in musical phrasing. We suggest that the perceptual segmentation of the surface of the auditory stream is made possible through musical cues, and we try to utilize such cues as parameters for an auditive analysis of music. We then proceed to test this idea by investigating musical features at the chunk level using signal processing technology.

In the testing procedure, common signal processing methods are employed to extract features with valid relations to music and perception. Music can be characterized by dynamics and pitch. Therefore, three features that can be extracted from the audio, which are related to dynamics and note values, are identified. For the sake of simplicity they are called loudness, pitch and brightness. The loudness and brightness are related to the dynamical aspect of music, and the pitch is related to the note values.

2 Chunks

A century ago, the Gestalt psychologists claimed that human beings perceive objects, states and events in the world as unified wholes (Gestalts), and consequently as more than the sum of their sensed properties. In other words, a chair is perceived as a chair, not as a compilation of brown surfaces and lines, a ball is perceived as a ball and not as a white round thing with black dots on it, etc. According to this idea, the human mind/brain has built into its perceptual apparatus a self-organizing ability that mediates the transition from sensory input at the perceptual level to mental representations or concepts that are operational at a higher cognitive level [3, 4].

Having been pushed in the background for a generation or two by the dominating behaviorist trend in psychology, the idea of a high-level structuring of perceptual cues resurfaced with the advent of cognitive science, which holds, in the words of Ray Jackendoff [5], that "there is a single level of mental representation [...] at which linguistic, sensory and motor information are compatible" (p. 17). A particularly pertinent example of this development can be found in Peter Gärdenfors' theory of Conceptual Spaces [6]. According to this theory, a conceptual space is "... built upon geometrical structures based on a number of quality dimensions" (p. 2). Thus, Gärdenfors aims to build a bridge between the level of mental representation as described by Jackendoff, at which information can be exchanged between different sensory modalities, and mathematical models, where the dynamic and functional values of "quality dimensions" can be understood computationally as "geometrical structures".

2.1 Chunking in the Temporal Domain

The move from mental to computational structures, as proposed by Gärdenfors, seems fairly straightforward in the spatial domain, where sensorial quality dimensions like color, verticality, and distance can be plotted mathematically. But what about the temporal domain, where music resides? Here, the sequential organization of information seems to be constrained by a mechanism called *chunking* by Miller [7], which is tied to the limitations of our short-term memory. (Miller's notion of chunking can in this context be seen as an updated version of the gestalt concept of *grouping*.) At the sonic level, we are grouping together or 'chunking' information from the surface of the auditory stream into words, clauses, and melodic and rhythmic figures. The ability of chunking is seen as an integral part, not only of our memory structure, but also of our conceptualization of temporal events.[1]

The cognitive organization of musical phrases has been said to be hierarchical and recursive [8]. In spoken language, for instance, the segmentation of transients and formant structure leads us to perceive words that are embedded or nested in clauses and sentences. The effect of this organizational principle is that it can be difficult to determine to determine whether a musical 'chunk' is in fact two or three chunks embedded in one larger chunk [9]. This indeterminacy, however, should not be seen as an argument against the chunking theory, but rather as yet another indication of the elegance of human temporal perception. Chunking performs a compression of highly complex, richly structured information, too extensive to keep in working memory for any length of time, into manageable units, concepts, gestalts, gestures, names, listed items, etc.

The extent of a chunk was shown by Miller to be in part determined by the number of items stored in it: seven plus or minus two [7]. However, there is also evidence indicating that chunks have a temporal limitation or closedness. Pöppel [10] has done

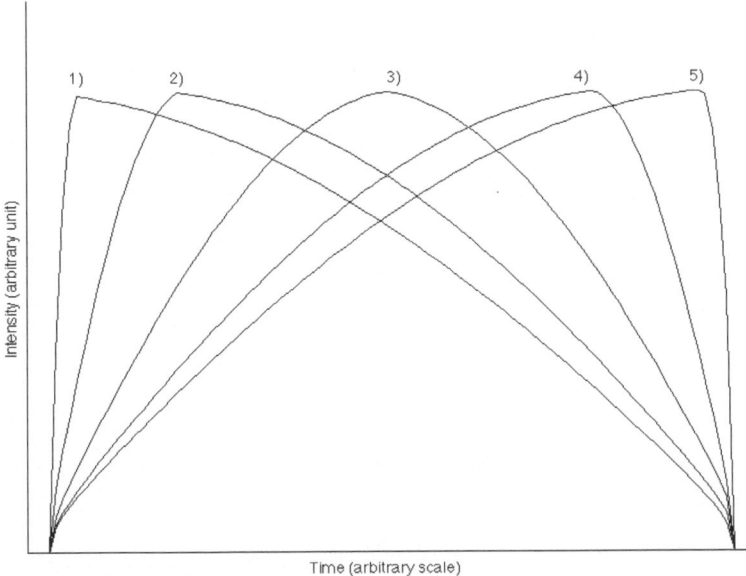

Fig. 1. The internal structure of a chunk. A chunk has a beginning and an end (closedness). Further, it will most often have a focus point, where its dynamic intensity peaks. Five possible positions of the focus point are shown: at the start (1), between the start and the middle (2), in the middle (3), between the middle and the end (4), and at the end (5).

---

[1] The phenomenological aspect of this phenomenon, where chunks are seen as the audible aspect of expressive gestures, is discussed extensively in [9].

extensive research in human temporal perception, and states "a mechanism of temporal integration binds successive events into perceptual units of 3 sec duration" (p. 56). This claim has often been challenged however, and, although this time window in human temporal perception can be seen referred to as "the 3-sec window", in practice it is variable: not less than 500 ms and not more than 5-8 sec. The variation seems to be dependent on not only the number of items, but also on such factors as training (see [11] for a discussion).

3 Perception-Based Segmentation and Classification

We see the chunk as a closed unit with an internal structure, and we aim to describe this structure mathematically (see figure 1). As can easily be observed in simple motor actions ('gestures'), a chunk will not only have a beginning and an end (closedness), but it will also have a peak or focus point. This is the point of maximum intensity of its dynamic curves. For a motor action it is the point where the energy is released for instance the impact point (when we hit the ball or the drum), or the point where we release the ball when throwing it. For a spoken sentence it may be where the highest pitch or the stress occurs, and where an accompanying gesture will 'beat' the air [12].

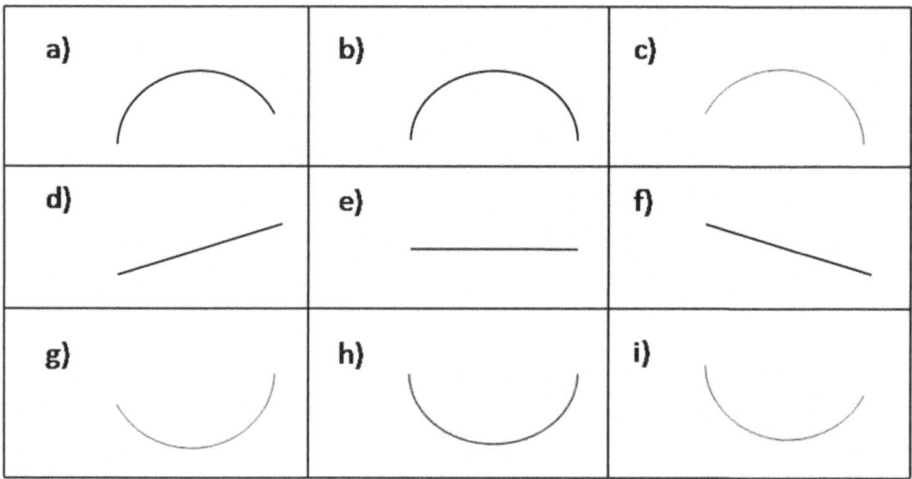

Fig. 2. Different shapes of a chunk. Positive (a-c) or negative peak (g-i), rising (a,d,g) or falling slope (c,f,i).

The internal organization of a chunk structures such dynamic factors as: the intensity of the brightness curve (timbre); the pitch curve; and the amplitude envelope of the phrase (micro-dynamics). In this process, the focus point serves at least two purposes: First, the musician can execute the phrase more rapidly, more precisely, and more relaxed, when his motoric execution is organized as a unit-curve with a peak. And second, the phrase/chunk is easier to pick out from its acoustic surroundings for the listener, when it is equipped with a sonic handle in the form an intensity peak. It communicates better, because it offers auditory cues that facilitate the segmentation. In fact, such sound-shaping marks the primary distinction between humanly shaped sound and machine-generated sound. Computer-based research offers new ways of investigating these features (see [13] for an overview).

3.1 Method

In an earlier study [3], we prepared a segmentation of three pieces of music from different genres, where we "perceptually" identified the most likely chunk boundaries from the auditory cues. This provided us with a list of times for the points, where the individual chunks start and end. Identifying the chunks for two of the pieces, *First Song (for Ruth)* with Stan Getz [14] and *Hold On* with Jamie Walters [15], was pretty straight forward, as jazz and rock music mostly are generic in the sense that they are song-based, (the phrasing of the saxophone emulates singing) and the sung phrases offer a natural segmentation. However, for the third piece, Barenboim's rendition of the *allegretto* from Mozart's *Allaturca* [16] the procedure was not so straightforward. Here, the phrasing is co-determined by the notated metrical structure, and any deviations from this practice will often be notated by the composer. It follows that the intensity peaks that we see as the focus points of the phrasing often will coincide with the barlines. Thus, the phrasing proposed here may be arguable, but we claim that the general tendency of segmentation will be towards chunks of a certain size organized around the focus points as indicated by the barlines.

We ended up with several sets of data for each song. For *Allaturca* we tested three sets, one for each hierarchical level of segmentation. The shortest chunk at level 1 was 600 ms, and the longest at level 3 was 3.5 sec. As the musical surface of a pop song has several other salient elements besides the song, we generated five sets for *Hold On*, including acoustic guitar, electric guitar, drums and chorus. Most of the chunks here averaged between 3 and 4 sec. Finally, we had two sets of nested chunks for the saxophone in *People Time*, as the phrasing of Stan Getz in a natural way pairs into larger, dramatic curves. Here the shortest chunk at level 1 was slightly less than one second, while at level 2 the chunks averaged at 5-6 sec. For the three songs perceptually segmented, the chunk length was found to lie between 600ms and 7-8 seconds. For more details on this, please see [3].

On the basis of this segmentation we performed a 'manual' classification of the chunks. We wanted to compare the (subjective) perception of chunks with the automatic feature extraction (see below). Each chunk was classified according to two parameters: 1) The position of the focus point in the chunk, numbered one through five (see fig. 1 above), and 2) a categorization of the chunk in one of nine possible types, 'a' through 'i'. This involves seeing chunks as curved or linear, rising or falling, and any combination of these (see fig. 2 above).

For each chunk this results in a description of its overall curve and its dynamic structure as determined by the position of the focus point. In the perceptual organization it was often found that the curve is determined by the internal pitch organization, while the focus point is positioned by listening for the dynamic peak (maximum loudness) and the degree of brightness, as these two features often go hand in hand.

The histogram for the curve shape of the chunks, according to the classification in figure 2, are shown in figure 3. For all three songs, a falling linear slope (f) is most common, followed by either a rising linear slope (d) and a falling peaked slope (c) for *Allaturca*, or stable peak (b) and rising linear slope (d) for *Hold On*, or rising peaked slope (a) and rising linear slope for *First Song*. Generally, the falling linear slope is most common, followed by the rising linear slope and the positive peaked slopes. The stable linear slope is the least common, together with the negatively peaked slopes.

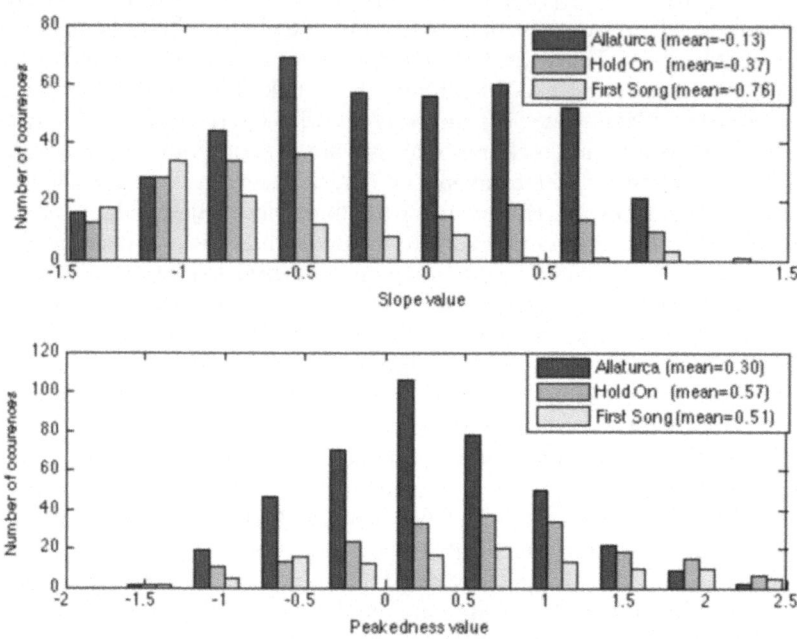

Fig. 3. Histogram of chunk shapes, according to perception-based categorization for three songs

4 Feature Extraction

Having established perception-based description and classification of chunks for the three songs, we turned to the question whether a similar description can be accomplished using automatic feature extraction. The first question is what are the features that shape the music into chunks. We chose to investigate common features with a strong relevance to perception: loudness, pitch, and brightness. These features are closely related to the factors used in the listening procedure. Therefore, the perceptual terms are used henceforth. It is believed that the pitch, as calculated here using an autocorrelation function, is more faithfully capturing the melody line than the chroma [18]. This was also indicated in the results in the previous work [3].

4.1 Feature Calculation

Here, the audio of the chunks found through the perceptual segmentation is processing in order to find estimates of the features loudness, pitch, and brightness. This renders a time-varying vector for each chunk and each feature.

All features are calculated on chunks extracted from the manual segmentation points, as explained above. For all features a step size of 10 msec has been used. The loudness is calculated using the DIN45631 standard as defined by Zwicker ([17], chapter 8.7). The pitch (fundamental frequency) is calculated using pre-processing and autocorrelation [19], and the brightness (spectral centroid, [20]) is calculated as the sum of the amplitude weighted frequencies divided by the sum of amplitudes. As the spectral centroid is high for high loudness, generally, and low for weak sounds, but high for noisy silence, it is weighted with the loudness, in order to remove the high values for silence artefacts.

4.2 Curve Fitting

A vector is now available for all chunks and for the loudness, pitch and brightness. In order to compare the features to the perceptual categories, parameters corresponding to the height, slope and peakedness is extracted from the features.

Each feature is fitted to a second-order curve in order to determine the relative number of occurrences of each category of curve shapes. The curve is made in order to have three characteristics, the height, the slope and the peakedness. The curve in eq(1) is fitted to each chunk for each feature $f(x)$,

$$\hat{f}(x) = A + Bx + Cx^2 \tag{1}$$

The curve is estimated by minimizing the lms error using the Levenberg-Marquardt algorithm [21]. From this match, the parameters A, B, and C, from eq (1) are found, and the height, slope and peakedness parameters, a, b, and c, respectively, are found as follows by rewriting eq. 1 into the sum of three parts, corresponding to the height (a), the slope (from $-b$ to b) and the peakedness (from 0 to c to 0),

$$a = A + \frac{B+C}{2}, \; b = \frac{B+C}{2}, \; c = -\frac{C}{4}. \tag{2}$$

The corresponding values for the perceptive found chunk shapes, according to figure 2, are as follows; a is not given, b is positive for shapes a), d) and g), zeros for shapes b), e) and h) and negative for shapes c), f) and i), and c is positive for shapes a)-c), zero for shapes d)-f) and negative for shapes g)-i).

The focal point, corresponding to the peak position, is denoted d. In order to determine the focal point of each chunk from the features, the time centroid would be preferred over the maximum or minimum of the feature, as it is considered more robust to noise. The time centroid is calculated as,

$$d = \frac{\sum x \, \hat{f}(x)}{\sum \hat{f}(x)} \tag{3}$$

where x is the feature time, normalized between zero and one, and $\hat{f}(x)$ is the feature.

Unfortunately, it is clear that if the sum of $\hat{f}(x)$ is zero, then d is not defined. This may not be the case for common uses of the time centroid, i.e. for determining the balance point of the amplitude envelope, but in the current case, it may very well have a mean zero. Therefore, the top point is used. While it may have other shortcomings, non-unique position, not robust to noise, it still has the advantage that it reaches all the way to the beginning and the end, while the time centroid generally would give values closer to the middle.

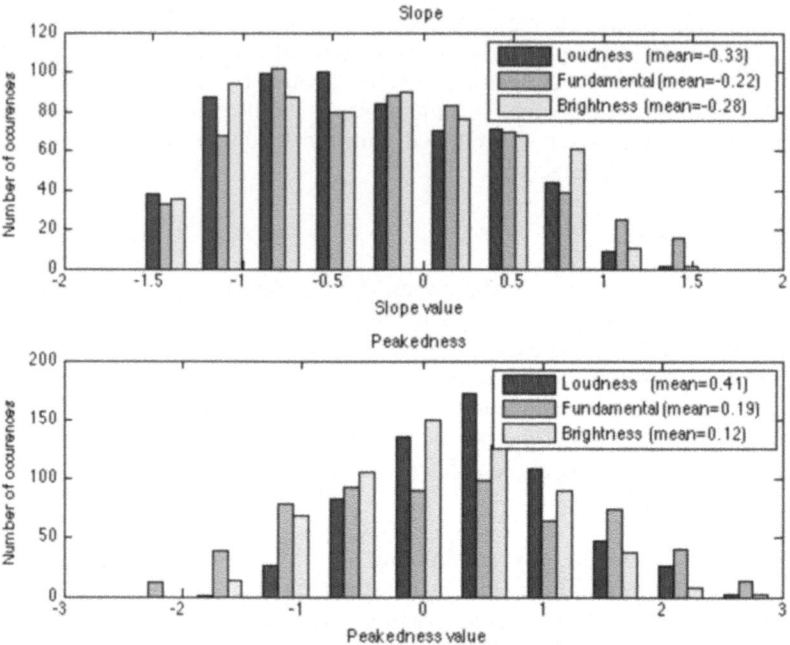

Fig. 4. The slope value (top) and peakedness value (bottom) for loudness, fundamental frequency and spectral centroid for all the chunks of three songs. The mean values of the parameters of the features are shown in the legends.

4.3 Feature Histograms

In this section, the categories and peak positions obtained from the perceptual segmentation in section 3 is compared with the slope, peakedness and peak position obtained from the audio of the chunks above.

We now have a parameterization from the features obtained from the audio files of the music. Each chunk, as defined by the manual perception-based segmentation is used for the calculation of loudness, brightness and fundamental frequency. Each feature is then fitted to a second order equation (1), from which the height (**a**), slope (**b**) and peakedness (**c**) is obtained. In order to be able to compare the parameters between each other and to the manual parameters, a solid curve fitting method is applied to the features, and their mean and standard deviation is normalized before the curve fitting. The height and peakedness of the combined three songs are shown in figure 4.

The slope values (as shown in figure 4, top) are clearly more inclined to the negative values, with a negative mean for all features. Each feature seems to have the same distribution for the slopes. These values correspond well with the histograms for the perceptually obtained chunk shapes in figure 3, in which the negative slopes were more common. The peakedness values are shown in figure 4 (bottom). These values are inclined more towards the positive values, in particular for the loudness.

The histogram for the perceptually obtained chunk parameters converted into slope and peakedness are shown in figure 6 (below). While they contained only three values each, positive, zero, or negative, it is still clear that the negative slope and positive peakedness also occur more often in the case of perceptually obtained chunks.

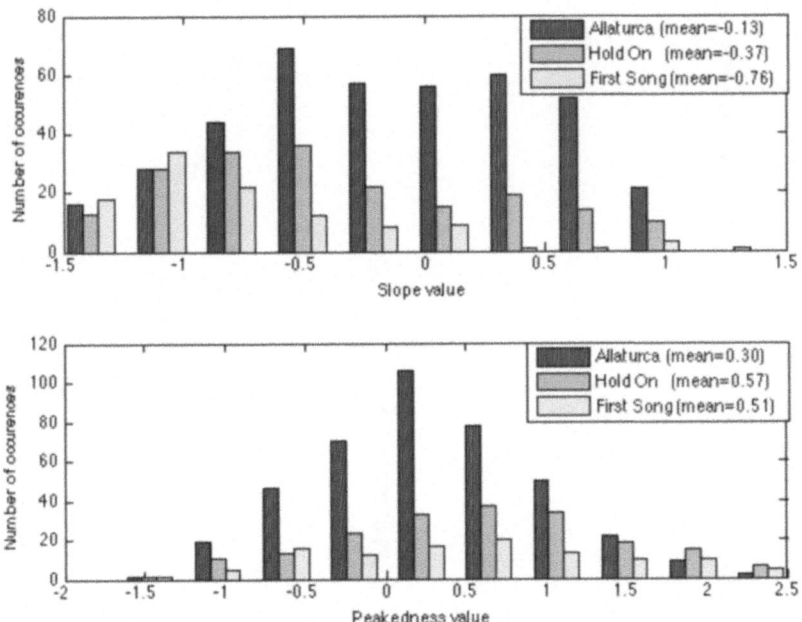

Fig. 5. Histogram of slope and peakedness parameters for loudness and three songs

It is possible to conclude from the current values that the slope is more often negative (in 68%, 62% and 64% of the chunks for the loudness, pitch and brightness features, respectively), and with a positive peak (in 69%, 54%, 55% of the chunks for the loudness, pitch and brightness). The corresponding values for the perceptually obtained shapes are 75% for negative slope, and 57% for positive peaks. As a great deal of the perceptual categorizations contain zero values, half of the zero values are counted for positive and negative respectively. It is difficult to compare the parameters obtained from the audio of the chunks to the non-parametric data obtained from the perceptual classification, but the percentages indicate that the slopes are found best by the loudness, followed by the brightness, and the peakedness best by the brightness and the pitch.

The same slope and peakedness values (**a** and **b** from eq. 2) are shown in figure 5 for the loudness only, but for the three songs individually. Here it is shown that the Stan Getz song has more negative slope chunks, and the Mozart song has less positive peaked chunks. The corresponding mean values for the perceptually obtained chunk shapes are -0.09, -0.36, -0.17 for the slope, and 0.09, 0.16, 0.23 for the peakedness for *Állaturca*, *Hold On*, and *First Song*, respective. This shows a good correspondence to the features for the peakedness, which in both cases give lower peakedness mean for the Mozart song. For the slope, the loudness feature gives more negative slopes for the Stan Getz song than the perceptually obtained chunk slopes. All in all, a good correspondence for the slope too.

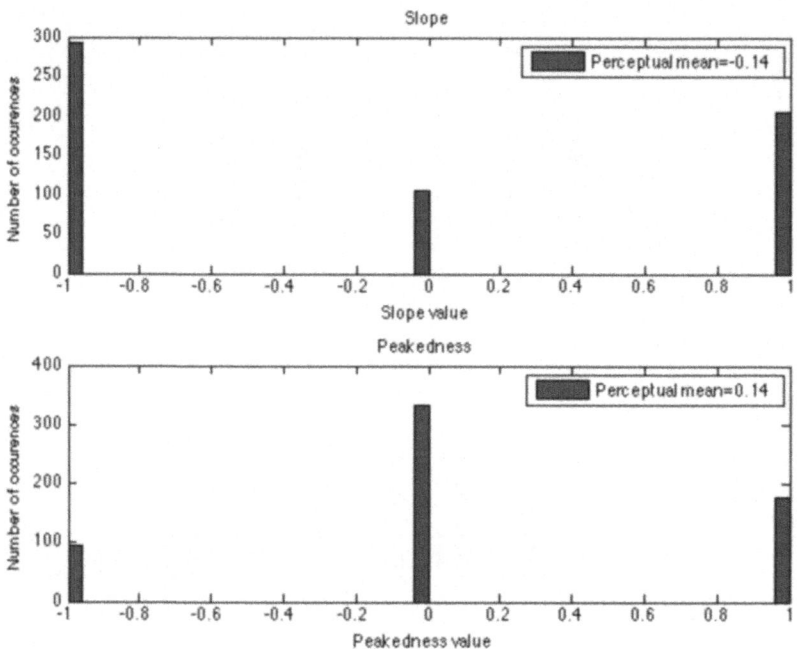

Fig. 6. Histogram of slope and peakedness parameters for perceptually obtained chunk shapes

4.3 The Peak Position

In the case of peaked chunks, the question arises where in the chunks the peaks are located (the peak position). The perceptually obtained shapes are categorized into five positions, as seen in figure 1. In the case of the shapes obtained from the features, it is calculated as the position of the maximum of each chunk, and normalized between zero and one. To facilitate comparison between the peak positions obtained from the features and from the perceptually obtained chunk shapes, the five positions are supposed to be parametric variables with values 1/10, 3/10, 5/10, 7/10 and 9/10, respectively. The histogram for the peak positions for all three songs is shown in figure 7 for the loudness (top) and perceptual chunks (bottom).

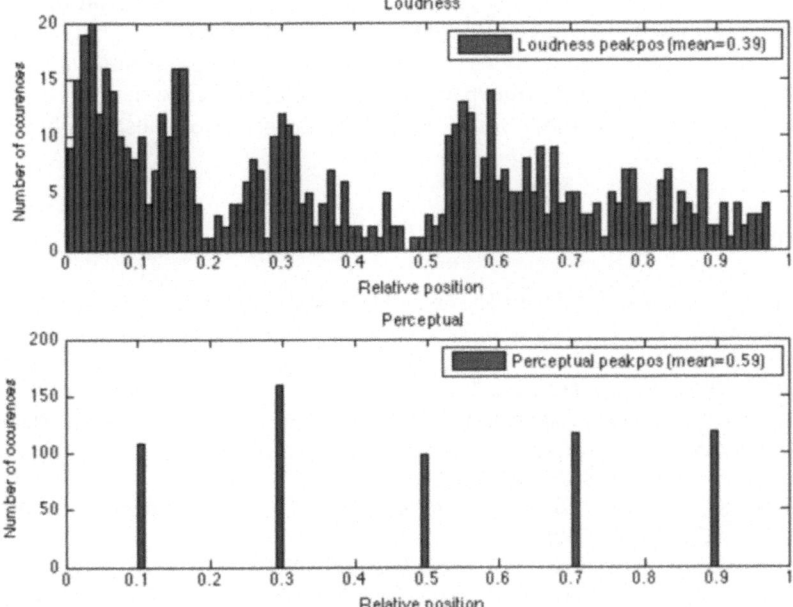

Fig. 7. Histogram for the peakposition for loudness (top) and perceptually obtained chunk shapes (bottom)

5 Discussion

This paper has investigated the chunking phenomenon from a musico-cognitive and a signal processing point of view. A chunk is seen as a short sequence of notes, performed within a short time-span (approximately 3 seconds). We define the chunk as a closed entity (having a beginning and an end) containing a focus point (peak). This description is then used for a perception-based segmentation of the musical surface into chunks at different levels for three representative songs. The chunks are then classified in 9 different categories with distinct descriptions of slope and peak.

In the next step, the musical chunks are extracted and analyzed using standard signal processing methods. Three features are selected for examination: loudness, pitch, and brightness. A second-order curve is fitted to each chunk for each feature, and parameters corresponding to the height, slope, and peakedness are obtained from the second-order curve. These parameters are investigated for three songs. The chunks are shown to be most often with a negative slope (in 68% of the cases according to the loudness feature), and with a positive peak (in 69%, again according to the loudness). This peak is further investigated, and its peak position is found for each chunk. The results obtained from the two strategies (perceptual-based and automatic) are compared, and found to be in good correspondence.

The investigation is one in a series of studies that aims to provide a theoretical foundation for a more naturalized generation of musical phrases. In the first study [3] we investigated the perceptual segmentation of the auditory stream. Here, we have studied the internal structure of a chunk. A more detailed comparison of automatic and perceptual-based chunking will bring us closer to the goal.

Although we need to investigate a larger number of songs in order to be able to make broader generalizations, this paper has supported the view that it is possible to use signal processing methods for a better understanding of musical phrasing and expressivity.

References

1. "Phrase". In: Kennedy, M. (ed.) The Oxford Dictionary of Music, 2nd ed. rev. Oxford Music Online,
   http://www.oxfordmusiconline.com/subscriber/article/opr/t237/e7894 (accessed October 5, 2008)
2. Chew, G.: "Articulation and phrasing". In Grove Music Online. Oxford Music Online,
   http://www.oxfordmusiconline.com/subscriber/article/grove/music/40952 (accessed October 5, 2008)
3. Jensen, K., Kühl, O.: Retrieving Musical Chunks. In: Proceedings of ICMC 2008. Re:New, Copenhagen (2008)
4. Wertheimer, M.: 'Gestalt Theory'. Social Research 11 (1944)
5. Jackendoff, R.: Semantics and Cognition Cambridge. The MIT Press, Mass (1983)
6. Gärdenfors, P.: Conceptual Spaces. The MIT Press, Cambridge (2000)
7. Miller, G.: The Magical Number Seven, Plus or Minus Two. Psychological Review 63, 81–97 (1956)
8. Lerdahl, F., Jackendoff, R.: A Generative Theory of Tonal Music. The MIT Press, Cambridge (1983)
9. Kühl, O.: Musical Semantics. Peter Lang, Bern (2007)
10. Pöppel, E.: A hierarchical model of temporal perception. Trends in Cognitive Science 1/2, 56–61 (1997)
11. Snyder, B.: Music and Memory. The MIT Press, Cambridge (2000)
12. McNeill, D.: Gesture and Thought. The University of Chicago Press, Chicago (2005)
13. Clarke, E.: Empirical Methods in the Study of Performance. In: Clarke, E., Cook, N. (eds.) Empirical Musicology, pp. 77–102. Oxford University Press, Oxford (2004)
14. Getz, S.: People Time, Mercury (1992)
15. Walters, J.: Jamie Walters, Atlantic (1994)
16. Barenboim, D.: Mozart: Complete Piano Sonatas and Variations, EMI Classics (1991)
17. Zwicker, E., Fastl, H.: Psychoacoustics: Facts and Models. Springer, Heidelberg (1990)
18. Bartsch, M.A., Wakefield, G.H.: To catch a chorus: Using chroma-based representations for audio thumbnailing. In: Proceedings of the Workshop on Applications of Signal Processing to Audio and Acoustics, pp. 15–18 (2001)
19. Rabiner, L.R.: On the use of autocorrelation analysis for pitch detection. IEEE Trans. ASSP ASSP-25(1) (February 1977)
20. Beauchamp, J.: Synthesis by spectral amplitude and "Brightness" matching of analyzed musical instrument tones. J. Acoust. Eng. Soc. 30(6) (1982)
21. Moré, J.J.: The Levenberg-Marquardt algorithm: Implementation and theory. In: Watson, G.A. (ed.). Lecture notes in mathematics. Springer, Heidelberg (1977)

Does Social Interaction Activate Music Listeners?

Leen De Bruyn, Marc Leman, Dirk Moelants, and Michiel Demey

Ghent University, Department of Musicology – IPEM,
Blandijnberg 2, 9000 Ghent, Belgium
{Leen.DeBruyn,Marc.Leman,Dirk.Moelants,Michiel.Demey}@UGent.be

Abstract. Over the last years, embodiment has gained a lot of interest in the field of music research. Researchers began to focus on the study of body movements and gestures in relationship with music. In the study presented here, we empirically quantified the impact of social interaction on movements made by groups of subjects listening and moving to music. Both children (average age 9) and adolescents (average age 16) were tested. The methodology was based on motion capturing using wireless Wii Nintendo Remote sensors, and subsequent statistical analysis. Participants were asked to move along with the beat of the music in two conditions: Individual, without social contact, and in groups of four, encouraging social interaction. Data analysis shows that the influence of the social environment has an effect that can be measured and quantified. In general, the social context stimulates participants to move more intensively to the music. Furthermore, adolescent participants even show a significantly improved synchronization with the beat of the music in the social condition, illustrating social facilitation.

Keywords: Music, Embodiment, Synchronization, Social interaction.

1 Introduction

Embodiment and embodied music cognition have gained a lot of attention over the past few years. In this approach, the human body is seen as a link between the physical level of the musical signal and the mental level at which musical meaning processes take place [1]. Although embodiment is a relatively unexplored paradigm in cognitive science [2,3], research on musical gesture and expressiveness is not entirely new. Reference can be made to the historical work of Truslit [4], Becking [5] and Clynes [6]. They were pioneers in approaching music and body movement from an empirical and phenomenological point of view. In *Gestaltung und Bewegung in der Musik* [4] Alexander Truslit describes inner movement as the most essential characteristic of music. He states that it is necessary to get access to this inner movement, through body movement, in order to fully understand music. In *Musikalische Rhythmus als Erkenntnisquelle* [5], Gustav Becking starts from the idea that the rhythmical structures of two musical pieces can be the same, but the interpretation of these rhythms can differ a lot. He suggests that the interpretation given to rhythmical structures is composer specific. Becking inspired Manfred Clynes who set up a series of experiments that give a more clear and analytical view on the relation between music

S. Ystad, R. Kronland-Martinet, and K. Jensen (Eds.): CMMR 2008, LNCS 5493, pp. 93–106, 2009.
© Springer-Verlag Berlin Heidelberg 2009

and movement. Clynes further developed Beckings ideas by arguing that there exists an inner pulse in the music. This inner pulse is defined as a special aspect of the beat that is a vehicle for a most intimate revelation of the composers' personality. He asked people to push the button of the sentograph in a repetitive way while listening to music. Analyzing all these pressure patterns made Clynes conclude that for different composers different pressure patterns exist. Furthermore, Clynes connected music and movement to the emotion domain. In *Sentics* [6], his main starting point is that each emotion relates to a certain dynamic shape (essentic form). He found that making simple body movements in synchrony with the musical pulse can give us a view on the most elementary movement unit that speaks from the music and that these movement patterns were composer specific.

Research on the relation between music and body movements has developed a lot over the last few years. Reference can be made to the more recent work of Camurri et al. [7], Wanderley and Battier [8], Leman et al. [1] and others. Current research explores the use of video and sensing systems in order to capture body movement during musical activities. Recently, a number of studies have focused on gesture analysis of performers [9,10] and on gestural interaction between musicians [7,11]. The research presented here, however, studies the relationship between music and body movement from the viewpoint of the listener.

Music is without doubt a highly social phenomenon. Research has shown that music has an impact on people's social behavior. It has, for example, been shown that music can be used to improve interaction and social skills in children diagnosed with autism spectrum disorder [12], or in individuals with acute and traumatic brain injury and stroke [13]. Experiments by DeNora [14] have also shown that music can have a great impact on the social behavior of customers in shopping malls or in bars. Besides this, there is a whole area of music related social activity on Internet [15]. People love to consume music in a social environment. Hence the popularity of pop and other public concerts, bars, disco's, dance classes, and also the rapid development of internet pages which allow to exchange music and ideas about music, such as last.fm. This raised the question why music listeners often prefer to experience music in a group. How does this social context contribute to the music listening experience?

The study presented here aims at gaining a deeper insight in the way this social interaction between music listeners affects music perception and musical meaning formation processes. To obtain this, we adopt the paradigm of embodied listening [1]. Corporeal articulations are assumed to express the active personal involvement of a subject listening to music. This can be related to the perceived musical structure, and to emotions that are attributed or experienced in response to music. The approach also assumes that embodiment is a strong factor in the disambiguation of perceived musical structures. In this paper, we aim at extending this paradigm of embodied music cognition to the social interactive domain. We assume that through social interaction, corporeal responses can be perceived and picked up by other subjects that perform a similar task. If this task involves synchronization of movements, and if the synchronization movements of different participants influence each other, then we speak of *entrainment* [11]. Entrainment supposes interaction between the participants in a way that they will adjust their movements to each other and eventually 'lock in' to a common phase and/or periodicity. In this respect, reference should be made to the literature of McNeill. In his book *Keeping together in time* [16] McNeill gives a number of examples throughout history of people using synchronized movement, singing and dancing to enhance a fellow-feeling, a feeling of belonging, a sense of community. For example, festive village dancing has the function to smooth out frictions and consolidate fellow-feeling among participants. Movement in unison was also used to make collective tasks more efficient, think about war dances, rhythmic exercises among hunters, synchronized rowing and others. Even today, we can still find proof for a human tendency to move together in time, think of cheering football crowds, patriotic parades, community dancing or audiences applauding in synchrony [17]. Based on his findings, McNeill developed his theory of muscular bonding: *Muscular bonding is the most economical label I could find for the euphoric fellow feeling that prolonged and rhythmic muscular movement arouses among nearly all participants in such exercises* [16]. McNeill refers to the feelings expressed by soldiers marching together, such as a sense of pervasive well-being, a strange sense of personal enlargement, a sort of swelling out, becoming bigger than life due to prolonged movement in unison that drilling involved. Although we can find numerous examples of the tendency in human beings to move together in synchrony, scientific investigation of what happens to those who engage in such behavior remains scarce. The present research investigates whether the social environment has an effect on the embodiment of groups of music listeners moving rhythmically to music. Based on findings of McNeill [16] and DeNora [14], that moving together to music creates a feeling of well-being and makes a task more efficient, we hypothesize that when people listen to music in a group, they will (1) synchronize their movements with each other (entrainment), (2) synchronize better to the beat of the music, hence executing the task more efficiently, and (3) move more intense to the music, caused by the *euphoric fellow-feeling* due to the muscular bonding between the music listeners.

The results presented in this paper are based on two exploratory studies, using new sensing technologies and statistical methods to investigate the impact of social interaction on subjects' – adolescents and children - movements to music in an objective way. These studies are a first step towards more profound research on the impact of social interaction on people's embodiment to music and can lead to more insight in the social processes involved in musical meaning formation and to the development of applications in music education, music therapy and revalidation.

2 Experimental Setup

2.1 Study I: Individual and Social Embodiment of Adolescents

2.1.1 Participants

32 groups of 4 adolescents participated in this experiment (mean age 16; standard deviation 3). All participants were recruited from the third and fifth grade of several secondary schools in Flanders. It was requested that participants had normal hearing and normal motor abilities for inclusion in this study. The experiment included a pre-questionnaire, which aimed at gathering information about participant's age, gender, musical education and dance experience. There were 80 female and 48 male participants, of which 21 participants had a formal musical education.

2.1.2 Stimuli

Six musical excerpts, each with a duration of 30 seconds, were selected. The excerpts varied in tempo, level of familiarity and rhythmical ambiguity, and were presented with an intersection of 5 seconds pause. Three songs were chosen from the top of the pop charts at the time of the experiment (September 2007). It was assumed that these three songs would be very familiar to the teenage participants. The three unfamiliar excerpts comprised non-mainstream music (electronic/experimental, classical, non-western). It was assumed that this music would not be familiar to the teenage participants. To increase the contrast between the familiar and the unfamiliar songs, the metric structures of the latter was ambiguous. The rhythm of songs 3 and 5 allowed a binary or ternary interpretation, whereas song 2 had an unclear beat. Table 1 gives an overview of the 6 musical excerpts and their characteristics.

Table 1. Overview of the 6 musical excerpts used as stimuli in the experiment. The column 'Level' stands for the level of Familiarity (F = Familiar; Uf = Unfamiliar) and level of Rhythmical Ambiguity (U = Unambiguous; A = Ambiguous) of the excerpts.

Nr	Title	Performer	Tempo [BPM]	Level
1	Sunrise	Milk Inc.	140	F / U
2	Window Licker	Aphex Twin	123	Uf / A
3	Follia	Anonymous	47/141	Uf / A
4	Vietnam	Vorwerk	142	F / U
5	Akacham Yaghwa	Rashid Anas	72/216/144	Uf / A
6	The way I are	Timbaland	115	F / U

2.1.3 Method and Equipment

Participants were given a wireless Wii Nintendo Remote sensor in the dominant hand and were asked to move in synchrony with the beat of the six musical excerpts as shown in Figure 1. Half of the groups (N = 16) performed this task in two conditions: individual, in which case participants were blindfolded, and social, without blindfolds and facing each other. The other 16 groups performed the task only in the group condition. Acceleration data were recorded on the hard drive of a PC, communicating with the Wii remotes via bluetooth. A Pd patch [18] was used to this purpose.

2.2 Study II: Individual and Social Embodiment of Children

2.2.1 Participants

14 groups of 4 participants participated in this experiment (mean age 9, standard deviation 1). All participants were recruited from the 3rd and 5th grade of a primary school in Flanders. It was requested that participants had normal hearing and normal motor abilities for inclusion in the study. The experiment included a pre-questionnaire, aimed at gathering information about participants' age, gender, musical education and dance experience. There were 33 female and 23 male participants, of which 11 participants were enrolled in a music school at the time of the experiment.

Fig. 1. Group of participants performing the experiment in the social condition, with a Wii Nintendo Remote sensor in their dominant hand

2.2.2 Stimuli

Ten 30 second musical excerpts were selected. The excerpts varied in tempo, level of familiarity and level of rhythmical ambiguity, and were presented with an intersection of 5 seconds pause. Familiarity of the songs was established using a questionnaire in the participating classes, previous to the experiment, in which the children were asked about their musical preferences. The three songs that were most often cited were included as 'familiar' songs. Next to these three songs, three pieces that were similar in style and tempo, but unknown to the children were added. With the four remaining songs rhythmical ambiguity was introduced. The rhythm of song 3 allowed a binary and ternary interpretation, whereas songs 6, 8 and 9 had an unclear beat. Table 2 gives an overview of the 10 musical excerpts and their characteristics.

Table 2. Overview of the 10 musical excerpts used as stimuli in the experiment. The column 'Level' stands for the level of Familiarity (F=familiar; Uf = Unfamiliar) and level of Rhythmical ambiguity (A=Ambiguous) of the excerpts.

Nr	Title	Performer	Tempo (BPM)	Level
1	Relax	Mika	122	F
2	Spraakwater	Extince	90	Uf
3	Akacham Yaghwa	Rachid Anas	144	Uf / A
4	Freefall	Jeckyll & Hyde	143	F
5	Kaantalaga	DJ Doll Remix	122	Uf
6	March of the Pigs	Nine Inch Nails	133	Uf / A
7	Say yeah!	Morning Musume	143	Uf
8	Window Licker	Aphex Twin	123	Uf / A
9	Hiyamikachi Bushi	Traditional	143	Uf / A
10	Straight to the bank	50 cent	89	F

2.2.3 Method and Equipment

Participants were given a wireless Wii Nintendo Remote sensor in the dominant hand and were asked to move along in synchrony with the beat of the ten musical excerpts. Each group had to perform this task in two conditions: individual, in which case participants were separated using screens (Figure 2a), and social, moving together in groups of four and facing each other (Figure 2b). All groups performed the task during three trials, of which two were individual and one was social. Half of the groups performed the task first two trials individually and the third trial social (IIS), the other 7 groups performed the task first individually, then social and the third trial again individually (ISI). This randomisation was used to enable distinction between the impact of the social context and the impact of learning effects.

Acceleration data were recorded using the same method as in study I. The whole experiment was also recorded on video, for further interpretation of the data.

Fig. 2a. Group of participants performing the experiment in the individual condition, separated by screens, with a Wii Nintendo Remote in their dominant hand

Fig. 2b. Group of participants performing the experiment in the social condition, facing each other, with a Wii Nintendo Remote in their dominant hand

3 Data Processing

The data captured by the Wii Remote consists of three acceleration time series, one for each axis of the local reference frame of the accelerometer. These data were sampled at a rate of 100Hz. The data-analysis had a focus on (i) the amount of synchronization of each participant with the music, (ii) the amount of movement intensity of each participant.

3.1 Synchronization Analysis

To analyze the individual synchronization with the beat of the music, the amount of seconds the participants synchronized correctly with the music is calculated from the raw data. First, the three time series (three axes) are summed up and the resulting signal is filtered to a 0.5Hz to 4Hz band. The filter eliminates the constant offset in the acceleration data due to the gravitation force, as well as the higher frequencies irrelevant to human rhythm perception (4Hz corresponds to a BPM-value of 240). In a next step, the dominant frequency component (beat) in the movement is calculated for each block of 2 seconds by applying a FFT over a 4-second moving window with a

2-second overlap. The dominant peak in the Fourier spectrum is identified and compared with the nominal BPM of the excerpt, allowing a tolerance of ±5BPM for deciding on correctness of synchronization. Also the half and the double of the nominal tempo are considered, with tolerance windows of ±2.5BPM and ±10BPM, respectively. The result of this calculation is defined as the number of 2-second blocks in which the participant successfully synchronized with the music [18].

3.2 Intensity of Movement Analysis

In the second approach, the raw data are converted to a measure for the intensity of the participant's movements. This is done through Eq. (1), giving the cumulative sum of the norms of the acceleration differences for each two consecutive samples in the 30 second series (3000 samples, at 100Hz).

$$I = \sum_{i=1}^{2999} \sqrt{(a_x(t_{i+1}) - a_x(t_i))^2 + (a_y(t_{i+1}) - a_y(t_i))^2 + (a_z(t_{i+1}) - a_z(t_i))^2} \qquad (1)$$

The resulting single number is a measure for the intensity of the movements of the participant: the more intense the movements, the larger the differences in acceleration between consecutive samples will be, resulting in a larger cumulative sum over the excerpt. In order to optimize the data for a comparison between the individual and group conditions and between the musical excerpts (rather than for differences between individual participants), the resulting intensity for each excerpt (and for each condition) is normalized over the mean of the intensities over all excerpts for that participant. This corrects for a 'natural' difference in intensity of movement between the participants, which is partly related to their body characteristics.

4 Results

4.1 Study I: Individual and Social Embodiment of Adolescents

First we will analyse the data of the 16 groups that performed the taks in both the individual and the social conditions. Prior to the analysis of these data a modified Levene test and a Kolmogorov-Smirnov test (KS-test) were used to check for homogeneity of variances and normality. Both assumptions could be accepted enabling an ANOVA-analysis for both synchronization and intensity of movement data. For the synchronization with the music, the results summarized in Table 3 show that participants synchronize significantly better in the social condition in comparison to the individual condition ($p<.05$, $\alpha=0.05$). The main effects are visualized in an interaction plot in Figure 3, which shows that the mean synchronization is higher in the social condition for all songs. Statistical analysis shows that the songs themselves have a great impact on the synchronization results, which is also evident from Figure 3. A multiple comparison Tukey analysis shows that participants score significantly lower for songs 3 and 5 than for songs 1, 4 and 6. As songs 3 and 5 are the unfamiliar excerpts with rhythmical ambiguity, these characteristics of the music clearly have an impact on the difficulty the participants experience in synchronizing with the beat. Songs 3 and 5 can be interpreted either binary or ternary, whereas songs 1, 4 and 6 are pop songs with a clear beat. Furthermore, for song 2, an unfamiliar excerpt with an unclear beat, the Tukey analysis shows the scores lie in between the scores for the ambiguous and the pop songs.

Results of the ANOVA-analysis on the intensity of movement data are shown in Table 4. Participants move significantly more intense in the social condition ($p<.05$, $\alpha=0.05$) for all songs. These results are visualized in the interaction plot in Figure 4. Not only do the participants synchronize better with the music in the social condition, they also move more intensively. For the intensity of movement again there is a definite impact of songs themselves. In this case however, a multiple comparison Tukey analysis did not reveal subgroups in the influence of songs with respect to rhythmical ambiguity and familiarity and it is yet unclear which characteristics of the songs are dominant. However it can still be noted that the only classical music example clearly evokes the least intensive movements.

Table 3. Overview of the results of the ANOVA-analysis on the synchronization data for the variable Condition

ANOVA: synchronization		
	F-value	**p-value**
Song1	2.40	0.12
Song2	10.13	<.01
Song3	5.37	<.05
Song4	5.69	<.05
Song5	9.46	<.01
Song6	6.97	<.01

Table 4. Overview of the results of the ANOVA-analysis on the intensity of movement data for the variable Condition

ANOVA: intensity of movement		
	F-value	**p-value**
Song1	20.06	<.01
Song2	66.13	<.01
Song3	26.53	<.01
Song4	41.09	<.01
Song5	46.40	<.01
Song6	45.61	<.01

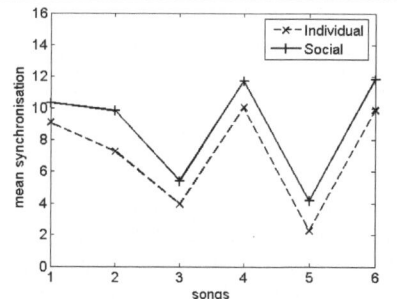

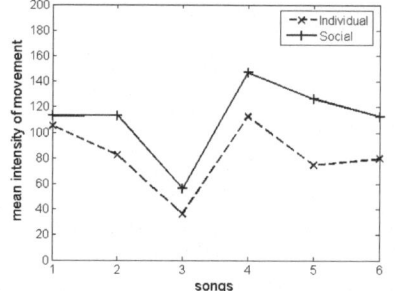

Fig. 3. Visualization of the mean synchronization results per song in the individual and the social condition for Study I

Fig. 4. Visualization of the mean intensity of movement data per song in the individual and the social condition for Study I

From these results we could conclude that there is a significant difference in gestural response to musical stimuli in a social compared to an individual context. However, it could be premature to conclude that this is solely due to the social impact. Since all participants performed the experiment in the same order, first the individual and then the social condition, it is not possible to distinguish between the impact of learning processes or familiarity with the task and the impact of the social condition. To be able to correct for the learning effects, we can compare these results with those of the second group of participants, who only performed the task in the social condition.

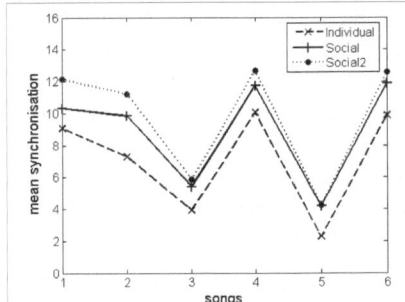

Fig. 5. Comparison of the synchronization results per song of the first set of participants in Study I, that performed the experiment in the individual and the social condition (Individual – Social), with the second set of participants, that performed the experiment only in the social condition (Social2)

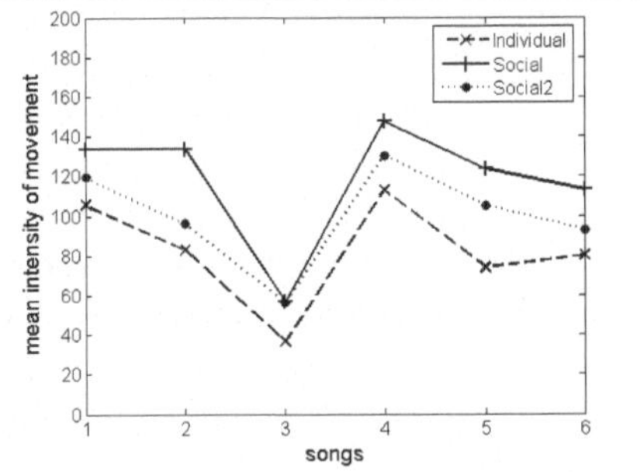

Fig. 6. Comparison of the intensity of movement per song of the first set of participants in Study I (Individual – Social) with the intensity of movement of the second set of participants, that only performed the experiment in the social condition (Social2)

Results of this second set of participants show that the synchronization results and level of intensity of movement is immediately as high as the amount of movement in the second condition of the first set of participants. Learning effects or familiarity with the task can not explain this immediate high level of synchronization and intensity. The mean synchronization results for the second set of participants are shown in Figure 5, where the data are compared with the results of the first set of participants (Figure 3). Figure 5 shows that there are no significant differences in synchronization results in both social conditions, which confirms the assumption that the social context did indeed stimulate the participants to synchronize better with the beat of the music. Similarly, Figure 6 shows the interaction plot for mean intensity of movement. Again, the results confirm that the social context did stimulate the participants to move more intensively to the music.

4.2 Study II: Individual and Social Embodiment of Children

One could argue that it is rather the deprivation of sight in the individual condition of study I that made the participants move differently in both conditions than the effect of the social context. Thus, to test whether the present results are a reflection of this deprivation of sight rather than an effect of social condition, we did a second study (Study II) in a school environment where the individual condition was created using separate boxes (Figure 2a).

Analysis of the synchronization with the music data shows that participants did not synchronize significantly better in the social condition in comparison to the individual condition (p>.05,α=0.05) (Figure 7). This contradicts the findings of Study I that with adolescents synchronization with the beat of the music did improve significantly from the individual to the social condition. Statistical analysis did show that the songs themselves, more particularly the complexity of the songs, have a great impact on the synchronization results in both conditions, which is also evident in Figure 7. A multiple comparison Tukey analysis shows that participants score significantly lower for songs 3, 6, 8 and 9 than for songs 1, 2, 4, 5, 7 and 10. As songs 3, 6, 8 and 9 were the songs with an ambiguous rhythm, this characteristic of the music clearly has an impact on the difficulty the participants experience in synchronizing with the beat. This confirms the findings of Study I, where we also found a significant impact of rhythmical ambiguity on the synchronization results. No significant difference in synchronization was found between the familiar songs and the unfamiliar songs in a similar style.

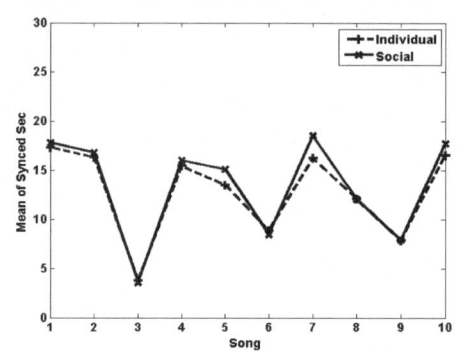

Fig. 7. Visualization of the mean synchronization results per song in the individual and the social condition in Study II, showing no effect of social facilitation on beat synchronization in children

Table 5. Overview of the results of the ANOVA-analysis on the intensity of movement data in Study II

ANOVA: Intensity of Movement		
	F-value	p-value
Song 1	36,94	<.01
Song 2	14,75	<.01
Song 3	17,18	<.01
Song 4	26,72	<.01
Song 5	16,09	<.01
Song 6	29,06	<.01
Song 7	18,37	<.01
Song 8	15,81	<.01
Song 9	10,62	<.01
Song 10	8,83	<.01

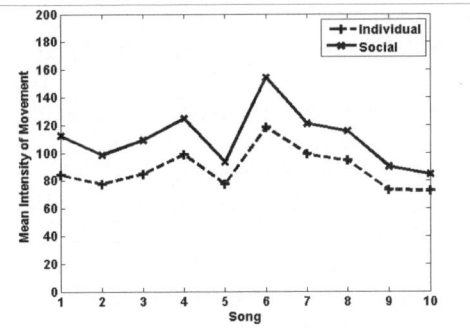

Fig. 8. Visualization of the mean intensity of movement data per song in the individual and the social condition in Study II

For the intensity of movement, the results summarized in Table 5 show that participants move significantly more intense in the social condition ($p<.05, \alpha=0.05$) compared to the individual condition. The main effects are visualized in an interaction plot in Figure 8. For the intensity of movement, again there is a definite impact of the songs themselves. In this case however, a multiple comparison Tukey analysis did not reveal subgroups in the influence of songs with respect to rhythmical ambiguity and familiarity and it is yet unclear which characteristics of the songs are dominant. Music education and gender, nor age had a significant impact on the intensity of the movements of the participants.

As a first conclusion, the analysis showed that the social context did not have an effect on the synchronization with the beat of the music, but did cause an increase in movement intensity. In other words, the children did not synchronize better in the social condition, but their movements did become more intense. The fact that we did not establish social facilitation in beat synchronization in children can have different causes: difficulty of the task, motor development or social development. Video analysis showed that children had much more difficulties than adolescents to keep to the given task, in that the children did not focus on their hand movements and were dancing and jumping around and even break dancing on the floor. This disturbs the measurements by the Wii Remotes and leads to a decrease in the score of the periodicity analysis. Hence, for future research with children, the use of more sensors, enabling the measurement of different body parts would be preferred.

The results did show that when children synchronize to music in a social context, there is a significant increase in movement intensity. However, the design of the experiment could have an effect on this increase in movement intensity; in particular a learning effect over the trials could be the cause of this increase in the intensity of the movements. Hence, using ANOVA and multiple comparison Tukey analysis, we investigated the effect of the order of the trials (IIS and ISI) on the movement intensity. This analysis shows that for the IIS design there is a significant difference in mean intensity of movement between trials. The main effects are visualized in Figure 9, showing that the intensity of movement increases quasi linear over the trials. This suggests that the increase of movement intensity may be caused by a learning effect. However, analysis of the data from the ISI design (Figure 10) is clearly different from the IIS design (Figure 9). For songs 1, 2, 3 and 7 we see that the movement intensity is highest in the social condition, whereas for songs 4, 5, 6 and 8 we see an increase from the first individual trial to the second social trial and then the movement intensity remains at the same level in the third individual trial. This could be explained by the fact that participants imitate movements in the third individual trial that they saw and did in the second social trial. We can refer here to the concept of *social memory* [19]. Social memory implies that the intrinsic parameters of the individual components have been altered by virtue of the social interaction. In the IIS design, the social condition generates the highest intensity for all songs. In the ISI design, the social condition is equally high or higher than the individual condition, depending on the type of song. Hence, we can conclude that the social context does indeed have an impact on how participants embody the music.

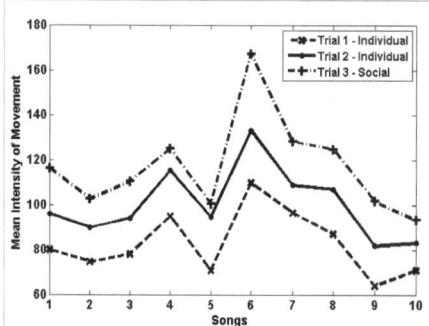

Fig. 9. Interaction plot visualizing the mean intensity of movement data per song for the 3 trials in the **IIS** design

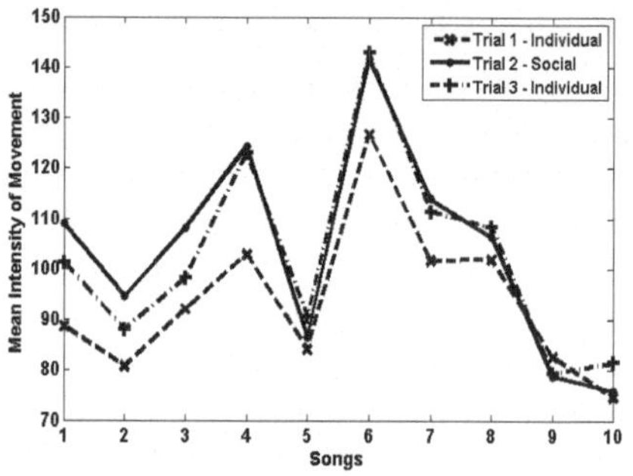

Fig. 10. Interaction plot visualizing the mean intensity of movement data per song for the 3 trials in the **ISI** design

5   Conclusion

The studies presented here are an example of the use of wireless motion sensors and new analysis methods to measure and quantify the embodiment of music listeners in individual versus group settings. It should be noted here that this new motion capturing technology allowed us to step outside of the laboratory environment and execute the studies in more ecological settings. However, concerning the used technology and analysis methods, we are aware that some challenges still have to be met. In future experiments it is desirable to increase the amount of sensors per participant and to make them more non-obtrusive, this in order to obtain a more complete image of the participants' embodiment. We are also developing more profound analysis methods for the time series data obtained by the sensors [20]. In future experiments, the developed methodology will be used to test larger groups of participants and to compare specific target groups.

The results presented here show that there is a social factor which can be measured and quantified. Results of both studies show a significant increase in intensity of movement when moving to music in a group situation. The experiment with groups of adolescents also shows a significant improvement of synchronization with the beat of the music in the social condition. Hence, the present findings support the muscular bonding theory of McNeill [16] and the findings of DeNora [14], showing that moving together in time with the music stimulates and activates people to move more intense and more efficient. The developed methodology can now be used in future experiments with specific target groups for studying influence of social context on musical gestures, music perception and musical meaning formation. These insights can lead to new applications in various fields, such as music education, music therapy and music production.

Acknowledgements

Leen De Bruyn acknowledges the Ghent University BOF fund for a doctoral grant. The authors also wish to thank all participants in the experiments at the Accenta fair Ghent and the primary school Henri D'Haese of Gentbrugge, and in particular the head of the school Frank Henry and the teachers Ann Trouvé and Iris Bouché, for allowing their pupils to participate in the experiment. Special thanks also goes to Ivan Schepers, Liesbeth De Voogdt and Frederik Styns for technical and practical support during execution of the experiments.

References

1. Leman, M.: Embodied Music Cognition and Mediation Technology. The MIT Press, Cambridge (2007)
2. Varela, F.J., Thompson, E., Rosch, E.: The Embodied Mind. In: Cognitive Science and Human Experience. The MIT Press, Cambridge (1991)
3. Gallagher, S., Cole, J.: Body Schema and Body Image in a Deafferented Subject. J. Mind Behav. 16, 369–390 (1995)
4. Truslit, A.: Gestaltung und Bewegung in der Musik. Chr. Friedrich Vieweg, Berlin-Lichterfelde (1938)
5. Becking, G.: Der Musikalische Rhythmus als Erkenntnisquelle. Ichthys Verlag, Stuttgart (1958)
6. Clynes, M.: Sentics, the touch of emotions. Doubleday Anchor, New York (1977)
7. Camurri, A., Castellano, G., Cowie, R., Glowinski, D., Knapp, B., Krumhansl, C.L., Villon, O., Volpe, G.: The Premio Paganini Experiment: a multimodal gesture-based approach for explaining emotional processes in music performance. In: 7th International Workshop on Gesture in Human-Computer Interaction and Simulation, Lisbon (May 2007)
8. Wanderley, M., Battier, M. (eds.): Trends in Gestural Control of Music. Ircam-Centre Pompidou (2000)
9. Dahl, S., Grossbach, M., Altenmuller, E.: Influence of Movement and Grip on Perceptual and Measured Tone Quality in Drumming. In: 10th International Conference on Music Perception and Cognition, Sapporo, Japan (2008)
10. Thompson, M., Luck, G.: Effect of Pianists' Expressive Intention on Amount and Type of Body Movement. In: 10th International Conference on Music Perception and Cognition, Sapporo, Japan (2008)
11. Clayton, M., Sager, R., Will, U.: In time with the music: The concept of entrainment and its significance for ethnomusicology. In: ESEM Counterpoint I (2004)

12. Kern, P., Aldridge, D.: Using embedded music therapy interventions to support outdoor play of young children with autism in an inclusive community-based child care program. J. Mus. Ther. 43, 4 (2006)
13. Nayak, S., Wheeler, B., Shiflett, S., Agostinelli, S.: Effect of Music Therapy on Mood and Social Interaction among individuals with acute and traumatic brain injury and stroke. Rehab. Psych. 45(3), 274–283 (2000)
14. DeNora, T.: Music in everyday life. The MIT Press, Cambridge (2000)
15. Kiraly, Z.: Solfeggio 1: A Vertical Ear Training Instruction Assisted by the Computer. Int. J. Music Educ., 40–41 (2003)
16. McNeill, W.H.: Keeping together in time: Dance and Drill in Human History. Harvard University Press, Cambridge (1995)
17. Néda, Z., Ravasz, E., Brechet, Y., Vicsek, T., Barabasi, A.L.: The sound of many hands clapping: Tumultuous applause can transform itself into waves of synchronized clapping. Nature 403, 849–850 (2000)
18. Demey, M., Leman, M., Bossuyt, F., Vanfleteren, J.: The Musical Synchrotron: Using wireless motion sensors to study how social interaction affects synchronization with musical tempo. In: 8th International Conference on New Interfaces for Musical Expression, Genova, Italy, pp. 372–373 (2008)
19. Oullier, O., de Guzman, G.C., Jantzen, K.J., Lagarde, J., Kelso, J.A.S.: Social coordination dynamics: Measuring human bonding. Soc. Neur. 3(2), 178–192 (2008)
20. Desmet, F., De Bruyn, L., Leman, M., Lesaffre, M.: Statistical analysis of human body movement and group interactions in response to music. In: 32nd Annual Conference of the German Classification Society, Hamburg, Germany (2008) (submitted)

Musically Meaningful or Just Noise?
An Analysis of On-line Artist Networks

Kurt Jacobson and Mark Sandler

Centre for Digital Music, Queen Mary University
{kurt.jacobson,mark.sandler}@elec.qmul.ac.uk
http://www.elec.qmul.ac.uk/digitalmusic/

Abstract. A sample of the Myspace social network is examined. Using methods from complex network theory, we show empirically that the structure of the Myspace artist network is related to the concept of musical genre. A modified assortativity coefficient calculation shows that artists preferentially form network connections with other artists of the same genre. We also show there is a clear trend relating the geodesic distance between artists and genre label associations - that is artists with the same genre associations tend to be closer in the network. These findings motivate the use of on-line social networks as data resources for musicology and music information retrieval.

1 Introduction

Music is an inherently social phenomenon. Of course music can be practiced in solitude, providing the individual with personal satisfaction and even profound inner-vision. But it is the social element - performance, participation, dance - that makes music a truly universal cultural foundation.

Musicologists have long recognized that in discussing music, it is important to consider its context - who created the music? where? why? One important aspect of this is the social context - who were the artist's contemporaries? her friends? her influences? [1].

Today, online social networking websites can provide a concise cross section of this information in an easily accessible format. Myspace [1] has become the de-facto standard for web-based music artist promotion. Although exact figures are not made public, recent blogosphere chatter suggests there are around 7 million artist pages[2] on Myspace.

Artists ranging from bedroom electronica amateurs to multi-platinum mega-stars publish Myspace pages. These Myspace artist pages typically include some media - usually streaming audio, video, or both - and a list of "friends" specifying social connections. This combination of media and a user-specified social network

---

[1] http://myspace.com

[2] http://scottelkin.com/archive/2007/05/11/Myspace-Statistics.aspx
~25 million songs, ~3.5 songs/artist, ~7 million artists
last accessed 26/11/2008.

S. Ystad, R. Kronland-Martinet, and K. Jensen (Eds.): CMMR 2008, LNCS 5493, pp. 107–118, 2009.

provides a unique data set that is unprecedented in both scope and scale. We examine a sample of this on-line social network of artists. Comparing the network topology with a collection of genre tags associated with each artist, we show there is a tendency towards *homophily* - artists are more likely to be friends with artists of the same genre. This suggests such networks are meaningful in the context of several music-related studies including music information retrieval and social musicology.

We begin with a review of some concepts from the complex networks literature and their applications to musician and listener networks. In section 3 we describe the methods used to gather our sample of the Myspace artist network. This is followed by our empirical results in section 4 and a discussion of the results and suggestions for applications and future work in section 5.

2   Complex Networks

Complex network theory deals with the structure of relationships in complex systems. Using the tools of graph theory and statistical mechanics, researchers have developed models and metrics for describing a diverse set of real-world networks - including social networks, academic citation networks, biological protein networks, and the World-Wide Web. All these networks exhibit several unifying characteristics such as small worldness, scale-free degree distributions, and community structure [2],[3]. Let us briefly discuss some definitions and concepts that will be used throughout this work.

2.1   Network Properties

A given network G is described by a set of *nodes* N connected by a set of *edges* E. Each edge is defined by the pair of nodes it connects (i, j). If the edges imply directionality, $(i, j) \neq (j, i)$, the network is a *directed network*. Otherwise, it is an *undirected network*. The number of edges incident to the a node i is the *degree* k_i. In a directed network there will be an *indegree* k_i^{in} and an *outdegree* k_i^{out} corresponding to the number of edges pointing into the node and away from the node respectively.

Degree distribution. The *degree distribution* $P(k)$ is the proportion of nodes that have a degree k. The shape of the degree distribution is an important metric for classifying a network - "scale-free networks" have a power-law distribution [3] while "random networks" have a Poisson distribution. The scale-free degree distribution is a property common to many real-world networks. Conceptually, a scale-free distribution indicates the presence of a few very-popular *hubs* that tend to attract more links as the network evolves [2] [3].

Average shortest path. Two nodes i and j are connected if a path exists between them following the edges in the network. The path from i to j may not be unique. The *geodesic path* d_{ij} is the shortest path distance from i to j in number of edges traversed. For the entire network, the average shortest path or mean geodesic distance is l.

$$l = \frac{1}{\frac{1}{2}n(n+1)} \sum_{i \geq j} d_{ij} \tag{1}$$

where d_{ij} is the geodesic distance from node i to node j and n is the total number of nodes in the network. In a "small-world network" the mean geodesic distance is small relative to the number of nodes in the network [3], [2]. The largest geodesic distance in a network is known as the *diameter*.

Transitivity. The transitivity or clustering coefficient estimates the probability that two neighbors of a given node are neighbors themselves. In the terms of social networks, the friend of your friend is also likely to be your friend. In terms of network topology, transitivity means a heightened number of triangles exist - sets of three nodes that are each connected to each other. For a given undirected unweighted network the transitivity is defined as

$$C = \frac{3N_{\triangle}}{N_3} \tag{2}$$

where $N_{\triangle}$ is the number of triangles in the network and N_3 is the number of connected triples. A connected triple is a set of three nodes where each node can be reached from every other node.

2.2   Networks and Music

Quite naturally, networks of musicians have been studied in the context of complex network theory - typically viewing the artists as nodes in the network and using either collaboration, influence, or similarity to define network edges. These networks of musicians exhibit many of the properties expected in social networks [4], [5], [6], [7].

However the networks studied are generally constructed based on expert opinions (e.g. AllMusicGuide[3]) or proprietary algorithms based on user listening habits (e.g. Last.fm[4]). The Myspace artist network is unique in that the edges - the "friend" connections - are specified by the artists themselves. This makes the Myspace artist network a true social network. It has been shown that significantly different network topologies result from different approaches to artist network construction [5]. Since the Myspace artist network is of unique construction - owing its structure to the decisions and interactions of millions of individuals - we are motivated to analyze its topology and explore how this network structure relates to music.

It should be noted that networks of music listeners and bipartite networks of listeners and artists have also been studied [8] [9]. While such studies are highly interesting in the context of music recommendation, and while the Myspace

---

[3] http://www.allmusic.com/
[4] http://last.fm

network could potentially provide interesting data on networks of listeners, we restrict our current investigation to the Myspace artist network.

Previous analysis of the Myspace social network (including artists and non-artists) suggests that it conforms in many respects to the topologies commonly reported in social networks - having a power-law degree distribution and a small average distance between nodes [10].

3   Sampling Myspace

The Myspace social network presents a variety of challenges. For one, the massive size prohibits analyzing the graph in its entirety, even when considering only the artist pages. Therefore we sample a small yet sufficiently large portion of the network as described in section 3.2. Also, the Myspace social network is filled with noisy data - plagued by spammers and orphaned accounts. We limit the scope of our sampling in a way that minimizes this noise. And finally, there currently is no interface for easily collecting the network data from Myspace. Our data is collected using web crawling and screen scraping techniques.

3.1   Artist Pages

Again, it is important to note we are only concerned with a subset of the Myspace social network - the Myspace *artist* network. Myspace artist pages are different from standard Myspace pages in that they include a distinct audio player application. We use the presence or absence of this player to determine whether or not a given page is an artist page.

A Myspace page will most often include a top friends list. This is a hyper-linked list of other Myspace accounts explicitly specified by the user. The top friends list is limited in length with a maximum length of 40 friends (the default length is 16 friends). In constructing our sampled artist network, we use the top friends list to create a set of directed edges between artists. Only top friends who also have artist pages are added to the sampled network; standard Myspace pages are ignored. We also ignore the remainder of the friends list (i.e. friends that are not specified by the user as top friends), assuming these relationships are not as relevant. This reduces the amount of noise in the sampled network but also artificially limits the outdegree of each node. Our sampling method is based on the assumption that artists specified as top friends have some mean-ingful musical connection for the user – whether through collaboration, stylistic similarity, friendship, or artistic influence.

Each Myspace artist page includes between zero and three genre tags. The artist selects from a list of 119 genres specified by Myspace. These genre label as-sociations were also collected. In our sample set, around 2.6% of artists specified no genre tags.

3.2   Snowball Sampling

For the Myspace artist network, snowball sampling is the most appropriate method [10]. Alternative methods such as random edge sampling and random node sampling would result in many small disconnected components and not provide any insight to the structure of the entire network [11]. In snowball sampling, a first seed node (artist page) is included in the sample. Then the seed node's neighbors (top friends) are included in the sample. Then the neighbors' neighbors. This breadth-first sampling is continued until a particular sampling ratio is achieved. We randomly select one seed node[5] and perform 6 levels of sampling - such that in an undirected view of the network, no artist can have a geodesic distance greater than 6 with respect to the seed artist - to collect 15,478 nodes. If the size of the Myspace artist network is around 7 million, then this is close to the 0.25% sampling ratio suggested in [12].

With snowball sampling there is a tendency to over-sample hubs because they have many links and are easily picked up early in the breadth-first sampling. This property would reduce the degree distribution exponent and produce a heavier tail but preserve the power-law nature of the network [11].

4   Empirical Results

The Myspace artist network sample conforms in many respects to the topologies expected in social networks. The network statistics for our sample are summarized in Table 1.

Table 1. The network statistics for the Myspace artist network sample where n is the number of nodes, m is the number of edges, $\langle k \rangle$ is the average degree, l is the mean geodesic distance, d_{max} is the diameter, and C is the clustering coefficient. The clustering coefficient is undefined for directed networks

	n	m	$\langle k \rangle$	l	d_{max}	C
undirected	15,478	91,326	11.801	4.479	9	. 219
directed	15,478	120,487	15.569	6.426	16	-

The values for the mean geodesic distance l and the diameter d_{max} are relatively small and suggest a small-world network - any node can be reached from any other node in a small number of steps. The value of the clustering coefficient $C = 0.219$ indicates a high level community structure - an equivalent random network would have a transitivity of $C_r = \frac{\langle k \rangle}{n} = 7.26 \cdot 10^{-4}$. Both of these properties are commonly reported in social networks [3], [2]. While our sample size is large enough for estimating the degree distributions of the entire network, it is insufficient to assume the C, l, and d_{max} values hold true for the entire Myspace artist network [12].

The cumulative degree distributions for the network sample are plotted in Fig. 1. Both the in-degree and out-degree distributions are plotted. Notice the

---

[5] Our randomly selected artist is French rapper Karna Zoo http://www.myspace.com/karnazoo

in-degree distribution is plotted on a log-log scale. For moderate degree values $(35 < k_{in} < 200)$, the in-degree distribution follows a power-law decay [6]. The power-law fit breaks down for high and low values of k_{in}. Similar "broad-scale" degree distributions have been reported for citation networks and movie actor networks [13] as well as in online social networks [10].

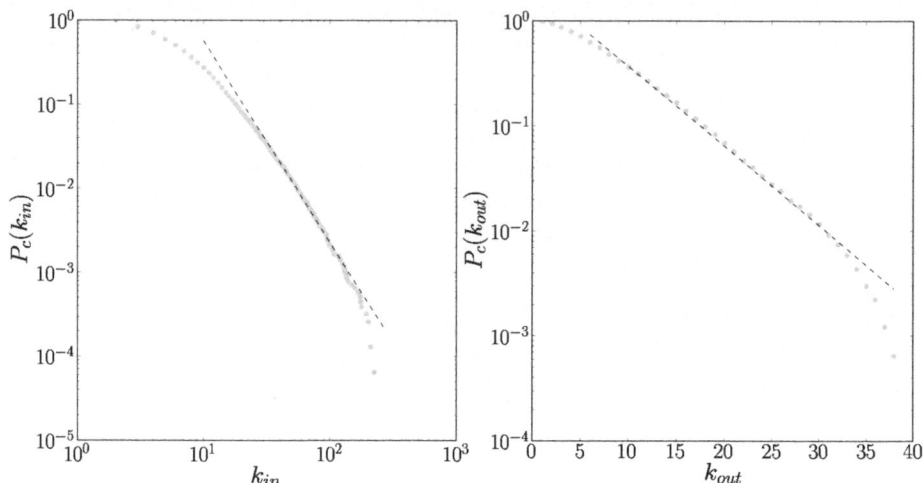

Fig. 1. The cumulative degree distributions for (a) the in degree plotted on a log-log scale and (b) the out degree plotted on a log-linear scale

The cumulative out-degree distribution is plotted on a linear-log scale. For moderate values of follows of k^{out} we see an exponential decay[7] indicated by the fit of a straight line in the linear-log scale. Such distributions have been reported in a variety of networks including some music artist networks and it has been suggested that artist networks with imposed degree limits tend to follow exponential degree distributions [5]. Recall that there is an out-degree limit imposed by Myspace which restricts the maximum number of top friends $(k^{out} \leq 40)$.

From the degree distributions, we can see that there exists a few very well-connected hub artists with an in-degree much higher than the average - a common finding in social networks as well as many other network structures [3]. In the primary network sample the artist with the most in-links ($k^{in} = 222$) is Grammy-award-winning rapper *T.I.*[8] immediately followed by Grammy-award-winning producer *Timbaland.*[9] The 10 most highly connected artists in the primary sample are exclusively popular American and French rap artists. Examining the genre tag distributions for our sample puts this result into context.

---

[6] $P_c(k) \sim k^{-(\alpha-1)}$

[7] $P_c(k) \sim e^{-k/\kappa}$

[8] http://www.myspace.com/trapmuzik

[9] http://www.myspace.com/timbaland

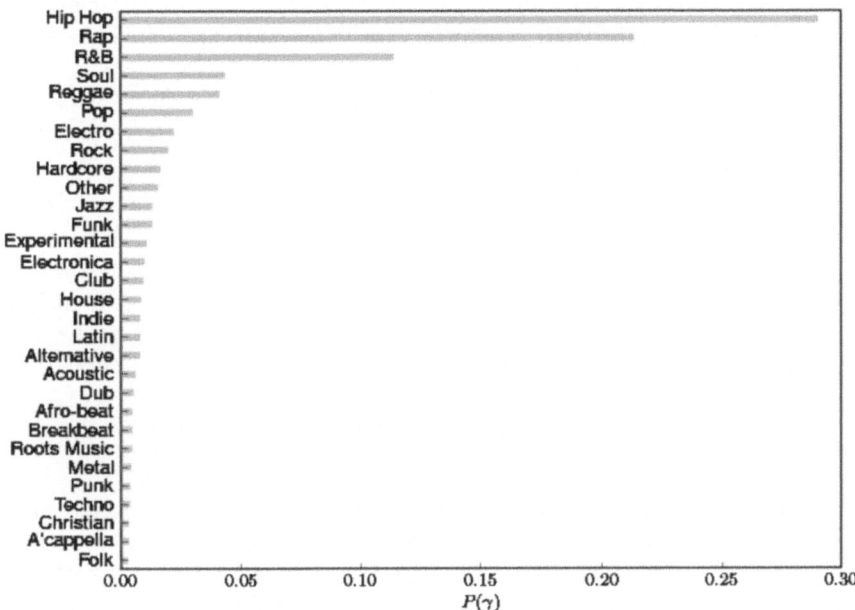

Fig. 2. The distribution for the top 30 genre labels found in the artist network sample

In Figure 2 we see the distribution for the 30 most popular genre tags in our sample. The genre tags "Hip-Hop", "Rap", and "R&B" account for 61.7% of all the genre tags found in the network sample. The most connected artists in our network sample are closely associated with these genre tags and widely recognized as some of the top performers in these genres. This suggests the most connected artists are not only popular but also influential.

These genre tag distributions in themselves suggest the Myspace artist network structure is closely related to concepts of musical genre. Smaller informal network samples, independent of our main data set, are also dominated by a handful of conceptually similar genre tags (i.e. "Alternative", "Indie", "Punk"). In the context of our snowball sampling method, this suggests the network sample is essentially "stuck" in a community of Myspace artists associated with these particular genre inclinations. However, it is possible, although unlikely, that these genre distributions are indicative of the entire Myspace artist network.

4.1 Assortativity with Respect to Genre

In addition to the distribution of genre labels found, we are interested in the mixing patterns found in our network sample. Do artists tend to form friendships with artists of the same genre? To answer this question we look at the homophily or *assortative mixing* with respect genre tags in our network. If a network exhibits assortative mixing, nodes tend to form links with nodes of the same type, or in our case, artists tend to form friendships with other artists of the same genre. The assortativity coefficient for our network sample is calculated following [14].

Let E be an $N \times N$ matrix with elements $E_{\gamma_i \gamma_j}$. For genre labels $\gamma_1, \gamma_2, \ldots, \gamma_N$, let $E_{\gamma_i \gamma_j}$ be the number of edges in a network that connect vertices of genre γ_i and γ_j. The normalized mixing matrix is defined as

$$e = \frac{E}{\|E\|} \tag{3}$$

where $\|x\|$ means the sum of all elements in the matrix x. The elements $e_{\gamma_i \gamma_j}$ measure the fraction of edges that fall between nodes of genre γ_i and γ_j. The assortativity coefficient r is then defined as

$$r = \frac{\text{Tr}(e) - \|e^2\|}{1 - \|e^2\|} \tag{4}$$

The assortativity coefficient will be nearly 0 in a randomly mixed network, 1 in a perfectly assortative network, and negative for a dissassortative network where nodes only connect with nodes of different types. However, this assortativity calculation assumes each node can only be of one type. In our sample, each artist is associated with between 0 and 3 genre types. A visual representation of this is presented in Figure 3. For simplicity, we truncate the list of genre labels for each artist taking only the first label. Artists with no genre label are excluded from the calculation. Using this approach the assortativity coefficient with respect to genre for our sample is $r = 0.350$. Of course this calculation assumes an overly strict definition of genre type, excluding all but one genre label. Also, this calculation makes no allowance for genre types that are conceptually very similar such as "Hip-Hop" and "Rap." Therefore we can assume this value of r underestimates the actual level of assortative mixing in the network sample.

We can ease these restrictions by applying another approach that preserves the entire genre label set and uses a weaker definition for genre type – two artists are of the same genre type if they have one or more label in common. Again, artists with no genre label are excluded. Then for each artist pair, if one or more genre labels are shared, the first shared label γ_i is selected and one count is added at $E'_{\gamma_i \gamma_i}$. If no genre labels are shared, the first genre label for each artist is selected and one count is added off the diagonal at $E'_{\gamma_i \gamma_j}$. In this way, only one count is added for each node pair in the network. The assortativity calculation follows equation (4) replacing e with $e' = \frac{E'}{\|E'\|}$.

Using this relaxed definition of genre type, the assortativity coefficient for our sample with respect to genre is $r' = 0.778$. Of course this is allowing each node to be recast as different genre types to facilitate matches, somewhat inflating the assortativity coefficient. However, this reflects the reality of artist-genre associations where a single artist is often associated with several genres.

We can define a third variation on the assortativity coefficient calculation by introducing fractional counts into E''. Let use assume artist x has a set of genre labels $\Gamma_x = \{\gamma_1, \gamma_2, \gamma_3\}$ and an artist y has genre labels $\Gamma_y = \{\gamma_2, \gamma_3\}$ and an

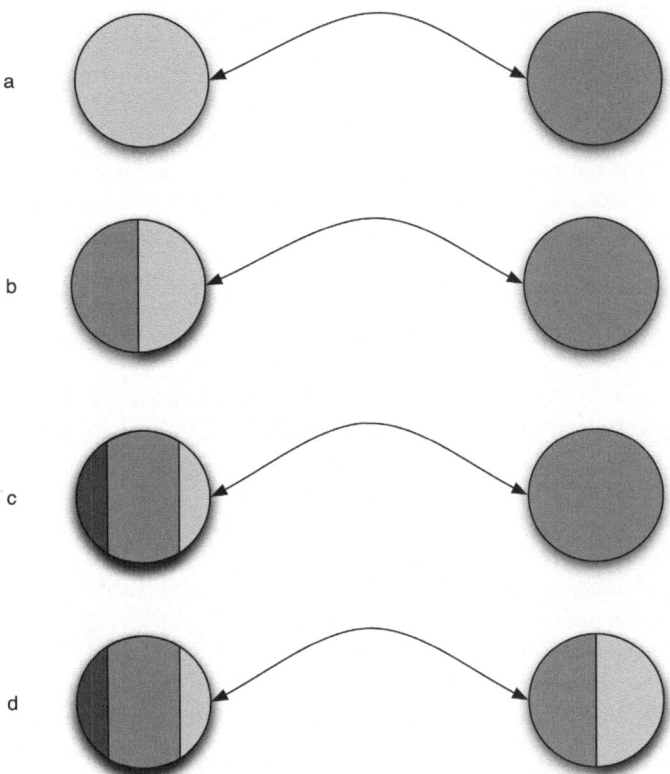

Fig. 3. Examples of various genre mixing present in the network sample. The shading corresponds to a specific genre label or node 'color.' In (a) each artist has one genre label, in (b) an artist with two distinct genre labels connects to an artist with one genre label, in (c) an artist with 3 labels connects to an artist with 1 label, and in (d) an artist with 3 labels connects to an artist with 2 labels.

edge exists $(x, y) \in G$. This is analogous to the situation illustrated in Figure 3.d. For the edge (x, y) the following entry would be made in E'':

$$E'' = \begin{bmatrix} 0 & 0 & 0 \\ +1/6 & +1/6 & +1/6 \\ +1/6 & +1/6 & +1/6 \end{bmatrix} \quad (5)$$

As there are $|\Gamma_x| \times |\Gamma_y| = 6$ possible combinations of genre labels between the nodes x and y we add $1/6$ to the appropriate elements of E''. Again, after populating E'' in this manner the assortativity coefficient calculation follows equation (4) replacing e with $e'' = \frac{E''}{\|E''\|}$.

This method reflects the tendency of artists to maintain multiple genre associations and captures multiple genre matches between artist pairs. However, this measure also captures multiple mismatches and results in the lowest valued assortativity coefficient $r'' = 0.216$. This still suggests a significantly higher degree of assortative mixing with respect to genre than would be present in a randomly mixed network.

Note that none of these assortativity calculations make any allowance for genres that are conceptually very similar, underestimating assortative mixing in this sense. Even so, the values of r, r', and r'' show that artists prefer to maintain friendship links with other artists in the same genre in the Myspace artist network.

4.2   Distance and Genre

Let us also examine the number of shared genre labels as a function of geodesic distance between artists. That is, do artist that are closer to each other in the network have more genre labels in common?

For this analysis let us take an undirected view of the graph. Each edge is considered bi-directional, that is $(i, j) = (j, i)$, and if a reflexive pair of edges existed in the directed graph, only one bi-directional edge exists in the undirected graph. This reduces the edge count by about 24% (see Table 1).

For each node pair i and j in the undirected network, we calculate the geodesic distance d_{ij}. Then, we count how many genre labels are shared between the nodes $\|\gamma_i \cap \gamma_j\|$, where node i has a set of genre labels γ_i and node j has labels γ_j. For each value of d_{ij} we plot the average value of $\|\gamma_i \cap \gamma_j\|$. This shows how the

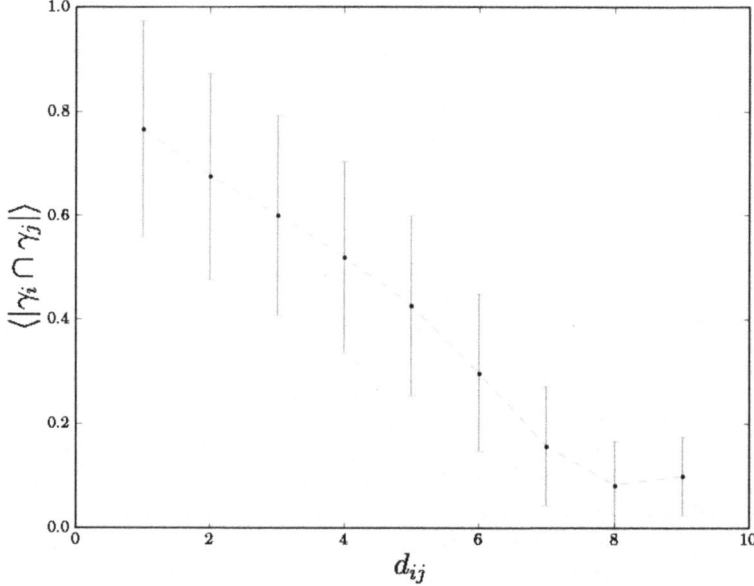

Fig. 4. The geodesic distance d_{ij} vs. the average number of shared genre labels between nodes $\langle |\gamma_i \cap \gamma_j| \rangle$

number of genre labels shared between node pairs is related to geodesic distance. The results are shown in Fig. 4. The averages are plotted with standard deviation error bars. There is a clear decrease in the number of shared genre labels as the geodesic distance increases.

However we do see an increase at $d_{ij} = 9$. It should be noted that in our network sample a geodesic distance of 9 is extremely rare. For the $1.2 \cdot 10^8$ node pairs in the undirected network, only 20 have $d_{ij} = 9$. The rarity of this value of geodesic distance is related to the "small world" effect first observed by Milgram in his famous experiments tracing chain letters through a social network of acquaintances [15]. In a small world network any node can reach any other node in just a small number of steps. This property is commonly observed in social networks as well as many other real world network structures [2], [3] and, as mentioned above, the Myspace artist network is no exception. Given small worldness, the clear relationship between geodesic distance and shared genre labels is all the more exceptional and is strong evidence of the tie between musical concepts and artist network structure.

5   Conclusion

Studying the sample of the Myspace artist network indicates that its structure is quite relevant to music. There is evidence of high assortativity with respect to genre. In our on-line social network sample, artists tend to form friendships with artists of the same genre.

The genre distributions seen in Figure 2 suggests large-scale community structures related to musical genre exist in the artist network beyond the scope of our sample.

The plot in Figure 4 indicates a clear relationship between genre similarity and geodesic distance. In our on-line social network sample, artists tend to be more closely connected to other artists that share some of the same genre labels.

These findings indicate that the structure of the Myspace artist network reflects the genre structures traditionally used to classify music. This result is not surprising, but it is significant - motivating new network-based genre-fication approaches - grouping artists based on network topologies. A similar approach is taken in [9], although the focus is on listener-generated data. Musicological metrics could be developed for quantifying the level of influence of a particular artist based on network structure. A simple and intuitive metric would be the in-degree k^{in} of a particular artist as an indicator of her influence.

An intuitive music recommendation application could be created by simply following the social connections in the music artist network. If a user of the system likes a particular artist, then recommend music by the neighbors of that artist. More advanced hybrid recommendation techniques could be developed, also taking into account audio signal-based similarity between artists [16] and collaborative filtering of user preference data [17].

Analysis of this data set has shown, despite the unregulated nature of the Myspace artist network, its structure reflects the top-down genre structures traditionally used to classify music. This suggests such social network data could be of interest in a variety of contexts including music recommendation, music information retrieval, and musicology.

Acknowledgements

The authors would like to acknowledge the assistance of Ben Fields at Goldsmiths University of London for his assistance in collecting the data set. This work is supported as a part of the OMRAS2 project, EPSRC grants EP/E02274X/1 and EP/E017614/1.

References

1. Shepherd, J.: Sociology of music, http://www.grovemusic.com
2. Costa, L.F., Rodrigues, F.A., Travieso, G., Boas, P.R.V.: Characterization of complex networks: A survey of measurements. Advances In Physics 56, 167 (2007)
3. Newman, M.E.J.: The structure and function of complex networks. SIAM Review 45, 167 (2003),
   http://www.citebase.org/abstract?id=oai:arXiv.org:cond-mat/0303516
4. Gleiser, P., Danon, L.: Community structure in jazz. Advances in Complex Systems 6, 565 (2003)
5. Cano, P., Celma, O., Koppenberger, M., Buldu, J.M.: The topology of music recommendation networks. arXiv.org:physics/0512266 (2005), http://www.citebase.org/abstract?id=oai:arXiv.org:physics/0512266
6. Park, J., Celma, O., Koppenberger, M., Cano, P., Buldu, J.M.: The social network of contemporary popular musicians. Physics and Society (2006)
7. Celma, O., Lamere, P.: Music recommendation. ISMIR Tutorial (2007)
8. Anglade, A., Tiemann, M., Vignoli, F.: Virtual communities for creating shared music channels. In: Proc. of Int. Conference on Music Information Retrieval (2007)
9. Lambiotte, R., Ausloos, M.: On the genre-fication of music: a percolation approach (long version). The European Physical Journal B 50, 183 (2006)
10. Ahn, Y., Han, S., Kwak, H., Moon, S., Jeong, H.: Analysis of topological characteristics of huge online social networking services. In: WWW 2007: Proceedings of the 16th international conference on World Wide Web, pp. 835–844. ACM, New York (2007), http://portal.acm.org/citation.cfm?id=1242685
11. Lee, S.H., Kim, P.-J., Jeong, H.: Statistical properties of sampled networks. Physical Review E 73, 102–109 (2006)
12. Kwak, H., Han, S., Ahn, Y.-Y., Moon, S., Jeong, H.: Impact of snowball sampling ratios on network characteristics estimation: A case study of cyworld. KAIST, Tech. Rep. CS/TR-2006-262 (November 2006)
13. Amaral, L.A.N., Scala, A., Barthélémy, M., Stanley, H.E.: Classes of small-world networks. In: Proceeding of the National Academy of Sciences (2000)
14. Newman, M.E.J.: Mixing patterns in networks. Phys. Rev. E 67(2), 026126 (2003)
15. Milgram, S.: The small world problem. Psychol. Today 1(61-67) (1967)
16. Logan, B., Salomon, A.: A music similarity function based on signal analysis. In: Multimedia and Expo ICME, pp. 745–748 (2001)
17. Goldberg, D., Nichols, D., Oki, B.M., Terry, D.: Using collaborative filtering to weave an information tapestry. Commun. ACM 35(12), 61–70 (1992)

The Pursuit of Happiness in Music: Retrieving Valence with Contextual Music Descriptors

José Fornari[1] and Tuomas Eerola[2]

[1] Interdisciplinary Nucleus for Sound Communication (NICS),
University of Campinas (Unicamp), Brazil
[2] Music Department, University of Jyvaskyla (JYU), Finland
tutifornari@gmail.com, tuomas.eerola@campus.jyu.fi

Abstract. In the study of music emotions, Valence is usually referred to as one of the dimensions of the circumplex model of emotions that describes music appraisal of happiness, whose scale goes from sad to happy. Nevertheless, related literature shows that Valence is known as being particularly difficult to be predicted by a computational model. As Valence is a contextual music feature, it is assumed here that its prediction should also require contextual music descriptors in its predicting model. This work describes the usage of eight contextual (also known as higher-level) descriptors, previously developed by us, to calculate happiness in music. Each of these descriptors was independently tested using the correlation coefficient of its prediction with the mean rating of Valence, reckoned by thirty-five listeners, over a piece of music. Following, a linear model using this eight descriptors was created and the result of its prediction, for the same piece of music, is described and compared with two other computational models from the literature, designed for the dynamic prediction of music emotion. Finally it is proposed here an initial investigation on the effects of expressive performance and musical structure on the prediction of Valence. Our descriptors are then separated in two groups: performance and structural, where, with each group, we built a linear model. The prediction of Valence given by these two models, over two other pieces of music, are here compared with the correspondent listeners' mean rating of Valence, and the achieved results are depicted, described and discussed.

Keywords: music information retrieval, music cognition, music emotion.

1 Introduction

Music emotion has been studied by many researches in the field of psychology, such as the ones described in [1]. The literature mentions three main models used in the study of music emotion: 1) categorical model; originated from the work of [2], that describes music in terms of a list of basic emotions [3], 2) dimensional model; originated from the research of [4], who proposed that all emotions can be described in a Cartesian coordinate system of emotional dimensions, also named as circumplex model [5], and 3) component process model; from the work of [6] that describes

S. Ystad, R. Kronland-Martinet, and K. Jensen (Eds.): CMMR 2008, LNCS 5493, pp. 119–133, 2009.
© Springer-Verlag Berlin Heidelberg 2009

emotion appraised according to the situation of its occurrence and the current listener's mental (emotional) state.

Computational models, for the analysis and retrieval of emotional content in music, have also been studied and developed, in particular by the Music Information Retrieval (MIR) community, that maintains a repository of publication on its field (available at the International Society for MIR link: www.ismir.net). To name a few: in [7] it was developed a computational model for musical genre classification that is similar, although simpler, to the retrieval of emotions in music. In [8] it was provided a good example of audio feature extraction using multivariate data analysis and behavioral validation of its features. There are also several examples of computing models developed for the retrieval of emotional features evoked by music, such as in [9] and [10] that studied the retrieval of higher-level features of music, such as tonality, in a variety of music audio files.

1.1 The Dynamic Variation of Appraised Valence

In the study of the dynamic aspects of music emotion, [11] used a two-dimensional model to measure emotions appraised by listeners along time, in several music pieces. The emotional dimensions described are the classical ones: Arousal (that ranges from calm to agitated) and Valence (that goes from sad to happy). This one used Time Series techniques to create linear models with five acoustic descriptors to predict each of these two dimensions, for each music piece. In [12] it was used the same listener's mean ratings collected by [11] to develop and test a general model for each emotional dimension (i.e. one general model for Arousal and another one for Valence). This one used System Identification techniques to create its two models of prediction.

In any case, these two studies described above, there was not made any effort to distinguish between musical aspects predicted by the descriptors that are related to the composition, given by its muscal structure or to its expressive performance.

1.2 The Balance between Expressive Performance and Musical Structure for the Appraisal of Valence

Music emotion is influenced by two groups of musical aspects. One, that is given by the structural features created by the composer and described in terms of musical notation. The other one relates to the emotions aroused in the listeners during the musician(s) expressive performance. The first group is here named as structural aspects and the second one, performance aspects. Sometimes the difference between a mediocre and a breathtaking interpretation of a musical structure relies on the performers' ability of properly manipulate basic musical aspects such as: tempo, dynamics and articulation. Such skill often seems to be the key for the musician to re-create the emotional depths whose composer supposedly tried to convey in the musical structure.

About this subject, in [13] it is mentioned that: "expert musical performance is not just a matter of technical motor skill; it also requires the ability to generate expressively different performances of the same piece of music according to the nature of intended structural and emotional communication". Also, in [14] it is said that: "Music performance is not unique in its underlying cognitive mechanisms". These arguments seem to imply that, in music, structure and performance both cooperate to evoke emotion. The question is to know how the musical structure and expressive performance cooperate and interact with each other on the appraisal of music emotion.

There are several researches on this subject. For instance, [15] provided an overview of the state of the art in the field of computational modeling of expressive music performance. He mentioned three important ones. The KTH model; that consists in a set of performance rules that predict timing, dynamics, and articulation based on the current musical context [16]. The Todd model; that, in contrast, applies the notion of "analysis-by-measurement", once that their empirical evidence comes directly from the ratings of the expressive performances [17]. Finally, there is the Mazzola model that is mainly based on mathematical modeling [18] (see the link: www.rubato.org).

Recently, a Machine Learning approach has also been developed. This one builds computational models of expressive performance from a large set of empirical data (precisely measured performances made by skilled musicians) where the system autonomously seeks out significant regularities on the data, via inductive machine learning and data mining techniques [19].

As seen, finding the hidden correlations between musical structure and performance and its effects on music emotion is a broad field of research. Obviously, fully mapping this relation is beyond our scope. Here we intend to initiate an investigation on the subject, using our contextual descriptors as structural and performance ones.

The underlying musical aspects that influence the emotional state of listeners have been subject of research in a number of previous studies, although few isolated the influence of each other, sometimes leading to conflicting qualitative results. In fact, it seems that a thorough attempt of combining these aspects of music are still to be done, despite some researches, such as in [20] that described a quite comprehensive study with the "adjective circle". There have been some other researches, such as [21], that studied the interaction of mode and tempo with music emotion, also studied by [22]. It would be, however, rather ambitious the intent of evaluating the interactions between tempo, dynamics, articulation, mode, and timbre in a large factorial experiment.

We aim here to initiate an investigation, using our eight higher-level descriptors, on the prediction of appraised Valence and on how structural and performance features contribute to this particular musical emotion. Here we first show the prediction of Valence for each of our descriptors and for a linear model using them all. Following, we separate these descriptors in two groups: structural and performance, and create with each one a linear model to calculate Valence. This experiment firstly takes one piece of music, its correspondent Valence ground-truth, and calculates its prediction with each descriptor and with the linear model using all descriptors. Next, we take two other pieces of music and their Valence ground-truths to calculate their prediction with the structural and performance models.

2 The Difficulty of Predicting Valence

As seeing in the results shown in [11] and [12], these models successfully predicted the dimension of Arousal, with high correlation with their ground-truths. However, the retrieval of Valence has proved to be difficult to measure by these models. This may be due to the fact that the previous models did not make extensive usage of higher-level descriptors. The literature in this field named as descriptor a model (usually a computational model) that predicts one aspect of music, emulating the perception, cognition or emotion of a human listener. While low-level descriptors account for perceptual aspects of music, such as: loudness (perception of sound intensity) or pitch (perception of fundamental partial), the higher-level ones account for contextual musical features, such as: pulse, tonality or complexity. These refer to the cognitive and aspects of music and deliver one prediction for each overall music excerpt.

If this assumption is true, it is understandable why Valence, as a highly contextual dimension of music emotion, is poorly described by models using mostly low-level descriptors.

Intuitively, it was expected that Valence, as the measurement of happiness in music, would be mostly correlated to the prediction of higher-level descriptors such as key clarity (major versus minor mode), harmonic complexity, and pulse clarity. However, as described further, the experimental results pointed to another direction.

3 Designing Contextual Musical Descriptors

In 2007, during the *Braintuning* project (see Discussion section for details) we were involved in the development of computational models for contextual descriptors of specific musical aspects. This effort resulted in the development of eight higher-level music descriptors. Their design used a variety of audio processing techniques (e.g. chromagram, similarity function, autocorrelation, filtering, entropy measurement, peak detection, etc.) to predict specific contextual musical aspects. Their output is a normalized between zero (normally meaning the lack of that feature in the analyzed music excerpt) and one (referring to the clear presence of such contextual music aspect).

These eight descriptors were designed and simulated in *Matlab*, as algorithms written in the form of script files that run music stimuli as digital audio files, in 16 bits of resolution, 44.1 KHz of sampling rate and 1 channel (mono).

To test and improve the development of these descriptors, behavioral data was collected from thirty-three listeners that were asked to rate the same features predicted by these descriptors. They rated one hundred short excerpts of music (five seconds of length each) from movie sound tracks. Their mean rating was then correlated with the descriptors predictions. After several experiments and adjustments, all descriptors presented coefficient of correlation from 0.5 to 0.65 with their respective ground-truths. They are briefly described as following below.

3.1 Pulse Clarity

This descriptor measures the sensation of pulse in music. Pulse is here seen as a fluctuation of musical periodicity that is perceptible as "beatings", in a sub-tonal frequency (below 20Hz), therefore, perceived not as tone (frequency domain) but as pulse (time domain). This can be of any musical nature (melodic, harmonic or rhythmic) as long as it is perceived by listeners as a fluctuation in time. The measuring scale of this descriptor is continuous, going from zero (no sensation of musical pulse) to one (clear sensation of musical pulse).

3.2 Key Clarity

This descriptor measures the sensation of tonality, or tonal center, in music. This is related to the sensation of how tonal an excerpt of music is perceived by listeners, disregarding its specific tonality, but focusing on how clear its perception is. Its scale is also continuous, ranging from zero (atonal) to one (tonal). Intermediate regions, neighboring the middle of its scale tend to refer to musical excerpts with sudden tonal changes, or dubious tonalities.

3.3 Harmonic Complexity

This descriptor measures the sensation of complexity conveyed by musical harmony. In communication theory, musical complexity is related to entropy, which can be seen as the degree of disorder of a system. However, here we are interested in measuring the perception of its entropy, instead of the entropy itself. For example, in acoustical terms, white-noise could be seen as a very complex sound, yet its auditory perception is of a very simple, unchanging stimuli. The challenge here is finding out the cognitive sense of complexity. Here we focused only on the complexity of musical harmony, leaving the melodic and rhythmic complexity to further studies. The measuring scale of this descriptor is continuous and goes from zero (no harmonic complexity perceptible) to one (clear perception of harmonic complexity).

3.4 Articulation

In music theory, the term articulation usually refers to the way in which a melody is performed. If it is clearly noticeable a pause in between each note in the melodic prosody, it is said that the articulation of its melody is *staccato*, which means "detached". In the other hand, if there is no pause in between the notes of the melody, then it is said that this melody is *legato*, meaning "linked". This descriptor attempts to grasp the articulation from musical audio files and attributing to it an overall grade that ranges continuously from zero (staccato) to one (legato).

3.5 Repetition

This descriptor accounts for the presence of repeating patterns in a musical excerpt. These patterns can be: melodic, harmonic or rhythmic. This is done by measuring the similarity of hopped time-frames along the audio file, tracking repeating similarities happening within a perceptibly time delay (around 1Hz to 10Hz). Its scale ranges continuously from zero (not noticeable repetition within the musical excerpt) to one (clear presence of repeating musical patterns).

3.6 Mode

Mode is the musical term referring to one of the eight modes in the diatonic musical scale. The most well-known are: major (first mode) and minor (sixth mode). In the case of our descriptor, mode refers to a computational model that calculates out of an audio file an overall output that continuously ranges from zero (minor mode) to one (major mode). It is somewhat fuzzy to intuit what its middle range grades would stand for, but the intention of this descriptor is mostly to distinguish between major and minor excerpts, as there is still ongoing discussion on whether major mode carries in itself valence of appraised happiness, as well as minor mode accounts for sadness (see Discussion section for counter-intuitive result on this subject).

3.7 Event Density

This descriptor refers to the overall amount of perceptually distinguishable, yet simultaneous, events in a musical excerpt. These events can also be: melodic, harmonic and rhythmic, as long as they can be perceived as independent entities by our cognition. Its scale ranges continuously from zero (perception of only one musical event) to one (maximum perception of simultaneous events that the average listener can grasp).

3.8 Brightness

This descriptor measures the sensation of how bright a music excerpt is felt to be. It is intuitive to know that this perception is somehow related to the spectral centroid, which accounts for the presence of partials with higher frequencies in the frequency spectrum of an audio file. However other aspects can also be of influence in its perception, such as: attack, articulation, or the unbalance or lacking of partials in other regions of the frequency spectrum. Its measurement goes continuously from zero (excerpt lacking brightness, or muffled) to one (excerpt is clearly bright).

4 Building a Model to Predict Valence

In the research on temporal dynamics of emotion, described in [11], Schubert created ground-truths with data collected from thirty-five listeners that dynamically measured the emotion categories depicted into a two-dimensional emotion plan that was then mapped into two coordinates, or dimensions: Arousal and Valence. Listener's ratings variations were sampled every one second. The pruned data of these measurements, mean rated and mapped into Arousal and Valence, created the ground-truths that was used later in [12] by Korhonen, as well as in this work. Here, we calculated the correlation between each descriptor prediction and Schubert's Valence ground-truth for one music piece, named "Aranjuez concerto", by Joaquín Rodrigo. During the initial minute of this 2:45' long piece of music, the guitar plays alone (solo). Then, it is suddenly accompanied by full orchestra, whose intensity fades towards the end, till the guitar, once again, plays the theme alone.

For this piece, the correlation coefficient presented between the descriptors predictions and its Valence ground-truth are: event density: $r = 0.59$, harmonic complexity: $r = 0.43$, brightness: $r = 0.40$, pulse clarity: $r = 0.35$, repetition: $r = 0.16$, articulation: $r = 0.09$, key clarity: $r = 0.07$, mode: $r = 0.05$.

Then, a multiple regression linear model was created with all eight descriptors. The model employs a time frame of three seconds (related to the cognitive "now time" of music) and hop-size of one second to predict the continuous development of Valence. This model presented a correlation coefficient of $r = 0.6484$, which leaded to a coefficient of determination of: $R^2 = 42\%$.

For the same ground-truth, Schubert's model used five music descriptors: 1) Tempo, 2) Spectral Centroid, 3) Loudness, 4) Melodic Contour and 5) Texture. The descriptors output differentiation was regarded as the model predictors. Using time series analysis, he built an ordinary least square (OLS) model for this particular music excerpt. Korhonen's approach used eighteen low-level descriptors (see [12] for details) to test several models designed with System Identification techniques. The best general model reported in his work was an ARX (Auto-Regressive with eXtra inputs).

Table 1 shows below the comparison of results for all three models, in terms of best achieved R^2 (coefficient of determination) in the measurement of Valence for the Aranjuez concerto.

Table 1. Emotional dimension: VALENCE. Ground-truth: Aranjuez concerto.

	Schubert's	Korhonen's	(our model)	Event Density
Model type	OLS	ARX	Multiple Regression	One Descriptor
R^2	33%	-88%	42%	35%

This table shows that our model performed significantly better than the previous ones, for this specific ground-truth. The last column of table 1 shows the achieved result for the descriptor prediction "event density", the one that presented the highest correlation with the ground-truth. This descriptor alone presented better results than the two previous models. The results shown seem to suggest that higher-level descriptors can in fact be successfully used to improve the dynamic prediction of Valence.

Figure 1 depicts the comparison between this ground-truth, given by the mean rating of Valence for the Aranjuez concerto ranked by listeners, and the prediction given by our multiple-regressive model, using all eight descriptors.

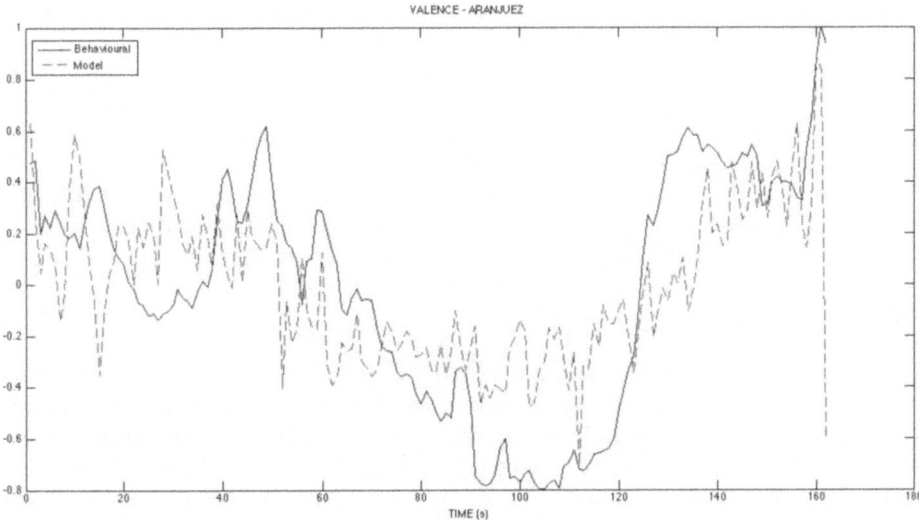

Fig. 1. Mean rating of the behavioral data for Valence (continuous line) and our model prediction (dashed line)

It is seen here that, in spite of the prediction curve presents some rippling effect, when visually compared with the ground-truth (the mean-rating behavioral data), in overall, its prediction follows the major variations of Valence along with the music performing time, what resulted in a high coefficient of determination.

As described in the next sections, the next step of this study was to distinguish between performance and structural aspect of music and to study how they account for the prediction of Valence. Hence, we separated our eight contextual descriptors into these two groups and created with them two new linear models; one to predict the performance aspects influencing the appraisal of Valence, and another one to predict its structural aspects.

4.1 Performance Model

This model is formed by the higher-level descriptors related to the dynamic aspects of musical performance. These descriptors try to capture music features that are manipulated mostly by the performer(s) instead of the aspects already described in the musical structure (i.e. its composition). They are commonly related to musical features such as: articulation, dynamics, tempo and micro-timing variability.

As the "dynamics" aspect is related to Arousal, as seen in [11, 12] and the examples studied here had their "tempo" aspect approximately unchanged, here we focused on "pulse clarity" and "brightness" aspects, as they also have been used as descriptors of expressive performance in other studies, such as in [21].

We considered as belonging to the performance, the following descriptors: 1) articulation, 2) pulse clarity and 3) brightness.

Articulation is a descriptor that measures how much similar musical events are perceptually separated to each other. This is a fundamental component of expressive performance that has been studied in many researches, such as in [22] where was analyzed the articulation strategies applied by pianists in expressive performances of the same scores. Articulation may also be seen as a musical trademark or fingerprint to help identifying a musical genre or the performing artist style.

Pulse clarity is the descriptor that measures how clear, or perceptible, is the pulse in a musical performance. This is chiefly in the distinction between expressive performances characterized by an interpretation more towards the *Ad Libitum* (without clear pulse), or the *Marcato* (with clear pulse).

Brightness is the descriptor that accounts for the musical aspects related to the variation of the perception of brightness along of an expressive performance. It scale will cover from Muffled (without brightness) to Bright (or brilliant).

4.2 Structural Model

Structural descriptors are the ones that account for the static or structural aspects of a piece of music given by the composition musical score, or any other kind of notation, so they are supposed to be little influenced by the expressive performance aspects. Several researches have studied them, such as in [23]. We considered as structural descriptors the following: 1) mode, 2) key clarity, 3) harmonic complexity, 4) repetition and 5) event density.

Mode is the descriptor that grades musical structure tonality. If the structure of the excerpt analyzed is clearly minor, the scale will have value near to zero, otherwise, if it is clearly major, the scale will have value towards one. If the music excerpt presents ambiguity in its tonality, or if it is atonal, its scale will have values around 0.5.

Key Clarity measures how tonal a particular excerpt of music structure is. Its scale goes from atonal (e.g. electro-acoustic, serialistic, spectral music structures) to clearly tonal structures (e;g; diatonic, modal, minimalist structures).

Harmonic Complexity is a descriptor that refers to the complexity of an structure in terms of its harmonic clusters, what is related to the perceptual entropy of: 1) chords progression and 2) chord structures.

Repetition describes the amount of repeating similar patterns found in the musical structure. This repetition has to happen in a sub-tonal frequency, thus perceived as rhythmic information.

Event Density is the descriptor that accounts for the amount of perceptible simultaneous musical events found in a structure excerpt. They can be melodic, harmonic or rhythmic as long as they can be aurally distinctively perceived.

4.3 Valence Prediction with Structural and Performance Models

As before, here we also used the ground-truth developed by the work of [13] where thirty-five listeners rated the music emotion dynamically appraised in a circumplex model, for several pieces of music, and then mapped to the dimensions of Arousal and Valence.

For this part we chose the Valence ratings of two musical pieces: 1) "Pizzicato Polka" by Strauss, and 2) "Morning" by Peer Gynt. The Valence ground-truths of them were chosen mainly because they presented a repeating musical structure with slight changes in the expressive performance, so both structural and performance models could be tested and compared.

Figures 2 and 3 show the comparison between each Valence ground-truth and its prediction for the structural and performance models. These ones were created using multiple regression technique.

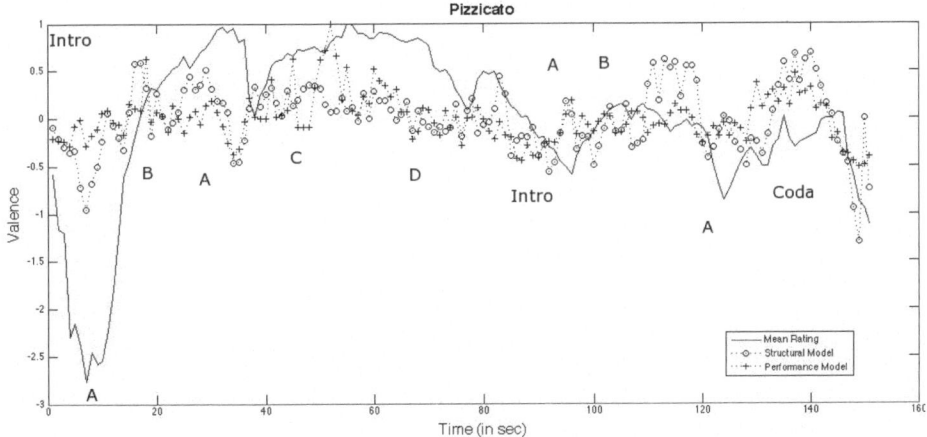

Fig. 2. Structural and performance models for "Pizzicato Polka", by Strauss

Figure 1 shows the "Pizzicato Polka" example. It is seen here three curves over-lapped: mean-rating, structural model prediction and performance model prediction. The "Mean Rating" curve is the Valence ground-truth. "Structural Model" curve is the prediction for the structural linear model, the same way as the "Performance Model" curve is the prediction for the performance model.

"Pizzicato" is a simple and tonal orchestral piece where the strings are mostly played in *pizzicato* (i.e. strings plucked). Its musical parts are repeated several times. Each part has even two similar sub-parts (i.e. A = A1 + A2). The musical parts that compound this piece of music are shown in table 2.

Table 2. Musical parts of "Pizzicato"

Time (s)	Musical Part
0	Intro
6	A
19	B
35	A
48	C
68	D
86	Intro
92	A
105	B
120	A
133	Coda

The second and most complex example is shown in Figure 3. It is the rating and predictions of Valence for the piece of music named "Morning". This figure describes the results for the Rating (Valence ground-truth) and its predictions for the structural and performance models.

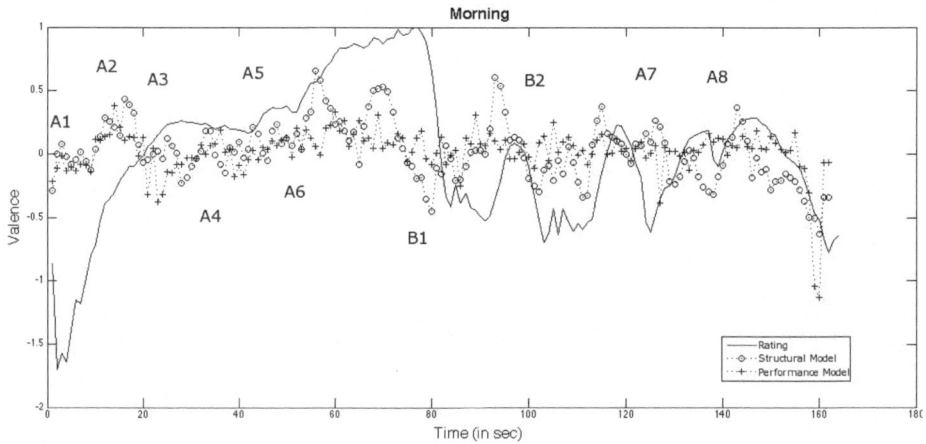

Fig. 3. Structural and performance models for "Morning", by Peer Gynt

"Morning" has a more advanced orchestration, whose melody swaaps between solo instruments and tonalities (key changes), although it still has a repetitive musical structure. The musical parts that constitute this piece are shown in table 3. Here, an extra column was included to describe what these changes represent in terms of musical structure.

Table 3. Musical parts of "Morning"

Time (s)	Musical Part	Descrition
0	A1	Flute in melody
10	A2	Oboe in melody
20	A3	Flute. Key change (3rd Major upward)
30	A4	Oboe in melody
40	A5	Flute&Oboe. Key change (3rd minor up)
50	A6	Strings unison. back to the original key
78	B1	B1 Cello unison
98	B2	Cello. key change (2nd Major down.)
123	A7	Horns in melody
138	A8	Coda

Finally, table 4 shows the coefficient of correlation for each piece of music, for the structural and performance models.

Table 4. Experimental results for the overall correlation between the Valence ground-truths and the Performance and Structural models

Piece of Music	Time of Duration	Performance Model	Structural Model
Pizzicato	02m33s	r=0.31	r= 0.44
Morning	02m44s	r=0.34	r= 0.45

As seen on the table above, the coefficient of correlation for these two pieces of music are approximately the same, where the structural model correlation is higher than the performance one, for the overall prediction of Valence.

5 Discussion

This work was developed during the project named: "Tuning you Brain for Music", the *Braintuning* project (www.braintuning.fi). An important part of it was the study of acoustic features retrieved from musical excerpts and their correlation with specific emotions appraised. Following this goal, we designed the contextual descriptors, here briefly described. They were initially conceived because of the lack of such descriptors in the literature. In *Braintuning*, a fairly large number of studies for the retrieval of emotional connotations in music were investigated. As seem in previous models, for the dynamic retrieval of contextual emotions such as the appraisal of happiness (represented here by the dimension of Valence), low-level descriptors are not enough, once they do not take into consideration the contextual aspects of music.

It was interesting to notice that the prediction of Valence done by the descriptor "Event Density" presented the highest correlation with Valence ground-truth, while the predictions of "Key Clarity" and "Mode" correlated very poorly. This seems to indicate that, at least for this particular case, the perception of major or minor tonality in music (represented by "Mode") or its tonal center (given by "Key Clarity") is not relevant to predict Valence, as it could be intuitively inferred. What counted the most here was the amount of simultaneous musical events (given by "event density"), remembering that by "event", it is here understood any perceivable rhythmic, melodic or harmonic stimuli. The first part of this experiment chose the music piece "Aranjuez" because it was the one that the previous models presented the lowest correlation with Valence ground-truth. Although the result presented here is enticing, further studies are definitely needed in order to establish any solid evidence.

The second part of this experiment studied the effects of expressive performance and musical structure on the appraisal of Valence. In "Pizzicato", the rating curve starts near zero and then abruptly plummets to negative values (i.e. sad). During the musical part A, the rating rises until it becomes positive (i.e. happy), when part B starts. Both models approximately follow the rating and present a peak where the rating inverts, as part B starts. They both present a negative peak around 35s, where part A repeats for the first time. At the same time the rating declines a little but still remains positive (happy). Maybe this is related to the listeners' memory of part A, and the models don't take into consideration their previous predictions. When part C starts, the rating rises sharply, as this is appraised as a particular "happy" passage of this music. Here, the performance model seems to present higher values (although wavy) than the structure model, until the beginning of part D, around 68s. Parts A-B-A repeats again around 92s where the rating shows a similar shape as before, although much narrower, maybe because the listeners have "recognized" this part. Here the performance model follows the rating closely. The structural model presents an abrupt rising between 110s and 120s where part B is taking place. In Coda, both models present positive predictions, but the rating is negative.

In "Morning", the rating starts from negative (sad) and rises continuously until it reaches positive values (happy), when part A3 stars. This is understandable once that part A3 begins with an upward key change, which in fact delivers the appraisal of an joy. The rating keeps raising until the next "key change" in part A5, and reaches its highest values in part A6, from 50s to 80s, when the whole orchestra plays together the "A" theme, back to the original key. Both models start from values close to zero. They show a steep rise in values from part A1 to part A2 (more visible in the performance model prediction). When part A3 starts, both models predictions decrease and the performance model goes to the negative side. This may have happened because articulation and pulse clarity, as the descriptors within the performance model, decrease in values at this passage, as well as in 40s, when A5 starts. During part A6, the structural model prediction is more similar to the rating than the performance model, which makes sense once that this is mostly a structural change and the performance parameters almost remain still. The rating decreases when part B1 starts in 78s. This is expected once that, in this part, the music mode changes from major to minor. Consequently, at this moment, the performance model prediction almost remains unchanged. The structural model prediction rises from negative to near zero (or positive) values and shows a peak around the beginning of part B2. When A7 starts in

123s the rating drops to negative values and rises continuously until 138s, when Coda starts. Both models do not follow this behavior. Structural model prediction remains positive as well as in any other part "A". Performance model is also little affected by this passage.

6 Conclusion

This work intended to investigate the usage of contextual descriptors for the prediction of the dynamic variation of music emotions. We chose to study the emotional dimension of Valence (here referred to as the perception of happiness in music) because this is a highly contextual aspect of music and known to be particularly difficult to be predicted by computational models.

We briefly introduced eight contextual descriptors previously developed by us. They are: event density, harmonic complexity, brightness, pulse clarity, repetition, articulation, key clarity and mode.

We used the same music stimuli and correspondent Valence ground-truths of two important models from the literature. Firstly, we selected a piece of music whose previous models did not reach satisfactory correlations in the prediction of Valence. We then predicted Valence with each descriptor and with a linear model made with all descriptors. The highest correlation descriptor was the "event density", presenting coefficient of determination higher than the ones presented by the previous models.

Secondly, we studied the relation between the appraisal of Valence with the expressive performance aspects and musical structure ones. Our descriptor were then separated in two groups, one covering the structural aspects (mode, key clarity, harmonic complexity, repetition and event density) and the other for the performance ones (articulation, pulse clarity and brightness). Two models with each descriptor group were then created and named as: structure and performance. Although these models did not reach outstanding coefficients of correlation with ground-truths (around 0.33 for performance model and 0.44 for the structural one) they reached very similar coefficients for two pieces of music stylistically very distinct. This seems to indicate that the results of these models, despite their simplicity and limitations, are pointing to a further promising outcome.

It also seems to make sense the results showing that the structural model presents a higher correlation with ground-truth than the performance one. The structural model accounts for a greater portion of musical aspects. The structure comprehends the musical composition, arrangement, orchestration, and so forth. In theory, it conveys "the seed" of all emotional aspects whose expressive performance is supposed to bring about.

There is a great number of topics that can be tested in further investigations on this subject. For instance, we did not take into consideration the memory aspects that will certainly influence the emotional appraisal of Valence. New models including this aspect, should consider principles found in the literature such as the forgetting curve and the novelty curve.

We used rating data from the ground-truth of another experiment that, in spite of bringing enticing results, was not meant for this kind of experiment. In a further investigation, a new listeners' rating data should be collected, with different performances of the same musical structure, as well as different structures of similar performances. This is a quite demanding task but that seems to be the correct path to be followed in order to enable the development of better descriptors and models.

Acknowledgements

We would like to thank the *BrainTuning* project (www.braintuning.fi) FP6-2004-NEST-PATH-028570, the Music Cognition Group at the University of Jyväskylä (JYU), and the Interdisciplinary Nucleus of Sound Communication (NICS) at the State University of Campinas (UNICAMP). We are specially grateful to Mark Korhonen, for sharing the ground-truth data from his experiments with us.

References

1. Sloboda, J.A., Juslin, P.: Music and Emotion: Theory and Research. Oxford University Press, Oxford (2001)
2. Ekman, P.: An argument for basic emotions. Cognition & Emotion 6(3/4), 169–200 (1992)
3. Juslin, P.N., Laukka, P.: Communication of emotions in vocal expression and music performance: Different channels, same code? Psychological Bulletin (129), 770–814 (2003)
4. Russell, J.A.: Core affect and the psychological construction of emotion. Psychological Review 110(1), 145–172 (2003)
5. Laukka, P., Juslin, P.N., Bresin, R.: A dimensional approach to vocal expression of emotion. Cognition and Emotion 19, 633–653 (2005)
6. Scherer, K.R., Zentner, K.R.: Emotional effects of music: production rules. In: Juslin, P.N., Sloboda, J.A. (eds.) Music and emotion: Theory and research, pp. 361–392. Oxford University Press, Oxford (2001)
7. Tzanetakis, G., Cook, P.: Musical Genre Classification of Audio Signals. IEEE Transactions on Speech and Audio Processing 10(5), 293–302 (2002)
8. Leman, M., Vermeulen, V., De Voogdt, L., Moelants, D., Lesaffre, M.: Correlation of Gestural Musical Audio Cues. In: Camurri, A., Volpe, G. (eds.) GW 2003. LNCS, vol. 2915, pp. 40–54. Springer, Heidelberg (2004)
9. Wu, T.-L., Jeng, S.-K.: Automatic emotion classification of musical segments. In: Proceedings of the 9th International Conference on Music Perception & Cognition, Bologna (2006)
10. Gomez, E., Herrera, P.: Estimating The Tonality Of Polyphonic Audio Files: Cogtive Versus Machine Learning Modelling StrategiesI. Paper presented at the Proceedings of the 5th International ISMIR 2004 Conference, Barcelona, Spain (October 2004)
11. Schubert, E.: Measuring emotion continuously: Validity and reliability of the two-dimensional emotion space. Aust. J. Psychol. 51(3), 154–165 (1999)
12. Korhonen, M., Clausi, D., Jernigan, M.: Modeling Emotional Content of Music Using System Identification. IEEE Transactions on Systems, Man and Cybernetics 36(3), 588–599 (2006)
13. Slodoba, J.A.: Individual differences in music performance. Trends in Cognitive Sciences 4(10), 397–403 (2000)
14. Palmer, C.: Music Performance. Annual Review of Psychology 48, 115–138 (1997)
15. Gerhard, W., Werner, G.: Computational Models of Expressive Music Performance: The State of the Art. Journal of New Music Research 2004 33(3), 203–216 (2004)

16. Friberg, A., Bresin, R., Sundberg, J.: Overview of the KTH rule system for music performance. Advances in Experimental Psychology, special issue on Music Performance 2(2-3), 145–161 (2006)
17. Todd, N.P.M.: A computational model of Rubato. Contemporary Music Review 3, 69–88 (1989)
18. Mazzola, G., Göller, S.: Performance and interpretation. Journal of New Music Research 31, 221–232 (2002)
19. Widmer, G., Dixon, S.E., Goebl, W., Pampalk, E., Tobudic, A.: Search of the Horowitz factor. AI Magazine 24, 111–130 (2003)
20. Hevner, K.: Experimental studies of the elements of expression in music. American Journal of Psychology 48, 246–268 (1936)
21. Gagnon, L., Peretz, I.: Mode and tempo relative contributions to "happy - sad" judgments in equitone melodies. Cognition and Emotion 17, 25–40 (2003)
22. Dalla Bella, S., Peretz, I., Rousseau, L., Gosselin, N.: A developmental study of the affective value of tempo and mode in music. Cognition 80(3), B1–B10 (2001)
23. Juslin, P.N.: Cue utilization in communication of emotion in music performance: relating performance to perception. J. Exp. Psychol. Hum. Percept. Perform. 26(6), 1797–1813 (2000)
24. Bresin, R., Battel, G.: Articulation strategies in expressive piano performance. Journal of New Music Research 29(3), 211–224 (2000)
25. BeeSuan, O.: Towards Automatic Music Structural Analysis: Identifying Characteristic Within-Song Excerpts in Popular Music. Doctorate dissertation. Department of Technology, University Pompeu Fabra (2005)

Perception of Impacted Materials: Sound Retrieval and Synthesis Control Perspectives

Mitsuko Aramaki[1,2], Loïc Brancheriau[3], Richard Kronland-Martinet[4], and Sølvi Ystad[4]

[1] CNRS - Institut de Neurosciences Cognitives de la Méditerranée,
31, chemin Joseph Aiguier 13402 Marseille Cedex 20, France
aramaki@incm.cnrs-mrs.fr
[2] Aix-Marseille - Université,
58, Bd Charles Livon 13284 Marseille Cedex 07, France
[3] CIRAD - PERSYST Department,
TA B-40/16, 73 Rue Jean-Franois Breton, 34398 Montpellier Cedex 5, France
loic.brancheriau@cirad.fr
[4] CNRS - Laboratoire de Mécanique et d'Acoustique,
31, chemin Joseph Aiguier 13402 Marseille Cedex 20, France
{kronland,ystad}@lma.cnrs-mrs.fr

Abstract. In this study, we aimed at determining statistical models that allowed for the classification of impact sounds according to the perceived material (Wood, Metal and Glass). For that purpose, everyday life sounds were recorded, analyzed and resynthesized to insure the generation of realistic sounds. Listening tests were conducted to define sets of typical sounds of each material category by using a statistical approach. For the construction of statistical models, acoustic descriptors known to be relevant for timbre perception and for material identification were investigated. These models were calibrated and validated using a binary logistic regression method. A discussion about the applications of these results in the context of sound synthesis concludes the article.

1 Introduction

Sound classification systems are based on the calculation of acoustic descriptors that are extracted by classical signal analysis techniques such as spectral analysis or time-frequency decompositions. In this context, many sound descriptors depending on the specificities of sound categories were defined in the literature, in particular in the framework of MPEG 7 [1]. Indeed, descriptors were proposed for speech recognition [2], audio indexing [3,4], music classification [5] or for psycho-acoustical studies related to timbre [6,7]. Nevertheless, these classification processes would be significantly improved if perceptually relevant information conveyed in acoustic signals could be identified to enable fewer and more relevant descriptors to characterize the signal.

In this current study, we aim at determining statistical models that allow categorization of impact sounds as a function of the perceived material based on few acoustic descriptors. For that purpose, we investigated the acoustic descriptors that are known to be relevant for timbre perception and material identification. In practice, a sound

S. Ystad, R. Kronland-Martinet, and K. Jensen (Eds.): CMMR 2008, LNCS 5493, pp. 134–146, 2009.
© Springer-Verlag Berlin Heidelberg 2009

data bank constituted of realistic impact sounds from different materials (Wood, Metal, Glass) was generated using analysis-synthesis techniques. Then, a morphing process allowed us to build sound continua that simulate continuous transitions between sounds corresponding to different materials. Listening tests were conducted and we used a statistical approach to determine the sets of sounds that were judged as typical and non typical for each material category. The use of sound continua allowed for the determination of perceptual borders between these typical and non typical sounds as a function of the position along the continua to identify the variation range of parameters for each material category. A statistical model of binary logistic regression was calibrated and validated based on the calculation of selected descriptors for each sound category. We finally address some perspectives of this study in particular, in the domain of sound synthesis.

2 Categorization Experiment

Twenty-two participants (11 women, 11 men), 19 to 35 years old were tested in this experiment. They were all right-handed, non-musicians (no formal musical training) and had no known auditory or neurological disorders. They all gave written consent to participate in the test and were paid for their participation.

Sounds were pseudo-randomly presented through one loudspeaker (Tannoy S800) located 1 m in front of the participants who were asked to categorize sounds as from impacted Wood, Metal or Glass materials, as fast as possible, by pressing one response button out of three. The association between response buttons and material categories was balanced across participants. Participants' responses were collected and were averaged for each sound.

To design stimuli, we first recorded (at 44.1 kHz sampling frequency) impact sounds from everyday life objects of various materials (i.e., impacted wooden beams, metallic plates and various glass bowls) that unambiguously evoked each material category. Then, based on the analysis-synthesis model described in [8], we resynthesized these recorded sounds. To minimize timbre variations induced by pitch changes, all sounds were tuned to the same chroma (note C), but not to the same octave, due to the specific properties of the different materials. For instance, Glass sounds could not be transposed to low pitches as they would no longer be recognized as Glass sounds. The synthesized sounds therefore differed by 1, 2 or 3 octaves depending upon the material. The new pitches of the tuned sounds were obtained by transposition (dilation of the original spectra). In practice,Wood sounds were tuned to the pitch C4, Metal sounds to the pitches C4 and C5 and Glass sounds to the pitches C6 and C7. Based upon previous results showing high similarity ratings for tone pairs that differed by octaves [9], an effect known as the octave equivalence, we presumed that the octave differences between sounds should not influence categorization. Each time the pitch was modified, the new value of the damping coefficient of each tuned frequency component was recalculated according to a damping law measured on the original sound [10], since the frequency-dependency of the damping is fundamental for material perception [11]. Sounds were finally equalized by gain adjustments to avoid an eventual influence of loudness in the categorization judgments.

The resynthesized sounds were further used to create 15 sound continua that simulate a progressive transition between the different materials. In particular, we built 5 continua for each of the following 3 transitions: {Wood-Metal}, {Wood-Glass} and {Glass-Metal}. Each continuum, composed of 20 hybrid sounds, is built using a morphing process. The interpolation on the amplitudes of the spectral components was computed by a crossfade technique. Concerning the damping, the coefficients were estimated according to a hybrid damping law calculated at each step of the morphing process. This hybrid damping law was computed from an effective linear interpolation between the 2 extreme damping laws. In practice, 15 continua (5 for each of the 3 transitions) were built. Sound examples are available at http://www.lma.cnrs-mrs.fr/~kronland/Categorization/sounds.html.

3   Determination of Sound Categories

Based on participants' responses, we aim at determining sounds considered as *typical* of each material category (Wood, Metal or Glass) by using a statistical approach. Actually, the sounds were produced to form progressive transitions from one category to another. The limits between categories along the continua are thus not known. This causes an intermediate zone with sounds that represent a mixture of the two extreme sounds. From a perceptual point of view, the sounds contained in this zone are perceived as ambiguous.

The limits of each category along continua have to be estimated to define sets of sounds that are typical of Wood, Metal and Glass categories. The specific perceptive space used to address this problem is defined by the three material axes {Wood, Metal, Glass}. Since the experimental protocol was based on a categorization task with three-choice answers, the percentages of responses obtained for material categories are correlated as shown in Table 1. Thus, these axes are not orthogonal and a principal component analysis is therefore carried out (Table 2).

Table 1. Pearson correlation coefficients of percentages of responses obtained in Wood, Metal and Glass material category (N= 300). The correlations are significant at the .01 level (2-tailed) and are represented by **.

	Wood	Metal
Metal	-0.68**	1
Glass	-0.33**	-0.48**

Two principal components are extracted; the third component can be neglected (Table 2). The perceptive space is thus totally defined in a plane and sounds are grouped inside a triangle as shown in Figure 1. This data representation shows the repartition of responses between the three material categories. In a case of a clear discrimination between categories, all sounds should be distributed in three distinct groups located

Table 2. Total variance explained by principal component analysis on percentages of responses obtained for Wood, Metal and Glass categories (N = 300)

Component	Eigenvalue	% of variance	Cumulative (%)
1	1.7	57	57
2	1.3	43	100
3	0	0	100

at the apexes of the triangle and the gaps between groups would mark the limits between categories. Figure 1 does not show three distinct groups and in this sense, reveals difficulties encountered by participants to classify sounds at intermediate position of the continua. Moreover, sounds located on the Metal-Glass side of the triangle are well-aligned, meaning that these sounds were classified as Metal or Glass but never as Wood. By contrast, sounds located on the Wood-Metal side are not well-aligned, meaning that these sounds were classified as Wood or Metal but also as Glass. Consequently, it is not possible to determine the limits of the categories directly from the perceptive space because of the high number of sounds scattered inside the triangle (ambiguous zone).

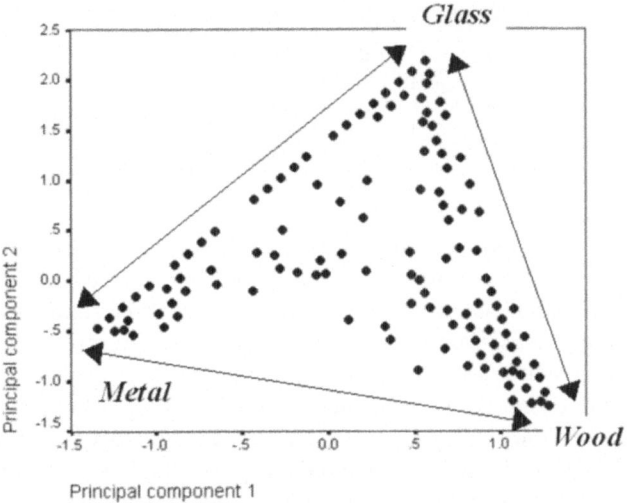

Fig. 1. Perceptive space defined by the two principal components (factor score plot, N = 300)

In order to determine the limits of the categories, a hierarchical cluster analysis is carried out on the principal components in a second stage. As presented previously, the two principal components completely define the perceptive space and are orthogonal. The distance measurement used is then the Euclidian distance. The method used for combining clusters is the furthest neighbor (complete linkage). This method is adapted to the research of globular groups with unequal variances and unequal sizes. Table 3

Table 3. Simplified agglomeration schedule of the hierarchical clustering procedure (N = 292; 8 sounds were missing because their distance does not allow an attribution to one of the three groups A, B or C). At each agglomerating step, the type of continua, the Min and Max indices, the number of samples in the agglomerate (S), the identified group (A, B or C) and the associated category (Wood, Metal or Glass) are indicated.

Agglomerating step	Continua	Min index	Max index	S	Identified group	Associated category
1	W-G	14	21	20	A	Glass
2	G-M	2	9	35	A	Glass
3	W-G	13	21	9	A	Glass
4	G-M	2	12	11	A	Glass
5	W-M	9	12	8	B	Metal
6	G-M	10	13	4	B	Metal
7	W-M	10	21	52	B	Metal
8	G-M	11	21	50	B	Metal
9	W-M	2	10	23	C	Wood
10	W-G	2	17	62	C	Wood
11	W-M	4	11	12	C	Wood
12	W-G	9	19	6	C	Wood

presents the simplified diagram of agglomeration obtained by hierarchical cluster analysis. The agglomeration procedure first identifies a group denoted A (from step 1 to 4) to which we associated the Glass category, because Glass is the common element of the first 4 agglomerating steps. From the relative position between sounds in the perceptive space, Glass thus constitutes the most easily identifiable category. The procedure identifies a second group denoted B (from step 5 to 8) to which we associated the Metal category. Finally, the third group C (from step 9 to 12) was associated with the Wood category. Wood thus constitutes the material category which is most difficult to identify. Interestingly, for most agglomerating steps (except for steps 5 and 6), the clustering procedure identified groups of sounds (A, B or C) located at the extreme of continua since the Min or Max index corresponds to an extreme position of the continua (i.e., position 2 or 21) or to a position close to an extreme (i.e., 4 or 17). This procedure is relevant from a perceptual point of view since it means that sets of typical sounds were located at the extreme of the continua.

Then, the values of "Min" and "Max" indices in Table 3 were used as far as possible to define sound indices delimiting categories. As an example, the step 2 revealed an agglomerate from index 2 (beginning of the Glass agglomerate) to 9 (end of the Glass agglomerate approaching Metal) associated to Glass category. In this case, the retained index delimiting the Glass category along Glass-Metal continua is 9. This process is

Table 4. Indices delimiting categories for each type of continua. The indices from steps linked with symbol - mark the membership to an agglomerate in an intermediate zone. The mark X indicates the inconsistency in the agglomerating step 12.

Transition	Indices from steps	Indices delimiting categories
Glass-Metal	9, 12, 10-13, 11	{9-13}
Wood-Metal	9-12, 10, 10, 11	{9-12}
Wood-Glass	14, 13, 17, X	{13-17}

Table 5. Percentages of responses in each category (Wood, Metal or Glass) for sounds located at the indices delimiting the categories for the 5 different continua. Sounds are denoted G_i-M_i-K, W_i-M_i-K and W_i-G_i-K for the ith continua with K the index along the continua (09 or 13 for Glass-Metal, 09 or 12 for Wood-Metal and 13 or 17 for Wood-Glass transition). Averaged percentage values (Mean) across the 5 continua of a given transition in the associated categories (e.g., mean values of G and M columns for Glass-Metal transition) and bilateral errors (Error) associated to the mean estimation with an unknown variance (significance level of .05).

GLASS-METAL				WOOD-METAL				WOOD-GLASS		
	W	M	G		W	M	G		W	M	G
G_1-M_1-09	8	36	**56**	W_1-M_1-09	**44**	40	16	W_1-G_1-13	**28**	12	60
G_2-M_2-09	0	28	**72**	W_2-M_2-09	**96**	4	0	W_2-G_2-13	**92**	0	8
G_3-M_3-09	0	20	**80**	W_3-M_3-09	**12**	68	20	W_3-G_3-13	**96**	0	0
G_4-M_4-09	0	36	**64**	W_4-M_4-09	**16**	52	32	W_4-G_4-13	**64**	8	28
G_5-M_5-09	0	24	**76**	W_5-M_5-09	**20**	60	20	W_5-G_5-13	**72**	4	24
Mean			70		38				70		
Error			12		43				34		

	W	**M**	G		W	**M**	G		W	M	**G**
G_1-M_1-13	0	**96**	4	W_1-M_1-12	12	**80**	8	W_1-G_1-17	4	16	**80**
G_2-M_2-13	0	**96**	4	W_2-M_2-12	20	**52**	28	W_2-G_2-17	68	4	**28**
G_3-M_3-13	0	**72**	28	W_3-M_3-12	8	**92**	0	W_3-G_3-17	60	4	**36**
G_4-M_4-13	0	**96**	4	W_4-M_4-12	4	**80**	16	W_4-G_4-17	24	4	**72**
G_5-M_5-13	0	**88**	12	W_5-M_5-12	4	**92**	0	W_5-G_5-17	12	4	**80**
Mean		90				79					59
Error		13				20					31

repeated for all the agglomerates of each step. The agglomerating step 12 is withdrawn from the analysis since the indices of the agglomerate (i.e., 9-19 on Wood-Glass continua) delimit a zone on the Glass side, that is incoherent with the identified group (C)

Table 6. Criterion of category membership according for each transition

Transition	Criterion	
Glass-Metal	Glass if	G ≥ 70%
	Metal if	M ≥ 90%
Wood-Metal	Wood if	W ≥ 38%
	Metal if	M ≥ 79%
Wood-Glass	Wood if	W ≥ 70%
	Glass if	G ≥ 59%

and associated category (Wood). The indices delimiting categories (and consequently delimiting intermediate zones) are defined for each type of continua in Table 4. For instance, along the Glass-Metal continua, the Glass category goes until index 9 and the Metal category starts from index 13.

Then, from these indices delimiting categories, we define the criteria of category membership as a threshold of percentage of responses in a category for each type of transition. In practice, we define these criteria as equal to the average of the percentages of responses obtained for sounds at the indices defined in Table 4 across the 5 different continua of a given transition. The calculation of these average values is shown in Table 5. The membership criteria for each transition are summarized in Table 6. Note that all criteria are superior to 50% except for the Wood membership criterion in the Wood-Metal continua (i.e., 38% ± 43%). This value is not accurate from a perceptual point of view since it would lead to define the sounds (issued from Wood-Metal continua) that were categorized in the Wood category by only 38% of participants as typical Wood sounds (actually, these sounds were more often classified in the Metal category, see Table 5). This incoherency can be explained by the fact that the average calculation is based on a small number of values (average on 5 values). In order to minimize the uncertainty associated with these membership criteria (revealed by large intervals of confidence, see error values in Table 5) that directly influences the construction and the validation of predictive models, we determine an unique category membership criterion equal to the average value of all the membership criteria, i.e., 67.6% ± 9.9% (N=30). For the sake of simplicity, we defined a criterion of category membership equal to 70% (value that belongs to the interval of confidence) for this current study.

4   Relationship between Acoustic Descriptors and Sound Categories

4.1   Acoustic Descriptors

To characterize sounds from an acoustic point of view, we considered the following sound descriptors known to be relevant for timbre perception and material identification: attack time AT, spectral centroid CGS, spectral bandwidth SB, spectral flux SF, roughness R and normalized sound decay α.

The attack time AT is defined as the time necessary for the signal energy to raise from 10% to 90% of the maximum amplitude of the signal. The spectral centroid CGS and the spectral bandwidth SB were defined by:

$$CGS = \frac{1}{2\pi} \frac{\sum_k \omega(k) \mid \hat{s}(k) \mid}{\sum_k \mid \hat{s}(k) \mid} ; SB = \frac{1}{2\pi} \sqrt{\frac{\sum_k \mid \hat{s}(k) \mid (\omega(k) - 2\pi \times CGS)^2}{\sum_k \mid \hat{s}(k) \mid}} \qquad (1)$$

where ω and $\hat{s}$ respectively represent the frequency and the Fourier transform of the signal. The spectral flux SF is a spectro-temporal timbre descriptor quantifying the time evolution of the spectrum. The definition presented in [12] was chosen. The roughness R of a sound is commonly associated to the presence of several frequency components within the limits of a critical band. In particular, R is closely linked to the concept of consonance/dissonance [13]. The definition presented in [14] was chosen.

Finally, the sound decay quantifies the global amplitude decrease of the temporal signal and is directly correlated to the damping. Since the damping is a fundamental cue for material perception [11,15,16,17], the sound decay is assumed to be a relevant acoustic descriptor for our sounds. In practice, the sound decay is estimated from the slope of the logarithm of the envelope of the temporal signal. Nevertheless, since the damping is frequency dependent, this decrease depends on the spectral content of the sound. In our case, typical sounds present a high variability of spectral content across material categories. Consequently, to allow comparisons between sound decay values, we further chose to consider a sound decay that was normalized with respect to a reference that takes into account the spectral localization of the energy, i.e., the CGS value.

4.2 Binary Logistic Regression Analysis

From classifications obtained from perceptual tests, we aim at estimating the membership of a sound in a material category starting from the calculation of the 6 acoustic descriptors presented in the previous section: {AT, CGS, SB, SF, R, α}.

In our case, the dependent variables are qualitative; they represent the membership (True) or the non membership (False) of the category. In order to build statistical models to estimate the membership to a category, the binary logistic regression method is used. The associated method of multinomial logistic regression is not adapted to the problem because the best estimators can be different from one category to another.

One statistical model of binary logistic regression for each material category (Wood, Metal and Glass) are then built based on the acoustic descriptors. The problem of collinear parameters is overcome by a forward stepwise regression. Logistic regression allows one to predict a discrete outcome, such as group membership, from a set of variables that may be continuous, discrete, dichotomous, or a mixture of any of these. The dependent variable in logistic regression is usually dichotomous, that is, the dependent variable can take the value 1 (True) with a probability of success π, or the value 0 (False). This type of variable is called a Bernoulli (or binary) variable. Logistic regression makes no assumption about the distribution of the independent variables. They do not have to be normally distributed, linearly related or of equal variance within each group. The relationship between the predictors and response variables is not a linear function in logistic regression. The logistic regression function which is the logit transformation of π is used:

$$\pi(x) = P(Y = 1/X = x) = \frac{e^{L_{Cat}(x)}}{1 + e^{L_{Cat}(x)}} \tag{2}$$

with

$$L_{Cat}(x) = \beta_0 + \sum_i \beta_i x_i \tag{3}$$

The function $L_{Cat}(x)$ was calibrated and validated for each category (Cat={Wood, Metal, Glass}). Because we are dealing with sound continua, a segmented cross validation procedure was used. The validation set was built by selecting 1 of 3 sounds (corresponding to a set of 67 sounds). The calibration set was composed by the remaining sounds (corresponding to a set of 133 sounds). Note that for a given material model, the validation and calibration sets were built by excluding sound continua that did not contain the material. For instance, the Metal category model is not concerned by the 5 sound continua of the transition {Wood-Glass}. For each category, the membership of sounds corresponded to the set of "typical" sounds that were defined from the results of the listening test and from a statistical approach (cf. sections 2 and 3). A stepwise selection method was used and the statistical analysis was conducted with SPSS software (Release 11.0.0, LEAD Technologies).

4.3   Results and Discussion

For each category model, the step summary is given in Table 7. The statistics Cox & Snell R^2 and Nagelkerke adjusted R^2 try to simulate determination coefficients which, when used in linear regression, give the percentage variation of the dependent variable explained by the model. Because a binary logistical model is used, the interpretation of R^2 is not quite the same. In this case, the statistics give an idea of the strength of the association between the dependent and independent variables (a pseudo-R^2 measure).

The results for calibration and validation processes are given in Table 8. Thus, the predictive models are expressed by the function $\pi(x)$ in Eq. (2) and $L_{Cat}(x)$ for each category {Wood, Metal, Glass} is respectively given by:

$$L_{Wood}(\alpha, CGS, SB) = -38.5 - 196\alpha - 0.00864CGS + 0.0161SB$$

$$L_{Metal}(\alpha, SB) = 14.7 + 322\alpha - 0.00253SB$$

$$L_{Glass}(SB, CGS, R, \alpha, SF) = 14.33 - 0.006SB + 0.002CGS - 3.22R$$

$$+52.69\alpha - 0.001SF$$

(4)

Table 7. Step summary (Nagelkerke R^2 adjusted value and the variable entered) of the logistic regression method for each material category (Wood, Metal, Glass)

Category	Step	Nagelkerke R^2 adjusted	Variable entered
WOOD	1	.616	α
	2	.644	CGS
	3	.854	SB
METAL	1	.637	α
	2	.718	SB
GLASS	1	.086	SB
	2	.164	CGS
	3	.300	R
	4	.377	α
	5	.410	SF

Table 8. Classification table for each category (Wood, Metal, Glass) calculated on the calibration (N=133) and validation (N=67) populations. The cut value is .5.

		Calibration			Validation		
	Observed / Predicted	False	True	% correct	False	True	% correct
WOOD	False	78	4	95.1	40	1	97.5
	True	8	43	84.3	4	22	84.6
	Overall %	90.7	91.5	91	91	95.6	92.5
METAL	False	50	12	80.6	27	7	79.4
	True	6	65	91.5	1	32	97
	Overall %	89.3	84.4	86.5	96.4	82	88
GLASS	False	91	7	92.9	43	3	93.4
	True	17	19	52.8	10	10	50
	Overall %	84.2	73	82.1	81.1	77	80.3

The logistic regression method revealed that the α parameter was the main predictor for Wood (overall percentage correct equal to 85% at step 1) and Metal (82.7%)

categories. This result was in line with several studies showing that the damping is an important acoustic feature for the material perception. Following α, the other important descriptors revealed by the analyses were related to the spectral content of the sounds ({CGS, SB} for Wood and SB for Metal), meaning that spectral information are also important to explain material categorization. For the Glass category, the majority of the descriptors were of equal importance in the classification model (all descriptors were taken into account except AT). Thus, by contrast with the Wood and Metal categories, the membership of the Glass category could not be accurately predicted with few descriptors. Moreover, the most relevant predictors for this category revealed by the analyses were the spectral descriptors, ({SB, CGS, R}), while the temporal α parameter which was the main predictor for Wood and Metal only was relegated at the 4th rank. This may be due to the fact that Glass sounds presented a higher variability in sound decay values than Wood or Metal sounds. More interestingly, another explanation can be found in the specificity of the Glass category for which the material perception is intricately associated to drinking glasses (as everyday life objects). The corresponding sounds are generally characterized by high pitches (associated to small objects) and crystal-clear sounds (few spectral components, due to the structure's characteristics). Consequently, the discrimination between Glass sounds and the other sound categories can be explained by the spectral properties of Glass sounds rather than by the damping.

5   Sound Synthesis Perspectives

In addition to sound classification processes, these results are of importance in the context of synthesis control. In particular, we are currently interested in offering an intuitive control of synthesis models for an easy manipulation of intrinsic sound properties such as timbre. This aspect is for instance of importance within the Virtual Reality domain. Indeed, the use of synthesis models can dramatically be improved in "sonification" processes which generally deal with the choice of optimal synthesis parameters to control sounds directly from a verbal description (in our case, directly from the label of the material category: Wood, Metal or Glass). According to this perspective, we assume that the acoustic descriptors highlighted in the predictive models would constitute a reliable reference. In this section, we propose a discussion on their actual relevancy from a synthesis point of view.

First, the parameter α (related to the damping) was confirmed as an important predictor coherent with previous psychoacoustical studies showing that damping is an essential cue for material perception. The parameter α was kept as an accurate control parameter and was integrated in the control of the percussive synthesizer developed in our group [18]. Moreover, the determination of typical and non typical sounds on each sound continuum allowed us to define characteristic domains of parameter range values for each material category.

In addition to α, the statistical analyses further highlighted CGS and SB as most relevant parameters in the predictive models. These results are in line with post hoc synthesis experiences which revealed that, in addition to the damping, another parameter controlling the spectral content of sounds is necessary for a more complete manipulation of the perceived materials. To address this control, we also aim at integrating data from brain imaging that point out the perceptual/cognitive relevancy of descriptors. Actually, a separate analysis reflecting the temporal dynamics of the brain processes observed through electrophysiological data (also collected during the listening tests), revealed that spectral aspects of sounds may account for the perception and categorization of these different categories (see companion article [19]). This argument supports the fact that the control of the synthesis model can be accurately improved by adding control parameters related to spectral characteristics of sounds. Nevertheless, direct manipulations of the statistically relevant parameters CGS or SB of a given impact sound do not allow intuitive modifications of the nature of the perceived material. Based on these considerations, we are currently investigating the possibilities to define a control space for material categories where the control of spectral characteristics of sounds should particularly render the typical dissonant aspect of Metal sounds [20].

Acknowledgments

This research was supported by a grant from the French National Research Agency (ANR, JC05-41996, "senSons") to Sølvi Ystad.

References

1. Martínez, J.M.: Mpeg-7 overview, version 10,
   http://www.chiariglione.org/mpeg/standards/mpeg-7/mpeg-7.htm
   (last checked March 25, 2008)
2. Foote, J.: Decision-tree probabilty modeling for HMM speech recognition. Ph.D thesis, Cornell university (1994)
3. Roy, P., Pachet, F., Krakowski, S.: Improving the classification of percussive sounds with analytical features: A case study. In: Proceedings of the 8th International Conference on Music Information Retrieval, Vienna, Austria (2007)
4. Slaney, M.: Mixtures of probability experts for audio retrieval and indexing. In: Proceedings of the IEEE International Conference on Multimedia and Expo, Lausanne, Switzerland (2002)
5. Pachet, F., Zils, A.: Evolving automatically high-level music descriptors from acoustic signals. In: Wiil, U.K. (ed.) CMMR 2003. LNCS, vol. 2771, pp. 42–53. Springer, Heidelberg (2004)
6. McAdams, S., Winsberg, S., Donnadieu, S., De Soete, G., Krimphoff, J.: Perceptual scaling of synthesized musical timbres: Common dimensions, specificities, and latent subject classes. Psychological Research 58, 177–192 (1995)
7. Peeters, G., McAdams, S., Herrera, P.: Instrument sound description in the context of mpeg-7. In: Proceedings of the International Computer Music Conference, Berlin, Germany (2000)
8. Aramaki, M., Kronland-Martinet, R.: Analysis-synthesis of impact sounds by real-time dynamic filtering. IEEE Transactions on Audio, Speech, and Language Processing 14(2), 695–705 (2006)
9. Parncutt, R.: Harmony - A Psychoacoustical Approach. Springer, Heidelberg (1989)
10. Aramaki, M., Baillères, H., Brancheriau, L., Kronland-Martinet, R., Ystad, S.: Sound quality assessment of wood for xylophone bars. Journal of the Acoustical Society of America 121(4), 2407–2420 (2007)

11. Wildes, R.P., Richards, W.A.: Recovering material properties from sound. In: Richards, W.A. (ed.), ch. 25, pp. 356–363. MIT Press, Cambridge (1988)
12. McAdams, S.: Perspectives on the contribution of timbre to musical structure. Computer Music Journal 23(3), 85–102 (1999)
13. Sethares, W.A.: Local consonance and the relationship between timbre and scale. Journal of the Acoustical Society of America 94(3), 1218–1228 (1993)
14. Vassilakis, P.N.: Sra: A web-based research tool for spectral and roughness analysis of sound signals. In: Proceedings of the 4th Sound and Music Computing (SMC) Conference, pp. 319–325 (2007)
15. Tucker, S., Brown, G.J.: Investigating the perception of the size, shape and material of damped and free vibrating plates. Technical Report CS-02-10, Université de Sheffield, Department of Computer Science (2002)
16. Giordano, B.L., McAdams, S.: Material identification of real impact sounds: Effects of size variation in steel, wood, and plexiglass plates. Journal of the Acoustical Society of America 119(2), 1171–1181 (2006)
17. Klatzky, R.L., Pai, D.K., Krotkov, E.P.: Perception of material from contact sounds. Presence: Teleoperators and Virtual Environments 9(4), 399–410 (2000)
18. Aramaki, M., Kronland-Martinet, R., Voinier, T., Ystad, S.: A percussive sound synthetizer based on physical and perceptual attributes. Computer Music Journal 30(2), 32–41 (2006)
19. Aramaki, M., Besson, M., Kronland-Martinet, R., Ystad, S.: Computer Music Modeling and Retrieval - Genesis of Meaning of Sound and Music. In: Ystad, S., Kronland-Martinet, R., Jensen, K. (eds.) Timbre perception of sounds from impacted materials: behavioral, electrophysiological and acoustic approaches. LNCS, vol. 5493, pp. 1–17. Springer, Heidelberg (2009)
20. Aramaki, M., Kronland-Martinet, R., Voinier, T., Ystad, S.: Timbre control of a real-time percussive synthesizer. In: Proceedings of the 19th International Congress on Acoustics, CD-ROM (2007) ISBN: 84-87985-12-2

Refinement Strategies for Music Synchronization

Sebastian Ewert[1] and Meinard Müller[2]

[1] Universität Bonn, Institut für Informatik III
Römerstr. 164, 53117 Bonn, Germany
ewerts@cs.uni-bonn.de
[2] Max-Planck-Institut für Informatik
Campus E1-4, 66123 Saarbrücken, Germany
meinard@mpi-inf.mpg.de

Abstract. For a single musical work, there often exists a large number of relevant digital documents including various audio recordings, MIDI files, or digitized sheet music. The general goal of music synchronization is to automatically align the multiple information sources related to a given musical work. In computing such alignments, one typically has to face a delicate tradeoff between robustness, accuracy, and efficiency. In this paper, we introduce various refinement strategies for music synchronization. First, we introduce novel audio features that combine the temporal accuracy of onset features with the robustness of chroma features. Then, we show how these features can be used within an efficient and robust multiscale synchronization framework. In addition we introduce an interpolation method for further increasing the temporal resolution. Finally, we report on our experiments based on polyphonic Western music demonstrating the respective improvements of the proposed refinement strategies.

1 Introduction

Modern information society is experiencing an explosion of digital content, comprising text, audio, image, and video. For example, in the music domain, there is an increasing number of relevant digital documents even for a single musical work. These documents may comprise various audio recordings, MIDI files, digitized sheet music, or symbolic score representations. The field of music information retrieval (MIR) aims at developing techniques and tools for organizing, understanding, and searching multimodal information in a robust, efficient and intelligent manner. In this context, various alignment and synchronization procedures have been proposed with the common goal to automatically link several types of music representations, thus coordinating the multiple information sources related to a given musical work [1, 3–6, 9, 12, 13, 15–21].

In general terms, *music synchronization* denotes a procedure which, for a given position in one representation of a piece of music, determines the corresponding position within another representation. Depending upon the respective data formats, one distinguishes between various synchronization tasks [1, 13].

S. Ystad, R. Kronland-Martinet, and K. Jensen (Eds.): CMMR 2008, LNCS 5493, pp. 147–165, 2009.

For example, *audio-audio* synchronization [5, 17, 20] refers to the task of time aligning two different audio recordings of a piece of music. These alignments can be used to jump freely between different interpretations, thus affording efficient and convenient audio browsing. The goal of *score-audio* and *MIDI-audio* synchronization [1, 3, 16, 18, 19] is to coordinate note and MIDI events with audio data. The result can be regarded as an automated annotation of the audio recording with available score and MIDI data. A recently studied problem is referred to as *scan-audio* synchronization [12], where the objective is to link regions (given as pixel coordinates) within the scanned images of given sheet music to semantically corresponding physical time positions within an audio recording. Such linking structures can be used to highlight the current position in the scanned score during playback of the recording. Similarly, the goal of *lyrics-audio* synchronization [6, 15, 21] is to align given lyrics to an audio recording of the underlying song. For an overview of related alignment and synchronization problems, we also refer to [4, 13].

Automated music synchronization constitutes a challenging research field since one has to account for a multitude of aspects such as the data format, the genre, the instrumentation, or differences in parameters such as tempo, articulation and dynamics that result from expressiveness in performances. In the design of synchronization algorithms, one has to deal with a delicate tradeoff between robustness, temporal resolution, alignment quality, and computational complexity. For example, music synchronization strategies based on chroma features [3] have turned out to yield robust alignment results even in the presence of significant artistic variations. Such chroma-based approaches typically yield a reasonable synchronization quality, which suffices for music browsing and retrieval applications. However, the alignment accuracy may not suffice to capture fine nuances in tempo and articulation as needed in applications such as performance analysis [22] or audio editing [3]. Other synchronization strategies yield a higher accuracy for certain classes of music by incorporating onset information [16, 19], but suffer from a high computational complexity and a lack of robustness. Dixon et al. [5] describe an online approach to audio synchronization. Even though the proposed algorithm is very efficient, the risk of missing the optimal alignment path is relatively high. Müller et al. [17] present a more robust, but very efficient offline approach, which is based on a multiscale strategy.

In this paper, we introduce several strategies on various conceptual levels to increase the time resolution and quality of the synchronization result without sacrificing robustness and efficiency. First, we introduce a new class of audio features that inherit the robustness from chroma-based features and the temporal accuracy from onset-based features (Sect. 2). Then, in Sect. 3, we show how these features can be used within an efficient and robust multiscale synchronization framework. Finally, for further improving the alignment quality, we introduce an interpolation technique that refines the given alignment path in some time consistent way (Sect. 4). We have conducted various experiments based on polyphonic Western music. In Sect. 5, we summarize and discuss the results indicating the respective improvements of the proposed refinement strategies. We conclude in Sect. 6 with a discussion of open problems and prospects on future work. Further references will be given in the respective sections.

2   Robust and Accurate Audio Features

In this section, we introduce a new class of so-called DLNCO (decaying locally adaptive normalized chroma-based onset) features that indicate note onsets along with their chroma affiliation. These features posses a high temporal accuracy, yet being robust to variations in timbre and dynamics. In Sects. 2.1 and 2.2, we summarize the necessary background on chroma and onset features, respectively. The novel DLNCO features are then described in Sect. 2.3.

2.1   Chroma Features

In order to synchronize different music representations, one needs to find suitable feature representations being robust towards those variations that are to be left unconsidered in the comparison. In this context, chroma-based features have turned out to be a powerful tool for synchronizing harmony-based music, see [2, 9, 13]. Here, the chroma refer to the 12 traditional pitch classes of the equal-tempered scale encoded by the attributes $C, C^\sharp, D, \ldots, B$. Note that in the equal-tempered scale, different pitch spellings such $C^\sharp$ and $D^\flat$ refer to the same chroma. Representing the short-time energy of the signal in each of the 12 pitch classes, chroma features do not only account for the close octave relationship in both melody and harmony as it is prominent in Western music, but also introduce a high degree of robustness to variations in timbre and articulation [2]. Furthermore, normalizing the features makes them invariant to dynamic variations. There are various ways to compute chroma features, e. g., by suitably pooling spectral coefficients obtained from a short-time Fourier transform [2] or by suitably summing up pitch subbands obtained as output after applying a pitch-based filter bank [13, 14]. For details, we refer to the literature.

In the following, the first six measures of the Etude No. 2, Op. 100, by Friedrich Burgmüller will serve us as our running example, see Fig. 1a. For short, we will use the identifier **Burg2** to denote this piece, see Table 1. Figs. 1b and 1c show a chroma representation and a normalized chroma representation, respectively, of an audio recording of **Burg2**. Because of their invariance, chroma-based features are well-suited for music synchronization leading to robust alignments even in the presence of significant variations between different versions of a musical work, see [9, 17].

2.2   Onset Features

We now describe a class of highly expressive audio features that indicate note onsets along with their respective pitch affiliation. For details, we refer to [13, 16]. Note that for many instruments such as the piano or the guitar, there is sudden energy increase when playing a note (attack phase). This energy increase may not be significant relative to the entire signal's energy, since the generated sound may be masked by the remaining components of the signal. However, the energy increase relative to the spectral bands corresponding to the fundamental pitch and harmonics of the respective note may still be substantial. This observation motivates the following feature extraction procedure.

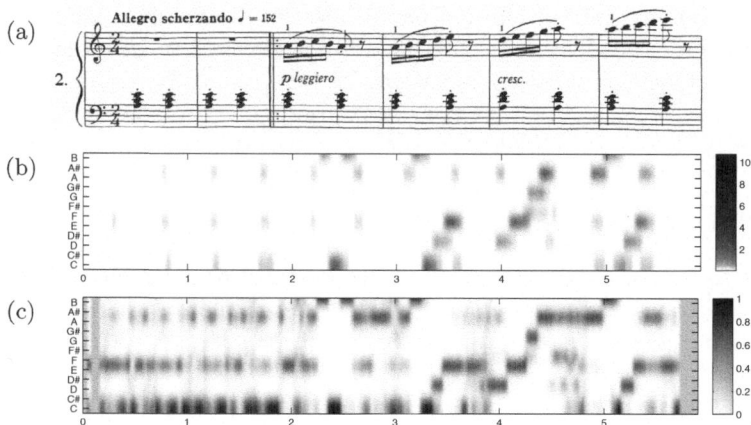

Fig. 1. **(a)** First six measures of Burgmüller, Op. 100, Etude No. 2 (**Burg2**, see Table 1). **(b)** Chroma representation of a corresponding audio recording. Here, the feature resolution is 50 Hz (20 ms per feature vector). **(c)** Normalized chroma representation.

First the audio signal is decomposed into 88 subbands corresponding to the musical notes A0 to C8 (MIDI pitches $p = 21$ to $p = 108$) of the equal-tempered scale. This can be done by a high-quality multirate filter bank that properly separates adjacent notes, see [13, 16]. Then, 88 local energy curves are computed by convolving each of the squared subbands with a suitably window function. Finally, for each energy curve the first-order difference is calculated (discrete derivative) and half-wave rectified (positive part of the function remains). The significant peaks of the resulting curves indicate positions of significant energy increase in the respective pitch subband. An onset feature is specified by the pitch of its subband and by the time position and height of the corresponding peak.

Fig. 2 shows the resulting onset representation obtained for our running example **Burg2**. Note that the set of onset features is sparse while providing information of very high temporal accuracy. (In our implementation, we have a pitch dependent resolution of $2 - 10$ ms.) On the downside, the extraction of onset features is a delicate problem involving fragile operations such as differentiation and peak picking. Furthermore, the feature extraction only makes sense for music with clear onsets (e. g., piano music) and may yield no or faulty results for other music (e. g., soft violin music).

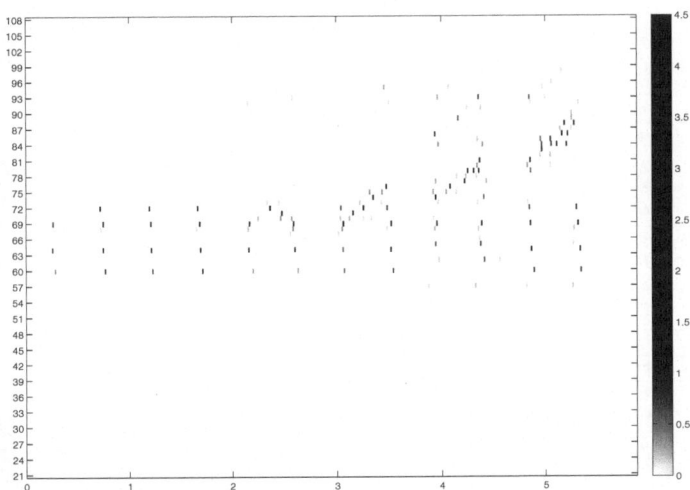

Fig. 2. Onset representation of **Burg2**. Each rectangle represents an onset feature specified by pitch (here, indicated by the MIDI note numbers given by the vertical axis), by time position (given in seconds by the horizontal axis), and by a color-coded value that correspond to the height of the peak. Here, for the sake of visibility, a suitable logarithm of the value is shown.

2.3   DLNCO Features

We now introduce a new class of features that combine the robustness of chroma features and the accuracy of onset features. The basic idea is to add up those onset features that belong to pitches of the same pitch class. To make this work, we first evenly split up the time axis into segments or frames of fixed length (In our experiments, we use a length of 20 ms). Then, for each pitch, we add up all onset features that lie within a segment. Note that due to the sparseness of the onset features, most segments do not contain an onset feature. Since the values of the onset features across different pitches may differ significantly, we take a suitable logarithm of the values, which accounts for the logarithmic sensation of sound intensity. For example, in our experiments, we use $\log(5000 \cdot v + 1)$ for an onset value v. Finally, for each segment, we add up the logarithmic values over all pitches that correspond to the same chroma. For example, adding up the logarithmic onset values that belong to the pitches A0,A1,. . .,A7 yields a value for the chroma A. The resulting 12-dimensional features will be referred to as *CO (chroma onset) features*, see Fig. 3a.

The CO features are still very sensitive to local dynamic variations. As a consequence, onsets in passages played in piano may be marginal in comparison to onsets in passages played in forte. To compensate for this, one could simply normalize all non-zero CO feature vectors. However, this would also enhance small noisy onset features that are caused by mechanical noise, resonance, or beat effects thus leading to a useless representation, see Fig. 3b. To circumvent

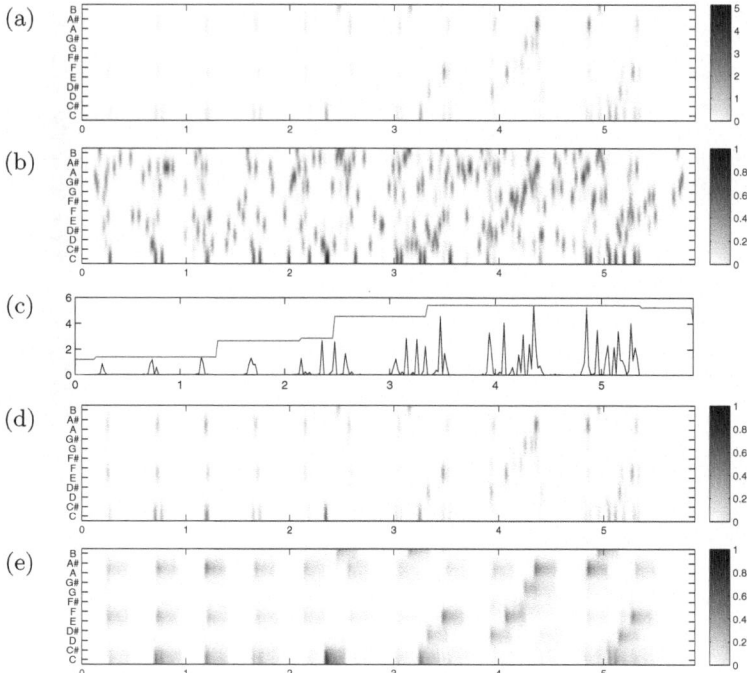

Fig. 3. (a) Chroma onset (CO) features obtained from the onset representation of Fig. 2. (b) Normalized CO features. (c) Sequence of norms of the CO features (blue, lower curve) and sequence of local maxima over a time window of ±1 second (red, upper curve). (d) Locally adaptive normalized CO (LNCO) features. (e) Decaying LNCO (DLNCO) features.

this problem, we employ a locally adaptive normalization strategy. First, we compute the norm for each 12-dimensional CO feature vector resulting in a sequence of norms, see Fig. 3c (blue curve). Then, for each time frame, we assign the local maxima of the sequence of norms over a time window that ranges one second to the left and one second to the right, see Fig. 3c (red curve). Furthermore, we assign a positive threshold value to all those frames where the local maximum falls below that threshold. The resulting sequence of local maxima is used to normalize the CO features in a locally adaptive fashion. To this end, we simply divide the sequence of CO features by the sequence of local maxima in a pointwise fashion, see Fig. 3d. The resulting features are referred to as *LNCO (locally adaptive normalized CO) features*. Intuitively, LNCO features account for the fact that onsets of low energy are less relevant in musical passages of high energy than in passages of low energy.

In summary, the octave identification makes LNCO features robust to variations in timbre. Furthermore, because of the locally adaptive normalization, LNCO features are invariant to variations in dynamics and exhibit significant onset values even in passages of low energy. Finally, the LNCO feature representation is sparse in the sense that most feature vectors are zero, while the non-zero vectors encode highly accurate temporal onset information.

In view of synchronization applications, we further process the LNCO feature representation by introducing an additional temporal decay. To this end, each LNCO feature vector is copied n times (in our experiments we chose $n = 10$) and the copies are multiplied by decreasing positive weights starting with 1. Then, the n copies are arranged to form short sequences of n consecutive feature vectors of decreasing norm starting at the time position of the original vector. The overlay of all these decaying sequences results in a feature representation, which we refer to as *DLNCO (decaying LNCO) feature* representation, see Figs. 3e and 6a. The benefit of these additional temporal decays will become clear in the synchronization context, see Sect. 3.1. Note that in the DLNCO feature representation, one does not loose the temporal accuracy of the LNCO features—the onset positions still appear as sharp left edges in the decays. However, spurious double peaks, which appear in a close temporal neighborhood within a chroma band, are discarded. By introducing the decay, as we will see later, one looses sparseness while gaining robustness.

As a final remark of this section, we emphasize that the opposite variant of first computing chroma features and then computing onsets from the resulting chromagrams is not as successful as our strategy. As a first reason, note that the temporal resolution of the pitch energy curves is much higher ($2 - 10$ ms depending on the respective pitch) then for the chroma features (where information across various pitches is combined at a common lower temporal resolution) thus yielding a higher accuracy. As a second reason, note that by first changing to a chroma representation one may already loose valuable onset information. For example, suppose there is a clear onset in the C3 pitch band and some smearing in the C4 pitch band. Then, the smearing may overlay the onset on the chroma level, which may result in missing the onset information. However, by first computing onsets for all pitches separately and then merging this information on the chroma level, the onset of the C3 pitch band will become clearly visible on the chroma level.

3   Synchronization Algorithm

In this section, we show how our novel DLNCO features can be used to significantly improve the accuracy of previous chroma-based strategies without sacrificing robustness and efficiency. First, in Sect. 3.1, we introduce a combination of cost matrices that suitably captures harmonic as well as onset information. Then, in Sect. 3.2, we discuss how the new cost matrix can be plugged in an efficient multiscale music synchronization framework by using an additional alignment layer.

3.1   Local Cost Measures and Cost Matrices

As discussed in the introduction, the goal of music synchronization is to time align two given versions of the same underlying piece of music. In the following,

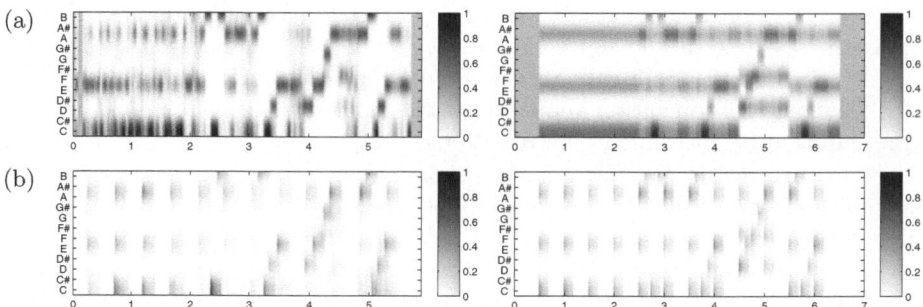

Fig. 4. (a) Sequences of normalized chroma features for an audio version (left) and MIDI version (right) of **Burg2**. (b) Corresponding sequences of DLNCO features.

we consider the case of MIDI-audio synchronization. Other cases such as audio-audio synchronization may be handled in the same fashion. Most synchronization algorithms [3, 5, 9, 16, 17, 19, 20] rely on some variant of dynamic time warping (DTW) and can be summarized as follows. First, the two music data streams to be aligned are converted into feature sequences, say $V := (v_1, v_2, \ldots, v_N)$ and $W := (w_1, w_2, \ldots, w_M)$, respectively. Note that N and M do not have to be equal, since the two versions typically have a different length. Then, an $N \times M$ cost matrix C is built up by evaluating a local cost measure c for each pair of features, i.e., $C(n, m) = c(v_n, w_m)$ for $1 \leq n \leq N, 1 \leq m \leq M$. Finally, an optimum-cost alignment path is determined from this matrix via dynamic programming, which encodes the synchronization result. Our synchronization approach follows these lines using the standard DTW algorithm, see [13] for a detailed account on DTW in the music context. For an illustration, we refer to Fig. 5, which shows various cost matrices along with optimal alignment paths.

Note that the final synchronization result heavily depends on the type of features used to transform the music data streams and the local cost measure used to compare the features. We now introduce three different cost matrices, where the third one is a simple combination of the first and second one.

The first matrix is a conventional cost matrix based on normalized chroma features. Note that these features can be extracted from audio representations, as described in Sect. 2.1, as well as from MIDI representations, as suggested in [9]. Fig. 4a shows normalized chroma representations for an audio recording and a MIDI version of **Burg2**, respectively. To compare two normalized chroma vectors v and w, we use the cost measure $c_{\mathbf{chroma}}(v, w) := 2 - \langle x, y \rangle$. Note that $\langle v, w \rangle$ is the cosine of the angle between v and w since the features are normalized. The offset 2 is introduced to favor diagonal directions in the DTW algorithm in regions of uniformly low cost, see [17] for a detailed explanation. The resulting cost matrix is denoted by $C_{\mathbf{chroma}}$, see Fig. 5a.

The second cost matrix is based on DLNCO features as introduced in Sect. 2.3. Again, one can directly convert the MIDI version into a DLNCO representation

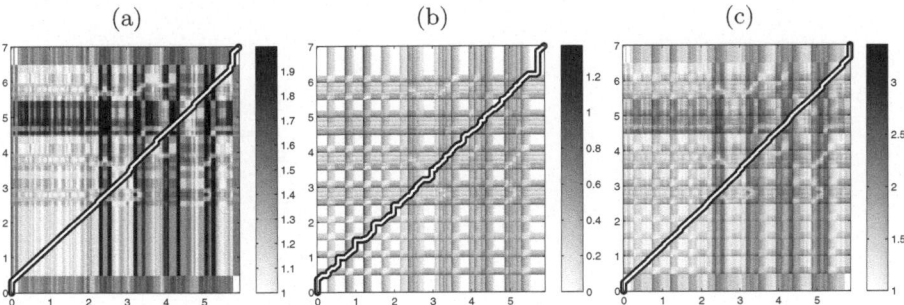

Fig. 5. (a) Cost matrix C_{chroma} using normalized chroma features and the local cost measure c_{chroma}. The two underlying feature sequences are shown Fig. 4a. A cost-minimizing alignment path is indicated by the white line. (b) Cost matrix C_{DLNCO} with cost-minimizing alignment path using DLNCO features and c_{DLNCO}. The two underlying feature sequences are shown Fig. 4b. (c) Cost matrix $C = C_{\text{chroma}} + C_{\text{DLNCO}}$ and resulting cost-minimizing alignment path.

by converting the MIDI note onsets into pitch onsets. Fig. 4b shows DLNCO representations for an audio recording and a MIDI version of **Burg2**, respectively. To compare two DLNCO feature vectors, v and w we now use the Euclidean distance $c_{\text{DLNCO}}(v, w) := \|v - w\|$. The resulting cost matrix is denoted by C_{DLNCO}, see Fig. 5b. At this point, we need to make some explanations. First, recall that each onset has been transformed into a short vector sequence of decaying norm. Using the Euclidean distance to compare two such decaying sequences leads to a diagonal corridor of low cost in C_{DLNCO} in the case that the directions (i. e., the relative chroma distributions) of the onset vectors are similar. This corridor is tapered to the lower left and starts at the precise time positions of the two onsets to be compared, see Fig. 6c. Second, note that C_{DLNCO} reveals a grid like structure of an overall high cost, where each beginning of a corridor forms a small needle's eye of low cost. Third, sections in the feature sequences with no onsets lead to regions in C_{DLNCO} having zero cost. In other words, only significant events in the DLNCO feature sequences take effect on the cost matrix level. In summary, the structure of C_{DLNCO} regulates the course of a cost-minimizing alignment path in event-based regions to run through the needle's eyes of low cost. This leads to very accurate alignments at time positions with matching chroma onsets.

The two cost matrices C_{chroma} and C_{DLNCO} encode complementary information of the two music representations to be synchronized. The matrix C_{chroma} accounts for the rough harmonic flow of the two representations, whereas C_{DLNCO} exhibits matching chroma onsets. Forming the sum $C = C_{\text{chroma}} + C_{\text{DLNCO}}$ yields a cost matrix that accounts for both types of information. Note that in regions with no onsets, C_{DLNCO} is zero and the combined matrix C is dominated by C_{chroma}. Contrary, in regions with significant onsets, C is dominated by C_{DLNCO}, thus enforcing the cost-minimizing alignment path to run trough

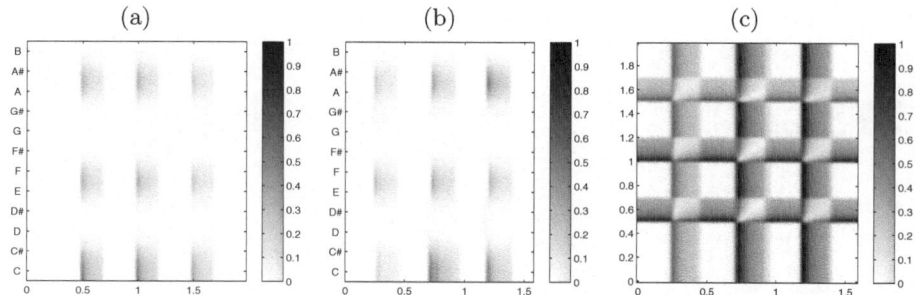

Fig. 6. Illustration of the effect of the decay operation on the cost matrix level. A match of two onsets leads to a small corridor within the cost matrix that exhibits low costs and is tapered to the left (where the exact onsets occur). **(a)** Beginning of the DLNCO representation of Fig. 4b (left). **(b)** Beginning of the DLNCO representation of Fig. 4b (right). **(c)** Resulting section of $C_{\mathbf{DLNCO}}$, see Fig. 5b.

the needle's eyes of low cost. Note that in a neighborhood of these eyes, the cost matrix $C_{\mathbf{chroma}}$ also reveals low costs due to the similar chroma distribution of the onsets. In summary, the component $C_{\mathbf{chroma}}$ regulates the overall course of the cost-minimizing alignment path and accounts for a robust synchronization, whereas the component $C_{\mathbf{DLNCO}}$ locally adjusts the alignment path and accounts for highly temporal accuracy.

3.2 Multiscale Implementation

Note that the time and memory complexity of DTW-based music synchronization linearly depends on the product $N \cdot M$ of the lengths N and M of the feature sequences to be aligned. For example, having a feature resolution of 20 ms and music data streams of 10 minutes of duration, results in $N = M = 30000$ making computations infeasible. To overcome this problem, we adapt an efficient multiscale DTW (MsDTW) approach as described in [17]. The idea is to calculate an alignment path in an iterative fashion by using multiple resolution levels going from coarse to fine. Here, the results of the coarser level are used to constrain the calculation on the finer levels, see Fig. 7.

In a first step, we use the chroma-based MsDTW as described in [17]. In particular, we employ an efficient MsDTW implementation in C/C++ (used as a MATLAB DLL), which is based on three levels corresponding to a feature resolution of 1/3 Hz, 1 Hz, and 10 Hz, respectively. For example, our implementation needs less than a second (not including the feature extraction, which is linear in the length of the pieces) on a standard PC for synchronizing two music data streams each having a duration of 15 minutes of duration. The MsDTW synchronization is robust leading to reliable, but coarse alignments, which often reveal deviations of several hundreds of milliseconds.

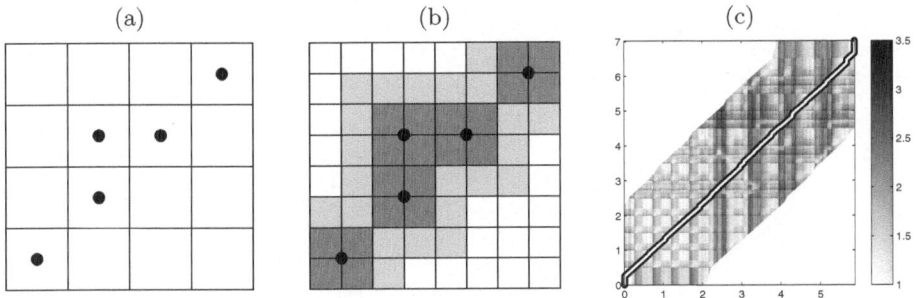

Fig. 7. Illustration of multiscale DTW. (**a**) Optimal alignment path (black dots) computed on a coarse resolution level. (**b**) Projection of the alignment path onto a finer resolution level with constraint region (dark gray) and extended constraint region (light gray). (**c**) Constraint region for **Burg2**, cf. Fig. 5c. The entries of the cost matrix are only computed within the constraint region. The resulting MsDTW alignment path indicated by the white line coincides with the DTW alignment path shown in Fig. 5c.

To refine the synchronization result, we employ an additional alignment level corresponding to a feature resolution of 50 Hz (i. e., each feature corresponds to 20 ms). On this level, we use the cost matrix $C = C_{\mathbf{chroma}} + C_{\mathbf{DLNCO}}$ as described in Sect. 3.1. First, the resulting alignment path of the previous Ms-DTW method (corresponding to a 10 Hz feature resolution) is projected onto the 50 Hz resolution level. The projected path is used to define a tube-like constraint region, see Fig. 7b. As before, the cost matrix C is only evaluated within this region, which leads to large savings if the region is small. However, note that the final alignment path is also restricted to this region, which may lead to incorrect alignment paths if the region is too small [17]. As our experiments showed, an extension of two seconds in all four directions (left, right, up, down) of the projected alignment path yields a good compromise between efficiency and robustness. Fig. 7c shows the resulting extended constraint region for our running example **Burg2**. The relative savings with respect to memory requirements and running time of our overall multiscale procedure increases significantly with the length of the feature sequences to be aligned. For example, our procedure needs only around $3 \cdot 10^6$ of the total number of $15000^2 = 2.25 \cdot 10^8$ matrix entries for synchronizing two versions of a five minute piece, thus decreasing the memory requirements by a factor of 75. For a ten minute piece, this factor already amounts to 150. The relative savings for the running times are similar.

4   Resolution Refinement through Interpolation

A synchronization result is encoded by an alignment path, which assigns the elements of one feature sequence to the elements of the other feature sequence. Note that each feature refers to an entire analysis window, which corresponds to a certain time range rather than a single point in time. Therefore, an alignment path should be regarded as an assignment of certain time ranges. Furthermore,

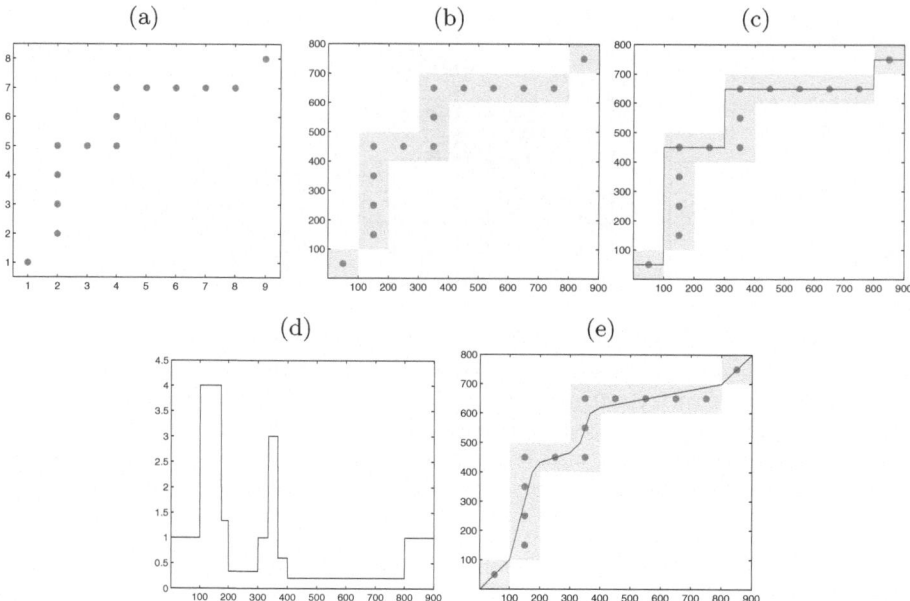

Fig. 8. (a) Alignment path assigning elements of one feature sequence to elements of the other feature sequence. The elements are indexed by natural numbers. (b) Assignment of time ranges corresponding to the alignment path, where each feature corresponds to a time range of 100 ms. (c) Staircase interpolation path (red line). (d) Density function encoding the local distortions. (e) Smoothed and strictly monotonic interpolation path obtained by integration of the density function.

an alignment path may not be strictly monotonic in its components, i. e., a single element of one feature sequence may be assigned to several consecutive elements of the other feature sequence. This further increases the time ranges in the assignment. As illustration, consider Fig. 8, where each feature corresponds to a time range of 100 ms. For example, the fifth element of the first sequence (vertical axis) is assigned to the second, third, and forth element of the second sequence (horizontal axis), see Fig. 8a. This corresponds to an assignment of the range between 400 and 500 ms with the range between 100 and 400 ms, see Fig. 8b. One major problem of such an assignment is that the temporal resolution may not suffice for certain applications. For example, one may want to use the alignment result in order to temporally warp CD audio recordings, which are typically sampled at a rate of 44,1 kHz.

To increase the temporal resolution, one usually reverts to interpolation techniques. Many of the previous approaches are based on simple staircase paths as indicated by the red line of Fig. 8c. However, such paths are not strictly monotonic and reveal abrupt directional changes leading to strong local temporal distortions. To avoid such distortions, one has to smooth the alignment path in such a way that both of its components are strictly monotonic increasing. To this end, Kovar et al. [10] fit a spline into the alignment path and enforce the strictness condition by suitably adjusting the control points of the splines. In the following, we introduce a novel strictly monotonic interpolation function that closely reflects the course of the original alignment path. Recall that the original alignment path encodes an assignment of time ranges. The basic idea is that each assignment defines a local distortion factor, which is the proportion of the ranges' sizes. For example, the assignment of the range between 400 and 500 ms with the range between 100 and 400 ms, as discussed above, defines a local distortion factor of 1/3. Elaborating on this idea, one obtains a density function that encodes the local distortion factors. As an illustration, we refer to Fig. 8d, which shows the resulting density function for the alignment path of Fig. 8a. Then, the final interpolation path is obtained by integrating over the density function, see Fig. 8e. Note that the resulting interpolation path is a smoothed and strictly monotonic version of the original alignment path. The continuous interpolation path can be used for arbitrary sampling rates. Furthermore, as we will see in Sect. 5, it also improves the final synchronization quality.

5   Experiments

In this section, we report on some of our synchronization experiments, which have been conducted on a corpus of harmony-based Western music. To allow for a reproduction of our experiments, we used pieces from the RWC music database [7, 8]. In the following, we consider 16 representative pieces, which are listed in Table 1. These pieces are divided into three groups, where the first group consists of six classical piano pieces, the second group of five classical pieces of various instrumentations (full orchestra, strings, flute, voice), and the third group of five jazz pieces and pop songs. Note that for pure piano music, one typically has concise note attacks resulting in characteristic onset features. Contrary, such information is often missing in string or general orchestral music. To account for such differences, we report on the synchronization accuracy for each of the three groups separately.

To demonstrate the respective effect of the different refinement strategies on the final synchronization quality, we evaluated eight different synchronization procedures. The first procedure (MsDTW) is the MsDTW approach as described in [17], which works with a feature resolution of 10 Hz. The next three procedures are all refinements of the first procedure working with an additional alignment layer using a feature resolution of 50 Hz. In particular, we use in the second procedure (Chroma 20ms) normalized chroma features, in the third procedure (DL-NCO) only the DLNCO features, and in the forth procedure (Chroma+DLNCO) a combination of these features, see Sect. 3.1. Besides the simple staircase interpolation, we also refined each of these four procedure via smooth interpolation as discussed in Sect. 4. Table 2, which will be discussed later in detail, indicates the accuracy of the alignment results for each of the eight synchronization procedures.

To automatically determine the accuracy of our synchronization procedures, we used pairs of MIDI and audio versions for each of the 16 pieces listed in

Table 1. Pieces of music with identifier (ID) contained in our test database. For better reproduction of our experiments, we used pieces from the RWC music database [7, 8].

ID	Comp./Interp.	Piece	RWC ID	Instrument
Burg2	Burgmüller	Etude No. 2, Op. 100	–	piano
BachFuge	Bach	Fuge, C-Major, BWV 846	C025	piano
BeetApp	Beethoven	Op. 57, 1st Mov. (Appasionata)	C028	piano
ChopTris	Chopin	Etude Op. 10, No. 3 (Tristesse)	C031	piano
ChopBees	Chopin	Etude Op. 25, No. 2 (The Bees)	C032	piano
SchuRev	Schumann	Reverie (Träumerei)	C029	piano
BeetFifth	Beethoven	Op. 67, 1st Mov. (Fifth)	C003	orchestra
BorString	Borodin	String Quartett No. 2, 3rd Mov.	C015	strings
BrahDance	Brahms	Hungarian Dance No. 5	C022	orchestra
RimskiBee	Rimski-Korsakov	Flight of the Bumblebee	C044	flute/piano
SchubLind	Schubert	Op. 89, No. 5 (Der Lindenbaum)	C044	voice/piano
Jive	Nakamura	Jive	J001	piano
Entertain	HH Band	The Entertainer	J038	big band
Friction	Umitsuki Quartet	Friction	J041	sax,bass,perc.
Moving	Nagayama	Moving Round and Round	P031	electronic
Dreams	Burke	Sweet Dreams	P093	voice/guitar

Table 1. Here, the audio versions were generated from the MIDI files using a high-quality synthesizer. Thus, for each synchronization pair, the note onset times in the MIDI file are perfectly aligned with the physical onset times in the respective audio recording. (Only for our running example **Burg2**, we manually aligned some real audio recording with a corresponding MIDI version.) In the first step of our evaluation process, we randomly distorted the MIDI files. To this end, we split up the MIDI files into N segments of equal length (in our experiment we used $N = 20$) and then stretched or compressed each segment by a random factor within an allowed distortion range (in our experiments we used a range of $\pm 30\%$). We refer to the resulting MIDI file as the *distorted MIDI file* in contrast to the original *annotation MIDI file*. In the second evaluation step, we synchronized the distorted MIDI file and the associated audio recording. The resulting alignment path was used to adjust the note onset times in the distorted MIDI file to obtain a third MIDI file referred to as *realigned MIDI file*. The accuracy of the synchronization result can now be determined by comparing the note onset times of the realigned MIDI file with the corresponding note onsets of the annotation MIDI file. Note that in the case of a perfect synchronization, the realigned MIDI file exactly coincides with the annotation MIDI file.

For each of the 16 pieces (Table 1) and for each of the eight different synchronization procedures, we computed the corresponding realigned MIDI file. We then calculated the mean value, the standard deviation, as well as the maximal value over all note onset differences comparing the respective realigned MIDI file with the corresponding annotation MIDI file. Thus, for each piece, we obtained 24 statistical values, which are shown in Table 2. (Actually, we also repeated all experiments with five different randomly distorted MIDI files and averaged all statistical values over these five repetitions). For example the value 73 in the first row of Table 2 means that for the piece **Burg2** the difference between the note onsets of the realigned MIDI file and the annotation MIDI file was in average 73 ms when using the MsDTW synchronisation approach in combination with a staircase interpolation. In other words, the average synchronization error of this approach is 73 ms for **Burg2**.

We start the discussion of Table 2 by looking at the values for the first group consisting of six piano pieces. Looking at the averages of the statistical values over the six piece, one can observe that the MsDTW procedures is clearly inferior to the other procedures. This is by no surprise, since the feature resolution of MsDTW is 100 ms compared to the resolution of 20 ms used in the other approaches. Nevertheless the standard deviation and maximal deviation of MsDTW is small relative to the mean value indicating the robustness of this approach. Using 20 ms chroma features, the average mean values decreases from 100 ms (MsDTW) to 51 ms (Chroma 20 ms). Using the combined features, this value further decreases to 26 ms (Chroma+DLNCO). Furthermore, using the smooth interpolation instead of the simple staircase interpolation further improves the accuracy, for example, from 100 ms to 67 ms (MsDTW) or from 26 ms to 19 ms (Chroma+DLNCO). Another interesting observation is that the pure DLNCO approach is sometimes much better (e. g. for **ChopBees**) but also sometimes much worse (e. g. for **BeetApp**) than the Chroma 20ms approach. This shows that the DLNCO features have the potential for delivering very accurate results but also suffer from a lack of robustness. It is the combination of the DLNCO features and chroma features which ensures robustness as well as accuracy of the overall synchronization procedure.

Next, we look at the group of the five classical pieces of various instrumentations. Note that for the pieces of this group, opposed to the piano pieces, one often has no clear note attacks leading to a much poorer quality of the onset features. As a consequence, the synchronization errors are in average higher than for the piano pieces. For example, the average mean error over the second group is 136 ms (MsDTW) and 134 ms (DLNCO) opposed to 100 ms (MsDTW) and 56 ms (DLNCO) for the first group. However, even in the case of missing onset information, the synchronization task is still accomplished in a robust way by means of the harmony-based chroma features. The idea of using the combined approach (Chroma+DLNCO) is that the resulting synchronization procedure is at least as robust and exact as the pure chroma-based approach (Chroma 20 ms). Table 2 demonstrates that this idea is realized by the implementation of our combined synchronization procedure. Similar results are obtained for the third group of jazz/pop examples, where the best results were also delivered by the combined approach (Chroma+DLNCO).

At this point, one may object that one typically obtains better absolute synchronization results for synthetic audio material (which was used to completely automate our evaluation) than for non-synthetic, real audio recordings. We therefore included also the real audio recording **Burg2**, which actually led to similar results as the synthesized examples. Furthermore, our experiments on the synthetic data are still meaningful in the relative sense by revealing relative performance differences between the various synchronization

Table 2. Alignment accuracy for eight different synchronization procedures (MsDTW, Chroma 20 ms, DLNCO, Chroma+DLNCO with staircase and smooth interpolation, respectively). The table shows for each of the eight procedures and for each of 16 pieces (Table 1) the mean value, the standard deviation, and the maximal value over all note onset difference of the respective realigned MIDI file and the corresponding annotation MIDI file. All values are given in milliseconds.

ID	Procedure	staircase			smooth		
		mean	std	max	mean	std	max
Burg2	MsDTW	73	57	271	71	65	307
	Chroma 20ms	49	43	222	50	48	228
	DLNCO	31	20	94	21	17	73
	Chroma+DLNCO	**28**	**16**	**77**	**18**	**14**	**61**
BachFuge	MsDTW	97	55	319	55	41	223
	Chroma 20ms	34	34	564	27	33	554
	DLNCO	20	30	318	18	27	296
	Chroma+DLNCO	**18**	**15**	**96**	**14**	**12**	**81**
BeetApp	MsDTW	116	102	1197	77	94	1104
	Chroma 20ms	62	58	744	54	58	757
	DLNCO	136	318	2323	131	318	2335
	Chroma+DLNCO	**37**	**41**	**466**	**29**	**40**	**478**
ChopTris	MsDTW	115	76	1041	72	62	768
	Chroma 20ms	66	69	955	57	64	754
	DLNCO	30	68	1318	22	68	1305
	Chroma+DLNCO	**31**	**34**	**539**	**22**	**33**	**524**
ChopBees	MsDTW	108	79	865	59	71	817
	Chroma 20ms	41	49	664	30	47	625
	DLNCO	20	14	104	12	9	95
	Chroma+DLNCO	**22**	**24**	**366**	**13**	**21**	**355**
SchuRev	MsDTW	93	95	887	66	77	655
	Chroma 20ms	51	80	778	46	72	567
	DLNCO	98	261	1789	94	264	1841
	Chroma+DLNCO	**22**	**38**	**330**	**15**	**36**	**315**
Average over piano examples	MsDTW	100	77	763	67	68	646
	Chroma 20ms	51	56	655	44	54	581
	DLNCO	56	119	991	50	117	991
	Chroma+DLNCO	**26**	**28**	**312**	**19**	**26**	**302**
BeetFifth	MsDTW	194	124	1048	142	116	952
	Chroma 20ms	128	98	973	116	96	959
	DLNCO	254	338	2581	241	338	2568
	Chroma+DLNCO	**128**	**99**	**1144**	**116**	**98**	**1130**
BorString	MsDTW	157	110	738	118	106	734
	Chroma 20ms	88	68	584	79	68	576
	DLNCO	275	355	2252	268	356	2233
	Chroma+DLNCO	**91**	**57**	**682**	**82**	**56**	**675**
BrahDance	MsDTW	104	62	385	64	54	470
	Chroma 20ms	58	54	419	50	54	427
	DLNCO	31	52	567	26	52	556
	Chroma+DLNCO	**24**	**22**	**185**	**17**	**20**	**169**
RimskiBee	MsDTW	99	48	389	50	32	196
	Chroma 20ms	51	17	167	41	17	155
	DLNCO	31	23	183	22	19	160
	Chroma+DLNCO	**37**	**17**	**108**	**27**	**15**	**91**
SchubLind	MsDTW	124	73	743	78	59	549
	Chroma 20ms	66	57	718	55	50	509
	DLNCO	79	175	1227	70	173	1206
	Chroma+DLNCO	**41**	**36**	**406**	**31**	**34**	**387**
Average over various intstrumentation examples	MsDTW	136	83	661	90	73	580
	Chroma 20ms	78	59	572	68	57	525
	DLNCO	134	189	1362	125	188	1345
	Chroma+DLNCO	**64**	**46**	**505**	**55**	**45**	**490**
Jive	MsDTW	97	105	949	58	93	850
	Chroma 20ms	44	61	686	34	59	668
	DLNCO	23	38	638	17	37	632
	Chroma+DLNCO	**22**	**18**	**154**	**14**	**15**	**158**
Entertain	MsDTW	100	67	579	66	58	492
	Chroma 20ms	52	44	407	45	46	414
	DLNCO	93	204	1899	85	204	1887
	Chroma+DLNCO	**40**	**65**	**899**	**31**	**64**	**889**
Friction	MsDTW	94	81	789	58	75	822
	Chroma 20ms	47	67	810	39	67	815
	DLNCO	44	120	2105	37	117	2106
	Chroma+DLNCO	**30**	**55**	**810**	**23**	**55**	**819**
Moving	MsDTW	114	76	497	76	64	473
	Chroma 20ms	77	51	336	68	50	343
	DLNCO	127	216	1443	124	217	1432
	Chroma+DLNCO	**53**	**45**	**284**	**46**	**43**	**275**
Dreams	MsDTW	136	105	659	115	106	674
	Chroma 20ms	97	94	702	91	95	673
	DLNCO	73	103	692	71	103	702
	Chroma+DLNCO	**43**	**57**	**429**	**40**	**58**	**434**
Average over jazz/pop examples	MsDTW	108	87	695	75	79	662
	Chroma 20ms	63	63	588	55	63	583
	DLNCO	72	136	1355	67	136	1352
	Chroma+DLNCO	**38**	**48**	**515**	**31**	**47**	**515**
Average over all examples	MsDTW	114	82	710	77	73	630
	Chroma 20ms	63	59	608	55	58	564
	DLNCO	85	146	1221	79	145	1214
	Chroma+DLNCO	**42**	**40**	**436**	**34**	**38**	**428**

Table 3. Dependency of the final synchronization accuracy on the size of the allowed distortion range. For each of the 16 pieces and each range, the mean values of the synchronization errors are given for the MsDTW and Chroma+DLNCO procedure both post-processed with smooth interpolation. All values are given in milliseconds.

		Distortion range				
ID	Procedure	±10%	±20%	±30%	±40%	±50%
Burg2	MsDTW	48	53	65	85	94
	Chroma+DLNCO	15	16	19	17	22
BachFuge	MsDTW	44	49	52	62	67
	Chroma+DLNCO	11	12	13	15	15
BeetApp	MsDTW	53	68	75	96	170
	Chroma+DLNCO	22	25	29	36	98
ChopTris	MsDTW	57	64	72	75	82
	Chroma+DLNCO	18	19	21	22	29
ChopBees	MsDTW	51	54	57	60	67
	Chroma+DLNCO	11	12	13	14	18
SchuRev	MsDTW	50	58	64	77	85
	Chroma+DLNCO	11	14	12	13	22
Average over piano examples	MsDTW	51	58	64	76	94
	Chroma+DLNCO	15	16	18	20	34
BeetFifth	MsDTW	119	126	141	143	184
	Chroma+DLNCO	101	106	113	113	145
BorString	MsDTW	86	97	109	118	153
	Chroma+DLNCO	75	78	82	84	101
BrahDance	MsDTW	52	58	66	70	81
	Chroma+DLNCO	13	15	18	19	25
RimskiBee	MsDTW	49	47	52	53	56
	Chroma+DLNCO	25	26	26	28	28
SchubLind	MsDTW	69	73	78	99	91
	Chroma+DLNCO	28	28	31	35	35
Average over various intstrumentation examples	MsDTW	75	80	89	97	113
	Chroma+DLNCO	48	51	54	56	67
Jive	MsDTW	44	62	50	63	77
	Chroma+DLNCO	12	13	14	14	15
Entertain	MsDTW	47	53	62	78	94
	Chroma+DLNCO	21	25	30	36	44
Friction	MsDTW	44	48	54	70	82
	Chroma+DLNCO	14	17	22	28	37
Moving	MsDTW	61	63	75	127	871
	Chroma+DLNCO	33	39	47	59	732
Dreams	MsDTW	71	84	114	142	178
	Chroma+DLNCO	24	28	39	52	85
Average over jazz/pop examples	MsDTW	53	62	71	96	260
	Chroma+DLNCO	21	24	30	38	183
Average over all examples	MsDTW	59	66	74	89	152
	Chroma+DLNCO	27	30	33	37	91

procedures. Finally, we also generated MIDI-audio alignments using real performances of the corresponding pieces (which are also contained in the RWC music database). These alignments were used to modify the original MIDI files to run synchronously to the audio recordings. Generating a stereo file with a synthesized version of the modified MIDI file in one channel and the audio recording in the other channel, we have acoustically examined the alignment results. The acoustic impression supports the evaluation results obtained from the synthetic data. The stereo files have been made available on the website http://www-mmdb.iai.uni-bonn.de/projects/syncDLNCO/.

For the experiments of Table 2, we used a distortion range of ±30%, which is motivated by the observation that the relative tempo difference between two real performances of the same piece mostly lies within this range. In a second experiment, we investigated the dependency of the final synchronization accuracy on the size of the allowed distortion range. To this end, we calculated the mean values of the synchronization error for each of the 16 pieces using different distortion ranges from ±10% to ±50%. Table 3 shows the resulting vales for two of the eight synchronization procedures described above, namely MsDTW and Chroma+DLNCO both post-processed with smooth interpolation. As one may expect, the mean error values increase with the allowed distortion range.

For example, the average mean error over all 16 pieces increases from 59 ms to 152 ms for the MsDTW and from 27 ms to 91 ms for the combined procedure (Chroma+DLNCO). However, the general behavior of the various synchronization procedures does not change significantly with the ranges and the overall synchronization accuracy is still high even in the presence of large distortions. As an interesting observation, for one of the pieces (**Moving**) the mean error exploded from 59 ms to 732 ms (Chroma+DLNCO) when increasing the range from ±40% to ±50%. Here, a manual inspection showed that, for the latter range, a systematic synchronization error happened. Here, for an entire musical segment of the piece, the audio version was aligned to a similar subsequent repetition of the segment in the distorted MIDI version. However, note that such strong distortion (±50% corresponds to the range of having half tempo to double tempo) rarely occurs in practice and only causes problems for repetitive music.

6   Conclusions

In this paper, we have discussed various refinement strategies for music synchronization. Based on a novel class of onset-based audio features in combination with previous chroma features, we presented a new synchronization procedure that can significantly improve the synchronization accuracy while preserving the robustness and efficiency of previously described procedures. For the future, we plan to further extend our synchronization framework by including various features types that also capture local rhythmic information [11] and that detect even smooth note transitions as often present in orchestral or string music [23]. As a further extension of our work, we will consider the problem of partial music synchronization, where the two versions to be aligned may reveal significant structural differences.

References

1. Arifi, V., Clausen, M., Kurth, F., Müller, M.: Synchronization of music data in score-, MIDI- and PCM-format. Computing in Musicology 13 (2004)
2. Bartsch, M.A., Wakefield, G.H.: Audio thumbnailing of popular music using chroma-based representations. IEEE Trans. on Multimedia 7(1), 96–104 (2005)
3. Dannenberg, R., Hu, N.: Polyphonic audio matching for score following and intelligent audio editors. In: Proc. ICMC, San Francisco, USA, pp. 27–34 (2003)
4. Dannenberg, R., Raphael, C.: Music score alignment and computer accompaniment. Special Issue, Commun. ACM 49(8), 39–43 (2006)
5. Dixon, S., Widmer, G.: Match: A music alignment tool chest. In: Proc. ISMIR, London, GB (2005)
6. Fujihara, H., Goto, M., Ogata, J., Komatani, K., Ogata, T., Okuno, H.G.: Automatic synchronization between lyrics and music cd recordings based on viterbi alignment of segregated vocal signals. In: ISM, pp. 257–264 (2006)
7. Goto, M.: Development of the rwc music database
8. Goto, M., Hashiguchi, H., Nishimura, T., Oka, R.: Rwc music database: Popular, classical and jazz music databases. In: ISMIR (2002)

9. Hu, N., Dannenberg, R., Tzanetakis, G.: Polyphonic audio matching and alignment for music retrieval. In: Proc. IEEE WASPAA, New Paltz, NY (October 2003)
10. Kovar, L., Gleicher, M.: Flexible automatic motion blending with registration curves. In: Proc. 2003 ACM SIGGRAPH/Eurographics Symposium on Computer Animation, pp. 214–224. Eurographics Association (2003)
11. Kurth, F., Gehrmann, T., Müller, M.: The cyclic beat spectrum: Tempo-related audio features for time-scale invariant audio identification. In: Proc. ISMIR, Victoria, Canada, pp. 35–40 (2006)
12. Kurth, F., Müller, M., Fremerey, C., Chang, Y., Clausen, M.: Automated synchronization of scanned sheet music with audio recordings. In: Proc. ISMIR, Vienna, AT (2007)
13. Müller, M.: Information Retrieval for Music and Motion. Springer, Heidelberg (2007)
14. Müller, M., Kurth, F., Clausen, M.: Audio matching via chroma-based statistical features. In: Proc. ISMIR, London, GB (2005)
15. Müller, M., Kurth, F., Damm, D., Fremerey, C., Clausen, M.: Lyrics-based audio retrieval and multimodal navigation in music collections. In: Kovács, L., Fuhr, N., Meghini, C. (eds.) ECDL 2007. LNCS, vol. 4675, pp. 112–123. Springer, Heidelberg (2007)
16. Müller, M., Kurth, F., Röder, T.: Towards an efficient algorithm for automatic score-to-audio synchronization. In: Proc. ISMIR, Barcelona, Spain (2004)
17. Müller, M., Mattes, H., Kurth, F.: An efficient multiscale approach to audio synchronization. In: Proc. ISMIR, Victoria, Canada, pp. 192–197 (2006)
18. Raphael, C.: A hybrid graphical model for aligning polyphonic audio with musical scores. In: Proc. ISMIR, Barcelona, Spain (2004)
19. Soulez, F., Rodet, X., Schwarz, D.: Improving polyphonic and poly-instrumental music to score alignment. In: Proc. ISMIR, Baltimore, USA (2003)
20. Turetsky, R.J., Ellis, D.P.: Force-Aligning MIDI Syntheses for Polyphonic Music Transcription Generation. In: Proc. ISMIR, Baltimore, USA (2003)
21. Wang, Y., Kan, M.-Y., Nwe, T.L., Shenoy, A., Yin, J.: LyricAlly: Automatic synchronization of acoustic musical signals and textual lyrics. In: MULTIMEDIA 2004: Proc. 12th annual ACM international conference on Multimedia, pp. 212–219. ACM Press, New York (2004)
22. Widmer, G.: Using ai and machine learning to study expressive music performance: Project survey and first report. AI Commun. 14(3), 149–162 (2001)
23. You, W., Dannenberg, R.: Polyphonic music note onset detection using semi-supervised learning. In: Proc. ISMIR, Vienna, Austria (2007)

Labelling the Structural Parts of a Music Piece with Markov Models

Jouni Paulus and Anssi Klapuri

Department of Signal Processing, Tampere University of Technology
Korkeakoulunkatu 1, Tampere, Finland
{jouni.paulus,anssi.klapuri}@tut.fi

Abstract. This paper describes a method for labelling structural parts of a musical piece. Existing methods for the analysis of piece structure often name the parts with musically meaningless tags, e.g., "p1", "p2", "p3". Given a sequence of these tags as an input, the proposed system assigns musically more meaningful labels to these; e.g., given the input "p1, p2, p3, p2, p3" the system might produce "intro, verse, chorus, verse, chorus". The label assignment is chosen by scoring the resulting label sequences with Markov models. Both traditional and variable-order Markov models are evaluated for the sequence modelling. Search over the label permutations is done with N-best variant of token passing algorithm. The proposed method is evaluated with leave-one-out cross-validations on two large manually annotated data sets of popular music. The results show that Markov models perform well in the desired task.

1 Introduction

Western popular music pieces often follow a sectional form in which the piece is constructed from shorter units. These units, or musical parts, may have distinct roles on the structure of the piece, and they can be named based on this role, for example, as "chorus" or "verse". Some of the parts may have several occurrences during the piece (e.g., "chorus") while some may occur only once (e.g., "intro").

To date, several methods have been proposed to perform automatic analysis of the structure of a musical piece from audio input, see [1] or [2] for a review. Majority of the methods do not assign musically meaningful labels to the structural parts they locate. Instead, they just provide information about the order, possible repetitions, and temporal boundaries of the found parts. There also exist a few methods that utilise musical models in the analysis, and the resulting structure descriptions have musically meaningful labels attached to the found parts [3,4].

The musical piece structure can be used, for example, in a music player user interface allowing the user to navigate within the piece based on musical parts [5]. The results of a user study with a music player having such a navigation ability suggest that the parts should be labelled meaningfully. The additional information of knowing which of the parts is for instance "chorus" and which is "solo" was judged to be valuable [6].

S. Ystad, R. Kronland-Martinet, and K. Jensen (Eds.): CMMR 2008, LNCS 5493, pp. 166–176, 2009.

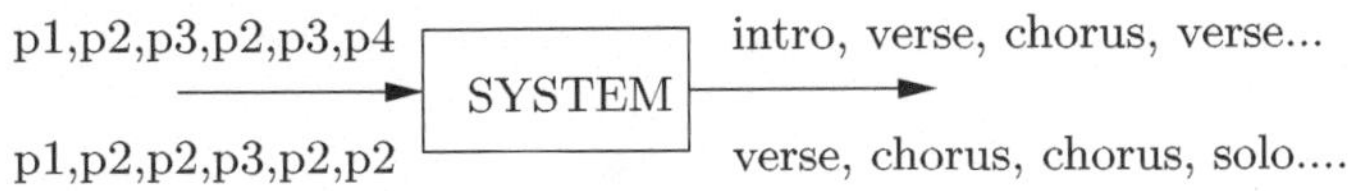

p1,p2,p3,p2,p3,p4 ──────▶ | SYSTEM | ──────▶ intro, verse, chorus, verse...

p1,p2,p2,p3,p2,p2   verse, chorus, chorus, solo....

Fig. 1. Basic idea of the system. The system assigns meaningful labels to arbitrary tags based on a musical model. The mapping from tags to labels is determined separately for each input.

The proposed method does not perform the musical structure analysis from audio, but only labels structural descriptions and should be considered as an add-on or an extension to existing structure analysis systems. So, the problem to be solved here is how to assign musically more meaningful part *labels* when given a sequence of *tags* describing the structure of a musical piece. The operation is illustrated in Figure 1. As an example, the structure of the piece "Help!" by The Beatles is "intro, verse, refrain, verse, refrain, verse, refrain, outro", as given in [7]. A typical structure analysis system might produce "p1,p2,p3,p2,p3,p2,p3,p4" as the result, which then would be the input to the proposed system. If the system operation was successful, the output would be the assignment: "p1 → intro, p2 → verse, p3 → refrain, p4 → outro".

It is often said more or less seriously that popular music pieces tend to be of the same form, such as "intro, verse, chorus, verse, chorus, solo, chorus".[1] The proposed method aims to utilise this stereotypical property by modelling the sequential dependencies between part labels (occurrences of musical parts) with Markov chains, and searching the label assignment that maximises the probability of the resulting label sequence. Evaluation show that the sequential dependencies of musical parts are so informative that they can be used in the labelling.

The rest of the paper is structured as following: Sect. 2 describes the proposed method. The labelling performance of the method is evaluated in Sect. 3. Sect. 4 gives the conclusions of the paper.

2 Proposed Method

The input to the system is a sequence of tags $R_{1:K} \equiv R_1, R_2, \ldots, R_K$, and the problem is to assign a musical label to each of the unique tags so that no two tags are assigned the same label. This assignment is defined as an injective mapping function $f : T \to L$ from input set T of tags to the output set L of musically meaningful labels, as illustrated in Figure 2. The mapping function transforms the input tag sequence $R_{1:K}$ into a sequence of labels $f(R_{1:K}) = S_{1:K}$.

The proposed methods assumes that the musical parts depend sequentially on each other in the form of a Markov chain and that it is possible to predict the next musical part given a finite history of the preceding parts. This predictability is used to score different mapping alternatives and the best mapping is then given as the output of the system.

---

[1] Though statistics from two data sets of popular music pieces show that the structures of the pieces are more heterogeneous than was initially expected, see Sect. 3.1.

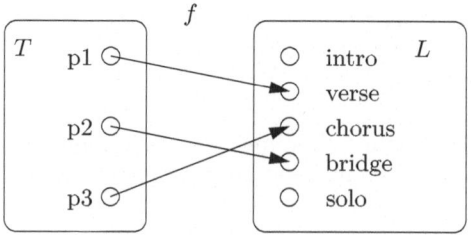

Fig. 2. An example of the mapping function $f : T \to L$. All tags in T are mapped to one label in L, but some labels in L may remain unused

2.1   Markov Models

Markov models assume that the probability of a continuation S_i for sequence $S_{1:(i-1)}$ depends only on a finite history of the sequence $S_{(i-(N-1)):(i-1)}$ instead of the full history, i.e., $p(S_i|S_{1:(i-1)}) = p(S_i|S_{(i-(N-1)):(i-1)})$, where $(N-1)$ is the length of the used history. This is also referred as the order of the resulting Markov model and gives rise to the alternative name of N-grams. Based on the Markov assumption, the overall probability of a sequence $S_{1:K}$ is obtained by

$$p(S_{1:K}) = \prod_{k=1}^{K} p(S_k|S_{(k-(N-1)):(k-1)}) \ . \tag{1}$$

In the beginning of the sequence where there is not enough history available, it is possible to use a lower order model or pad the sequence from the beginning with a special symbol [8].

The total N-gram probability of (1) is used to score different mapping functions by evaluating it for the output sequences after the mapping $f(R_{1:K}) = S_{1:K}$. The target is to find the mapping function f_{OPT} that maximises the total probability

$$f_{OPT} = \underset{f}{\mathrm{argmax}}\{p\left(f(R_{1:K})\right)\}, \ f : T \to L \text{ injective} \ . \tag{2}$$

2.2   Optimisation Algorithm

The maximisation problem is solved by using M-best[2] variant of token passing (TP) algorithm, more frequently used in speech recognition [9]. The main principle of TP is that tokens t are propagated time synchronously between the states of the model. Each token knows the path it has travelled and accumulates the total probability over it. Based on the path probabilities, the M tokens with the highest probabilities are selected for propagation in each state, they are

---

[2] Better known as the N-best token passing. The name is adjusted to avoid possible confusion with N-grams.

replicated and passed to all connected states. The token path probabilities are updated based on the transition probabilities between the states.

The state space of TP is formed from the possible labels in L, and the paths of the tokens encode different mapping functions. The optimisation of (2) can be done by searching the most probable path through the states (labels) defining the state transition probabilities with

$$p\left(f_k(R_k) = l_i | R_{1:(k-1)}, f_{k-1}\right) = \begin{cases} 0, & \text{if DME} \\ p(l_i | f_{k-1}(R_{1:(k-1)})), & \text{otherwise} \end{cases}, \quad (3)$$

where DME denotes the predicate "different mapping exists", which is used to guarantee that the mapping function is injective, and it is defined by

$$\text{DME} = \exists j : (R_j = R_k \wedge f_{k-1}(R_j) \neq l_i) \vee (R_j \neq R_k \wedge f_{k-1}(R_j) = l_i), j \in [1, k-1]. \quad (4)$$

In the equations above, $p\left(f_k(R_k) = l_i | R_{1:k}, f_{k-1}\right)$ denotes the probability of a token to transition to the state corresponding to label l_i after it has travelled the path $f_{k-1}(R_{1:(k-1)})$. The N-gram probability for label l_i when the preceding context is $f_{k-1}(R_{1:(k-1)})$, is denoted as $p(l_i | f_{k-1}(R_{1:(k-1)}))$. As the mapping is generated gradually, f_k is used to denote the mapping after handling the sequence $R_{1:k}$.

Pseudocode of the algorithm is given in Algorithm 1. It searches a mapping function $f : T \rightarrow L$ from tags in input sequence to the possible label set. For each label $l \in L$, the probability $\pi_0(l)$ of that label to be the first label in the sequence and the probability the label the be the last $\pi_E(l)$ are defined. In the middle of the sequence, the probability of the continuation given the preceding context is obtained from (3).

As the mapping depends on decisions done within the whole preceding history, the Markov assumption is violated and the search cannot be done with more efficient methods guaranteeing a globally optimal solution. This sub-optimality hinders also the traditional TP, since it might be that the optimal labelling may not be the best one earlier in the sequence, and is therefore pruned during the search. The M-best variant of TP alleviates this problem by propagating M best tokens instead of only the best one. If all tokens were propagated, the method would find the globally optimal solution, but at a high computational cost. With a suitable number of tokens, a good result can be found with considerably less computation than with an exhaustive search. An exhaustive search was tested, but due to the large search space, it proved to be very inefficient. However, it was used to verify the operations of TP with a subset of the data. In that subset, the TP showed to find the same result as the exhaustive search in almost all the cases when storing 100 tokens at each state.

2.3   Modelling Issues

The main problem with N-gram models is the amount of training material needed for estimating the transition probabilities: the amount increases rapidly as a

---

Algorithm 1. Search label mapping $f : T \to L$

Input sequence $R_{1:K}$.
Label space L. Associated with each label $l \in L$, there are input buffer I_l and output buffer O_l.
Tokens t with probability value $t.p$ and label mapping function $t.f$.
for $l \in L$ **do**   // initialisation
    Insert t to I_l and assign $t.p \leftarrow \pi_0(l)$
for $k \leftarrow 1$ **to** K **do**
    for $l \in L$ **do**
        $O_l \leftarrow I_l$ // propagate to output
        Clear I_l
    for $l \in L$ **do**   // transition source
        for $t \in O_l$ **do**
            for $\tilde{l} \in L$ **do**   // transition target
                $\tilde{t} \leftarrow t$ // copy token
                if $\exists j : R_j = R_k, j \in [1, k-1]$ **then**
                    if $\tilde{t}.f(R_k) = \tilde{l}$ **then**
                        $\tilde{t}.p \leftarrow \tilde{t}.p \times p(\tilde{t}.f(R_k)|\tilde{t}.f(R_{1:(k-1)}))$ // N-gram probability
                    else
                        $\tilde{t}.p \leftarrow 0$
                else
                    if $\forall j : \tilde{t}.f(R_j) \neq \tilde{l}, j \in [1, k-1]$ **then**
                      Set $\tilde{t}.f(R_k) \leftarrow \tilde{l}$
                      $\tilde{t}.p \leftarrow \tilde{t}.p \times p(\tilde{t}.f(R_k)|\tilde{t}.f(R_{1:(k-1)}))$
                    else
                        $\tilde{t}.p \leftarrow 0$
                Insert $\tilde{t}$ to $I_{\tilde{l}}$
    for $l \in L$ **do**
        Retain M best tokens in I_l
for $l \in L$ **do**
    $O_l \leftarrow I_l$
    for $t \in O_l$ **do**
        $t.p \leftarrow t.p \times \pi_E(l)$
Select token $\hat{t}$ with the largest $t.p$
return $\hat{t}.f$

---

function of the number of possible states and the length of used history (given A possible states and history length of N, there exist A^N probabilities to be estimated). It may happen that not all of the sequences of the required length occur in the training data. This situation can be handled by back-off (using shorter context at those cases), or by smoothing (assigning a small amount of the total probability mass to the events not encountered in the training material).

In some cases, it is possible that increasing the length of the context does not provide any information compared to the shorter history. Variable-order Markov models (VMMs) have been proposed to replace traditional N-grams. Instead of using a fixed history, VMMs try to deduce the length of the usable context from the data. If increasing the length of the context does not improve the prediction, then only the shorter context is used. VMMs can be used to calculate the total probability of the sequence in the same manner as in (1), but using a variable context length instead of fixed N [10].

3   Evaluations

Performance of the labelling method was evaluated in simulations using structural descriptions from real music pieces.

3.1   Data

The method was evaluated on two separate data sets. The first, *TUTstructure07*, was collected at Tampere University of Technology. The database contains a total of 557 pieces sampling the popular music genre from 1980's to present day.[3] The musical structure of each piece was manually annotated. The annotation consists of temporal segmentation of the piece into musical parts and naming each of the parts with musically meaningful labels. The annotations were done by two research assistants with some musical background. The second data set, *UPF Beatles*, consists of 174 songs by The Beatles. The original piece structures were annotated by musicologist Alan W. Pollack [7], and the segmentation time stamps were added at Universitat Pompeu Fabra (UPF)[4].

Though many of the forms are thought to be often occurring or stereotypical for music from pop/rock genre, the statistics from the data sets do not support this fully. In TUTstructure07, the label sequences vary a lot. The three most frequently occurring structures are

- "intro", "verse", "chorus", "verse", "chorus", "C", "chorus", "outro"
- "intro", "A", "A", "B", "A", "solo", "B", "A", "outro"
- "intro", "verse", "chorus", "verse", "chorus", "chorus", "outro",

each occurring four times in the data set. 524 (94%) of the label sequences are unique.

With UPF Beatles, there is a clearer top, but still there is a large body of sequences occurring only once in the data set. The most frequent label sequence is

- "intro", "verse", "verse", "bridge", "verse", "bridge", "verse", "outro",

occurring seventeen times in the data set. 135 (78%) of the label sequences are unique.

---

[3] List of the pieces is available at
    <http://www.cs.tut.fi/sgn/arg/paulus/TUTstructure07_files.html>

[4] <http://www.iua.upf.edu/%7Eperfe/annotations/sections/license.html>

3.2   Training the Models

Transition probabilities for the models were trained using the data sets. Each label sequence representing the structure of a piece was augmented with special labels "BEG" in the beginning, and "END" in the end. After the augmentation, the total number of occurrences of each label in the data set was counted. Because there exists a large number of unique labels, some of which occur only once in the whole data set, the size of the label alphabet was reduced by using only the labels that cover 90% of all occurrences. The remaining labels were replaced with an artificial label "MISC". The zero-probability problem was addressed by using Witten-Bell discounting (Method C in [11]), except for the VMMs.

In the original data sets, there were 82 and 52 unique labels (without the augmentation labels "BEG", "END", and "MISC") in the data set of TUT-structure07 and UPF Beatles, respectively. After augmentation and set reduction the label set sizes were 15 and 10. On the average, there were 6.0 unique labels and 12.1 label occurrences (musical parts) in a piece in TUTstructure07. The same statistics for UPF Beatles were 4.6 and 8.6. This suggests that the pieces in TUTstructure07 were more complex or they have been annotated on a finer level.

3.3   Simulation Setup

In simulations, the structural annotations from the data base were taken. The original label sequences (with the "MISC" substitution) was taken as the ground truth, while the input to the labelling algorithm was generated by replacing the labels with letters.

To avoid overlap in train and test sets whilst utilising as much of the data as possible, simulations were run using leave-one-out cross-validation scheme. In each cross-validation iteration one of the pieces in the data set was left as the test case while the Markov models were trained using all the other pieces. This way the model never saw the piece it was trying to label.

With conventional N-grams, the length of the Markov chain was varied from 1 to 5, i.e., from using just prior probabilities for the labels to utilising context of length 4. With VMMs, several different algorithms were tested, including: decomposed context tree weighting (DCTW), prediction by partial matching - method C, and a variant of Lempel-Ziv prediction algorithm. The implementations for these were provided by [12]. It was noted that DCTW worked the best of these three, and the result are presented only for it. The maximum context length for VMMs was set to 5. Also the maximum context lengths of 3 and 10 were tested, but the former deteriorated the results and the latter produced practically identical results with the chosen parameter value.

3.4   Evaluation Metrics

When evaluating the labelling result, confusion matrix C for the labels is calculated. The result of the best mapping function applied to the input sequence

Table 1. Performance comparison on TUTstructure07 with traditional Markov models of different order. The best VMM result is given for comparison. The given values are the average hit rates in percents. The row *average* is the total average of correct part labels. The best result on each row is typeset with bold.

label	N=1	N=2	N=3	N=4	N=5	VMM
chorus	68.1	76.3	**80.8**	76.6	74.9	78.5
verse	42.3	62.4	64.4	64.9	**66.0**	66.0
bridge	17.7	38.6	45.6	**47.4**	44.4	43.7
intro	27.6	97.6	**98.2**	97.8	97.8	96.4
pre-verse	4.2	40.7	**46.3**	43.3	41.7	43.3
outro	13.9	98.3	**98.6**	97.8	92.1	98.3
c	0.0	38.0	42.1	47.4	**54.8**	49.3
theme	0.0	0.0	2.7	**4.4**	3.3	3.3
solo	0.0	4.4	7.2	16.0	**18.2**	14.9
chorus_a	0.0	0.0	7.5	**15.7**	11.2	3.0
a	0.0	0.0	**32.5**	31.7	27.0	29.4
chorus_b	0.0	0.9	5.3	**12.4**	7.1	2.7
MISC	12.6	29.5	38.3	37.1	**40.3**	38.3
average	30.9	55.6	**60.3**	59.9	59.5	59.8

$f(R_{1:K})$ and the ground truth sequence $S_{1:K}$ are compared. At each label occurrence $S_i, i \in [1, K]$, the value in the element $[S_i, f(R_i)]$ of the confusion matrix is increased by one. This applies weighting for the more frequently occurring labels. The confusion matrix is calculated over all cross-validation iterations. The average hit rate for a target label was calculated as a ratio of correct assignments (main diagonal of confusion matrix) to total occurrences of the label (sum along rows of the confusion matrix).

3.5   Results

The effect of varying the context length in N-grams is shown in Tables 1 and 2 for TUTstructure07 and UPF Beatles, respectively. In addition to the different N-gram lengths, the tables contain also the result for the best VMM (DCTW with maximum memory length of 5). The tables contain the percentage of correct assignments for each label used. The total average of correct hits ("average") is calculated without the augmentation labels "BEG" and "END".[5]

Based on the results in Tables 1 and 2, it can be seen that increasing the order of traditional Markov model from unigrams to bigrams produce a large increase in the performance. The performance continues to increase when the context length is increased, but more slowly. With TUTstructure07, the performance peak is at $N = 3$, whereas with UPF Beatles, the maximum with traditional N-grams can be obtained with $N = 4$. It was also noted that with

---

[5] For an interested reader, the confusion matrices are given in a document available at <http://www.cs.tut.fi/sgn/arg/paulus/CMMR08_confMats.pdf>.

Table 2. Performance comparison on UPF Beatles with traditional Markov models of different order. The best VMM result is given for comparison. For description of the data, see the Table 1.

label	N=1	N=2	N=3	N=4	N=5	VMM
verse	72.4	79.9	86.7	85.7	83.7	**87.5**
refrain	30.1	32.1	62.2	66.3	68.7	**70.7**
bridge	36.7	40.7	**78.0**	74.0	74.0	70.6
intro	0.0	93.2	88.9	92.0	**93.8**	93.2
outro	0.0	99.3	**99.3**	97.2	93.0	97.9
verses	0.0	16.1	48.2	**50.0**	44.6	44.6
versea	0.0	5.9	7.8	17.6	**21.6**	5.9
MISC	0.0	15.9	22.3	**25.5**	23.6	22.3
average	33.5	58.9	72.1	72.8	72.1	**73.0**

TUTstructure07 the use of VMM did not improve the result. However, there is a small performance increase with VMMs in UPF Beatles.

Even though the use of VMM did not improve the result with TUTstructure07, there was one clear advantage with them: it was possible to use longer context in the models. With traditional N-grams, the transition probabilities will become very sparse even with bigrams. The large blocks of zero provide no information whatsoever and only consume memory. With VMMs, the context length is adjusted according to the available information.

From the results, it is notable that "chorus" can be labelled from the input over 80% accuracy, and "verse" almost at 65% accuracy in TUTstructure07. In UPF Beatles "verse" could be labelled with 87% accuracy and "refrain" with 71% accuracy.

3.6   Discussion

It should be noted that the proposed system performs the labelling purely based on a model of sequential dependencies of musical parts. Incorporating some acoustic information might improve the result somewhat (e.g., energetic repeated part might be "chorus"). Also, the knowledge of the high-level musical content, such as the lyrics, instrumentation or chord progressions, could provide valuable information for the labelling. However, the extraction of these from the acoustic input is still a challenging task, as well as creating a usable model for them. In addition, when discussing the principles used when assigning the ground truth labels with the annotators, the main cue was the location of the part in the "musical language model". Incorporating these other information sources in addition to the sequence model should be considered in the future work.

The difference in performance between the two data sets remains partly an open question. The main reason may be that the label sequences in TUTstructure07 are more diverse, as could be seen from the statistics presented in Sec. 3.1 (94% of sequences in TUTstructure are unique, compared to 78% in UPF Beatles). We tested the hypothesis that is was due to the smaller label set (10 vs. 15) by using only as many of the most frequent labels as were used with UPF Beatles. As a slight surprise, the performance on the remaining set was even worse compared label-wise to the larger set. The average result, however, increased slightly because the most rarely occurring (and most often mis-labelled) labels were omitted.

4   Conclusion

This paper has proposed a method for assigning musically meaningful labels to the parts found by music structure analysis systems. The method models the sequential dependencies between musical parts with Markov models and uses the models to score different label assignments. The paper has proposed applying M-best token passing algorithm to the label assignment search to be able to perform the assignment without having to test all possible permutations. The proposed method has been evaluated with leave-one-out cross-validations on two data sets of popular music pieces. The evaluation results suggest that the models for the sequential dependencies of musical parts are so informative even at low context lengths that they can be used alone for labelling. The obtained labelling performance was reasonable, even though the used model was relatively simple.

Acknowledgements

This work was supported by the Academy of Finland, project No. 5213462 (Finnish Centre of Excellence program 2006 - 2011). The TUTstructure07 was annotated by Toni Mkinen and Mikko Roininen.

References

1. Peeters, G.: Deriving musical structure from signal analysis for music audio summary generation: "sequence" and "state" approach. In: Wiil, U.K. (ed.) CMMR 2003. LNCS, vol. 2771, pp. 143–166. Springer, Heidelberg (2004)
2. Ong, B.S.: Structural analysis and segmentation of musical signals. Ph.D thesis, Universitat Pompeu Fabra, Barcelona (2006)
3. Shiu, Y., Jeong, H., Kuo, C.C.J.: Musical structure analysis using similarity matrix and dynamic programming. In: Proc. of SPIE. Multimedia Systems and Applications VIII, vol. 6015 (2005)
4. Maddage, N.C.: Automatic structure detection for popular music. IEEE Multimedia 13(1), 65–77 (2006)
5. Goto, M.: A chorus-section detecting method for musical audio signals. In: Proc. of IEEE International Conference on Acoustics, Speech, and Signal Processing, Hong Kong, pp. 437–440 (2003)
6. Boutard, G., Goldszmidt, S., Peeters, G.: Browsing inside a music track, the experimentation case study. In: Proc. of 1st Workshop on Learning the Semantics of Audio Signals, Athens, pp. 87–94 (December 2006)
7. Pollack, A.W.: 'Notes on...' series. The Official rec.music.beatles Home Page (1989-2001), http://www.recmusicbeatles.com

8. Jurafsky, D., Martin, J.H.: Speech and language processing. Prentice-Hall, New Jersey (2000)
9. Young, S.J., Russell, N.H., Thornton, J.H.S.: Token passing: a simple conceptual model for connected speech recognition systems. Technical Report CUED/F-INFENG/TR38, Cambridge University Engineering Department, Cambridge, UK (July 1989)
10. Ron, D., Singer, Y., Tishby, N.: The power of amnesia: Learning probabilistic automata with variable memory length. Machine Learning 25(2–3), 117–149 (1996)
11. Witten, I.H., Bell, T.C.: The zero-frequency problem: Estimating the probabilities of novel events in adaptive text compression. IEEE Transcations on Information Theory 37(4), 1085–1094 (1991)
12. Begleiter, R., El-Yaniv, R., Yona, G.: On prediction using variable order Markov models. Journal of Artificial Intelligence Research 22, 385–421 (2004)

Tree Representation in Combined Polyphonic Music Comparison

David Rizo[1], Kjell Lemström[2], and José M. Iñesta[1]

[1] Dept. Lenguajes y Sistemas Informáticos, Universidad de Alicante,
E-03080 Alicante, Spain
{drizo,inesta}@dlsi.ua.es
[2] Dept. of Computer Science
University of Helsinki
FIN-00014 Helsinki, Finland
klemstro@cs.helsinki.fi

Abstract. Identifying copies or different versions of a same musical work is a focal problem in maintaining large music databases. In this paper we introduce novel ideas and methods that are applicable to metered, symbolically encoded polyphonic music. We show how to represent and compare polyphonic music using a tree structure. Moreover, we put for trial various comparison methods and observe whether better comparison results can be obtained by combining distinct similarity measures. Our experiments show that the proposed representation is adequate for the task with good quality results and processing times, and when combined with other methods it becomes more robust against various types of music.

1   Introduction

The recent dramatic increase in the number of music databases available in the Internet has made the automatic music comparison/retrieval systems attractable, not only to researchers working in the area, but also to music consumers downloading midi files or new ringing tones, and organising personal music databases.

In this paper we consider and develop methods comparing symbolically encoded (e.g. MIDI) musical works. A central problem in music information retrieval is to recognise copies/versions of a same musical work, although the versions may considerably differ from each other. A relevant, intrinsic feature of music is that music presented in different keys (i.e., *transposed* in higher or lower pitch) are perceived by human listeners as the same work. This phenomenon also applies to differences in tempo.

In the literature, several methods have been developed for comparing monophonic[1] musical works (see e.g., [11,13,15]). One possibility for comparing two

---

[1] In monophonic music only one note is played at any time, while in polyphonic music there are simultaneous notes.

S. Ystad, R. Kronland-Martinet, and K. Jensen (Eds.): CMMR 2008, LNCS 5493, pp. 177–195, 2009.

polyphonic works would be to use a monophonic reduction schema, such as the skyline algorithm [20]. However, even though the two versions to be compared may represent the same original work, because of differences in the accompaniments and harmonisations the reduction may produce two totally different monophonic melodies in which resemblance cannot be found.

If the musical works in hand are not allowed to be transposed and, therefore, the comparison algorithm does not have to be transposition invariant, one can apply a string representation based algorithm for the problem [3,6]. If transposition invariance is required, most of the string-based methods fail because of the combinatorial explosion in the number of possible strings to be taken into account. Doraisamy and Rüger [5] avoids the worst explosion by chopping the possible strings in n-grams. Recently, various algorithms based on geometric representation of music [9] which are capable of finding occurrences of both a monophonic and a polyphonic pattern within a polyphonic musical work have been introduced [4,10,21,22].

A tree structured comparison method was introduced in [15] for the corresponding monophonic task. Transposition and tempo invariances are obtained by conducting a preprocessing phase that finds the rhythm structure and the tonic of the music in hand [14]. In this paper we will elaborate this approach further and introduce novel tree based methods for the polyphonic task. Moreover, as it is well-known that by combining classifiers one can often achieve better results in accuracy and robustness when compared to the performance of the individual classifiers; see e.g., Moreno-Seco et al. [12]. We have also experimented on whether one can achieve better comparison results when combining our novel methods with some existing methods.

2   Tree Representations

2.1   Tree Representation for Monodies

A melody has two main dimensions: time (duration) and pitch. In linear representations, both pitches and note durations are coded by explicit symbols, but trees are able to implicitly represent time in their structure, making use of the fact that note durations are multiples of basic time units, mainly in a binary (sometimes ternary) subdivision. This way, trees are less sensitive to the codes used to represent melodies, since only pitch codes are needed to be established and thus there are less degrees of freedom for coding.

Duration in western music notation is designed according to a logarithmic scale: a *whole* note lasts twice than a *half* note, that is two times longer than a *quarter* note, etc. (see Fig. 1). The time dimension of music is divided into *beats*, and consecutive beats into bars.

In our tree model, each melody bar is represented by a tree, τ. Each note or rest resides in a leaf node. The left to right ordering of the leaves preserves the time order of the notes in the melody. The level of a leaf in the tree determines the duration of the note it represents, as displayed in Fig. 1: the root

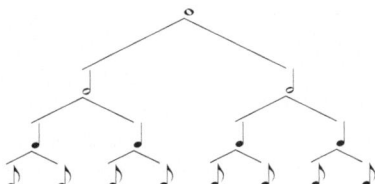

Fig. 1. Duration hierarchy for note figures. From top to bottom: whole (4 beats), half (2 beats), quarter (1 beat), and eighth (1/2 beat) notes

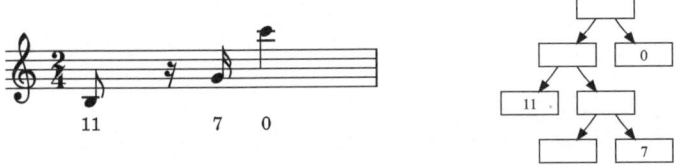

Fig. 2. Simple example of tree construction

(level 1) represents duration of the whole bar (a *whole* note), the two nodes in level 2 duration of a *half* note. In general, nodes in level i represent duration of a $1/2^{i-1}$ of a bar.

During the tree construction, internal nodes are created on demand to reach the appropriate leaf level. Initially, only the leaf nodes contain a label value. Once the tree is built, a bottom-up propagation of these labels is performed to fully label all the nodes. The rules for this propagation are described below.

The tree labels represent the corresponding pitch information. In order to have a transposition invariant representation, in this paper we use the interval from the main key of the song obtained using the algorithm introduced in [14]. The labels of the tree use the alphabet {0..11} corresponding to pitch classes relative to the tonality. This way, in 'G Major', pitch class 'G' is mapped to 0. Nodes representing rests have an empty label.

An example of this schema is presented in Fig. 2. In the tree, the left child of the root has been split into two subtrees to reach level 3 that corresponds to the first note duration (as eighth note lasts $1/2^2$ of the bar, pitch B coded as **11**). In order to represent the durations of the rest and note G, coded as **7** (both last 1/8 of the bar), a new subtree is needed for the right child in level 3, providing two new leaves for representing the rest (empty label) and the note G (**7**). The quarter note C (**0**) onsets at the third beat of the bar, so it is represented in level 2 according to its duration.

Fig. 2 depicts how the time order of the notes in the score is preserved by the tree from left to right. Note also how onset times and durations are implicitly represented in the tree, compared to the explicit encoding of time when using strings. This representation is invariant under time scalings, as for instance, different meter representations of the same melody (e.g. 2/2, 4/4, or 8/8).

Processing non binary durations. In some occasions the situation can be more complicated. There are note durations that do not match a binary division of the whole bar. This happens, for example, for dotted notes (duration is extended in an additional 50%) or tied notes whose durations are summed. (see Fig. 3). In such a case, a note cannot be represented just by one leaf in the proposed schema. However, it is well-known [11] that our auditory system perceives a note of a given duration the same way as two notes of the same pitch, played one after the other, whose durations sum to that of the single one. Therefore, when a note exceeds the considered duration, in terms of binary divisions of time, it is subdivided into notes of binary durations, and the resulting notes are coded in their proper tree levels. Fig. 3 depicts such an example and how it is handled by the schema.

Fig. 3. Tree representation of notes exceeding their notation duration: dotted and tied notes. Both 0 leaves correspond to the same dotted quarter note. The two 4 leaves represent the two tied notes.

Other frequently used non binary divisions are ternary rhythms. In that case, the length of one bar is usually 3 beats and it is split into 3 quarter notes, etc. This is not a problem, since neither the tree construction method nor the metrics used to compare trees need to be binary; there can be any arbitrary number of children for a node. So, in ternary meters or ternary divisions, the number of children for a node is three. This can be generalized to other more complicated cases that can appear in musical notations, like tuplets or compound meters. Fig. 4 gives an example of compound meter based on ternary divisions and the corresponding tree.

Fig. 4. The meter 9/8 is a compound one based on ternary divisions. The tree construction method can also represent this melody.

There are other subtle situations that may appear in a score, like for example grace notes[2], that are not included in the cases described above. Nevertheless, in

---

[2] A grace note is a very short note or a series or notes to achieve musical effects that occupies no time in the duration notation in a score. They are also known as *acciaccatura*.

digital scores (e.g. MIDI files) these special notes are represented by short notes that are subsequently coded in the level corresponding to their written duration by our schema.

Representation of complete melodies. The method described above is able to represent a single bar as a tree, τ. A *bar* (or a measure) is the basic unit of rhythm in music, but a melody is composed of a series of M bars. Let us now describe how to combine the set of trees $\{\tau_i\}_{i=1}^{M}$ representing the bars.

To build a tree, T, for a complete melody, the computed bar trees are joined in a particular order. For instance, the sub-trees can be grouped two by two, using always adjacent pairs. This operation is repeated hierarchically, bottom-up, with the new nodes until a single tree is obtained. Let us denote the depth (or height) of a tree T by $h(T)$. With this grouping method, the trees grow in depth quickly:

$$h(T) = \log_2 M + 1 + \max_i \; h(\tau_i),$$

making the tree edit distance computation very time consuming, as discussed in Section 4. The best choice is to build a tree with a root for the whole melody, whose children are the bar sub-trees. This way, the depth of a tree corresponding to a whole melody becomes

$$h(T) = 1 + \max_i \; h(\tau_i).$$

The smaller depth of the tree of the latter approach makes it the choice to be taken. Fig. 5 (to the left) displays an example of a simple melody, composed of three bars, and how it is represented by a tree composed of three sub-trees.

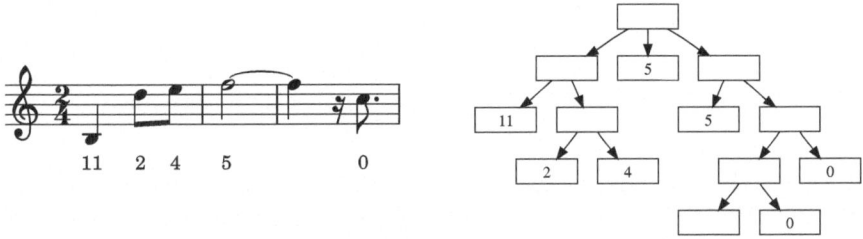

Fig. 5. Melody and the corresponding tree. The root of the tree connects all the bar sub-trees.

Tree representation of polyphonic music. To represent polyphonic music all voices are inserted in the same tree following the rules of the monophonic music representation. Node labels now represent sets of pitch classes. Under this approach, each leaf will contain all the notes played at a given time (whose depth is conditioned by the shortest one). A node representing only rests has an empty set as the label.

Fig. 6 contains a polyphonic example and its tree representation.

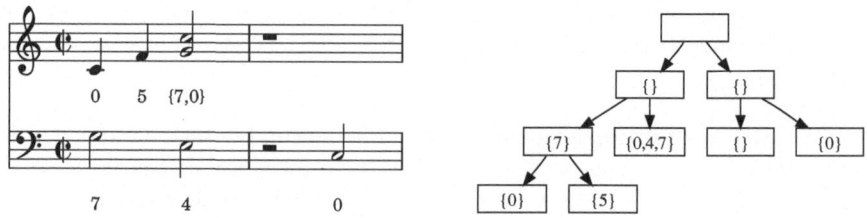

Fig. 6. An example of a polyphonic music and the corresponding tree. Note that in polyphonic trees empty labels are explicitly represented by the empty set.

Bottom-up propagation of labels. Once the tree is constructed, a label propagation step is performed. The propagation process is performed recursively in a post-order traversal of the tree. Labels are propagated using set algebra. Let $L(\tau)$ be the label of the root node of the subtree τ expressed as a set of pitch classes. When the label of the node is a rest, the label set is empty: $L(\tau) = \varnothing$. Then, given a subtree τ with children c_i, the upwards propagation of labels is performed as $L(\tau) = \bigcup_i L(c_i)$. The upwards propagation goes until level two, that is, the root representing the whole piece of music always remains empty. Fig. 7 shows the tree in Fig. 6 after propagating its labels.

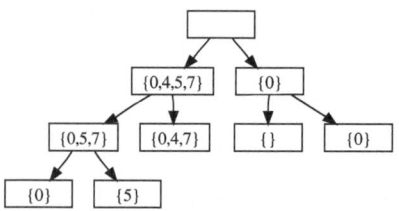

Fig. 7. Tree of Fig. 6 after bottom-up label propagation

In Fig. 7, the half note C (pitch class 0) in the second bar, which shared a parent with the rest, is promoted ($\varnothing \cup \{0\} = \{0\}$). In the first bar, the node containing label $\{0, 5, 7\}$ contained only the quarter note F (pitch class 5) before propagation. The propagation operation merges all pitches in that branch ($\{0\} \cup \{5\} \cup \{7\} = \{0, 5, 7\}$).

Multiset labels. The current polyphonic representation may have a drawback after the propagation step: if the lower levels of the tree contain scales covering a whole octave, the sets of propagated inner nodes would contain all the pitch classes. This way, the inner nodes representing two distinct musical works would be the same and the comparison methods would always consider the two similar to each other.

To overcome this problem the set label is replaced with a multiset, where longer notes have higher cardinality than short ones, i.e., giving lower importance to those pitch classes propagated from deeper levels of the tree.

A *multiset* (aka. a bag) is a pair (X, f), where X is an ordered set, and f is a function mapping $f : X \to \mathbb{N}$. For any $x \in X$, $f(x)$ is called the *multiplicity* of x. Using this definition and expressing f as an ordered set, we see that the multiset $\{1, 1, 3\} = (\{1, 3\}, \{2, 1\})$ meaning that $f(1) = 2$ and $f(3) = 1$.

Now, all the node labels in a tree are represented by an assigned multiset (B, f). Once again, we start from the leaves by setting:

$$B = \{p \mid 0 \le p \le 11\}, \tag{1}$$

$$f(p) = \begin{cases} 2^{h-l}/F, & \text{if } p \in L(\tau) \\ 0, & \text{otherwise} \end{cases} \tag{2}$$

where l gives the level of the node in the tree, and $F = \max_{0 \le q \le 11} f(q)$. Then the propagation is performed analogously to that of above, using the multiset union operation instead of that of sets.

Fig. 8 illustrates this representation. It can be noticed that the note 'F' has a low weight at root level as compared to the other longer notes.

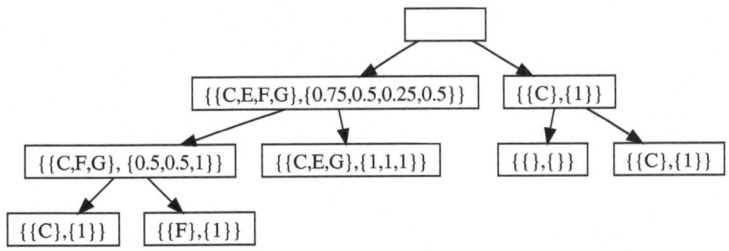

Fig. 8. Multiset label version of the tree in Fig. 7. Pitch names are used instead of pitch classes to avoid confusion with cardinalities. The labels contain multisets (B, f).

Prunning. Due to the presence of very short notes that eventually will have a low weight in the final node labels, the pruning of the trees has been considered thus making trees smaller and tree edit algorithms faster.

3   Geometric Algorithms for Polyphonic Pattern Matching

Clausen et al. [4] used inverted file indices with the geometric representation. The onset times of the notes are quantized to a pre-selected resolution so that both the pitch and time dimensions are discrete. Moreover, onset times are represented relatively to their metrical position within the measure. The information within a measure constitutes one unit for the query. The retrieval method finds occurrences (total and partial) that have a similar metrical positions as the query; local time and pitch fluctuations cannot be dealt with. Tempo invariance can be obtained by conducting a metrical structure analysis phase, transposition invariance by using a mathematical trick that outperforms the brute-force solution.

Wiggins et al. [22] suggested to use the piano-roll representation and work on the translation vectors between the points in the piano-rolls. In this way, finding a transposition invariant exact occurrence of a query pattern becomes straightforward: find a translation vector that translates each point in the pattern to some point within the studied musical work. Ukkonen et al. [21] showed how to process the translation vectors in a suitable order to obtain an algorithm of a linear expected and a quadratic worst case time complexity (algorithm G-P1). Their method is also modified to the case of finding all partial occurrences of the pattern. This is doable in $O(nm \log m)$ time, where n and m refer to the length of the musical work and the pattern, respectively (algorithm G-P2). Moreover, they also suggested to replace the points in the piano-rolls by horizontal line segments (thus considering the length of the notes instead of the bare note-on information) and modified their algorithm to solve the problem of *the longest common total length*. For this problem, their G-P3 algorithm requires some extra data structures but runs also in $O(nm \log m)$ time (with discrete input). This setting takes into account tempo fluctuations but not pitch fluctuations. One attempt in this direction was presented by Lubiw and Tanur [10]. More recently, Lemström et al. [8] have developed more efficient versions of the G-P2 algorithm using indexing. In our experiments we have used one of their novel algorithms called G-P2v6.

4   Tree Comparison Methods

The edit distance between two trees is defined accordingly to the string edit distance: it is the minimum cost sequence of all possible sequences of operations that transforms one tree into another [18]. The standard editing operations are deletion, insertion, and substitution of a node label. Thus, in the straightforward case where the operations are assigned with unit costs, the distance of the trees is obtained by counting the number of required operations.

Selkow tree edit distance. The Shasha and Zhang's [18] tree edit distance is a well known method for tree comparison, but it has a high time complexity. Instead of that, an alternative method introduced by Selkow [17] has been used in this paper. The main functional difference is that node insertions and deletions can be done only at the leaf level. If an inner node needs to be deleted, all the subtrees rooted by it have to be deleted first. This restriction makes the algorithm simpler but less accurate.

Having joined all the bar sub-trees in the root in the construction method, the Selkow method runs in time $O(n_A n_B h)$ where n_A, n_B and h are the maximum arities of the trees T_A and T_B, and their maximum depth, respectively.

Root edit distance. Since the nodes in level two represent all the bars, an overview of the whole musical work can be obtained by observing only the nodes at this level. In this way we compute the root edit distance.

To this end, let T be a tree representing a polyphonic musical work of M bars, and $\{T_2^k\}_{k=1}^M$ the siblings in level one of the tree rooted by T. The label function $l(T_2^k)$ returns the vector $\mathbf{v}_\mathcal{M}$ corresponding to the node T_2^k. The root edit distance RootED(T, T') between two trees T and T' is the unit cost string edit distance between strings $S(T)$ and $S(T')$, such that for a tree τ, $S(\tau) \in (\mathbb{N}^{12})^*$, is constructed using the sequence of labels of $\{\tau_2^i\}$: $S(\tau) = l(\tau_2^1), l(\tau_2^2), \ldots, l(\tau_2^M)$.

The algorithm is not dependent on the depth of the tree, as the Selkow tree distance; it works in time $O(M_T M_{T'})$, where M_T and $M_{T'}$ are the number of bars of the musical works represented by trees T and T', respectively.

4.1   Multiset Substitution Cost

Let $\mathcal{M} = (B, f)$ be a multiset that corresponds to a node label. We represent it by using a vector $\mathbf{v}_\mathcal{M} \in \mathbb{R}^{12}$, such that $\mathbf{v}_\mathcal{M}[p] = f(p), \forall p \in B$ according to definition in eq. (2). Then, the substitution cost c_{sbn} between two multisets $\mathcal{M}_a = (B_a, f_a)$ and $\mathcal{M}_b = (B_b, f_b)$ is defined as a distance between the corresponding vectors:

$$c_{sbn}(\mathcal{M}_a, \mathcal{M}_b) \triangleq d_{eq}(\mathbf{v}_{\mathcal{M}_a}, \mathbf{v}_{\mathcal{M}_b}) \tag{3}$$

For computing the distance d_{eq}, a number of distances between vectors have been tested. They are described in the appendix A.

5   Classifier Combination

The results for different similarity models may differ substantially. This feature can be exploited by combining the outcomes of individual comparisons. It has been proved [12] that the classifier ensemble produces equal or better performances than single methods and it is more robust against different datasets.

In this paper, two weighted voting methods (BWWV, QBWWV) [12] and a combiner of normalised distances (NDS) have been utilized. These approaches are described below.

Best-worst weighted vote (BWWV). In this ensemble, the best and the worst classifiers C_k in the ensemble are identified using their estimated accuracy. A maximum authority, $a_k = 1$, is assigned to the former and a null one, $a_k = 0$, to the latter, being equivalent to remove this classifier from the ensemble. The rest of classifiers are rated linearly between these extremes (see figure 9-left). The values for a_k are calculated using the number of errors e_k as follows:

$$a_k = 1 - \frac{e_k - e_B}{e_W - e_B} \quad,$$

where

$$e_B = \min_k\{e_k\} \quad \text{and} \quad e_W = \max_k\{e_k\}$$

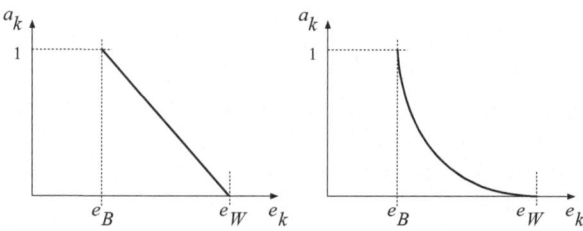

Fig. 9. Different models for giving the authority (a_k) to each classifier in the ensemble as a function of the number of errors (e_k) made on the training set

Quadratic best-worst weighted vote (QBWWV). In order to give more authority to the opinions given by the most accurate classifiers, the values obtained by the former approach are squared (see figure 9-right). This way,

$$a_k = (\frac{e_W - e_k}{e_W - e_B})^2 \quad .$$

Classification. For these voting methods, once the weights for each classifier decision have been computed, the class receiving the highest score in the voting is the final class prediction. If $\hat{c}_k(\mathbf{x}_i)$ is the prediction of C_k for the sample $\mathbf{x}_i$, then the prediction of the ensemble can be computed as

$$\hat{c}(\mathbf{x}) = \arg\max_j \sum_k w_k \delta(\hat{c}_k(\mathbf{x}_i), c_j) \quad , \tag{4}$$

being $\delta(a, b) = 1$ if $a = b$ and 0 otherwise.

Combination by normalised distances summation (NDS). For this combination the normalised similarity values from the included individual algorithms are summed. A normalisation of the similarity values is necessary due to the different result ranges of them. Given a collection G^N of N musical works, let $d_\alpha(G_x, G_y)$ be the similarity value between two musical works G_x and G_y $(1 \leq x, y \leq N)$ using the algorithm α. The normalized distance $\tilde{d}_\alpha$ is computed as:

$$\tilde{d}_\alpha(G_x, G_y) = \frac{d_\alpha(G_x, G_y) - \min_{1\leq i,j\leq N; i\neq j}\{d_\alpha(G_i, G_j)\}}{\max_{1\leq i,j\leq N; i\neq j} - \min_{1\leq i,j\leq N; i\neq j}\{d_\alpha(G_i, G_j)\}} \quad .$$

Finally, the combination $\mathcal{C}$ of the similarity measures of a set of M algorithms is performed as follows:

$$\mathcal{C}(\{\alpha\}_{m=1}^M, G_x, G_y) = \sum_{m=1}^M \tilde{d}_{\alpha_m}(G_x, G_y) \quad .$$

6   Experiments

We have devised four experiments. The first one is to ensure that the proposed tree representation is effective in comparing polyphonic music. In the second experiment we compare the multiset distance functions against each other. In the third experiment we explore the best trade-offs between success rates and processing times for various pruning levels. Finally, the last experiment takes the best multiset distance along with the ROOTED and the tree distance and combines them with the geometric methods to improve the success rates.

To evaluate the methods, we have used the *leave-one-out, all-against-all* scheme: given a problem work from the corpus the similarity values to the rest of the works in the corpus are computed, and a nearest-neigbour rule is used to make the decision.

In all the cases, given an algorithm and a corpus, the reported results are averages calculated from the corresponding trial. The reported execution times exclude all preprocessing. This is because preprocessings are executed only once, not when the actual comparison is carried out.

6.1   Proof of Concept

In order to check the competence of the proposed tree representation and multiset distances to distinguish between different songs and covers a little corpus named *ALIGNED* has been built. It consists of 43 polyphonic MIDI files of 12 bars length corresponding to different interpretations of 9 tunes, such that all variations of the same song have been aligned bar by bar: given two sequences $S(T)$ and $S(T')$ representing two different interpretations of the same song, $|S(T)| = |S(T')|$, and $\forall_{i=1}^{|S(T)|} S(T)_i \doteq S(T')_i$.

The comparison between sequences has been performed using a *Substitution Distance* defined as:

$$d_s(S(T), S(T')) = \sum_{i=1}^{min(|S(T)|,|S(T')|)} c_{sbn}(S(T)_i, S(T')_i) \qquad (5)$$

This distance is a classical edit distance where no insert or delete operations are allowed.

The plot in Fig. 10 shows the success rates for each multiset distance defined in appendix A using the *Substitution Distance* (eq. 5) for the corpus *ALIGNED*. Note that all success rates are above 77% showing that the proposed representation scheme is valid for the aimed task, leaving a smaller part of responsibility for the distance to be properly to be selected in order to achieve the best results according to the given data.

6.2   Multiset Distance Comparison

In order to evaluate the comparison algorithms and multiset distances, four corpora with different styles of polyphonic music have been built:

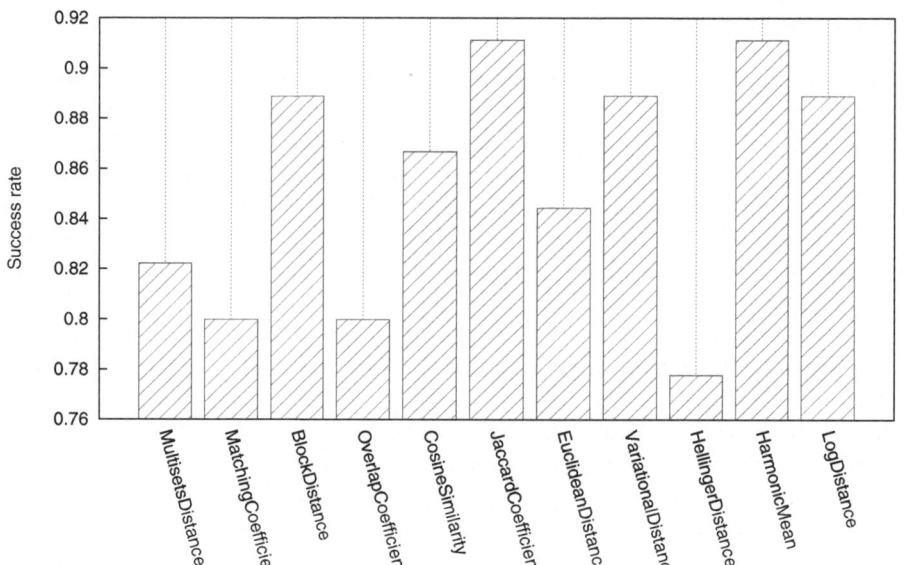

Fig. 10. Comparative of success rates for the different multiset distances evaluated

- The first one, called *ICPS*, has 68 MIDI files corresponding to covers of the incipits of seven musical works: Schubert's Ave Maria, Ravel's Bolero, the children songs Alouette, Happy Birthday and Frère Jacques, the Carol Jingle Bells and the jazz standard When The Saints Go Marching In. All the works in this corpus have a similar kind of accompaniment tracks.
- The second corpus, called *VAR*, consists of 78 classical works representing variations of 17 different themes as written by the composer: Tchaikovsky variations on a rococo theme op.33, Bach English suites BWV 806-808 (suite 1 courante II, suite 2, 3, and 6 sarabande), and Bach Goldberg variations.
- The third one, called *INET* is made of 101 MIDI files downloaded from the Internet corresponding to 31 different popular songs.
- Finally, a corpus called *ALL* contains all the previous corpora merged.

For computing the tree edit distance, in order to keep a reasonable processing time, the Selkow edit distance has been done using pruning the trees at level 2.

Table 1 show the success rates for all multiset distances and both editing algorithms. Note that the Cosine Similarity and the Log Distance outperform the rest in the comparison task.

A statistical test of null hypothesis has been applied to the average values of the success rates obtained by Selkow and RooTED in order to know whether the means o theses success rates are the same or not. This test based on the *T-Studend* distribution showed that the performance of both distances are the same, but only with a significance of a 90%, leaving room to say that Selkow performance is maybe slightly better.

Table 1. Results for all multiset distances and tree distance algorithms. Selk. = Selkow tree edit distance, R.ED = RootED.

Distance	ICPS Selk.	ICPS R.ED	VAR Selk.	VAR R.ED	INET Selk.	INET R.ED	ALL Selk.	ALL R.ED	Average Selk.	Average R.ED
Multiset	0.97	0.95	0.64	0.66	0.74	0.75	0.76	0.75	0.78±0.11	0.78±0.11
Matching	0.95	0.91	0.62	0.59	0.76	0.72	0.76	0.70	0.77±0.10	0.73±0.12
Manhattan	0.97	0.95	0.66	0.68	0.76	0.75	0.77	0.75	0.79±0.10	0.78±0.10
Overlap	0.95	0.93	0.68	0.61	0.76	0.72	0.75	0.72	0.79±0.09	0.75±0.12
Cosine	0.97	0.93	0.68	0.73	0.79	0.79	0.79	0.78	0.81±0.09	0.81±0.07
1/Jackard	0.95	0.93	0.60	0.65	0.73	0.79	0.74	0.77	0.76±0.11	0.79±0.10
Euclidean	0.97	0.95	0.65	0.66	0.70	0.71	0.74	0.73	0.77±0.11	0.76±0.11
Variational	0.97	0.97	0.63	0.64	0.69	0.71	0.74	0.74	0.76±0.12	0.77±0.12
Hellinger	0.99	0.85	0.62	0.76	0.71	0.75	0.74	0.75	0.77±0.12	0.78±0.04
Harmonic	0.96	0.93	0.67	0.64	0.79	0.79	0.79	0.77	0.80±0.09	0.78±0.10
Log	0.92	0.89	0.72	0.72	0.82	0.82	0.80	0.79	0.82±0.06	0.81±0.06

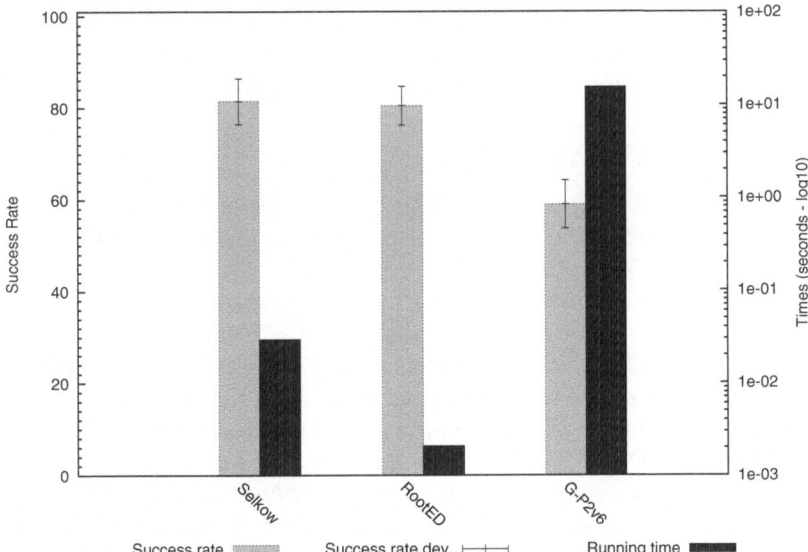

Fig. 11. Success rates and running times for the calculation of each distance. The results are averages and deviations for the four corpora. The Selkow and RootED were computed using the multiset Log Distance.

The success rates and processing times of the proposed edit distances have been compared to the reviewed geometric methods. The plot in Fig. 11 shows that the proposed tree methods performed better in time and success rates than the reviewed geometric methods. Note that geometric methods were designed to find an occurrence of a music query inside a whole song, and not for comparing complete pieces of music.

6.3   Tree Pruning

In this experiment the trade-off between processing time and success rate has been evaluated. Selkow edit distance has been used with all multiset distances. Only the Log Distance multiset distance results are presented in Table 2 as a picture of the performance of the other distances, since all of them they were similar.

Table 2. Processing times and success rates for different pruning levels of the trees. The results are averages for corpora *ICPS*, *VAR*, and *INET*.

Tree level	Avg.Success rate	Avg.Time per distance (ms.)
2	0.82	0.11
3	0.81	0.57
4	0.80	3.88

Not only the processing times are worse as pruning level increases, but also success rates decrease. This is due to the fact that the highest levels of the tree contain a summary of the information contained in the lower levels that is enough for the algorithms to perform their task efficiently.

6.4   Combination of Algorithms

This last experiment tries to explore the possibilities of combination using the methods proposed in Section 5 of the tree comparison methods and the geometric algorithms reviewed in Section 3.

For the classifier combination to improve the results, the errors made by the different algorithms should be diverse: different algorithms misclassify different data. If they agree in their errors, it must be supposed that the problem is related either to the data or to the representation model, and therefore the combination is unable to improve the results. We have tested this issue and verified that the errors were indeed diverse, so the combination makes sense.

First, an ensemble using the geometric algorithms G-P1 and G-P2v6 and all the combinations using the tree algorithms Selkow and RooTED with all the multiset distances as substitution costs has been built, thus the number of algorithms involved in the ensemble is 24. The *NDS* combination (see Section sec:clascomb) needs no training, and therefore only one result is given for the test set cosideered. From the results in Table 3, all the ensembles performed clearly better than the individual classifier in average, and comparable or even better than the best of them. This fact shows that this classification method is more robust against different single algorithms and datasets.

The processing time of an ensemble is roughly the sum of those of the individual algorithms involved. For keeping the running times in a reasonable magnitude, the next experiment uses only one algorithm from each family of algorithms, namely G-P1, G-P2v6, RooTED with Log Distance, and Selkow

Table 3. Performance of the ensembles using all the algorithms. The best individual method and the average sucess rates for all the single algorithms are shown as a reference for comparing the results.

Train	Test	BWWV	QWWV	NDS	Selkow+Log Dist	Average
ICPS	VAR	0.75	0.73	0.74	0.72	0.63±0.13
INET		0.75	0.75			
ICPS	INET	0.80	0.80	0.81	0.82	0.72±0.14
VAR		0.80	0.80			
VAR	ICPS	0.99	0.99	0.99	0.92	0.90±0.17
INET		0.99	0.99			

Table 4. Performance of the ensembles using four algorithms representative of each of the families. The best individual method and the average sucess rates for all the single algorithms are shown as a reference for comparing the results.

Train	Test	BWWV	QWWV	NDS	Selkow+Log Dist	Average
ICPS	VAR	0.75	0.75	0.77	0.72	0.62±0.28
INET		0.78	0.78			
ICPS	INET	0.83	0.83	0.89	0.82	0.79±0.31
VAR		0.82	0.82			
VAR	ICPS	0.91	0.91	0.96	0.92	0.86±0.32
INET		0.90	0.90			

with Log Distance. Table 4 shows the results of this new ensemble compared to those obtained with best individual classifier and the average of them. These new ensembles are six times faster than those built using all the algorithms, and the results are comparable to the former ones.

7   Conclusions

We have introduced a new paradigm to represent and compare polyphonic musical works based on a tree representation. In the reported experiments, the method obtained good results with different sets of musical pieces sequenced as MIDI files. Some sets of the songs were built using files sequenced by the authors with different covers of popular songs, while others were made up with files downloaded from the Internet.

The tree based algorithms performed better than geometric methods in terms of both accuracy and processing time. The combination of both approaches has improved the results with respect to those obtained with individual decisions.

The way the propagation in the tree is performed is a key issue, because it determines the way the song is summarized. Some experiments using different weights fore the nodes propagation in the tree, depending on a number of factors (harmonicity, position in the tree, etc.)are currently being explored.

The extraction of musical motives from the whole song is another line of work. The in-depth study of the motive extraction is a key feature that will be developed in the near future.

Finally, as the tree representation requires a metered input, we are now including some existing methods for automatic meter extraction from unmetered sequences, such as those described in [1,19] in the preprocessor of our tree algorithm.

A   Appendix: Multiset Distances

The similarity computation between vectors of features has been widely studied in the pattern matching and information retrieval literature [24,23,25]. In this paper we have selected some of the well known vector distances and in some cases they have been adapted to our problem.

Manhattan, L1

$$\frac{\sum_{p=0}^{11} |\mathbf{v}_{\mathcal{M}_a}[p] - \mathbf{v}_{\mathcal{M}_b}[p]|}{12} \tag{6}$$

Cosine similarity

$$1 - \frac{\sum_{p=0}^{11} (\mathbf{v}_{\mathcal{M}_a}[p])(\mathbf{v}_{\mathcal{M}_b}[p])}{\sqrt{\sum_{i=1}^{12} \mathbf{v}_{\mathcal{M}_a}[p]^2 \sum_{i=1}^{12} \mathbf{v}_{\mathcal{M}_b}[p]^2}} \tag{7}$$

If the denominator takes a 0 value, the expression returns 1.

Euclidean distance, L2

$$\frac{\sqrt{\sum_{p=0}^{11} (\mathbf{v}_{\mathcal{M}_a}[p] - \mathbf{v}_{\mathcal{M}_b}[p])^2}}{12} \tag{8}$$

1/Jaccard coefficient

$$1 - \frac{count_{p=0}^{11}(\mathbf{v}_{\mathcal{M}_a}[p] > 0 \wedge \mathbf{v}_{\mathcal{M}_b}[p] > 0)}{count_{p=0}^{11}(\mathbf{v}_{\mathcal{M}_a}[p] > 0 \vee \mathbf{v}_{\mathcal{M}_b}[p] > 0)} \tag{9}$$

The possible singular case of $0/0$ is solved to 0.

Log distance. Even though the absolute difference between two short notes can be the same as the difference between two long notes, the perceived difference is not the same. With this distance we try to reflect that situation.

$$\frac{\sqrt{\sum_{p=0}^{11} (ln(\mathbf{v}_{\mathcal{M}_a}[p] + 1) - ln(\mathbf{v}_{\mathcal{M}_b}[p] + 1))^2}}{12} \tag{10}$$

Matching coefficient

$$1 - \frac{count_{p=0}^{11}(\mathbf{v}_{\mathcal{M}_a}[p] > 0 \wedge \mathbf{v}_{\mathcal{M}_b}[p] > 0)}{12} \tag{11}$$

Multisets distance

$$\frac{\sum_{p=0}^{11} min(1, (\mathbf{v}_{\mathcal{M}_a}[p] - \mathbf{v}_{\mathcal{M}_b}[p])^2)}{12} \tag{12}$$

Note that the maximum difference between two components of the multiset has been limited to 1. Initially, unit cost has been assigned to insertion and deletion operations.

Overlap coefficient

$$\frac{count_{p=0}^{11}(\mathbf{v}_{\mathcal{M}_a}[p] = \mathbf{v}_{\mathcal{M}_b}[p])}{12} \tag{13}$$

Note the equality between floats is performed as $|\mathbf{v}_{\mathcal{M}_a}[p] - \mathbf{v}_{\mathcal{M}_b}[p]| < 0.001$

Probabilities. The next distances make use of probabilities. We have used the normalized form of the vectors as an approach to express these probabilities:

$$\forall_{p=0}^{11} p(\mathbf{v}_{\mathcal{M}_a}[p]) = \frac{\mathbf{v}_{\mathcal{M}_a}[p]}{\sum_{q=0}^{11} \mathbf{v}_{\mathcal{M}_a}[q]} \tag{14}$$

Variational distance

$$\sum_{p=0}^{11} (p(\mathbf{v}_{\mathcal{M}_a}[p]) - p(\mathbf{v}_{\mathcal{M}_b}[p])) \tag{15}$$

Hellinger distance

$$1 - \frac{\sum_{p=0}^{11} (p(\mathbf{v}_{\mathcal{M}_a}[p])p(\mathbf{v}_{\mathcal{M}_b}[p]))}{12} \tag{16}$$

Harmonic Mean

$$\sum_{i=1}^{12} \frac{p(\mathbf{v}_{\mathcal{M}_a}[p]) \, p(\mathbf{v}_{\mathcal{M}_b}[p])}{p(\mathbf{v}_{\mathcal{M}_a}[p]) + p(\mathbf{v}_{\mathcal{M}_b}[p])} \tag{17}$$

Acknowledgments

David Rizo and José M. Iñesta are supported by the Spanish CICyT PROSE-MUS project (TIN2006-14932-02), partially supported by EU ERDF, and Consolider Ingenio 2010 programme (MIPRCV project, CSD2007-00018). Kjell Lemström is supported by the Academy of Finland.

References

1. Meudic, B., Staint-James, E.: Automatic Extraction of Approximate Repetitions in Polyphonic Midi Files Based on Perceptive Criteria. In: Wiil, U.K. (ed.) CMMR 2003. LNCS, vol. 2771, pp. 124–142. Springer, Heidelberg (2004)
2. Bergroth, L., Hakonen, H., Raita, T.: A survey of longest common subsequence algorithms. In: Proc. 7th Int. Symp. on String Processing Inf. Retrieval, pp. 39–48 (2000)
3. Bloch, J.J., Dannenberg, R.B.: Real-time accompaniment of polyphonic keyboard performance. In: Proc. Int. Comp. Music Conference, pp. 279–290 (1985)
4. Clausen, M., Engelbrecht, R., Meyer, D., Schmitz, J.: Proms: A web-based tool for searching in polyphonic music. In: Proc. Int. Symp. on Music Inf. Retrieval (2000)
5. Doraisamy, S., Rüger, S.M.: A polyphonic music retrieval system using n-grams. In: Proc. Int. Symp. on Music Inf. Retrieval (2004)
6. Dovey, M.J.: A technique for "regular expression" style searching in polyphonic music. In: Proc. Int. Symp. on Music Inf. Retrieval, pp. 179–185 (2001)
7. Hyyrö, H.: Bit-parallel LCS-length computation revisited. In: Proc. 15th Australasian Workshop on Combinatorial Algorithms, pp. 16–27 (2004)
8. Lemström, K., Mäkinen, V., Mikkilä, N.: Fast index based filters for music retrieval (submitted)
9. Lemström, K., Pienimäki, A.: On comparing edit distance and geometric frameworks in content-based retrieval of symbolically encoded polyphonic music. Musicae Scientiae 4A, 135–152 (2007)
10. Lubiw, A., Tanur, L.: Pattern matching in polyphonic music as a weighted geometric translation problem. In: Proc. Int. Symp. on Music Inf. Retrieval, pp. 289–296 (2004)
11. Mongeau, M., Sankoff, D.: Comparison of musical sequences. Computers and the Humanities 24, 161–175 (1990)
12. Moreno-Seco, F., Iñesta, J.M., Ponce de León, P., Micó, L.: Comparison of classifier fusion methods for classification in pattern recognition tasks. In: Yeung, D.-Y., Kwok, J.T., Fred, A., Roli, F., de Ridder, D. (eds.) SSPR 2006 and SPR 2006. LNCS, vol. 4109, pp. 705–713. Springer, Heidelberg (2006)
13. Pienimäki, A., Lemström, K.: Clustering symbolic music using paradigmatic and surface level analyses. In: Proc. Int. Symp. on Music Inf. Retrieval, pp. 262–265 (2004)
14. Rizo, D., Iñesta, J.M., Ponce de León, P.J.: Tree model of symbolic music for tonality guessing. In: Proc. IASTED Int. Conf. on Artificial Intelligence and Applications, pp. 299–304 (2006)
15. Rizo, D., Iñesta, J.M.: Tree-structured representation of melodies for comparison and retrieval. In: Proc. 2nd Int. Conf. on Pattern Recognition in Inf. Systems, pp. 140–155 (2002)
16. Rizo, D., Ponce de León, P.J., Iñesta, J.M.: Towards a human-friendly melody characterization by automatically induced rules. In: Proc. Int. Symp. on Music Inf. Retrieval (2007) (to appear)
17. Selkow, S.M.: The tree-to-tree editing problem. Inf. Proc. Letters 6(6), 184–186 (1977)
18. Shasha, S., Zhang, K.: Approximate Tree Pattern Matching. In: Pattern Matching Algorithms, ch. 11, pp. 341–371. Oxford Press, Oxford (1997)
19. Temperley, D.: An evaluation system for metrical models. Comp. Music J. 28(3), 28–44 (2004)

20. Uitdenbogerd, A.L., Zobel, J.: Melodic matching techniques for large music databases. In: Proc. ACM Multimedia (1999)
21. Ukkonen, E., Lemström, K., Mäkinen, V.: Sweepline the music! In: Klein, R., Six, H.-W., Wegner, L. (eds.) Computer Science in Perspective. LNCS, vol. 2598, pp. 330–342. Springer, Heidelberg (2003)
22. Wiggins, G.A., Lemström, K., Meredith, D.: SIA(M)ESE: An algorithm for transposition invariant, polyphonic content-based music retrieval. In: Proc. Int. Symp. on Music Inf. Retrieval, pp. 283–284 (2002)
23. Borg, I., Groenen, P.: Modern multidimensional scaling - theory and applications. Springer, Heidelberg (1997)
24. Han, J., Kamber, M.: Data Mining: Concepts and Techniques. Morgan Kaufmann Publishers, San Francisco (2001)
25. Ryu, T.W., Eick, C.F.: A Unified Similarity Measure for Attributes with Set or Bag of Values for Database Clustering in. In: Proc. Sixth International Workshop on Rough Sets, Data Mining and Granular Computing (RSDMGrC 1998), Research Triangle Park (NC) (October 1998)

Interval Distinction on Melody Perception for Music Information Retrieval

Cihan Isikhan[1], Adil Alpkocak[2], and Yetkin Ozer[1]

[1] Dokuz Eylul University, Department of Musicology, Balcova,
35320 Izmir, Turkey
[2] Dokuz Eylul University, Department of Computer Engineering, Tinaztepe,
35160 Izmir, Turkey
{cihan.isikhan,adil.alpkocak,yozer}@deu.edu.tr

Abstract. The problem of musical query processing can be envisioned as a sub-string-matching problem when the melody is represented as a sequence of notes associated with a set of attributes. In comparison of two musical sequences, one of the important problems is to determine the weights of each operation. This paper presents an alternate weighting-scheme which is based on diatonic distinctions on melody perception. To achieve this, we run a cognitive experimentation applying Probe-Tone method. The results showed that perceptional hierarchy of pitches changes according to the interval distinction on melody, whether it has more disjunct interval than conjunct intervals, vice versa. Consequently, if the new weighting-scheme created in this study are used in sequenced-based melody comparison, melodies retrieved to user would have a more credible ranking. The details of experimentations and the results we reach are also presented in detail.

Keywords: Music Perception, Pitch Hierarchy, Melody Comparison, Music Information Retrieval.

1 Introduction

Recently, there is an increasing interest in Music Information Retrieval (MIR) as a result of large amount of music data becoming available both on the Internet and other resources. Although melodic similarity has been great interest to composers, ethnomusicologist and music analysts at the beginning, the issue have received new interest due to the development of the Internet. It is also starting to be a significant commercial interest in MIR. MIR is the ability to answer music queries framed musically. In its simplest form, such a system will receive a music query from the user, compare it against each one of the music in the collection, and finally return the music that approximately matches the given query if it's found [1]. In generally, the query is entered to system as a 'melody' using humming, whistling, singing, etc.

Melody is, in its broader sense, a succession of pitches each being heard when the previous ends. This structure is cause of a music sequence. Therefore, in MIR systems, one of the common ways to represent music data is to use a sequence of symbols [10], [11], [12], [13], [14], [15]. Thematic feature strings are extracted from

S. Ystad, R. Kronland-Martinet, and K. Jensen (Eds.): CMMR 2008, LNCS 5493, pp. 196–206, 2009.
© Springer-Verlag Berlin Heidelberg 2009

original music data and the treated as the meta-data to represent their content. The problem of content based music retrieval is then transformed into the string-matching problem. Under this definition, a MIR system can be envisioned as an application of sequence comparison techniques. Sequence comparison is an important technique in a large variety of applications, e.g., text editing, document retrieval, bio computing, linguistic analysis, and literary analysis. It will also play a central role in music retrieval or musicological analysis because music can also be regarded as a sequence of symbols. To date, many of the pattern matching techniques has been proposed [3], [16], [17], [18]. However, the topic is still an active research area due to different requirement of music matching.

The music retrieval task is to good enough occurrences of a given query pattern in a music database and pattern matching techniques for strings of symbols are used as essential components in a large variety of applications for music matching. The instruction to play a whole musical work can be given by a sequence of notes which may be completely serial or may contain simultaneous pitches. However, the terms *melody* and *pattern* represent particular appearances of such musical lines [17]. On the other hand, even though a melody is transposed from one key to another, it is perceived as similar and it is more conformable to use the string representation for this structure of music.

Western music has a hierarchical structure among intervals, where interval is, simply, a distance or a label between two pitches. The name of each interval indicates the number of scale it includes. For example, the first and main pitch of scale is tonic and the other pitches in a scale subordinates to tonic such as dominant, subdominant, etc. However, in this hierarchical structure, some pitches are used occasionally instead of the others and interval distinction influence how pitches are used in place of the other in hierarchy. If intervals have tonal pattern of a melody, the hierarchy among pitches are evaluated in tonal distinction. On the contrary, it is evaluated in diatonic distinction. Moreover, it has been shown that Disjunct Intervals (DI) in a melody has a different kind of hierarchy on perception the lapping Conjunct Intervals (CI) over a tonal evaluation in the theory of Western Music [19]. Therefore, this increases the importance of replacement transformation during similarity comparison of two music sequences.

In this study, we have investigated pitch hierarchy on perception of melody line in order to use melody comparison on MIR. To achieve this we made a cognitive research by applying Probe-Tone (P–T) method. Our experimentation showed that perceptional hierarchy of pitches changes according to the interval distinction on melody, whether it has more DI than CI. This phenomenon leads to the attempt to redefine the concepts of 'tonality' and 'diatonic', for DI interval melodies are more associated with tonality, emphasizing the significant pitches of tonality, while CI melodies are with diatonic, relating to the other pitches of diatonic scale as well, in the hierarchy.

The rest of the paper is organized as follows: The next section presents some background information, problem definition and related works. Section 3 presents the details of experimentation on tonal-diatonic distinction. Discussion and evaluation of experimentation results are given in section 4. The last, section 5, concludes the paper and gives a look at the future studies on this topic.

2 Background and Related Works

If the melody of a music object commonly represented as a sequence of notes associated with a set of attributes, then the problem of query processing becomes a substring-matching problem. More formally, a musical object is represented as an ordered set of sequence of notes as follows:

$$S = \{s_1, s_2, ..., s_n\} \tag{1}$$

where each term of the sequence is defined as follows,

$$s_i = \{p_i, d_i\} \tag{2}$$

where the first term, p_i, is pitch value and the second term, d_i, is duration. The *pitch* is defined as the perceived frequency of a note whereas duration defines how long that respective note lasts. For instance, in MIDI format, pitch values are in the range of 0 through 127 and duration is relative time interval. Formally, pitch values are from alphabet $\Sigma_p=\{0,1,...,r\}$, where $r=127$ for MIDI. Similarly, durations are from alphabet $\Sigma_d=\{0,1,...,m\}$, where m is the maximum time interval. Therefore, a musical object containing n notes represented as a sequence of numbers.

Furthermore, a music sequence can also be represented as two distinct sequences; one for pitch values and other is for durations of respective notes as follows:

$$S_p=p_1,p_2,...,p_n \text{ and } S_d=d_1,...,d_n$$

where each $p_i \in \Sigma_p$ and $d_i \in \Sigma_d$. It is obvious that $\|S_p\|=\|S_d\|$, where $\|S_p\|$ and $\|S_d\|$ denotes the length of the pitch and duration sequences, respectively. The sequences for musical object shown in Fig.1 can be written as follows:

$$S =\{\{64,1\},\{64,1\},\{64,2\},\{64,1\},\{64,1\},\{64,2\},\{64,1\},\{67,1\},\{60,1\},\{62,1\},\{64,4\}\}$$

Fig. 1. An example musical data on staff

Some of the comparison of the music sequence are used a measure for distance that is based on the concept of Edit Distance (ED). In general, the ED between two sequences is defined as the minimum total cost of transforming one sequence (the source sequence) A=a1, a2,.....,am into the other (the target sequence) B=b1, b2,....., bn, given a set of allowed edit operations and a cost function. This number is called the dissimilarity. The most common set of edit operations contains insertion, deletion, and replacement. Insertion is the operation of adding an element, or pitch, at some point in the target sequence. Deletion refers to the removal of an element from the source sequence. Replacement is the substitution of an element from the target sequence for an element of the source sequence [2]. Dynamic Programming (DP) algorithm is the most common algorithm to calculate edit distance for a given two sequences. Let us have a look at how string comparison works in conventional DP algorithm. As already mentioned, there are three types of edit operations which transform symbol in DP:

Insertion: To insert a symbol into a string, denotes as $\lambda \rightarrow a$, where λ symbol is used to denote nothing, null symbol.

Deletion: To delete a symbol a from string, denotes as $a \rightarrow \lambda$

Replacement: To replace a symbol a with another b, denotes as $a \rightarrow b$,

Let w be an arbitrary non-negative real cost function which defines a cost $w(a \rightarrow b)$ for each edit operation $a \rightarrow b$. Also, define the cost of an edit sequence $S = s_1, s_2, \ldots, s_n$ to be

$$w(S) = \sum_{i=1}^{n} w(s_i) \tag{3}$$

Finally, define the edit distance $D(A,B)$ from sequence A to sequence B to be the minimum of the costs of all the edit sequences taking A to B, i.e.,

d(A,B) = min{w(S) | S is and edit sequence A to B}

It is clear that the change operation, $a \rightarrow b$, assumes that the $\|a\| = \|b\| = 1$ in above definition. However, an algorithm for MIR should also have a change operation satisfying $\|a\| \geq 1$ and $\|b\| \geq 1$. This can be also called as a generalized replacement where $a \rightarrow b$, where $|a| \geq 1$ and $|b| \geq 1$, respectively. Finally, an arbitrary term in DP algorithm can be defined as follows:

$$d_{ij} = \begin{cases} d_{i-1} + w(a_i, \phi) & \text{(deletion)} \\ d_{i-1} + w(\phi, b_j) & \text{(insertion)} \\ d_{i-1,j-1} + w(a_i, b_j) & \text{(replacement)} \end{cases} \tag{4}$$

Although constant values such as 0,1,4,8 etc. are used for deletion and insertion operations, the most important problem is to determine how weights used especially for replacement operations are assigned. In literature, Mongeau and Sankoff (M&S) proposed a generalized approach to this problem [3]. They have simply suggested associating a weight that defines the cost of replacement edit operation. Then, the dissimilarity becomes the minimum sum of weights among all possible series of transformation converting sequence A to B. For example, M&S suggests the formula below to be used the replacement operation of ED in DP.

$$w(a,b) = w_{interval}(a,b) + k.w_{length}(a,b) \tag{5}$$

where w_{lenght} is a distinction of duration among two pitches, k with the coefficient and finally, $w_{interval}$ is a weight values between two pitches which will be come from ton(m) in formula 6.

M&S takes the weight value from tonal harmonic structure of Western Music. On the other hand, for weighting, M&S uses tonal evaluation on Western Music Theory according to which the most consonant intervals, perfect eighth and perfect fifth, respectively, and he uses deg(n) to define consonant or dissonant degree among interval of pitches (n). While the most dissonant degree has second or seventh interval, the most consonant one has tonic, third or fifth interval etc. Then, interval degrees are determined later, calculating ton(m) to remove the difference of major/minor and finally, they suggest the formula below:

$$ton(m) = \varsigma \deg(n(m)) + \Phi \qquad (6)$$

where ton(m) is, finally, the weight values of pitch (m) intervals. ς and Φ are the constant values (2 and 0.6) and deg(n) represents the interval degree in a scale.

Another solution comes from Krumhansl [4], indicating that some pitches use occasionally instead of the others, in a hierarchical structure. This is to increase the value of the perception and pitch hierarchy must be used as a weight of the replacement transformation during comparison two music sequences. Apart from Krumhansl , there are a lot of studies about perceptional pitch hierarchy. For example, Deutch [5] has explained that connection of all pitch on melody in Western Music head towards to a central pitch called tonic on music perception and this pitch bases the main factor for hierarchy. In addition to this, many studies (Lehrdal [6], Meyer [7], Schenker [8] and Narmour [9]) argue that it has to benefit from tonal framework for pitch hierarchy in Western Music. Schenker [8], using the name of *high level theory*, explains that pitch relation of Western Music has an important hierarchy which is formed by tonal distinction on perception. Meyer [7] states the same meaning through *Gestalt Principles* and he claims that only hierarchical structure consubstantiates the complexity of music on perception as a whole.

It is clearly explained that there is a hierarchical structure between pitches in Western Music. Some pitches replace with the others thanks to tonal evaluation on perception and it is the most benefit to take advantage of using a hierarchy for replacement operation in ED measurement for sequence-based melody comparison. In contrast to the situation, depending on an already determined tonal framework in Western Music theory and looking for a hierarchy in it however seems to be preconditioning the subjects. Because, MIR systems are based on actual melodic material rather than intervallic relations in a tonal structure, due to the assumption that intervallic relations in a melodic progression may not necessarily be perceived the same as the tonal perception. For example, the result of an experiment applied by Vurma [19] has pointed out that dissonance interval in a melody has discovered a kind of different hierarchy on perception the lapping consonance interval over a tonal evaluation in the theory of Western Music. Consequently, if consonance and dissonance intervals in a melody are the most significant fact of an evaluation of hierarchy on perception, it can be used separate weight values for some intervals which have conjunct or disjunct movements in a part of melody. On the other hand, the context independent, instead of context dependent, of melody in which the relations are horizontal leads to a more relevant both perceptional evaluation and ground for MIR.

The example on Figure 2 shows that if M&S's weight values come from tonal structure of Western Music are used for four different melodies in ED measurement, the first melody is zero distance (i.e., exact match) to the query, while the other melodies are dissimilar to the first melody 1.2 for A#, 1.7 for D, 2 for D# switches, respectively, whereas the expectation is that melody (b) should be ranked the last among the sample melodies due to the diatonic evaluation on perception.

Fig. 2. According to query and database example of MIR, in ED measurement M&S ranking results and expected results on perception of hierarchical structure of Western Music

3   Experimentation on Interval Distinction

The purpose of the experiment is to establish a new weighting-scheme that shows the values of pitch hierarchy in perception of Western Music. The values on the resulting scheme can be used replacement operations of melody comparison in DP as a weight. Thus, a more accurate ranking can be provided in the retrieved melodies, using the conclusion of cognitive query needed for direct MIR in the ED measurement switching of sequence comparisons in particular.

In this experiment, we have used the Probe – Tone (PT) method. PT method is based on replacing one or more pitches of a given stimulus with all the pitches in the chromatic scale, one by one. Each pitch of chromatic scale is called PT. The most important feature of PT method is to have the subjects put every PT in a rank on paper following the probing. Ranking goes from the most similar to the least. The data provided are evaluated through statistics method.

Experimental stimulus consists of four original melodies (*main melody*) in Fig.3, with two groups named DI and CI represent disjunct intervals and conjunct interval, respectively. Each main melody, after original one, is to have subjects listen with only one PT exchange. Thus, subjects listen to whole 13 different melodies randomly for only one main melody of each group, and make a decision how much similar to original melody or not.

In this experiment, we use a single personal computer equipped with a professional headphone, and running software with an interface in Cubase SX. Subjects sit in front of a table and they use a professional studio headphone connected to the computer which is placed in reverse position toward the subject. Each subject listens to a stimulus through Cubase SX as separate sessions. The experiment is scheduled allowing the subjects to follow one another.

The number of subjects is 20 consisting of students and faculty members in the department of musicology, at Dokuz Eylul University. Validation of subjects is made according to the 'control pitch' which is same as the pitch in the original melody. If anyone of the subjects doesn't perceive that the melody included in the control pitch matches to the original melody, he/she is not taken into account in evaluation.

Fig.3. Experimental stimulus with four original melodies separated two groups named DI and CI. For each melody, only one pitch (or note) has been taken PT to their places.

For each melody, subjects are given a 'measurement sheet' including scales on which subjects mark a PT number from the most similar to dissimilar, or left to right, comparing the original melody to the PT melody. As 13 melodies consist of 1 original and 12 PT, there are 13 markings, or numbers, on a scale.

4   Evaluation and Discussion

Table 1 shows the mean ratings for 13 PT in the experiment averaged across subjects within four main melodies of two groups.

Table 1. Mean Ratings of experiment results

M	N	C	C#	D	D#	E	F	F#	G	G#	A	A#	B	C'
DI 1	19	52,4	78,9	65,6	70,6	85,3	ϕ	54,0	71,5	54,8	57,9	41,8	65,6	90,8
DI 2	20	85,8	50,8	68,5	ϕ	89,5	69,5	71,0	74,8	61,3	55,0	62,3	60,3	61,5
CI 1	19	75,6	54,0	60,9	55,9	78,1	75,1	56,5	ϕ	64,3	77,3	71,7	50,4	69,5
CI 2	17	ϕ	58,8	79,2	71,3	71,6	73,7	68,5	45,4	48,8	72,6	45,1	55,1	49,8

M: Main Melody, N: Number of Subject, ϕ: Exchanged Pitch on Main Melody, C ~ C'= Notes

After calculating the average value, a series of statistical tests are performed to determine the existence or non-existence of reliability among the average. First, Kendall's Agreement Coefficient (W) is calculated. Second, as the cases in which subjects are more than 7 require questioning sense of W value according to Kendall, Chi-Squire (x^2) and Probability of Disagreement (p) are calculated. If x^2 is higher than %50 and p equals .00, the reliability among the values is significant. This provides to establish a more reliable basis for measurement of results of DI and CI. Table 2 shows the sum of arguments above.

Table 2. The results of agreement among subjects

Main Melodies	N	W	x^2	p
DI 1	19	0,58	122,09	0.005
DI 2	20	0,4	91	0.005
CI 1	19	0,27	58,2	0.005
CI 2	17	0,34	63,69	0.005

N: Number of Subject, W: Kendall's Agreement Coefficient, x^2: Chi-Square, p: Probability of Disagreement

As a last one, we use the factor analysis to fix whether an existing group between P-T pitches called variables or not. The purpose of factor analysis is to discover simple patterns in the pattern of relationships among the variables. In particular, it seeks to group if the observed variables can be explained largely or entirely in terms of a much smaller number of variables called factors.

The first condition in factor analysis, the variables higher than Eigen value of 1 can explain at least %50 of the feature to be grouped. If it is below %50, this shows that the factor analysis cannot be applied for experiment. All the values in this experiment are higher than % 73 and Table 3 shows the statistical results of factor analysis for four main melodies with two groups in this experiment.

Table 3. The results of factor analysis

CI 1	FACTOR				
	1	2	3	4	
E	-.798	.392	.109	.261	
A#	.690	.600	.176		
F	-.629	-.377	.291		
C'	.623	.496		.390	
C	-.590	.544	-.265		
D	-.530	-.464	.325	-.205	
B	.520		.375		
A	.293	-.732	.326	.229	
G#	.519	-.622	-.144		
C#	-.181		-.790	.321	
F#	.318	-.223	-.617	-.585	
D#		.554	.288	-.601	

CI 2	FACTOR			
	1	2	3	4
B	-.815	,194		-.292
A#	-.805	-.103	,443	,215
D	-,751	-,214	-,523	,217
F	,714		-,303	-,415
E	,631		,206	
G	,236	-,824	-,377	
C'	,355	,789	-,245	
D#	-,369	,750	-,195	-,150
C#	,504	,589	,311	
A	,120	-,120	,839	,349
G#	,114	-,573	,366	-,662
F#	,447	-,270	-,220	,644

DI 1	FACTOR				
	1	2	3	4	5
B	.735	-.284	.450	-.173	
A	-.726	.213	.159	-.452	.276
A#	-.710	-.248	.481	-.205	
G#	.617	-.331	-.263	-.213	.486
C#	-.602	-.434	-.484		-.339
E		.735		-.104	-.139
D	.327	.660	-.198	-.404	.115
D#	.621	-.638			
C'	.307	.343	.633	.340	.264
G	.306	.439	-.629	.358	.155
C	-.389		.157	.811	.269
F#	.474	.254	.250	.107	-.725

DI 2	FACTOR			
	1	2	3	4
F#	.810		-.301	.371
B	.802		-.450	.123
C'	-.735	.313	-.511	-.162
D	-.665	-.493		.310
A	.659	.302		-.147
A#	-.600	.559	-.437	
G	.135	.729	.368	-.119
F	-.120	-.700		-.469
G#	.483	-.641	.101	-.256
E	.379	.514	.496	-.251
C#	-.355	-.139	.807	
C			.229	.835

However, according to the results of factor analysis, while D# is the altered pitch on the melody DI1, E – C and G are, respectively, perceived to as the most similar to D# by subjects and while F is on melody DI2, C'- E - C# and G are, respectively, perceived as the most similar to F by subjects. It can be shown that the perception of hierarchy for DI melodies consist of in-tonality pitches. Several subjects perceive the third interval pitches as well the ones keeping the substance of melody as the ones in harmony with tonality. Moreover, the most similar pitches such as E - A - C and F are, respectively, on melody CI1 for changing of G; D - F - A and E are, respectively, on melody CI2 for changing of C. This shows that the hierarchy on CI depends on pitches of diatonic scale rather than pitches of tonality. Several subjects perceive the pitches of diatonic scale as the ones keeping the substance of melody. In DI type melodies, there seems to be no factor in which chromatic pitches gather, while in CI melodies, the first factor gathers diatonic pitches and the other factors do the chromatic pitches. Table 4 shows the sum of arguments above.

Table 4. The results of agreement among subjects as the factor analysis

Melodies	Exchanged Pitches	The highest mean ranking of pitches	Ranking of the pitches in the first factors	Pitch Distribution
DI 1	D#	C E G	D F# A A# B	No Ordering
DI 2	F	C' C# E G	C# G# A A# B	
CI 1	G	C E F A	C D E F A# B	Ordering
CI 2	C	D E F A	D E F A# B	

The results of experimentation shows that pitch hierarchy on perception have to be considered separately for melodies including DI and CI movements. On account of DI, the subjects have an inclination for consonant intervals of tonal evaluation. In contrast to tonal evaluation, diatonic evaluation is an important agent for CI. No matter what the tonality shows that melodies are perceived the context of tonal and diatonic in the event of the movement of DI or CI.

According to the results, in comparison of two melodies using ED, going on M&S's weights for CI, it is assigned to new weights which is shown Fig.4 below between pitches with DI.

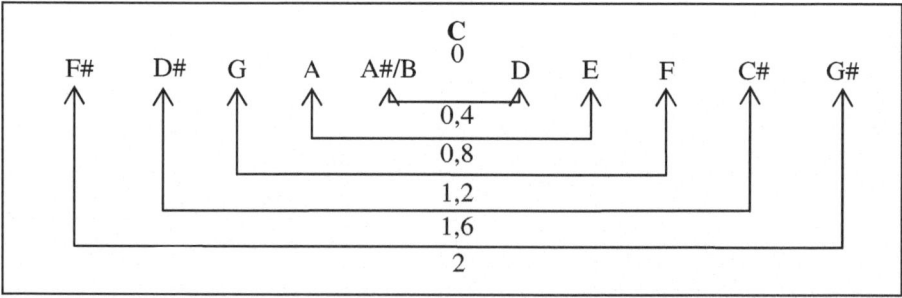

Fig. 4. New weight values between pitches with DI

Consequently, the perception is dependent of the context of DI or CI movement. Table 5 shows both weighting scheme of M&S and our findings. In row of M&S, values are calculated based western music theory, as shown in Equation 6. The new row shows our news values, which is based on cognitive results on perception of melodies with DI movements.

Table 5. M&S and our suggested weighting scheme of pitch E for sequences with DI movement

Scheme	C	C#	D	D#	E	F	F#	G	G#	A	A#	B	Rest
New	0,8	1,6	0,4	1,6	0	1,6	0,4	1,6	0,8	1,2	2	1,2	0,1
M&S	0,4	0,4	1,7	2	0	2	1,7	0,4	0,4	1	1,2	0,2	0,1

Recalling the main problem discussed in section two, it is clear that sequence comparison returns wrong ranking when weights based hierarchy of western music theory is used. The solution lies on taking DI movements into consideration in sequence comparison. As shown in Fig.2, it gives the exactly same order of ranking with expected column when we calculate the similarities of sequences using new weighting scheme.

4   Conclusion

In this study, we have an experiment, applying PT method, containing a melody which will be singing by user as a condition instead of western music theory and we try to be contented with having pitch hierarchy on perception to be a realistic dimension by horizontal relation of pitches on melody line. Experimental stimulus consists of four main melodies with two groups named DI and CI represents disjunct intervals and conjunct intervals, respectively. For each group, subjects return to us a measurement sheet including one main melody and 12 PT. After the experiment, calculating the average value, we have applied a series of statistical tests called Kendall's Agreement Coefficient, Chi-Squire, Probability of Disagreement and Factor Analysis.

The result of the experiment shows that tonal and diatonic are not an ankylosed concept accepted by Western Music Theory, distinctly, they have several potential context features when being a practical using on music. This situation has not contradicted that every diatonic scales are able to be connected with one or more tonality as theoretic. Because of the fact that, according to the experiment results, pitch relationship on music has a hierarchical structure on perception, being a conjunct/disjunct pitch movement in a melody determines that hierarchical structure is set up as a tonal or diatonic evaluation on perception. While tonal evaluation appears to exist of the CI movement on a melody, diatonic evaluation has a DI movement. According to this result, if interval distinction proved in this study is used in the Edit-Distance measurement for sequenced-based melody comparison on MIR, melodies retrieved to user would have a more credible ranking.

References

1. Garay, A.: Evaluating text-based similarity measures for musical content. In: Second International Conference on WEB Delivering of Music, p. 2. Darmstadt, Germany (2002)
2. Grachten, M., Arcos, J.L., Mántaras, R.L.: Melodic Similarity: Looking for a Good Abstraction Level. In: 5th International Conference on Music Information Retrieval (ISMIR), Barcelona, Spain (2004)
3. Mongeau, M., Sankoff, D.: Comparison of Musical Sequences. Computers and the Humanities 24, 161–175 (1990)
4. Krumhansl, C.L.: Cognitive Foundations of Musical Pitch. Oxford University Press, New York (1990)
5. Deutsch, D.: The Processing of Pitch Combinations. In: The Psychology of Music. Academic Press, New York (1990)
6. Lerdahl, F., Jackendoff, R.: A Generative Theory of Tonal Music. MIT Press, Cambridge (1983)
7. Meyer, L.B.: Emotion and Meaning in Music. University of Chicago Press, Chicago (1956)
8. Schenker, H.: Neue Musikalische Theorien und Phantasien: Der Freie Satz, Universal Edition, Vienna (1956)
9. Narmour, E.: The Analysis and Cognition of Basic Melodic Structures. University of Chicago Press, Chicago (1990)
10. McNab, R.J., Smith, L.A., Bainbridge, D., Witten, I.H.: The New Zealand Digital Library MELody inDEX. D-Lib Magazine 3(5) (1997)
11. Hoos, H.H., Hamel, K.: GUIDO music notation: Specification Part I, Basic GUIDO. Technical Report TI 20/97, Technische Universität Darmstadt (1997)
12. Ghias, A., Logan, J., Chamberlin, D., Smith, B.C.: Query by humming: Musical information retrieval in an audio database. In: Proceedings of the ACM International Multimedia Conference & Exhibition, pp. 231–236 (1995)
13. Uitdenbogerd, A.L., Zobel, J.: Matching techniques for large music databases. In: Proceedings of the 7th ACM International Multimedia Conference, pp. 57–66 (1999)
14. Droettboom, M., Fujianga, I., MacMillan, K., Patton, M., Warner, J., Choudhury, G.S.: Expressive and efficient retrieval of symbolic music data. In: Proceedings of the 2nd Annual International Symposium on Music Information Retrieval, pp. 173–178 (2001)
15. Sapp, C.S., Liu, Y.-W., Field, E.S.: Search Effectiveness Measures for Symbolic Music Queries in Very Large Databases. In: International Symposium on Music Information Retrieval, p. 11 (2004); Hoos, H.H., Hamel, K.: GUIDO music notation: Specification Part I, Basic GUIDO. Technical Report TI 20/97, Technische Universität Darmstadt (1997)
16. Downie, S., Nelson, M.: Evaluation of a simple and effective music information retrieval method. In: Proceedings of the 23rd Annual International ACM SIGIR Conference on Research and Development in Information Retrieval, pp. 73–80 (2000)
17. Lemstrom, K.: String Matching Techniques for Music Retrieval. Ph.D thesis, University of Helsinki, Department of Computer Science (2000)
18. Lemstrom, K., Tarhio, J.: Transposition invariant pattern matching for multi-track strings. Nordic Journal of Computing 10, 185–205 (2003)
19. Vurma, A., Ross, J.: Production and Perception of Musical Intervals. Music Perception 23(4), 331–345 (2006)

A Learning-Based Model for Musical Data Representation Using Histograms

Mehdi Naccache[1], Amel Borgi[2], and Khaled Ghédira[1]

[1] ENSI, Campus Universitaire Manouba, Manouba 2010, Tunisia
mehdi.naccache@isi.rnu.tn, khaled.ghedira@isg.rnu.tn
[2] INSAT, Centre Urbain Nord de Tunis, 1080, Tunisie
amel.borgi@insat.rnu.tn

Abstract. In this paper we are interested in musical data classification. For musical features representation, we propose to adopt a histogram structure in order to preserve a maximum amount of information. The melodic dimension of the data is described in terms of pitch values, pitch intervals, melodic direction and durations of notes as well as silences. Our purpose is to have a data representation well suited to a generic framework for classifying melodies by means of known supervised Machine Learning (ML) algorithms. Since such algorithms are not expected to handle histogram-based feature values, we propose to transform the representation space in the pattern recognition process. This transformation is realized by partitioning the domain of each attribute using a clustering technique. The model is evaluated experimentally by implementing three kinds of classifiers (musical genre, composition style and emotional content).

1 Introduction

The Computer Music field reveals plenty of works using all sorts of Machine Learning (ML) techniques. This domain's literature shows very promising achievements reached thanks to the use of ML. For instance, we can cite [1] [5] [12] for content based classification, [4] for musical style replication, [9] [13] for generating computer improvised responses, and [8] for modelling expressiveness in musical performances. In this paper, we are interested in content-based classification of musical data. This issue is related to the automatic discovery of what makes a human being build a judgement concerning some given melody and classify it with others according to some criterion (for example musical genre jazz/classic or emotional content joyful/sad). The underlying mental process is complex to some extent, even the definition of classes is somehow confusing, and the decision is more relevant to human intuition rather than to a thorough analysis linking well established musical rules to the outcome. Hence, musical data is concealing useful knowledge that is worth being discovered. This point of view motivates our work, that's why we propose a generic framework for structuring and representing musical data to be well adapted for supervised ML algorithms so that their potential could be exploited to fulfill the classification task. Our effort consisted, on one hand, in carrying out a study on the considered musical properties (i.e. measure space), and on the other, in figuring out how to structure them

S. Ystad, R. Kronland-Martinet, and K. Jensen (Eds.): CMMR 2008, LNCS 5493, pp. 207–215, 2009.

(i.e. representation space). Thus, our main objective is to find out a suitable data representation scheme. Moreover, this representation should not be dictated by the need of a particular classification problem (i.e. classification criterion). We settled up on adopting a discrete distribution (histogram) representation of the attributes. However, known ML algorithms cannot handle the resulting representation space since they operate on numeric or nominal values [3]. We propose to overcome this problem by transforming the complex histogram space into a nominal representation space that is a viable input to most common supervised ML algorithms. The idea consists in using a clustering technique in such a way that clusters represent the possible values of each attribute.

This paper is organized as follows: the next section provides an overview of the musical data representation in ML, and our choices concerning this issue. Section 3 describes in detail the proposed model and the whole supervised learning process. Section 4 deals with the experimental setup and exposes the results validating our model.

2 Musical Data Representation

When dealing with musical data processing, an observation is made of a succession of events because of the temporal aspect of musical objects. Musical objects are then more complex than other usual kinds of objects. Some works in the computer music field rely on capturing low level description made of MIDI[1] attributes [1]. Statistical descriptors are also an alternative for representing some selected musical features, and have been applied in classification [5]. However, the use of estimators such as average or variance implies some information loss. Another option is to represent the musical attributes in terms of discrete distributions [7] [13], which is a quite more precise measure. In fact this histogram-based representation has the advantage to preserve musical objects such as note pitches, rather than reporting aggregated numerical quantities. It is also more informative thanks to an abstraction level communicating some musical concepts that are not necessarily communicated by the initial raw data (the musical scale for example). Contributions in the field of intelligent musical composition adopt more complex representations, driven by the problematic or the algorithm that is dealt with [9] [10].

In our case, raw data is constituted of MIDI files of different sources, whose content fits the criterion of the classifier to be implemented. For example, if classification is to be made according to the compositional style, files are selected in such a way so that they reflect well their composer's style. The MIDI tracks are segmented to obtain the observations that are labelled by means of human expertise, then features are coded according to the adopted representation scheme.

Since we focus on melody classification in general, we do not have prior knowledge concerning the structure and the abstraction level for a sufficient description of the data. In [13], melody representation is based on a histogram encoding of the note sequences, and this choice proved to be advantageous for perceiving and generating

---

[1] MIDI (Musical Instrument Digital Interface) is an industrial standard enabling communication between electronic equipments, musical instruments and computers. The MIDI format can enclose music playing instructions and is considered as a digital score.

computer improvisations. We opted for the same structure for representation since it provides a general view of the analysed sequences, and fosters the emergence of some similarity notions. Besides, separating elementary musical objects (pitches, durations, pitch intervals…) within the histograms reduces information loss and provides an expansible platform for representation, and in the future for generating new material.

Data preparation for learning consists then in producing a vector of histograms for each observation, each histogram corresponding to an attribute value. In this work, we are considering the following musical properties:

- Note pitches. This attribute summarizes the number of notes per pitch class for a given musical sequence (Fig. 1).
- Pitch intervals. Absolute pitch intervals are computed for each pair of consecutive notes. The corresponding histogram counts the number of pairs of notes for each possible interval (Fig. 1).
- Melodic direction. Ascending, descending and constant trends are summarized over ranges of 2 to 4 consecutive notes forming histograms having 9 possible values.
- Note durations. Note occurrences are reported over a set of fixed durations so that all histograms for this attribute have the same dimensionality.
- Silence durations. Histograms for silences are generated in the same manner as for note durations.
- Onset distances. The amount of time separating the starting time event of each pair of consecutive notes in the sequence is calculated. Histograms summarize then the number of note pairs over a set of fixed durations.

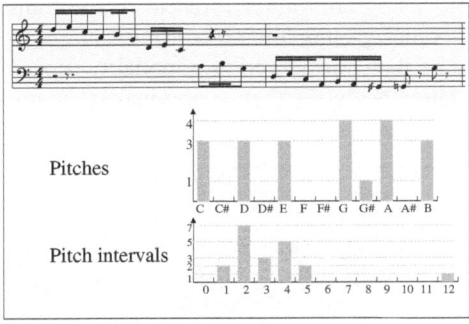

Fig. 1. An example of histogram representation for the two attributes pitches and pitch intervals

3   Implementation of the Machine Learning System

In this section we describe in detail the proposed framework for implementing supervised classifiers.

3.1   System Architecture

For the global system architecture, we follow a conventional pattern recognition scheme that implies three spaces (Fig. 2):

- The measure space. In our case, the examples of the training set are melodic MIDI tracks extracted from raw source files, segmented into small chunks and labelled by human expertise according to the considered classification criterion.
- The representation space. The features identified in section 2 correspond to an attributes vector $X=(X_1, X_2, \dots , X_{nf})$, with nf the total number of features. A function χ maps an example π to a representation vector $\chi(\pi)=(X_1(\pi), X_2(\pi), \dots, X_{nf}(\pi))$, $X_i(\pi)$ is the histogram value corresponding to feature i. The representation space R is the cartesian product $D_1 \times D_2 \times \dots \times D_{nf}$ of the respective domain of values of each attribute.
- The decision space. It is the set of the classes which are the possible outcomes of the classifier.

The objective of supervised learning is to define a function that associates one of the considered classes to an unlabeled random observation.

3.2 Transforming the Representation Space

Histogram encoding makes the representation space quite complex (Fig. 2). In opposition to conventional nominal or numeric spaces which are straightforward inputs to ML algorithms, histogram values' domains are not clearly defined. In fact, the domain of a "histogram" attribute would be all possible shapes of distributions and in practical terms this is not a suitable input for learning algorithms. To overcome this difficulty we propose to transform the representation space, the domain of each attribute will emerge from the available values within the learning data: having a particular attribute X_i, the set of all histogram values (present in the training examples) should present a structure of distinct groups (clusters) of histograms showing inner similarities. Each cluster could be then considered as a modality (possible value) for the considered attribute. The latter becomes then a nominal attribute with a discrete finite

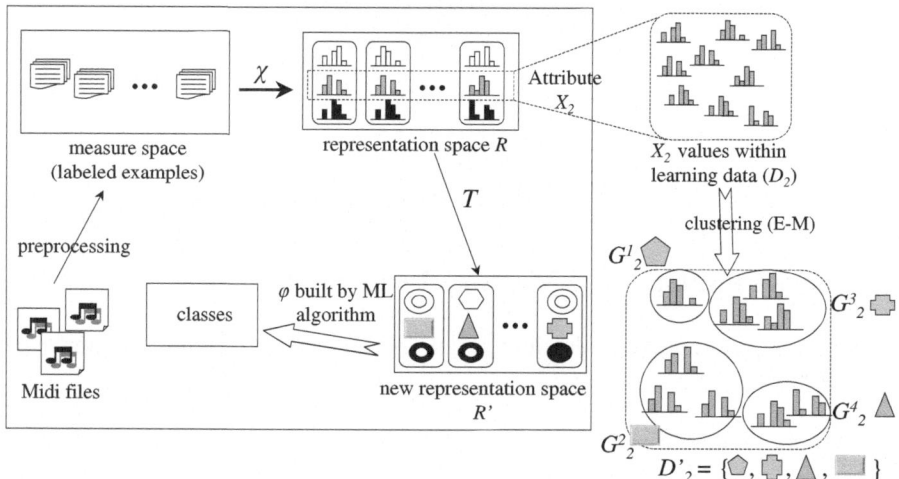

Fig. 2. The global learning process. The transformation of representation space is illustrated for the attribute X_2.

domain, where the values are the indexes of the identified groups. Then, given an observation, the effective value of an attribute is the mapping of the corresponding histogram to one of the clusters. This leads to a transformation of the initial representation space R, into an alternate space $R' = D'_1 \times D'_2 \times \ldots \times D'_{nf}$ by a transformation function T, having $D'_i = T(D_i)$ (Fig. 2).

3.3 Unsupervised Learning for Defining Attributes' New Domains

The representation space transformation task leads us to define a procedure that, for each attribute, should partition the set of learning values (histograms) into a number of homogeneous subsets. This could be achieved in unsupervised learning by clustering techniques. In [13] musical attributes have been encoded into histograms, and a clustering algorithm have been applied in order to discover playing modes from training data. We are inspired from this work to implement the transformation function T. Each attribute being treated independently, an Expectation-Maximization (E-M) [13] [6] based algorithm is applied so that K_i clusters are identified (i being the index of the attribute). The E-M algorithm produces a mixture model of multinomial distributions $G_i = < G_i^1, G_i^2, \ldots, G_i^{ki} >$ where each cluster G_i^j is described by the parameters of a multinomial distribution. The purpose of unsupervised learning is to compute a vector $\Omega_i = < \theta_i^1, \theta_i^2, \ldots, \theta_i^{ki} >$, each component θ_i^j being the probability vector describing the jth distribution. Thus, by assimilating each cluster to a modality of the considered attribute, we end up with a domain of K_i possible values (Fig. 2). Function T is then defined as follows:

$$T \quad : \quad \bigcup_{i=1}^{nf} D_i \quad \rightarrow \quad \bigcup_{i=1}^{nf} D'_i$$

$$D_i \quad \mapsto \quad D'_i = \{ G_i^1, G_i^2, \ldots, G_i^{K_i} \}$$

$$(1)$$

Having defined the new domains, we need to assign to the value (histogram) of each attribute X_i a new value (cluster index) within the transformed space. Deriving the attributes' values of a given example is made by associating a cluster to each attribute by applying the Bayes rule. Let h_i^0 be the histogram value of a particular attribute X_i from a given example. The corresponding value G_i^0 within the domain D'_i has parameters θ_i^0 given by the formula $\theta_i^0 = \underset{i \leq j \leq k_j}{\mathrm{argmax}} (Pr(\theta_i^j | h_i^0, \Omega_i))$. Hence, for each attribute X_i we define a mapping t_i that associates a cluster from D'_i to each histogram h_i^0 from initial domain D_i:

$$t_i: \quad D_i \quad \rightarrow \quad D'_i$$

$$(2)$$

$$h_i^0 \quad \mapsto \quad G_i^0, \ \theta_i^0 = \underset{i \leq j \leq k_j}{\mathrm{argmax}} (Pr(\theta_i^j | h_i^0, \Omega_i))$$

4   Experimental Validation

In order to assess the performance of the proposed system, we carried out various experiments based on different types of classifiers involving three classification criteria: composer, musical genre, and emotional content.

4.1   The Data

Eight bins of MIDI Files have been prepared each corresponding to one class of the classifiers implemented: J. S. Bach (111 examples), W. A. Mozart (112 examples), S. Joplin (112 examples) for the composer classifiers, classic (95 examples), jazz (105 examples), blues (103 examples) for musical genre, and joyful (81 examples), sad (72 examples) for emotional content. All the files underwent a preliminary filtering, which consisted in removing percussions, basses, accompaniments etc... so that the remaining score reflects their melodic content. Each file is segmented into 10 seconds sequences forming the dataset examples.

4.2   Experimental Set Up

Several classifiers have been implemented for the criteria cited above. Each classifier operates over two or three classes depending on the considered criterion. Moreover, each classifier has a scheme for data representation and uses a supervised learning algorithm. We evaluated our model by comparing it to a more traditional representation scheme. The latter relies on a "flat" encoding of the attributes using averages and standard deviations, that produces numerical one-dimensional spaces of values for the attributes. The detailed procedure of data representation for the two data representation schemes is described below:

- Note Pitches. For a given sequence, all pitches are reduced to one octave. The histogram has 12 bins with values ranging from C to B with a semitone step. To compute the average and standard deviation for this feature, pitches are converted to numeric values, C corresponding to 0, B corresponding to 11, and the semitone step is 1.
- Pitch intervals. The MIDI integer pitch value is used for this feature. One interval value is the absolute value of the difference in semitones between the pitches of two consecutive notes. For the histogram representation, intervals greater than two octaves (>24) are discarded. The histogram has then 25 bins. The average/standard deviation representation takes into account all the interval values of the sequence.
- Melodic direction. Since the trends cannot be quantified numerically, there is no possible average/standard deviation representation for this feature.
- Note, silence durations and onset distances. In order to avoid the effect of tempo differences between different files, all durations and onset (note starting event) values are converted into seconds. The average/standard deviation representation uses directly these values. For the histogram representation, we used 15 values $v_0..v_{14}$ as references corresponding to the histogram bins. A random duration d is assigned to reference $v_d = \underset{0 \leq i \leq 14}{\operatorname{argmin}} (d-v_i)$. The v_i values are computed by reducing the precision

of the considered duration feature to 1 decimal digit, and taking the 15 most frequent values found within the whole dataset.

4.3 Results

We carried out experiments by implementing classifiers using the Naive Bayes, C4.5 [11] decision tree and the rule-based RIPPER [2]. We used the WEKA[2] [14] implementations of these algorithms. The reported results (Fig. 3) are the rates of correct classifications (accuracy) using a 10-fold cross validation procedure. In Fig. 3, classifiers are labelled as follows: {A, B, C, D} are the composer classifiers, {E, F, G, H} are the musical genre classifiers and {I} is the joyful/sad classifier.

With the histogram space transformation, we obtained the best correct classification rates in almost all the classification tasks, especially those involving the composer. However, it is to be noticed that in the case of the joyful/sad classifiers the two representation schemes performed nearly the same for the three algorithms used.

The results exposed above rely on a cross validation procedure that allows examples coming from a same MIDI file to be scattered over different folds. In other words, excerpts from a same file have been frequently used for learning and testing within a same cross validation loop. One could then say : and what if the classifiers sometimes remember the song rather than the compositional style or musical genre structure? That's why we made a second series of tests, where the fold-making procedure ensures that examples belonging to the same MIDI file are always kept in the same fold (Fig. 4).

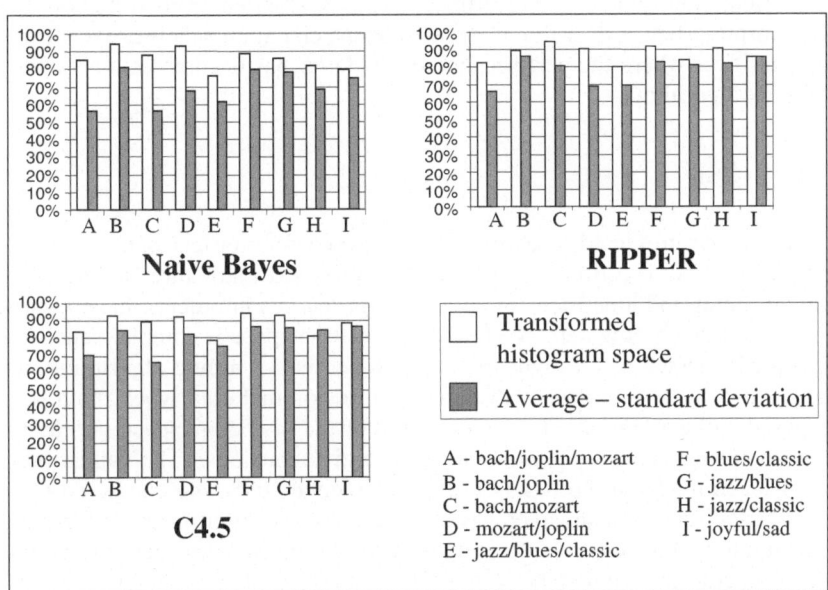

Fig. 3. Rates of correct classifications with cross validation tests

[2] Waikato Environment for Knowledge Analysis.

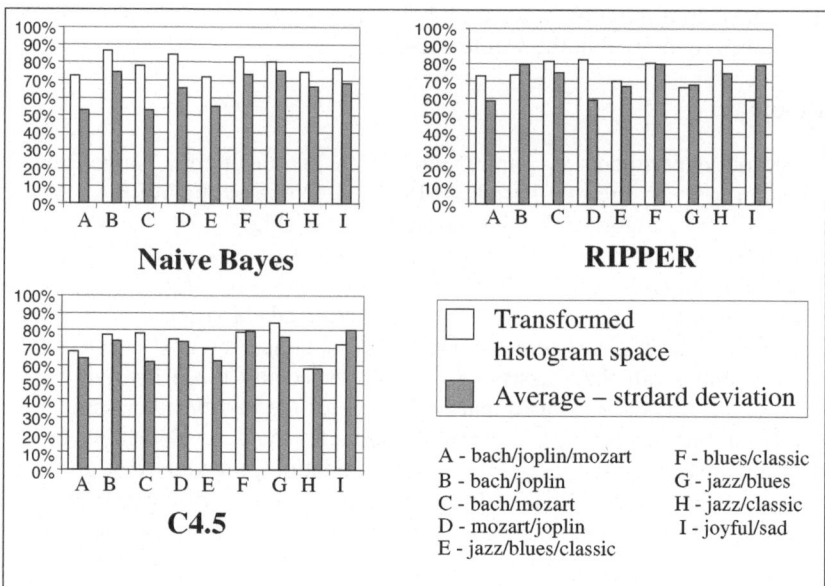

Fig. 4. Rates of correct classifications, second series of test

As expected, the overall performance of the classifiers has slightly decreased for both representation schemes. Nevertheless, our histogram transformation scheme keeps performing better than the average/standard deviation scheme, except the joyful/sad classifiers where the performance of the latter has become better for the C4.5 and RIPPER algorithms.

5 Conclusion

In this paper, we presented a learning-based model for musical data representation and supervised classification. We proposed a histogram structure for encoding the musical attributes and identified some melodic properties in order to have a sufficient description of the learning data. Such a representation space is complex since it could not be directly passed as an input to known supervised learning algorithms. Indeed, such algorithms generally deal with numerical or nominal data types. As a solution, we proposed a clustering-based transformation of the histogram space into a nominal space, each cluster being a potential value for a given attribute. The validation of the model has been made on the basis of an experimental study and compared to an aggregation-based scheme using averages and standard deviations instead of histograms. Our model allowed to obtain better results with several implemented classifiers. The classification criteria included the composer, the musical genre or emotional content.

This work has several perspectives. Improvements could be achieved by a better and more rational segmentation of the initial files. In addition, the procedure for defining the histogram bins of the duration, silences and onset features could be investigated further.

References

1. Basili, R., Serafini, A.: Stellato. A.: Classification of musical genre: a machine learning approach. In: Proceedings of the International Symposium on Music Information Retrieval, Barcelona (2004)
2. Cohen, W.W.: Fast effective rule induction. In: Proceedings of the 12th International Conference on Machine Learning, Tahoe city, California, USA, pp. 115–123 (1995)
3. Cornuéjols, A., Miclet, L.: Apprentissage artificiel, concepts et algorithms. Eyrolles (2003)
4. Dubnov, S., Assayag, G., Lartillot, O., Bejerano, G.: Using Machine-Learning Methods for Musical Style Modeling. IEEE Computer 36(10), 73–80 (2003)
5. de Leon, P.J.P., Inesta, J.M.: Statistical description models for melody analysis and characterisation. In: Proceedings of the 2004 International Computer Music Conference, Miami, USA, pp. 149–156 (2004)
6. Dempster, A.P., Laird, N.M., Rubin, D.B.: Maximum likelihood from incomplete data via the EM algorithm. Journal of the Royal Statistical Society, Series B 39(1), 1–38 (1977)
7. Eerola, T., Toiviainen, P.: A method for comparative analysis of folk music based on musical feature extraction and neural networks. In: Proceedings of the VII Int. Symposium of Systematic and Comparative Musicology and the III Int. Conference on Cognitive Musicology, University of Jyväskylä, pp. 41–45 (2001)
8. Lopez de Mantaras, R., Arcos, J.L.: AI and Music: From Composition to Expressive Performances. AI Magazine 23(3), 43–57 (2002)
9. Pachet, F.: The Continuator: Musical Interaction with Style. In: Proceedings of the 2002 International Computer Music Conference, pp. 211–218 (2002)
10. Ponsford, D., Wiggins, G., Mellish, C.: Statistical Learning of Harmonic Movement. Journal of New Music Research 28(2), 150–177 (1999)
11. Quinlan, R.: Programs for Machine Learning. Morgan Kaufmann Publishers, San Francisco (1993)
12. Ruppin, A., Yeshurun, H.: MIDI Music Genre Classification by Invariant Features. In: Proceedings of the International Symposium on Music Information Retrieval, Victoria, Canada, pp. 397–399 (2006)
13. Thom, B.: Machine Learning Techniques for Real-time Improvisational Solo Trading. In: Proceedings of the 2001 International Computer Music Conference, Havana, Cuba (2001)
14. Witten, I.H., Frank, E.: Data Mining Practical Machine Learning tools and techniques. Morgan Kaufmann, San Francisco (2005)

Ontological Substance and Meaning in Live Electroacoustic Music⋆

Jeffrey M. Morris

Texas A&M University, TAMU 4240, College Station, Texas 77843-4240, USA

Abstract. Philosopher Stephen Davies has used the terms "ontologically thin" and "ontologically thick" to describe compositions with varying amounts of flexibility under interpretation. Placing these two poles on a continuum of ontological *substance*, I extend Davies's ideas to shed light on issues concerning meaning in live electroacoustic music. I demonstrate that algorithmic and interactive elements lend an extra dimension to the existence of the musical work and that the apparent obsolescence of live performance caused by new technology is really an opportunity to develop meaning in a new parameter of musical structure.

1 Introduction

In discussing popular music, philosopher Stephen Davies (7, 180; 8) refers to some songs as "ontologically thin", because the compositions exist only as "lead sheets": melodies with chord progressions (and sometimes lyrics). For such songs, there can be great differences among performances of the same composition, because so much of it is left for the performer to decide—the performer acts in part as composer. An "ontologically thick" composition would be one in which every instrument's part is written out in detail. I find it useful to place these poles on a continuum of ontological *substance*. For example, in the case of the lead sheet, the composition's ontological thinness does not necessarily result in a disappointed audience, because the performer can contribute (or is responsible for most of the) substance in the performance of the work.

As a teacher of composition, I have found this concept useful in managing students who try to shirk by presenting shallow imitations of John Cage's silence or Anton Webern's brevity. If they are being graded for their work as composers, the ontological substance of their work must be taken into account. Surely brief or even silent works can be great and substantial ones, so ontological substance must not be merely a function of how many notes are in the score. Substance can be cultivated through massive effort, a very special structure, ingenious originality, or something else that makes it very special. Therefore, it may be argued that Cage's *4'33"* (6) is substantial in its originality (it is also not as careless as its reputation may make it seem, as many have not seen the score or

---

⋆ Special thanks to the performers who have helped me develop these concepts in live concerts (in alphabetical order): Gracie Arenas, Eric km Clark, Ulrich Maiß, Andy McWain, and Chapman Welch.

S. Ystad, R. Kronland-Martinet, and K. Jensen (Eds.): CMMR 2008, LNCS 5493, pp. 216–226, 2009.

attended a performance of it). Webern's bagatelles for string quartet are among the shortest of compositions, but they are substantial in the careful design of their pitch structures and meticulous performance directions.

Two works of mine for live electronics have, in retrospect, driven me to extend this concept to algorithmic or interactive electroacoustic music. I have always considered *Zur Elektrodynamik bewegter Musiker* (2004/13) to be a composition because it was created in response to a performer's request for something to play.[1] Around the same time, I created another similar work called *Motet* (2005/13). Both works exist as software applications that use live sampling of a human performer to build musical gestures, textures, and forms. The identity of the works use new, improvised material—the *Now* in sonic form—in order to illuminate their otherwise mute structures. I think of each work like a house a mirrors: it has structure even in darkness, but it only becomes apparent when there is content for it to distort. However, since neither work can make sound on its own (without having a source to sample first), and neither contains directions for a performer to make sounds, should they be called compositions? Are they ontologically substantial compositions even though they demand so much of the performer?

2   Open Works and Systems

George Lewis (12, 33) refers to his *Voyager* as an "interactive musical environment" that generates and performs an "automatic composition (or, of you will, improvisation)", but after this formal introduction, he refers to it as a composition. An "automated composition" system like this is more of a composer than a composition. If *Voyager* is to be called a composition, then I would refer not to *Elektrodynamik* and *Motet* as composition *systems* but simply compositions. The possibilities of their output are practically infinite, but they are, by design, much less versatile or intelligent than *Voyager*.

While *Elektrodynamik* and *Motet* exist only as software programs and neither contains explicit instructions for realizing particular sounds, they are still musical compositions. Like several other open works, every performance exhibits certain qualities that are characteristic of the specific work and are resultant from the structure of its program. In these works, the act of composition includes designing algorithms to bring about certain behavioral and musical tendencies, and the object of the composition, the *work*, exists in every performance. While a traditional composition is interpreted in performance, these compositions are instantiated. Inspired by mid-century musical developments, Umberto Eco wrote about "open" works of art:

> In fact, the form of the work of art gains its aesthetic validity precisely in proportion to the number of different perspectives from which it can

---

[1] The work was created in celebration of the centenary of Albert Einstein's special theory of relativity (Einstein, 11), and its name is inspired by the title of Einstein's paper introducing the theory.

be viewed and understood. These give it a wealth of different resonances and echoes without impairing its original essence. (Eco 10, 49)

An indeterminate acoustic work like *December 1952* (Brown 5, 4) is ontologically thin, because almost every aspect of its performance is coordinated by the performer. There are marks on the page, but the performer is even responsible for determining how to interpret them. *Elektrodynamik* and *Motet* are not thin in this way, because they contain within them sets of distinct contributions to each possible performance. Much effort has gone into their creation, and there is much detail to the structure of each, even though much is demanded of the performer. William Seaman discusses the creative possibilities of new technology and the composer's new challenge in using them for expression:

> The artist need no longer seek to define a singular artefact, but instead need develop systems that enable a series of sonic artefacts to become operational and polycombinational, thus engendering an emergent relational sonic artefact during exploration. (Seaman 15, 234)

This openness in a musical work can be seen as an extra dimension in the substance of the composition in addition to each quantifiable musical parameter (e.g., pitch, loudness). Imagine a simple traditional composition on staff paper: it is two-dimensional, with pitch on the vertical axis and time on the horizontal. While most traditional compositions can still allow for infinite variations in performance, these variations stay within a narrow margin in comparison with open works. Drawing from visual arts, this could be called "two and a half" dimensions. Performances of an open work present a much wider range of differences, each shedding new light on the true character of the composition.

When teaching algorithmic composition, I find it useful to explain how artists use (pseudo-)randomness through the analogy of sculpting. Rather than placing every atom of the sculpture (or every possible outcome in a musical work), the artist pares away the unwanted elements, restricting the remainder to a form that fulfills the character of the artist's design. One performance of such a musical work is equivalent to viewing a statue from one angle. Each performance/view is significantly different, but all support and illuminate the underlying structure. The substance of a work can exist in the "negative space"—how the artist has built structure by carving away rather than building up, or it can lie in the specialness of the structure—the ways in which it can be the same across widely varied performances.

3   Liveness as a Structural Element

3.1   Substance in Stage Presence

Effort, evident preparation, or other kinds of specialness in live performance can add ontological substance to a performance, and this is often where live electroacoustic music is found lacking. The fairly new possibility of using a laptop computer as a performer's primary or sole instrument has unsettled some audiences because of natural shortcomings in stage presence. When the performer on stage looks the same while doing office work, playing a video game, or giving a masterful musical performance—hunched over behind a computer interface—an audience may become as detached from the musical experience as the performer appears to be.

The increased use of technology in live performance has evoked varied responses. Many are troubled by the apparent disparity between performative acts and the sounds resulting from them. Others give it no thought, having become accustomed to valuing only the sound, because that is all most recorded music delivers. Perhaps a new performance practice is developing with different values, or perhaps the troubling qualities of this disparity can help us reflect on our understanding of the value of live performance. In my experience performing with computers, watching others do so, and speaking with audience members about it, I have observed that it is generally disconcerting to watch straight-faced pointing and clicking and perhaps even more troubling to watch repetitive jerking with a control interface if there is no visual clue regarding how those actions affect the music. I have experimented with pianistically-ornamented gestures while performing with gamepad and Nintendo Wii Remote controllers with good responses from audience members. I am not fond of adding superficial elements to a project, but the informal experiment has demonstrated that they do serve some kind of function. While some like Julio d'Escriván (9, 183–91) believe that younger audiences are increasingly less troubled by such disparity and that this will soon cease to be an issue, two things are still made clear: audiences *are* sensitive to the relationships between performative causes and effects, and because of that, it is possible to exploit liveness as a distinct element of a work of art.

Even when cause and effect are clear, however, a performance may still fall short because it lacks substance in its live component. There is something very disappointing about the performer who stands on stage and presses a button, triggering a looped sample. A scripted or automated process like playing this loop is the product of the composer (acting off stage, out of real time, at some time before the performance), and the contribution of the performer is menial: simply triggering events or changes in ongoing events. While the act of pressing the button is clearly related to the resulting sound, it is not a very substantial act, because the one effortless act corresponds to a larger set of musical events that have no performative counterparts. When the material triggered by that button is always the same, the substance of the composition is also lessened by virtue of its reproducibility. If it can be repeated identically any number of times, it can't be that special.

Over the time I have performed with electronics, I have experimented with mannered actions, taking after dramatic pianists that lunge their torsos into chords and raise their hands high above the keyboard before or after playing a run. I understand (as many pianists seem) that some of these motions have real effects on the sound, but I maintain that they are mostly superficial exaggerations and that the sonic effect is usually minimal. However, the overall effect of the performance may indeed be strengthened by such visual ornaments. In performance, I began to allow my face to reflect the intensity or fulfillment with which I meant to imbue my performance. I used higher-than-necessary hand strokes to push buttons or sliders, which let me feel more in control of timing, like a conductor's preparatory gesture. When expressively changing playback speed with a gamepad-controlled sampler approaching a climactic event, I began to let the gamepad tilt back and forth accordingly. I have received more positive comments on these performances, unsolicited. By acting as if I were playing a "real" instrument, it seems to have helped audiences process the fact that I actually was.

The computer performer may actually detract from the musical experience by omitting mannered or obvious causal actions, especially when the computer performer is joined by acoustic instrumentalists whose instruments demand a certain level of visible causality. There can be an intriguing counterpoint between causal performance and its effects.[2] It appears to be helpful for the performer to act as a surrogate or model for the audience in this way, demonstrating the emotional intensity, physiological engagement, sincerity of expression and enjoyment of the performance that a sensitive audience member might experience. It can be frustrating, confusing, or insulting to the audience if such signs are not present or congruent with the musical content of the performance.

I have seen this alienation in effect even among contemporary art specialists and musicians, for example after a performance at the International Society for Improvised Music conference, in which Eric km Clark performed on electric violin and I performed with him using a computer to mediate his sound. The sound heard through the single instrument amplifier did not always include the live violin. Sometimes the live violin's playing only caused past violin passages to be heard, and at other times there was no obvious relationship at all between Clark's actions and the sounds and silences coming from the amplifier. One observer, who was also performing at the conference, expressed discomfort with this performance: "If there's a violin there, I want to hear it", and other performers separately made similar remarks.

Members of my audience that came looking for meaningful relationships in only the usual places tended to see the overt mediation by the computer as a mistake or malfunction that only obstructed their experience of the performance. A more Cagean mindset, ready to appreciate anything for what it is, would more readily notice and appreciate the tension and release in the counterpoint between the live events and the resulting sounds (whether or not they were intentional). However, the effects of mediation at play here are indeed salient; they are only overlooked as a result of recent social conditioning. The fact is that the relationship between the

---

[2] By *causal performance* I mean any action of a performer during a performance that has some result in the performance, either generating a sound directly or triggering events or changes in the action of the software program. These actions can be ornamented or mannered. Other actions may be purely ornamental, having no effect outside themselves.

live and the mediated can establish tension. If it can be structured and resolved, liveness and mediation can be used as a new dimension for meaningful structure and expression in performance—one that gives new value to the authentic unmediated human experience, the *aura* of the Now.

3.2 Mediatization

Mediation refers to something coming between two other things, or for our purpose, the intervention of communications technology in the path between sender (performer or composer) and recipient (audience). Jean Baudrillard (2, 175–6) has adopted the term *mediatization* to discuss the transformation of events when they are recorded or transmitted by communications technology, originally to highlight more overt or intentional kinds of transformation of the symbols in play. It has come to be used by others in a more general way highlighting any result of the process of recording or transmitting once-live events (Auslander 1, 5). In this article, mediation refers to the intervening position of technology, and mediatization refers to the effects of that intervention (in the general way without Baudrillard's embedded implications).

Mediatization contains senses of both emasculation and preserved identity. What is lost is the aura as Walter Benjamin (3) described it, the sense of authenticity that comes from witnessing the "real thing", whether it be the original Mona Lisa or an unmediated live performance. Through mediatization, "real" live events become *hyperreal*: they enter an artificial world in which once-live moments are frozen in unrealistically extreme detail and are susceptible to endless manipulation by technology but still carry the reference to the authentic once-live event.

Modern audiences have become accustomed to granting the same authenticity to mediatized objects as the realities they symbolize. Philip Auslander (1) has carefully argued that contemporary society has become desensitized to the differences between live and recorded media, and so they are wholly equivalent. I do regret the apparent widespread sacrifice of quality for the sake of (not always legal) convenience, but as an artist, I see the playing field for expression as shifting into new territory instead of suffering a loss: as technology allows humans to communicate in new ways, structure and meaning can be manifest in new dimensions of a work. Auslander describes where audiences have placed value; it is not a prescription that inhibits artists from seeking new places where value could be found or created.

Peggy Phelan insists on recognizing the difference between the live and the mediated.

> Performance cannot be saved, recorded, documented, or otherwise participate in the circulation of representations of representations: once it does so, it becomes something other than performance... To the degree that performance attempts to enter the economy of reproduction it betrays and lessens the promise of its own ontology. Performance's being... becomes itself through disappearance. (Phelan 14, 146)

Something is lost when a performance is reproduced, and the loss weakens ontology, but is it the state of the performance or that of the recording that is affected? In Benjamin's terms, the aura of a work is lost in reproduction, so the copies are degraded, but the original is unaffected by the existence of the copies. However, Phelan refers to the ontological promise of the original performance. To "enter the economy of reproduction" is to do something that is reproducible, whether or not it is reproduced. The more that would be lost through reproduction, the more substantial it is, or the greater its aura is. When a sound is recorded, the sample does not have the aura of the original sound, but in the context of live sampling within the course of a musical performance, the sample can gain its own aura that reframes the original as an acoustic version of a musical idea that is later presented in an electronically- mediated form. Phelan writes,

> Performance occurs over a time which will not be repeated. It can be performed again, but this repetition itself marks it as "different." The document of a performance then is only to spur a memory, an encouragement of memory to become present. (Phelan 14, 147)

However, the sample that is a copy of an event earlier within the same live performance must lie somewhere between the often-sampled "Amen break" (The Winstons 16) and the return of a fugue subject: it is both the artificial reproduction of another musical event and the recurrence, prolongation, or imitation of musical material within a work. Live sampling during performance is like musique concrte come to life: it still concrete (in the sense of freezing sounds in recorded form), but it uses the Now as its subject. Live sampling facilitates structural phenomena, not just extramusical or intermusical (intertextual) signifiers. Not only does the aura of the original moment slip away, but the memory of that aura is replaced with a new one situated in a net of imitative references. Multiple copies of the musical idea, acoustic and electronic, reframe each other as particular references to an abstract musical form evoked by—but lying outside—the performed music. The original event becomes merely the first reference to a musical idea within the performance. In the works presented below, the sonic presence of the performer is prolonged and folded upon itself in time, taking along the gaze of the audience, to be continually revised.

3.3 Mediatization in Imitative Counterpoint

In order to explore this kind of structure, I developed live sampling instruments controlled by a gamepad or Nintendo Wii Remotes and have used them in performance with improvising musicians. I begin each performance without preloaded sounds; my sonic materials come only from the current performance. The process of exploring the live-sampled sound can become part of the developmental structure of the live performance. The once-live can become live again when it is replayed, but it becomes a new and distinct event happening in its own moment, Now, but connecting with (and escalating by that reference) the moment in which the referent was first performed. Live sampling within an improvised performance intensifies the connections made in this way, because the performers are not reading from a musical score. What they play cannot be reproduced in another performance. Even in composed works, I am working primarily with structuring improvised passages in order to magnify the sense of liveness and intensify the significance when those Nows are mediatized and manipulated. Replayed material can participate in and influence new Nows and be recontextualized within the new web of connections.

Through such a performance, cause and effect can become twisted or reversed: the authenticity of being the real musical idea can be passed among different re-iterations of it (for example, a theme followed by variations or a climax preceded by foreshadowing copies), it can be cast outside the musical work to refer to a series of events that never actually happens within the performance, or authenticity can be completely demolished. My goal is not simply to deconstruct the concept of authenticity and celebrate its demise but instead to use the establishment, distortion, and reinforcement of authenticity as a new way to create and manipulate tension. The elements that are lost through the mediation of technology expose new elements that are unique to the live performance, and this mediation itself can be included in the performance in the form of live audiovisual sampling to build imitative contrapuntal textures that explore the area between liveness and mediatization.

The following are two compositions of mine that apply mediatization as a device of imitative counterpoint for the purpose of developing musical meaning.

This is Not a Guitar. Six studies in mediation called *This is Not a Guitar* (2007) embraces the electric guitar as an instrument that is necessarily mediated. Its sound is disembodied, isolated from the physical acts that cause the sound, it is transformed by a series of "black boxes", and it is only heard through one or many loudspeakers that may be any distance from the guitar and performer. Despite this disparity, we are accustomed to watching the performer and listening to the speaker(s), considering them to be one seamless whole. This work explores various notions of presence and causality embedded in this construction, including the hum of the amplifier as the audible-but-ignored sensation of presence. It plays with the distance between physical cause and sonic effect and stretches the bonds between what is seen and what is heard by letting the two fall out of synchrony. It presents physical events without their expected sonic results, and it presents recognizable sounds like pitch bends and familiar riffs in the absence of the physical actions we expect to create them. This piece uses counterpoint in the dimension of liveness and mediation to create tension and release for the forward development of the music.

"Time is the Substance of Which I am Made." An extended composition for electric violin, digital piano, and electronics called "Time is the substance of which I am made." (2008) extends this exploration of mediation to include visual sampling.[3] Just as in the works described above, all sonic materials come from things played during the performance, even though they are not always presented in a recognizable way. Video clips are taken of the performers during

---

[3] The title of this work comes from a non-fiction essay by Jorge Luis Borges (4, 187).

the performance and are at times presented only as abstract textures moving in relation to the music. For example, a performer's arm or hair will often move in a way related to what he or she is playing but rarely in a strictly parallel way so that the music could be "read" just by watching the close-up video. While the performer's body is not completely independent of the sound it plays, the relationship between sight and sound shifts among parallel, similar, contrary, and oblique states in a way that can make it an effective intermedial counterpoint. The processed video is projected onto the performers, allowing their live motions to recombine with the mediatized visual materials.

The eye of a camera and processing by the computer can capture, highlight, and reintroduce the visual component of performance as more significant, but organically related, elements in the overall work. Much of the authenticity of Now comes from visually witnessing the live event. Visual Nows can be captured and recontextualized like the aural events during the performance. The inclusion of video also allows for the audiovisual recording of events not heard, in order to be replayed later, slicing the liveness away from both the sound and vision of the performance. (This is why digital piano is used instead of an acoustic instrument.) This also creates tension during the original live event, because it is clear to the audience that music is being played which is not heard. When the sound is presented later, it resolves that tension and can be an opportunity to illuminate significant structural relationships within the work.

Another technique used in the work is directing one performer to watch and play along audibly with another performer who is inaudible at the time. This allows the pure distilled liveness to function as a distinct influence in the work: the music heard from the violin is a sonic translation of the pianist's performative acts. The audio recording of the silenced digital piano can then be presented later in the work with some of the specialness of ordinary live performance, because it is the authentic performance of which the violinist had previously only performed a flawed copy.

The violin and keyboard/zither combination each plays through its own instrument amplifier, which, as with the electric guitar, is readily accepted as the live unmediated voice of each instrument. However, a computer-based instrument mediates these connections in order to distort the authenticity of liveness. The instruments' seemingly live sounds sometimes fall out of synchronization with the visible actions of the performers. In other moments, completely different material is heard, or the computer freely crossfades between the live performance and previously recorded moments. The computer can also impersonate the instruments by playing their sampled sound through the amplifiers at times when the performers are not playing. Finally, the performers may be seen to be playing but not be heard until that captured sound material is introduced at a later time in the performance.

Three loudspeakers are used in addition to the instrument amplifiers. One stereo pair will represent the main voice of the computer, through which clearly-manipulated material recorded earlier in the performance will be played in a live sampler instrument controlled primarily by game controllers including wireless Nintendo Wii Remotes. The live sampler instrument enables the performer to recompose sound material captured during performance, recontextualizing materials in new settings, recombining it with other recorded material, and warping it into new material that is organically related to previous events. It enables the Now to be captured, rewritten, and smeared across time. A third speaker is placed offstage for an obviously distant sound, which is used to play material in a way that is physically detached from the live Here and Now.

The visual artist has a tripod-mounted camera and video processing computer. During the performance, the visual artist is given instructions to focus the camera on some movement related to the music, for example the violin bridge as the bow glides by it or hands on the keyboard. More abstract visual sources include the arm, waist, or hair of the performer. Like the sounds in the performance, the visual material may be presented live, falling in and out of synchronization, or stored and replayed later. Visual material captured from the performers is represented and transformed again by using the performers as a partial projection surface, which can be recaptured by the camera. Visual material presented is also transformed by a live video processing instrument controlled by the visual artist using Nintendo Wii Remotes.

The vision of the performance is itself a visual dimension in counterpoint with the sounds and mediatized video of the performance. The goal of this project is to extend this counterpoint-through-mediatization to include these visual aspects of performance and to fold them into imitative contrapuntal structures as I have previously done with sonic materials. In that way, we can extract the "liveness" of the event from the recorded visuals and sound and develop liveness as its own element in the aesthetic structure of the work. The performers are used for visual material for the same reason the sounds they make are used for sonic material: to explore and exploit the imitative counterpoint in this newly feasible realm.

4   Conclusion

Communications technology is seemingly making the concert hall obsolete, and audiences are sacrificing quality and authenticity for the conveniences offered by the technology. This picture of the state of the arts is a depressing one, depicting a loss of humanity for the posthuman. However, the dimension of the live and the mediated is still salient to audiences; it is only ignored. Artists can use this dimension as a new venue for structure and meaningful expression. In this endeavor, indeterminacy may add to the ontological substance of the work, and therefore the power of that which it expresses, by embracing uniquely live events and highlighting the tension as they become mediatized. Works like those described here can illuminate the humanity amidst posthuman constructions: it has not disappeared but shifted into new realms.

References

Auslander, P.: Liveness: Performance in a Mediatized Culture. Routledge, New York (1999)

Baudrillard, J.: Simulacra and Simulation. Glaser, Sheila Faria (trans.). University of Michigan Press, Ann Arbor (1981)

Benjamin, W.: The Work of Art in the Age of Mechanical Reproduction [1936]. In: Arendt, H. (ed.) Illuminations: Essays and Reflections. Schocken, New York (1969)

Borges, J.L.: New Refutation of Time. In: Other Inquisitions: 1937–1952. Simms, Ruth (trans.). University of Texas Press (1975)

Brown, E., Shirmer, G.: Folio and 4 Systems (December 1952)

Cage, J.: 4'33": for Any Instrument or Combination of Instruments. Edition Peters, New York (1960)

Davies, S.: Musical Works and Performances: A Philosophical Exploration. Oxford University Press, Oxford (2001)

Davies, S.: Versions of Musical Works and Literary Translations. In: Stock, K. (ed.) Philosophers on Music: Experience, Meaning and Work. Oxford University Press, Oxford (2007)

d'Escrivan, J.: To Sing the Body Electric: Instruments and Effort in the Performance of Electronic Music. Contemporary Music Review 25(1-2) (2006)

Eco, U.: The Open Work. Harvard University Press, Cambridge (1989)

Einstein, A.: Zur Elektrodynamik bewegter Körper. Annalen der Physik und Chemie 17, 891–921 (1905)

Lewis, G.: Too Many Notes: Computers, Complexity and Culture in Voyager. Leonardo Music Journal 10 (2000)

Morris, J.M.: Live Sampling in Improvised Musical Performance: Three Approaches and a Discussion of Aesthetics. DMA diss. University of North Texas (2007)

Phelan, P.: Unmarked: The Politics of Performance. Routledge, New York (1993)

Seaman, W.: Recombinant Poetics: Emerging Meaning as Examined and Explored within a Specific Generative Virtual Environment. Ph.D. thesis. Centre for Advanced Inquiry in the Interactive Arts, University of Wales (1999)

The Winstons: "Amen Brother". On: Color Him Father (sound recording). Metromedia, New York (1969)

Dynamic Mapping Strategies for Expressive Synthesis Performance and Improvisation

Palle Dahlstedt*

Dept. of applied information technology, University of Gothenburg and
Chalmers University of Technology, SE41296 Gteborg, Sweden
Academy of Music and Drama, University of Gothenburg
palle@ituniv.se

Abstract. Realtime musical expression through synthesis is notoriously difficult. The complete potential of a sound engine is traditionally available only at design time. In this paper two mapping strategies are presented, adressing this problem. Based on dynamic and random many-to-many mappings between control space and synthesis space, they erase the line between sound editing and synthesizer performance, with an emphasis on free improvisation. One strategy is based on the addition of random vectors in synthesis space, weighted by control parameters. The other is based on a gravity analogy, interpolating between random points in synthesis space, with the gravities controlled by player interaction. Vectors and point sets can be scaled and shifted during performance, allowing dynamic exploration of vast soundspaces or minute timbral control. The mappings have been adopted to a wide range of musical interfaces. Together with suitable sound engines, surprisingly expressive performance instruments have been created, and they have been used in regular rehearsals, concerts and recording sessions over the last two years.

1 Introduction

Synthesizers[1] are very flexible instruments, which is at the same time their strongest and weakest point. Because of this very flexibility, their vast sonic potential and the sheer number of parameters involved, sound editing is difficult. Furthermore, how to really *play* them as expressive instruments is an open question. Synthesis parameters are traditionally accessed at design time through an interface based on one-to-one mapping, requiring extensive knowledge and patience to arrive at good sounds. In performance, a small number of essential synthesis parameters are mapped to realtime controllers, allowing some musical

---

* This research is part of the project Potential Music, funded by the Swedish Research Council. Parts of this paper were written during a visit to CEMA, Monash Univ., Melbourne, Australia.

[1] The word is used in a wide sense, denoting any kind of sound producing device in software and/or hardware that generates sound or sound textures. Note that this also includes parametrized generative realtime composition algorithms.

S. Ystad, R. Kronland-Martinet, and K. Jensen (Eds.): CMMR 2008, LNCS 5493, pp. 227–242, 2009.

expression, but essentially these variations consist of small deviations from the given timbre. The result is a division between two modes of operation. While editing sounds, we can theoretically access the whole parameter space, but it requires extensive time and expertise. While playing, we can only make slight variations to the sound, i.e., explore the immediate vicinity of the chosen preset.

This is especially limiting in a context of free improvisation, where instant flexibility – timbral and gestural – is required to respond to fellow players' actions. In this context, there is no time to browse for a suitable sound, or to fiddle with a large number of knobs. The musician needs to respond within milliseconds.

We have previously addressed the problem of sound editing, i.e., exploring the vast potential of sound engines at design time, by developing tools for interactive evolution of synthesis parameter sets (see, e.g., [1,2]). This offers the composer and sound designer a tool to explore unknown soundspaces by ear in an iterative process, and has proven very efficient for both sound design and composition. There are, however, a few problems with this approach, which makes it unsuitable for expressive performance. While it can be used to evolve musical material by exploring an unknown sound space in a live improvisational setting, the stepwise nature of the process excludes gestural expression. Also, while you may like a specific variation of a mother sound, you do not have continuous control over the amount of variation; i.e., you cannot access the continuum between the parent and the offspring. The evaluation process may not always be suitable for the audience's ears. Since an evolutionary process by definition involves some less fit sounds, you may end up with an unwanted sound playing at full volume, and the only way to get rid of it is to switch to another unknown sound. On a traditional instrument you can make something of your mistakes by quick adjustment or by developing them into new themes. The stepwise control of interactive evolution does not allow such flexibility.

In this paper, we present a series of mapping strategies that were developed in an attempt to solve these problems. Based on a scalable and dynamic vector mechanism, they allow realtime exploration of vast sound spaces, and simultaneous control over broad gestures and minute expression. This development was also motivated by a strong personal need to reintroduce musicianship in electronic music performance, including concepts well-known from traditional instruments: direct connection (in time and direction) between gesture and sound, and between physical effort and sound (no hands – no sound). Today, many electronic musicians look like they check their email on stage, controlling the music with a mouse, eyes staring at the screen. While the musical result can be great, there is something lacking, and the activity is more related to composition than to playing an instrument. The physical dimension of the instrument and the connection to the body are lost, and with them the microvariations of human activities and the sense of strain, which creates a natural phrasing between effort and rest in all kinds of acoustic musical performance. Another problem is the (lack of) visual component. There is no perceivable correlation between the computer operator's gestures and the musical results, which can be essential for the audience's perception, comrehension and appreciation of the music.

These thoughts are not new, and probably recognized by all traditionally trained musicians working with electronic music. The importance of effort has, e.g., been stressed by Ryan [3], while Wessel et al emphasize intimacy between gestural controller and sound generation [4]. Important collections on the subject of gestural control in general [5] and mappings in particular [6] have established the terminology and provided a foundation for discussion. Reviews of projects are given in [7,8], with [9,10] as notable early examples. Finally, high-dimensional control mappings are discussed in [11,12].

The presented mappings were inspired by our experiences with interactive evolution of synthesis parameter sets, and initially conceived as interpolated performance extensions of such tools. The evolutionary aspects of these mappings are further elaborated and discussed in [13].

2   Overview

First, a few essential definitions. The musician perform on an interface that consists of a set of *controllers* (keys, pads, ribbons, etc, usually based on sensors of some kind), each transmitting one or more values communicating its current state. Each sensor value is a *control parameter*, and together they define a point in *control parameter space* (or shorter, *control space*). The interface can be, e.g., a keyboard (clavier), where note numbers, velocities and pressure values contitute the essential control parameters, or an array of percussion pads, where the control parameters could be gate signals, initial and continuous pressure. By mapping, we mean a way to translate from a point in control parameter space to a point in *synthesis parameter space*. Based on the synthesis parameters, the sound is created by a sound engine.

Two general mapping strategies are presented, mathematically very similar but leading to different playing techniques and with different characteristics. They are both based on a set of random points in synthesis parameter space, i.e., randomized at design time. The set of points is not changed during performance (unless explicitly asked for). In the first strategy, these random points are interpreted as vectors, and each controller (e.g., key or pad) is assigned a specific vector. Each vector is scaled by its controller parameter (e.g., velocity or pressure) and by a global scaling control, and the vectors are added to arrive at a single point in synthesis space, effectively deciding the synthesis parameters of the monophonic sound (see Fig 1a). In the second strategy, the random points are instead interpreted as gravitational points in synthesis space. The gravity strength of each point is determined by its correponding control parameter (e.g., velocity or pressure). The resulting point in synthesis space is found somewhere between the gravitational points, decided by the ratio between the values of applied controllers (e.g., keys or pads). For example, if one controller is applied with more strength than others, the result will be closer to its corresponding gravitational point (see Fig 1b).

Both of these models are dynamic, i.e., the whole system can be shifted and scaled in synthesis space, allowing wild exploration of the whole space, or expression through refined nuances around a particular point.

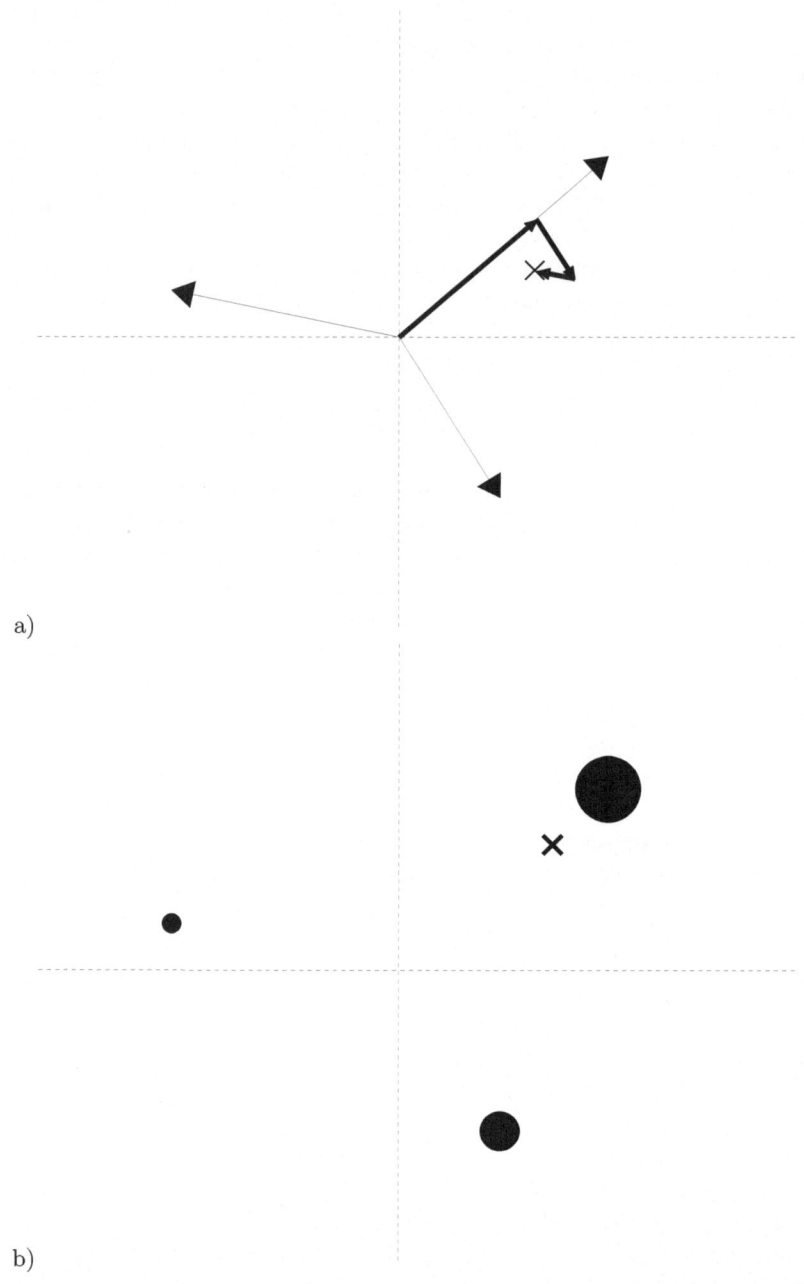

a)

b)

Fig. 1. The ideas behind the two mapping models. a) The vector model. Each controller corresponds to a vector in synthesis parameter space, which is scaled by the controller's value. The vectors are added to arrive at a resulting point in synthesis parameter space. b) The gravity model. Each controller corresponds to a point in synthesis parameter space, with gravity corresponding to the controller's value (shown as the size of the points). The equilibrium point determines the synthesis parameters.

Pitch data has to be treated independently. For some sound engines, pitch is not at all a relevant parameter, for others it is crucial, providing essential structure to the music. Some controllers (e.g., keyboard) provide a natural mapping for pitch, while others do not (e.g., percussion pads), and special pitch algorithms had to be designed.

The sound engines are only briefly discussed in this paper, since they are interchangable, and a range of different ones have been used.

In summary, the system consists of a controller surface, a mapping engine, a pitch engine and a sound engine (see Fig. 2). Not all control data from the surface goes to the mapping engine. Some of the controls, usually faders or knobs, regulate the behaviour of the mapping and pitch engines, and some controls are routed directly to the sound engine for global timbral control.

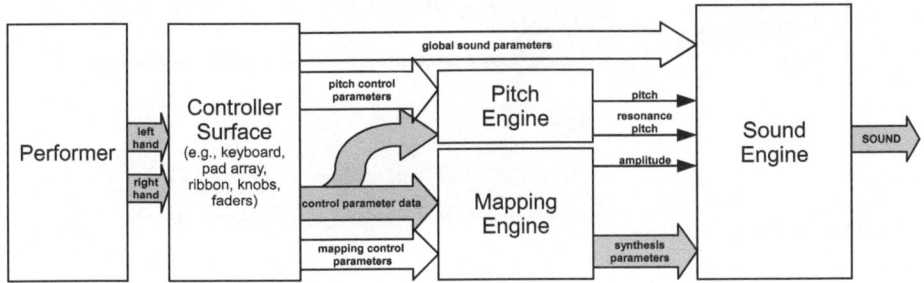

Fig. 2. A schematic of the performance system. Shaded arrows represent performance data going to the mapping engine and the synthesis parameters coming out of it. White arrows represent meta-parameters that control the behaviour of the pitch, mapping and sound engines.

3   The Interfaces

The choice of interface is crucial for any electronic instrument, and lots of effort has gone into the development of various gestural controllers (see, e.g., [5]). Because of time and economical constraints, we have chosen not to develop new interfaces, but to use existing controllers that fits our purpose. Our requirements were robustness (for extensive live use), flexibility of configuration (to be compatible with any sound engine), generality – a set of similar sensors/controllers that can be played singularily or together in any combination, and expressivity (capturing minute changes in physical effort, movement or force).

The vector model was first developed for and inspired by a controller based on an array of pressure sensors, allowing precise control over vector scaling by finger pressure. It has since been modified and further developed for a number of different controllers, primarily keyboard, percussion pads and mallet controllers, each requiring certain adaptations and modifications depending on performance idiomatics. For example, the lack of continuous performance data from a percussion controller led to the development of the gravity model. Some implementations have been used, tested and refined over a period of almost two years, while others are still in prototype stage, in particular the percussion-based implementations. The mappings can most certainly be applied to a wide variety of controllers in addition to the ones developed so far. So far, we have made implementations for the controllers shown in Fig. 3.

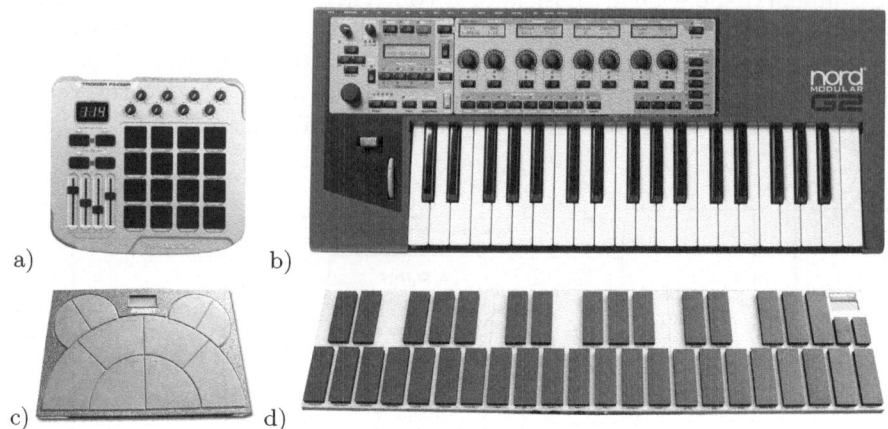

Fig. 3. The controllers for which implementations have been made so far: a) The M-Audio Trigger Finger, with sixteen finger pads transmitting note on/off, initial velocity, and individual continuous pressure. b) A traditional keyboard with velocity and aftertouch. c) The DrumKAT percussion pad controller, played with mallets or hands, transmitting note on/off, velocity and limited pressure data. d) The MalletKAT chromatic percussion controller, transmitting note on/off, velocity and polyphonic aftertouch. In performance, the percussion controllers are complemented by a fader box for meta-parameters and global timberal control.

The idea of generality should not be underestimated. All of these interfaces can be played with any number of fingers or mallets at a time, on any combination of controllers (pad or key); each controller is both discrete and continuous, allowing both triggering and continuous expression with one finger, hand or mallet; and finally, all controllers are equal. How would you play such a surface? In the simplest and most general case, any single controller should produce a sound and simultaneously affect the timbre, and any additionally applied controller should also affect the current timbre. This idea of generality triggered the development of a mapping based on weighted addition of random vectors, one per controller. Each controller affects the timbre in its own, arbitrary way.

No acoustic polyphonic instrument allows continuous timbral and pitch control over each note. There seems to be a trade-off between polyphony and control, probably beacuse of human limitations, both physical and cognitive [14].

Skilled instrumentalists use their full expressive capacity, regardless of instrument, monophonic or polyphonic. The amount of information can be assumed to be roughly equal. So, these are monophonic instruments.

4   The Mapping Engine - Timbral Control

Two related mapping strategies are described. The vector model, suitable for performance controllers with an emphasis on continuous control, and the gravity model, suitable for controllers where timing and attack velocity are the most important parameters from the musician.

4.1   The Vector Model

A controller (e.g., pad or key) i is assigned a vector $\mathbf{r}_i$ in $\mathbb{R}^n$, where n is the number of synthesis parameters. The vector components $r_{i,1}, r_{i,2}, ..., r_{i,n}$ are initialized to random floating point values in the range $[-1, 1]$, with equal distribution. Each vector is scaled by the current control parameter value p_i (pressure or velocity, depending on interface) of the controller and a global controller scaling knob p_{amt}. It is also affected by an attack-decay envelope function $\beta(t) \in [0, 1]$ scaled by the initial velocity v_i of the controller and a global envelope scaling knob v_{amt}. Short attack and decay times are preferred, since a slow envelope would reduce the performer's direct control over the sound. The main purpose of the envelope is to add a distinct timbral transient to the sound when needed, enabling more rhythmical playing (see Fig.4). At the outset, the departure point in synthesis parameter space $\mathbf{o} = (0, 0, ..., 0)$. The resulting point $\mathbf{s}$ in $\mathbb{R}^n$ is calculated by the following formula:

$$\mathbf{s} = \mathbf{o} + \sum_{i=1}^{m}(p_{amt}p_i + v_{amt}v_i\beta(t_i))\mathbf{r}_i, \quad p_{amt}, v_{amt}, v_i, p_i \in [0, 1] \qquad (1)$$

where m is the number of controllers and t_i is the time since pad i was last pressed. The components $s_1, s_2, ..., s_n$ of $\mathbf{s}$ are the synthesis parameters sent to the sound engine. Adjusting p_{amt} allows exploration of the whole sound space in search of interesting regions, or minute expressions around a particular point, while different values of v_{amt} allow different playing techniques, with more or less percussive attacks. The total pressure or velocity (depending on interface used) $\sum p_{1...m}$ is mapped to the overall amplitude of the sound.

At any time during performance, e.g., when an interesting region in sound space has been found, $\mathbf{o}$ can be shifted to the current sounding point $\mathbf{s}$ with a momentary switch/pedal, effectively recentering the whole vector exploration mechanism to the subspace around the current $\mathbf{s}$. This is usually followed by a reduction of p_{amt} to enable finer movement around the new center point. With another switch, $\mathbf{o}$ can be reset to $(0, 0, ..., 0)$, if one is lost in sound space. With each shifting of $\mathbf{o}$, the vectors can if desired be reinitialized to new random values. It is a choice between fresh exploration of the space and retained consistency of mapping directions.

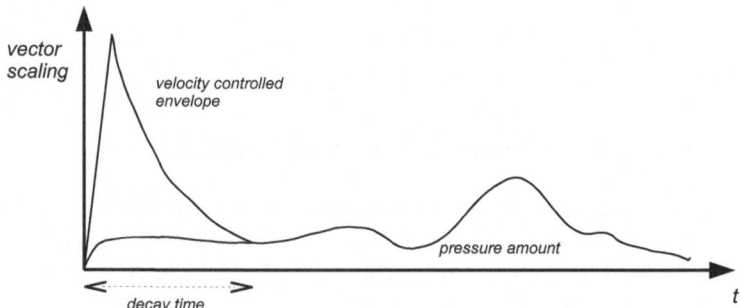

Fig. 4. A vector is scaled based on the sum of an attack envelope controlled by initial velocity, and the continuous pressure applied to the corresponding pad. Both timbre and amplitude are controlled by the vectors. The envelope amount and the pressure amount can be globally scaled, to make possible different kinds of playing — e.g., sharp attack with minute control through pressure, or no attack and coarse timbral control by pressure.

This mapping can be used to control timbre in many different ways. A high vector scaling setting allows wild exploration of the sound space in search of interesting regions, or very dynamic gestures. You can play on one controller at a time, or on all of them. One or more controllers can be held while another is varied. Rhythmic pulses can be played on one controller while others are varied smoothly. By scaling down the vectors, delicate control of timbre is achieved. The velocity amount control ranges from smooth pressure-based continuous sounds to discrete percussive playing. By alternating and overlapping two or more controllers, complex trajectories in sound space can be realized. With longer envelope decay times, several attack envelopes overlap, and create a progression in timbre space from a repeated note. The navigational controls allow zooming in to interesting subspaces, or instant escape from them if stuck. And since vectors components can be negative, controllers can have the effect of damping or muting, which can be exploited musically by the player.

4.2   The Gravity Model

The gravity model was developed specifically for percussion interfaces, since it involves a different kind of playing. Initial velocity and timing are the essential parameters, with pressure and sustain only occasionally applied.[2] With the vector model, the sound is literally shaped with the fingers, while a percussive sound primarily happens after the instant attack/release, when the player no longer can affect it. The infinitely short note length of a percussive hit also implies that there will be no overlapping notes. So some kind of decay function for the parameter mapping has to be introduced to deal with these particularities of the interface.

---

[2] Not all percussion controllers allow sustained notes and/or pressure. Ours do, and this is performed with the hand or the mallet on the pad.

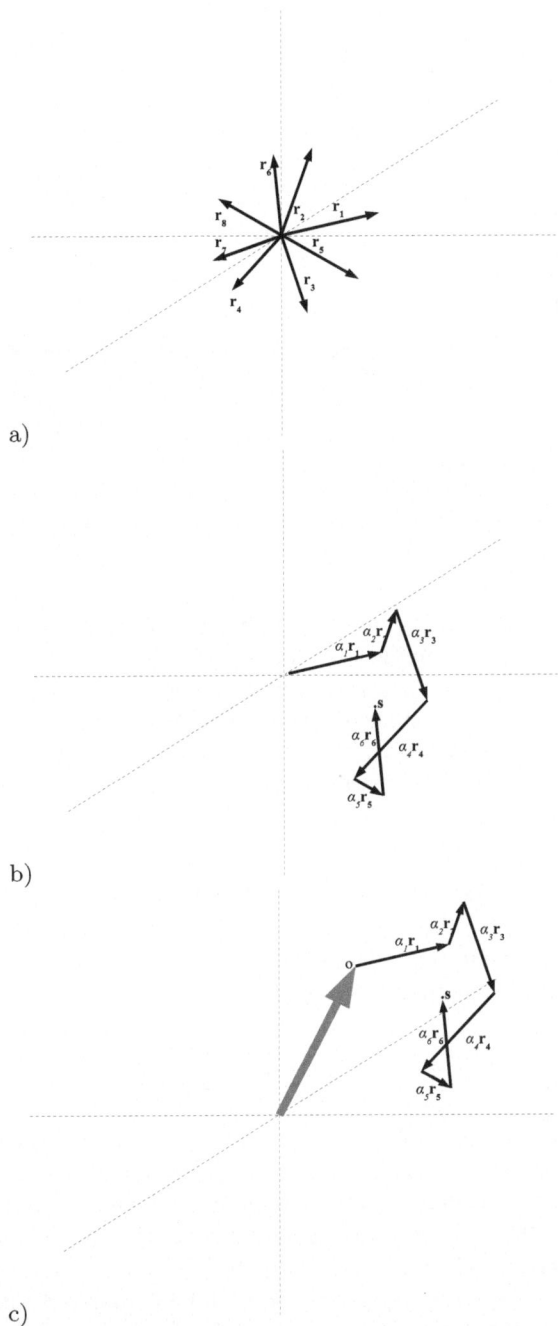

Fig. 5. A simplified illustration of the vector mapping. **a)** A set of vectors in synthesis parameter space, each corresponding to a control parameter. **b)** Vectors of active control parameters are scaled and added to arrive at the sounding point, **s**. **c)** The origin **o** of the vector addition can be reset during performance, allowing exploration of different subspaces.

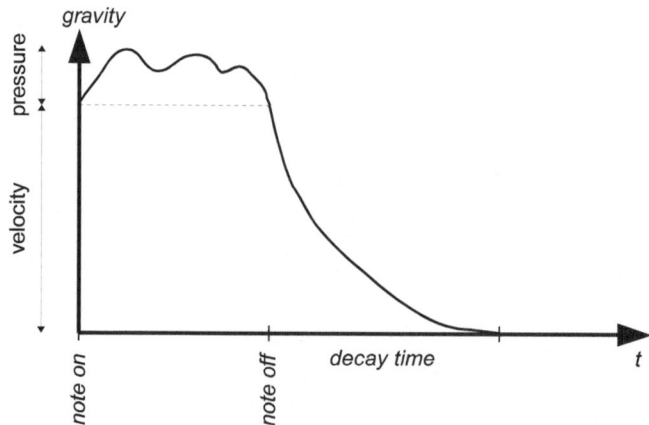

Fig. 6. A graph of α_i in 2, as a function of time, velocity and pressure. Velocity controls the base gravity, with pressure added on top. With percussive hits without sustain, only the decay section is used.

Mathematically, the gravity model is very similar to the vector model, except that each vector length is divided by the sum of all controller values (pressures and/or velocities, depending on interface). The global scaling of the point set, to make it cover a smaller or larger part of the synthesis space, also has to be slightly revised. With most variables from the vector model kept, the formula can be written as follows. First, we calculate the gravity α_i of point i as

$$\alpha_i = p_{amt}p_i + v_{amt}v_i\gamma_i(t_i), \quad p_{amt}, v_{amt}, v_i, p_i \in [0,1] \tag{2}$$

where $\gamma_i(t_i)$ is a sustain-release envelope function controlling how the gravity of point i changes over time (see Fig. 6). The ratio between p_{amt} and v_{amt} determines the relative importance of velocity and pressure. The resulting point in synthesis space is then calculated as

$$\mathbf{s} = \mathbf{o} + \frac{1}{\sum_{i=1}^{m}\alpha_i}\sum_{i=1}^{m}\alpha_i u\mathbf{r_i} \tag{3}$$

where u is a global scaling of the point set controlled by an expression pedal. The components $s_1, s_2, ..., s_n$ of $\mathbf{s}$ are the synthesis parameters sent to the sound engine. The amplitude is decided by the sum of the current gravities $\sum \alpha_{1...m}$. As with the vector model, the origin $\mathbf{o}$ can be shifted to the current $\mathbf{s}$ at any moment, controlled by a footswitch, and reset to $(0, 0, ..., 0)$ with another footswitch. In this way, different subspaces, small or large, can be explored during performance. A third footswitch triggers a re-randomization of the point set, effectively generating a new instrument on the fly, ready to be explored.

The vector model is based the vector directions from the origin and out. The actual vector end points are not so important since they are continuously rescaled based on pressure. Instead, the gravity model deals with a set of points, and the space they encapsulate. This is very evident when playing softly. With the gravity model, each pad has a distinct timbre when played alone, regardless of amplitude, while soft playing in the vector model will result in very similar timbres near the current origin.

Each controller's gravity envelope γ_t has a different decay time, so that different pads respond differently. Since the gravity and the sound volume decays gradually after the hit, subsequent notes are affected by the previous sound, if played within the decay tail. This is somewhat similar to how real sounding bodies work, and can be exploited to realize quite complex trajectories in synthesis space, especially with the added potential of pressure playing and sustained notes. Hence, the *sequence* of notes played is as important as *how* they are played. All these features together forms a very expressive instrument.

5   Pitch Control

Pitch has a different status than other synthesis parameters. In our first prototypes with the Trigger Finger pad array, pitch was simply mapped from one vector component, but the results were burdened with *glissandi*, tiring the ears of the listener. To avoid this, pitch has now been extracted from the mapping engine. Depending on interface and sound engine, different pitch algorithms have been used.

For interfaces with no obvious pitch mapping (Trigger Finger, DrumKAT), an additive pitch engine was developed. It is applied as an overlay to the mapping engine. Furthermore, two faders control global pitch offset. They are two, since some of the predominantly used sound engines are based on two intermodulating oscillators. They span from 1Hz to 10kHz, and can thus be used also for gestural and textural generation. Each pad is assigned a chromatic interval. A minor second is in the lower left corner, increasing to the right and then upwards, with a major tenth in the upper right corner. This layout corresponds both to our intuitive notion of high notes requiring more effort (stretching the hand further out) and to our clavier convention of placing low notes to the left. The interval of all pressed pads, regardless of velocity or pressure, are added together to form a result interval, in the same way as, e.g., the valves of a trumpet. This is scaled by a pitch amount fader (0 to 1), and added to the inherent pitch of the sound engine (set by the faders). This allows for a continuum from no pitch control via microtonality to chromatic pitch, over the whole audible range.

Many of our sound engines are chaotic and noisy. In these cases, when no distinct pitch exists, resonant filters of different kinds are used to create a sense of relative pitch. The pitch of the filter is controlled with a fader, and can be modulated by a vector component or by the additive pitch, with modulation amount on a knob. This mechanism helps create a sense of relative pitch with non-pitched sounds.

This mechanism allows for a wide range of playing styles. If global vector scaling is set to near zero and pitch modulation amount is at maximum, the current timbre can be played chromatically on one pad at a time. Melodies based on relative intervals can be produced by pressing and holding multiple pads. A motive

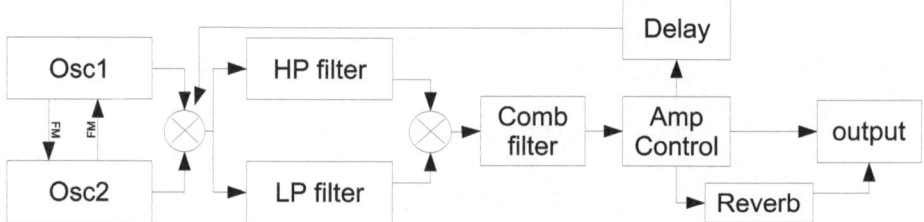

Fig. 7. Simplified schematics of a typical sound engine. Parameters controlled by vector mapping are: FM amounts, oscillator crossfade, filter cutoff frequencies, filter resonance amounts, comb filter feedback, delay time, panning and reverb amount. Other parameters, e.g., offsets for some of the above mentioned, are controlled directly by knobs.

can be transposed by holding an extra pad. Since it is relatively easy to press a pad without very low registered pressure, pitch can be controlled separately from timbre. There is a natural correspondence between effort (holding many pads) and high pitch. For sweeping gestures or sudden changes in register, the global pitch faders can be used as performance controllers.

There is a coupling of pitch and timbre, since they are controlled by the very same controllers. This could be regarded as a limitation, but could also be a quality. In traditional instruments, there is definitely a coupling between different pitch regions and specific timbral qualities (cf. the registers of a clarinet). The fact that certain pitch sequences can only be realized in connection with specific timberal gestures can help the musician in the improvisation, and creates an idiom. We could also call it a creative limitation.

6   Sound Engines

These controllers and mappings have been used with a number of different sound engines, of 7-30 synthesis parameters, controlled by 16-48 control parameters. More is probably possible. Because of the random exploratory nature of the system, it is suitable for wild, noisy sound engines, but equally capable of smooth expressive playing. Designing a sound engine for this system is similar to designing one for interactive evolution or other exploratory algorithms – you have think in potential, i.e., what is possible, and you have to try to consider all possible combinations of parameter values, which of course is impossible.

All essential timbral parameters are controlled by vector components. Some parameters are controlled directly by knobs, such as offsets for essential vector-controlled parameters and certain stepwise parameters (e.g., oscillator waveforms). These are not supposed to be altered in an expressive manner, but are changed intermittently to alter the fundamental conditions for the sound engine, in a "structural modification gesture" [15]. It may be compared to when a violinist changes between *arco* and *pizzicato*.

One sound engine that has been used frequently may serve as an example (see Fig. 7). Two intermodulating oscillators are mixed and sent to two filters, whose outputs are mixed and passed through a comb filter for resonance. Most essential parameters are controlled by the vector mapping. There is feedback through a modulated delay to make the sound more dirty, complex and organic. This, the feedback in the comb filter, and the intermodulation between the oscillators together cause nonlinear behaviour, creating different regions in parameter space with phase transitions that can be used to the performers advantage.

All sound engines so far have been implemented in the Nord Modular G2 synthesis system.

7 Discussion

Superficially, the vector mapping is a generalized version of most linear mappings, since any conventional mapping could be implemented as a vector addition, each vector defining how a specific controller affects the synthesis parameters. But our vectors are random, and every controller affects all sound parameters. It is a many-to-many mapping, which is not so common but has been discussed [16]. Experiments have shown that coupled mappings are easier to learn and more engaging to play [17], and this is here taken to its extreme. When playing, you cannot think in parameters. You have to use your ear, all of the time.

It has been said that a good mapping should be intuitive ([18]), in the sense that you should immediately understand the internals of the system. But this is not true for most acoustic instruments. Many musicians do not know their instrument from a physics point of view. Some phenomena are extremely complex, e.g., multiphonics in wind instruments, but instrumentalists learn to master them. Choi et al emphasize the feedback process through which we learn how an instrument works, and redefine the word intuitive to mean "the experience of participating in feedback systems where the participant can draw compatible conclusions from a small number of trials..." [11]. This is related to issues of consistency (same gesture, same result), continuity (small gesture, small effect) and coherence (works like the physical world) [12]. Our system has short term repetitivity and is mostly continuous (depending on sound engine). There is nothing random when you play, but the mapping is dynamic, i.e., it can be changed at will by scaling or shifting. After an origin shift or a change of vector scaling, gestures give different results. When global sound parameters are changed, the space is "warped" and all sounds are different. It is difficult to get back to the exact same settings. Still, based on months of playing, it is clear that you can learn and internalize the way the system works on a higher level. You learn how to read its current behavior, react to a musical context in a predictable way, and create specific expressions at will. In a conventional instrument the aural feedback teach you the correspondence between gestures and effects. Here, the learning is on another conceptual level – you learn how to extrapolate from the current reactions of the system, into meaningful musical gestures. The immediate feedback between actions and ear is essential. You cannot play this instrument if you can't hear yourself well. The mapping are random and complex, but they feel easy to work with. There is a natural alternation between exploratory (long vectors) and expressive playing (short vectors). The physical gestures (fingertip pressure, percussive playing with hand or mallets) feels natural, and the sound can be controlled with great precision, in a way unlike any other electronic instrument the authors have experienced. It works well visually, with a clear connection between physical gesture and sound, enhancing musical communication. There is instant gratification – people who try these instrument after demonstrations or concerts enjoy it and don't want to stop. But the real evaluations have been weekly rehearsals, a number of concerts and the recording of an album. For about a year the Trigger Finger system, with a single sound engine controlled by the vector mapping, was the author's main instrument. There is absolutely a potential for long term improvement and the development of skill.

These instruments are instrument for improvisation, and as such they work very well. It would be different with score-based music. In improvisation, the random aspects of the instrument is an advantage since they provide external input, as glitches and unexpected sounds, in the same way as an extra performer. Thanks to the direct control of the sound, you can react to it literally instantly, *in* the sound, not after, to "cover up" or modify it, or develop it into something useful.

These mapping strategies were inspired by interactive evolution of synthesis parameter sets, and there are still some close resemblances. Obviously, this is not an optimization process of any kind, but rather an exploration. The current origin is the parent sound, and each random vector corresponds to a mutated offspring. The global vector scaling has the effect of a mutation rate. By pressing one pad, you hear one offspring, but you can also hear combinations of different offspring (by interpolation, not recombination) by pressing several pads. When a good sound is found, it is reproduced by shifting the origo and re-randomizing the vectors, making the current point the parent sound. This process can be iterated. In essence, this amounts to mutation-based interactive evolution of synthesis parameter sets with continuous expressive interpolation *between* population members (gravity model) or *around* the parent in directions toward the offspring (vector model).

Looking at the system from a mathematical point of view, the relation between the numbers of control and synthesis parameters is crucial. In our case, the number of synthesis parameters has been slightly lower. If there were fewer controls or more synthesis parameters, the vectors would not span the whole space. Then, to maximize the volume of the search space, one could make the random vectors orthogonal. On the other hand, since they can be re-randomized at origin shift, all dimensions will eventually be explored. An analogy is the concept of mutations in evolutionary algorithms. You do not require every generation to have a mutation in every locus, but trust chance to supply, sooner or later, variation in all directions.

On the other hand, with a well-designed sound engine, a small number of controllers could provide interesting variation, since the mapping after each re-randomization produces an instrument very different from the previous one, since the span different subspaces of the synthesis space.

Mappings are sometimes categorized into explicit and generative (based on, e.g., neural nets) [16]. These systems are neither of these, but could be considered as *dynamic mappings*. They are randomly generated at design time, but explicit in the short term. Since the performer has direct control over essential mapping parameters (vector or point-set scaling, origin shift), the mapping can be changed at will, and these changes become integrated into the way of playing. Meta-control becomes part of control, and exploration and expression are merged into one process.

The vectors could be randomized in different ways. Currently, each controller affects all parameters (positively or negatively). Random values could be assigned to a small number of vector components and the others set to zero, in overlapping groups. Then each pad would have a different effect on the sound, and the playing technique would possibly be different. It is also conceivable to hand-tune all vectors, but then we are back to explicit instrument design, and the idea of random exploration inspired by evolutionary strategies is lost.

We have also started preliminary experiments with presets of vectors and points sets, to provide long-term repeatability and the ability to go back to a previous mapping.

8   Conclusions

We have described two mapping strategies from arbitrary control surfaces to synthesis parameters that merges exploration of a sound space with expressive playing, overcoming the expressive limitations of interactive evolutionary approaches. These mappings also allow exploration of the whole sonic potential of a sound engine during performance, erasing the border between sound editing and performance. They are based on random correlations and they are reconfigurable during performance, continuously and stepwise, making them essentially different from conventional mappings. Still, they satisfy criteria such as low learning threshold, short term repeatability and possibility of developing skill over time. Thanks to the emphasis on effort and direct connection between physical gesture and sonic output, the instruments feel, behave, and appear like traditional instruments, and they are very suitable for free improvisation with intimate and immediate control over timbre, pitch and dynamics. They are different from your average musical instrument, but extensive playing has proven that, while complex, they are fascinating and expressive partners on stage, much like acoustic instruments, and deserves to be heard, and to be further developed.

References

1. Dahlstedt, P.: Creating and exploring huge parameter spaces: Interactive evolution as a tool for sound generation. In: Proceedings of the 2001 International Computer Music Conference, Habana, Cuba, pp. 235–242 (2001)
2. Dahlstedt, P.: Evolution in creative sound design. In: Miranda, E.R., Biles, J.A. (eds.) Evolutionary Computer Music, pp. 79–99. Springer, London (2007)

3. Ryan, J.: Effort and expression. In: Proceedings of the 1992 International Computer Music Conference, San Jose, California, USA, pp. 414–416 (1992)
4. Wessel, D., Wright, M.: Problems and prospects for intimate musical control of computers. In: Workshop in New Interfaces for Musical Expression, Seattle (2001)
5. Wanderley, M., Battier, M. (eds.): Trends in gestural control of music (CDROM). Ircam/Centre Pompidou, Paris (2000)
6. Wanderley, M. (ed.): Theme issue on mapping. Organised Sound 7(2) (2002)
7. Mulder, A.: Virtual musical instruments: Accessing the sound synthesis universe as a performer. In: Proc. of the 1st Brazilian Symposium on Computers and Music
8. Wanderley, M.: Gestural control of music. In: Intl. Workshop on Human Supervision and Control in Engineering and Music, Kassel (2001)
9. Cadoz, C.: Instrumental gesture and musical composition. In: Proceedings of the 1988 International Computer Music Conference - Kologne, Germany, pp. 1–12. ICMA, San Francisco (1988)
10. Bowler, I., Purvis, A., Manning, P., Bailey, N.: On mapping n articulation onto m synthesiser-control parameters. In: Proceedings of the 1990 International Computer Music Conference (ICMC 1990), pp. 181–184 (1990)
11. Choi, I., Bargar, R., Goudeseune, C.: A manifold interface for a high dimensional control space. In: Proceedings of the 1995 International Computer Music Conference, Banff, pp. 89–92 (1995)
12. Garnett, G.E., Goudeseune, C.: Performance factors in control of high-dimensional spaces. In: Proceedings of the 1999 International Computer Music Conference, Beijing, China (1999)
13. Dahlstedt, P., Nilsson, P.A.: Free flight in parameter space: A dynamic mapping strategy for expressive free impro. In: Giacobini, M., Brabazon, A., Cagnoni, S., Di Caro, G.A., Drechsler, R., Ekárt, A., Esparcia-Alcázar, A.I., Farooq, M., Fink, A., McCormack, J., O'Neill, M., Romero, J., Rothlauf, F., Squillero, G., Uyar, A.Ş., Yang, S. (eds.) EvoWorkshops 2008. LNCS, vol. 4974, pp. 479–484. Springer, Heidelberg (2008)
14. Levitin, D.J., McAdams, S., Adams, R.L.: Control parameters for musical instruments: a foundation for new mappings of gesture to sound. Organised Sound 7(2), 171–189 (2002)
15. Cadoz, C., Wanderley, M.M.: Gesture-music. In: Wanderley, M., Battier, M. (eds.) Trends in Gestural Control of Music. Ircam/Centre Pompidou, Paris (2000)
16. Hunt, A., Wanderley, M.M., Kirk, R.: Towards a model for instrumental mapping in expert musical interaction. In: Proceedings of the 2000 International Computer Music Conference, pp. 209–212 (2000)
17. Hunt, A., Kirk, R.: Mapping strategies for musical performance. In: Wanderley, M., Battier, M. (eds.) Trends in Gestural Control of Music (CDROM). Ircam/Centre Pompidou, Paris (2000)
18. Norman, D.A.: The psychology of everyday things. Basic Books Inc. (1988)

Amplified Breath – (Dis)Embodied Habitat: Exploring Sonic Interfaces of Performance, Electronics, Space and Flautist Identity

Jean Penny

mjpenny@bigpond.net.au
http://www.hutes.com.au

Abstract. The electronic spatialization of flute sound represents an intersection of acoustic resonance and technology, ancient sonic imagining and present day cultural imprints. The performative impacts of technological interventions and the new responses thus stimulated in performance practice, invite rigorous exploration and reflection. In this paper I aim to articulate my personal responses to spatialization technologies and live interactive electronics, to explore the expanded capacities provided for the flautist, and the new performative elements introduced by this genre. Focusing on breath tone and gesture, transformations of sonority, performer identity, space, physicality and interactivity are investigated from the flautist's point of view. Much of the material of this paper is extracted from my doctoral thesis, 'The Extended Flautist: techniques, technologies and perceptions in the performance of music for flute and electronics', due for submission in early 2009.

Keywords: flute, electronics, performance, space, identity.

1 Introduction

Solo flute works characteristically exploit spatial tonal qualities, as composers and performers across the centuries have explored ways of capturing and expanding the instrument's translucent sonic qualities into evocative expression. This sonic ethos has stretched from the architectural structures of Baroque works, such as J. S. Bach's Partita in A minor or Jacob van Eyck's Der Fluyten Lust-hof, to the more recent works of composers such as Takemitsu and Saariaho, in which the resonance and malleability of the tone and breath are a critical element of composition. Edgard Varese's seminal composition for solo flute, Density 21.5 (1936), initiated new tonal directions through the use of key clicks, dynamics as sound manipulation and extremes of tessitura. This work generated immense change in the perception of flute sound and capabilities, and encouraged practitioners to explore new sonic paths [1]. New texts began to appear examining such techniques as microtones, whistle-tones, breath tones, tongue clicks, key slaps, multiphonics, harmonics, glissandi, new embouchure techniques, vocalization and varieties of articulation by such authors as Bruno Bartoluzzi [2], Pierre-Yves Artaud [3] and Robert Dick [4]. These texts became the source material of composers: the techniques were scrutinized for sonic properties and expanded out into the musical milieu through amplification and spatial projection.

S. Ystad, R. Kronland-Martinet, and K. Jensen (Eds.): CMMR 2008, LNCS 5493, pp. 243–252, 2009.

Contemporary flute players have embraced these techniques, especially in conjunction with electronic interventions, revelling in the expanded sonic palette, a fresh abundance of ideas and new discoveries in expression and performance. The overlapping layers of instrumental performance and extended practice through electronic techniques have evolved into a complex search for interpretative cohesion and confluence, an engrossing search that provokes new responses and analysis.

My focus in this paper is on transformations of sonority, identity, space and physicality, as they occur in the performance of music for flute and electronics. My vehicles for exploration are the breath tone, gesture and inter-activated space.

2   Transformed Sonority

...the microphone ... became an extension of the instrument, and the performer ... (it) made it possible to exalt the "shadow tones" with their resultant partials, it became possible to spatialise gradations of sound: "sinusoidal" or "pure sounds" derived from researching dynamics at the very limits of audibility and with total emission control. [5]

The sonic landscape of flute music has been transformed, the inaudible has become audible, the interior has become exterior, and performer explorations of identity and expression aroused. Amplification is the core electronic process that provides the technological means by which sonic transformations can be projected. This expanded territory incites a new set of sonic goals, far removed from the traditional resonance of the flute, and creates new performative freedoms and powers. Extended flute techniques are a major part of this new approach to sound, as techniques such as microsounds and percussion demand a reappraisal of the flautist's approach to the instrument. Multiphonics create layering and instability; microtones blur conventional note distinctions and scalic structures; glissandi smudge and meld, giving a new sense of placement and movement of flute tone. A kaleidoscope of musical inferences can be articulated as electronic processes combine with flute sounds, amplifying, merging and transforming timbres, mirroring, re-pitching and re-positioning to create changed sensations and expectations. I focus here on the breath tone.

The evolution of the breath tone from its lowly position of extraneous noise needing eradication (as expected in conventional flute music) to exquisite sonic material, is a striking example of the changed sonic goals of the contemporary flautist. The breath tone becomes a highly suggestive expressive element, imbued with eloquence and beauty. It is a new expressive tool, creating new layers of colour and meaning. Amplification of the breath tone creates illusions of proximity, sensations of extending the inner self into the music and out into the hall; a connection of inner and outer identities.

Breath tone begins with an unfocussed flute sound that can be manipulated acoustically and electronically to produce intense musical effects. Varied embouchure shape, internal mouth and throat shape, air stream direction, air speed, tongue positions, articulations, differing focus, use of vibrato, pitching, closed or open embouchure and body positions are used by the flautist to create the effects. These air sounds can be expanded into enormous wind noise, melded with normal flute tone, voice, percussive techniques, greater or lesser amounts of hissing, or create tentative wisps or dots of micro sound.

The map below (Fig.1) shows exploratory pathways as they pertain to breath tones in flute playing. The musical example included in the map is from Stroppa's little i, first movement, indicating a breath tone multiphonic changing to normal tone. Techniques are defined in the upper section of the map, and effects in the lower.

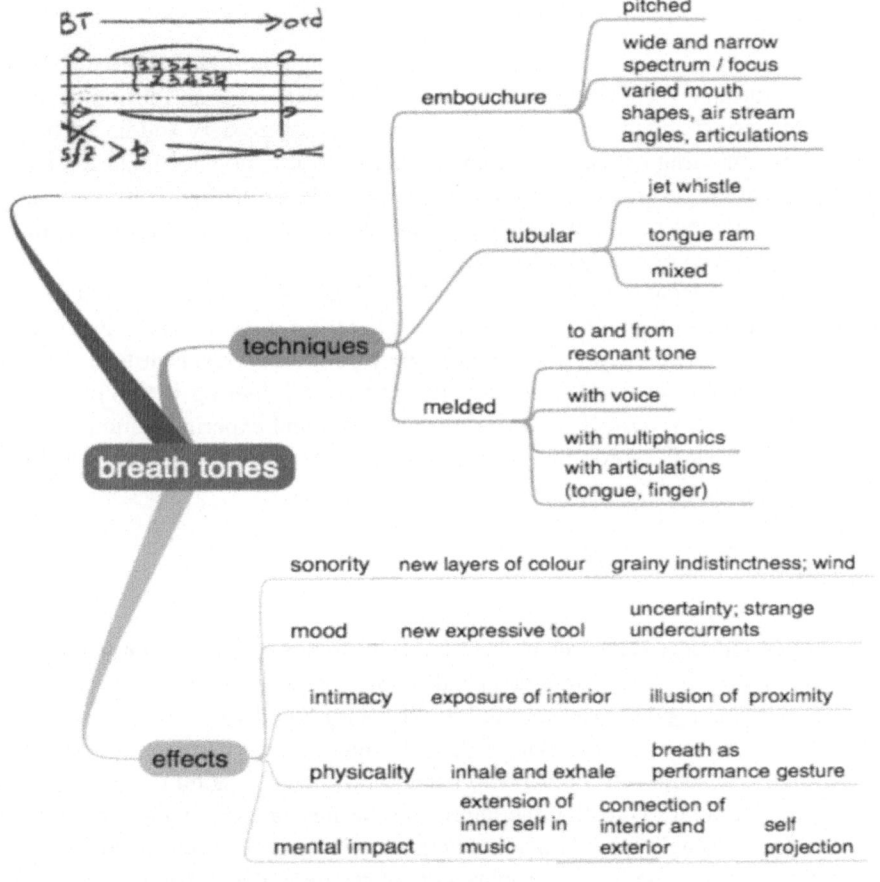

Fig. 1. Breath tone explorations

Percussive sounds on flute are usually key slaps or tongue clicks, and they are effectively used in combination with breath tones. A most astonishing sound-scape results from extensive use of amplified percussive sounds, as seen in the third movement of Marco Stroppa's *little i* for flutes and electronics: *Moderato Percusive - Molto Minuzioso*. (Fig. 2)

Fig. 2. Percussive articulations and breath tones in Stroppa's *little i*, third movement, bars 20 – 26

In this music, various combinations of pizzicato, tongue ram, key slaps and breath tone are sent through speakers away from the player, generating an illusion of invisible presences, an inhabited dialogical space. The sense of mystery and uncertainty is underlined by the fragmentary sonic interpolations. Diffusion techniques such as these, manipulations of timbre and sound placement, capturing and conversion techniques, expansion and contraction of the sound, all transform the breath tone into a viable and highly expressive musical device.

Working up the technique for breath tones is a remarkable journey, full of self-scrutinization and surprise. The very intimacy of the use of breath as a direct sound source places this technique in a different plane from normal resonant tone. Hearing this sound projected out into the room, shaping it and colouring it through minute mouth and blowing movements encourages much play and experimentation, generating a different physical approach, a re-positioning of the soloist in the space and new sense of identity.

3 Identity

The performer's identity is a combination of multiple interior and exterior factors. The outward identity (style, sound, interface) and inward identity (self awareness, interpretation, transformative potentials, musical background) blend to form the performing persona. This persona is a projection of the self, intermingled with compositions and artistic goals. The sonic self 'comes into being with sound', Naomi Cumming states, 'and the tone is central to creating the impression of musical personality.' [6] A musician's identity is strongly bound up with being a particular type of musician, and making specific musical sounds. As an extension of the self, the instrument acts as an amplifier [7]. Inward and outward identity is displayed through performance, revealing aspects of inner processes and thoughts, responses and emotional connections, through interpretational signals. This self-projection creates a perception in both player and listener, imprinting both visual and aural impressions on a listener, and a sense of positioning and potential to the player.

Timbre manipulations influence sonic identity, as new sound objects become familiar in one's sound world. Through memory, sounds become recognizable, "admissable" [8][1] and hence usable – and audiences also become significantly more comfortable with sounds they know or can relate to the known. The new sound worlds become elements you hold as part of yourself, part of your own "vocabulary", a representation of personality in sound.

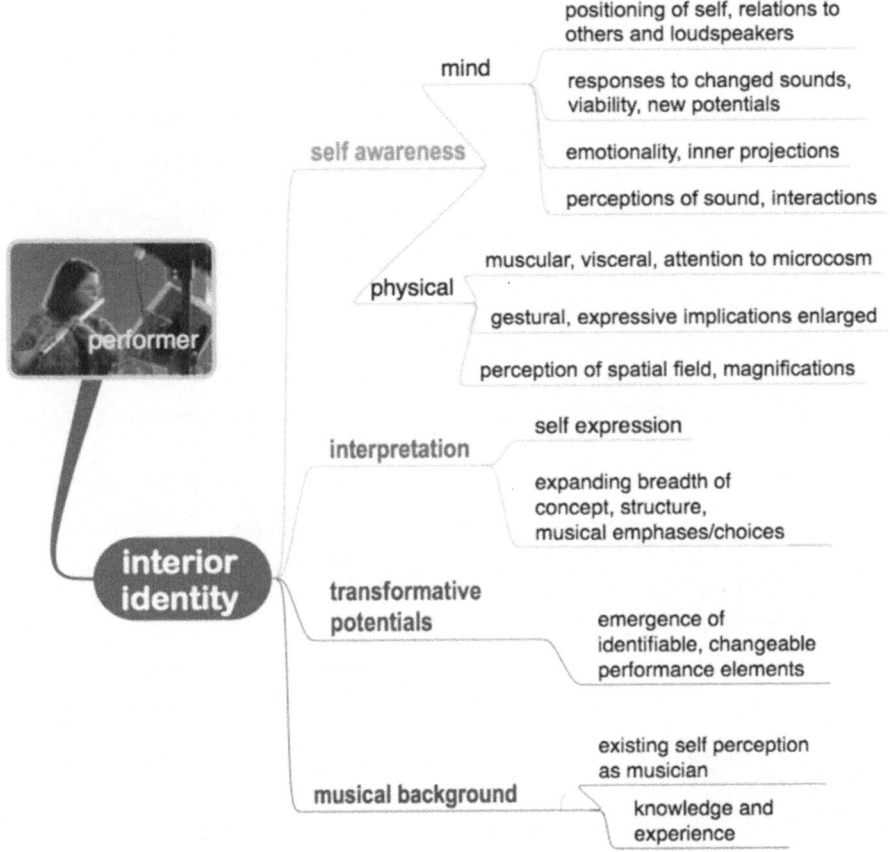

Fig. 3. Performer identity explorations: interior

A new sense of oneness in the sonic world can occur through electronic processes. These include the melding of techniques to give enhanced freedom of expression, sonic empowerment and flexibility. Simply enlarging the sound gives an immediate

---

[1] With live electronics, when electronics are performed in realtime like instruments and combined with instruments ... two worlds are brought together in a theatre of transformations. No-one listening knows exactly what is instrumental and what is electronic any more ... When they lack their connection to the familiar instrumental world electronics can be inadmissably alien, other, inhuman, dismissable ... When electronics are seamlessly connected to the physical, solid instrumental world an expansion of the admissable takes place, and the 'mad' world is made to belong. [8].

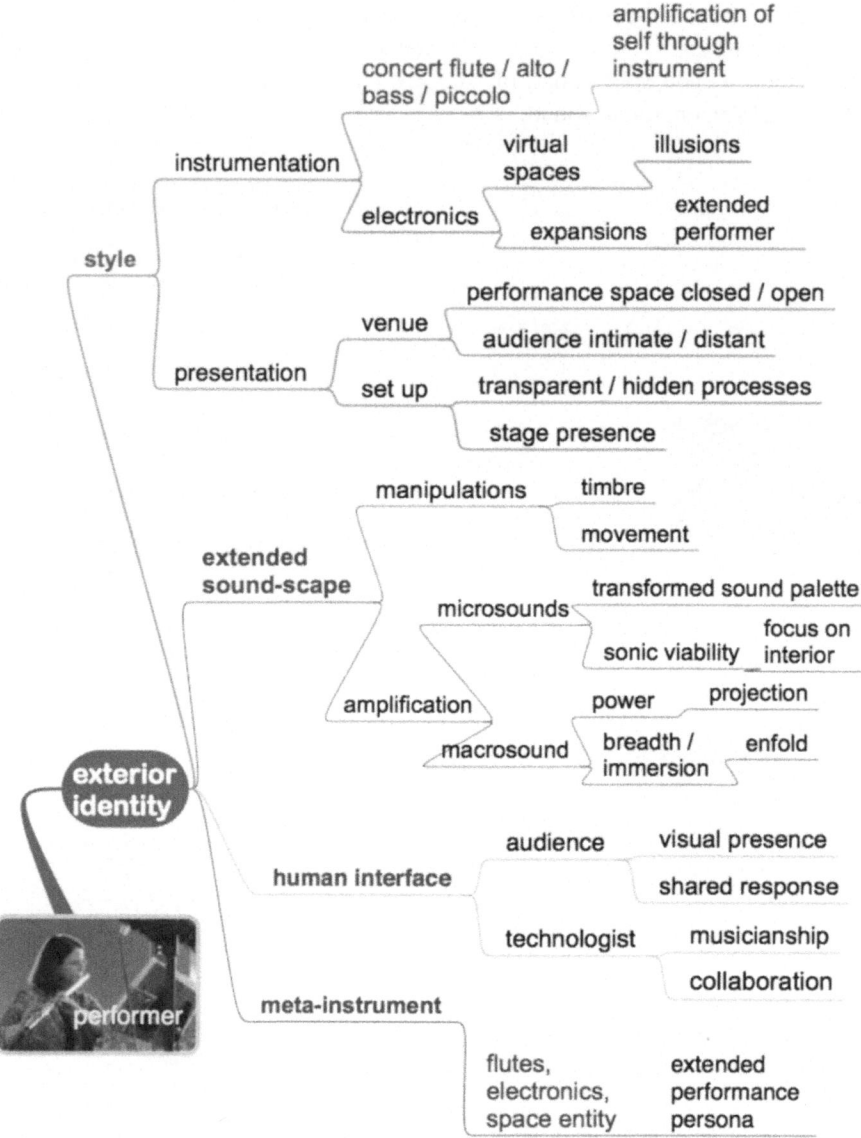

Fig. 4. Performer identity explorations: exterior

sense of power of projection and flexibility to the flute player; adding effects such as reverberation or delay alters the location of self and ensemble symbiosis; exposure of small body sounds out into the hall can give a sense of self discovery and also unveiling. These influences provide a vastly increased range of musical elements to activate, thus enlarging the personality in sound. There is an expanded sense of the energy source – the gestures, breath, interpretations - and increased sense of sonic choice. There is a new sense of ensemble, and (at times) a spatialization of solo playing into layers and illusions of other presences. There is a magnification of the micro, intimate elements of playing, and the possibility to mask and confuse.

The following maps (Fig. 3 and Fig. 4) indicate interior and exterior identity elements I have found in my own work. They represent inner explorations and pathways to new self-perception and awareness, positioning and projection, spatial and gestural implications, and transformative capabilities invoked by electronics. Outer explorations are represented by style and presentation, the extended sound world, and the human interface. Discussion of these elements, and the development of the meta-instrument, continues below.

4 Performer's Habitat

The play–as-text can be performed in a space, but the play-as-event belongs to the space, and makes the space perform as much as the actors perform. [9]

The creation of a performance space is an intriguing and integral part of a performer's world, influenced by many elements of historical context or tradition and physical practicalities. The spaces of music (hall, church, outdoors), the forms of presentation (formal, intimate, invisible), the position of the audience (opposite or around) and the natural acoustic within the playing space have major roles in projection and synthesis, and the listeners' and performers' perception (and reception) of the music. Electronic technologies and the new interactive dimensions of relationships within that space transform this performer's habitat.

4.1 New Spaces – New Effects

The transformation of space in a performance for instrument and electronics occurs with the combined physical set up and visible dynamics, the real space, and the virtual space of sonic illusion, invisible interconnections and processes. As the virtual spaces created through electronics do not necessarily follow natural rules of sonic behavior, the spatial field becomes a dynamic player in the performance, controlled in the main by the sound technologist, an expressive role that influences the relationship of performer and performance. Ambiguity can reign in this environment as, for example, sound sources become entirely mixed up through live and pre-recorded sound sources, a sense of invisible presence creates a distinctive dramaturgy, or unexpected interconnections generate re-positioning: the performer can be magnified or obscured, empowered or reduced. A sense of enclosure, or disorientation, uncertain proximity and passing of time can result, (for example, in Jean Claude Risset's *Passages*), or a dialogue with spatialized voices (as in Marco Stroppa's *little i*).

These expansions and contractions invoke changed expectations, impose new meanings and alter perceptions of the listener and performer. Added vocalizations can add the sense of other presences, and the electronic processes such as delay or harmonization collect layers or mirroring reverberations to increase density or texture. These sounds can traverse across the room, or dart from speaker to speaker, create an immersion, or disconnection, or further illusions of intimacy or distance through panning or delay.

Hyper-magnification through amplification influences this new sense of space by generating an increased capacity to draw the listener into the intimate sound world of the performer. The breath tone sound, for example, can be stunningly large, creating a broad spatial implication, or coloured by minute tongue or percussion sounds, expanded out into the room, creating an impression of intimacy. The proximity of the breath tone can give an illusion to the audience of moving into the performer's sound space, an access to a private space. This expansion of internal bodily actions out into the room has a two-fold impact. The performer experiences an exposure of self, an open sharing of the internal in pursuit of sonic and communicative pathways. The self at the same time is empowered, enlarged, and given a new context. The listener, on the other hand, experiences the extreme "close up", illusions and sensations of proximity and distance.

4.2 Partnerships and the Meta-instrument

The dominant partnership creating interconnections in this space is the instrumentalist – technologist relationship. This is an incontrovertibly vital, central element of electro-acoustic performance, but one that is rarely discussed from a performative point of view. The balance, the working methodology, the construction of a functional zone that activates and recreates the habitat for the piece are central elements to any performance. Developing this symbiosis, this meta-instrument, and working together for confluence and functionality, demands a relationship that is a very carefully balanced, yet vigorous dynamic. In the best situations, the divergent experience a technologist brings to this relationship is embellished with an understanding of the performance practice priorities of the instrumentalist, allowing for joint immersion in both worlds, and in a sharing of the musical and aesthetic ideals. In this happy situation, the context does not need redefinition: there is an equality of input, with a tilt towards the soloist's "right" of artistic license or leadership.

The relationship of instrumentalist and technologist is consequently one built on great trust, acceptance and a willingness to tread risky paths together. Most importantly, it also thrives when a commonality of artistic and aesthetic goals exist, when the myriad shades of balance, tonal softening or distortion, response and imagination create together a truly interactive environment and ensemble.

5   (Im)Perceptible (Inter)Activity

Performing involves the development of intelligence in the body and tactility in the mind. [10]

The emergence of sonic and performance identity through gesture and the shaping of musical material is founded on physical actions (posture, breathing, throat and mouth shaping, tonguing, arm and hand movement, emotionally reflective body language) learnt over many years of practice. Electronic processes have a robust impact on this physicality and kinaesthetic awareness, as techniques are adjusted to new dimensions, and new requirements, such as player activation of interface, have evolved. These may include the use of foot pedals, the computer keyboard, electronic flute attachments or whole body movements that activate effects and events. The physical memory shifts, the different actions required to produce musical outcomes not learned as part of previous instrumental training, extend the practice into new musculature and mental dimensions.

Kinaesthetic awareness is further heightened by the intensified focus on micro techniques, and the sense of physical freedom that comes from amplification. Amplification liberates the flautist's sense of energy: the sensation of projection is overwhelmingly overtaken by electronics, the audibility is no longer a matter for concern. The impact on the player is an increased relaxation of musculature, as the sound dimension is taken over, and an expanded sense of subtly available through minute movements. The focus is on this micro-sound world, on the link between physicality and sound texture and timbre, the projection of meaning in the interaction of breath, instrument and electronics.

The visible (physical) and invisible (virtual) dynamics between live performer and electronics has developed as an important expressive field, where the sonic universe of the performer is expanded into a multidimensional setting for performance. The invisibility of electronic functioning can be used as a compositional and performative feature, or revealed through gesture or transparent processes. Ambiguity and a cognitive dissonance with reality can occur through the removal or alteration of visual gestural cues, the blurring of sound sources, and the juxtaposition of virtual and real elements.

Invisible processing occurs in Russell Pinkston's *Lizamander* for flute and Max/MSP (2003), which utilizes pitch and threshold tracking. Two microphones are used in this work, one for tracking and one for amplification and audio processing. The computer program detects specific pitches played by the flute at precise moments in the score, at times searching for notes above or below a particular threshold, in other instances, an exact pitch. This identification allows movement to the next section, triggering such actions as capturing and granulating sounds, harmonization, and the playing of computer-generated material. The flute part is resonant and energetic, and the effects generate a compelling drive and rich sonic environment, but rehearsals of this work highlight a complexity in these seemingly simple arrangements. The characteristics of the acoustics in the performance space become critical as an over reverberation of the flute sound can fail to trigger the functions, and the sound technician must then step in to move the work on manually. When the functioning succeeds, the playing becomes something of a game, as 'matched' signals come up on the computer screen at each trigger point and the work drives on. This digital confirmation of engagement is amusing for the performers, but imperceptible to the audience.

Warren Burt's *Mantrae* (2007)[2] for flute and live interactive electronics uses full body gesture as interactive trigger. Sharply articulated flute tone provides the sonic base for this work, which captures the flautist's movements with a camera, and uses these to activate radical sound effects. The flautist moves randomly between the three Mantrae, lunging between three music stands, whilst maintaining a continuous chanting contour. The flute sound is processed by Cycling '74's *Hipno* sound processing modules, and a random mixing routine is set up in *Plogue Bidule*, the host program

---

[2] Burt, *Mantrae* for flute and live interactive electronics, self-published. (Commissioned by Jean Penny with assistance from the Australia Council for the Arts).

for the processing. The flautist thus aims to maintain a sense of focus and inner calm in the midst of dramatic sound treatments, representing the individual in a constantly changing and unpredictable world.

The experience of performing *Mantrae* is an unfolding focus on motion and location. New balances and sensations evolve, challenging acquired performance knowledge and merging with the desire to be completely free within this circle, to attempt to move with abandon, swiftness and grace, to dissolve into the music, to become the meditation through a semi-immersion. The movements are sharp and fast, turning with seeming unpredictability from one stand to another. There is some awkwardness, some difficulty sustaining vision of the scores, moving without unraveling basic flute playing techniques and postures. The performer is enclosed within a circular space, introspective, self-contained, entrained within the meditation; the surrounding diversity of manipulated sounds are shifted and altered through physical gestures far removed from that world. An intensified experience evolves, as the desire for control transforms into a response, as the individual turns away from outside events, embracing the vortex created by the technology.

Close

Technology reveals performance aspects that include musical structures, spaces in sounds, spaces in performance and illusions; it provides a focus for examining playing techniques, musician responses and interconnections in performance. This paper has touched on important intersections of flute performance and technology, highlighting the transformative elements of the genre. In this environment, the flautist becomes a re-shaped, re-located, renewed and re-invented musician in a field of shifting emphases, new processes and expanded symbiosis. New sonic goals and identities emerge as the performer's world attains an expanded meaning and refreshed understanding.

References

1. Artaud, P.-Y., Dale, C. (trans).: Aspects of the Flute in the Twentieth Century. Contemporary Music Review 8(2), 131–216 (1994)
2. Bartoluzzi, B.: New Sounds for Woodwind, 2nd edn. Oxford University Press, London (1982)
3. Artaud, P.-Y.: Present Day Flutes. Billaudot, Paris (1995)
4. Dick, R.: The Other Flute, 2nd edn. Multiple Breath Music Company, Missouri (1989)
5. Fabbriciano, R.: Walking with Gigi. Contemporary Music Review 18(1), 7–15 (1999)
6. Cumming, N.: The Sonic Self. Indiana University Press, Bloomington (2000)
7. Emmerson, S.: Music, Electronic Media and Culture. Ashgate Publishing Limited, Aldershot (2000)
8. Harvey, J.: The Metaphysics of Live Electronics. Contemporary Music Review 18(3), 79–82 (1999)
9. Wiles, D.: A Short History of Western Performance Space. Cambridge University Press, Cambridge (2003)
10. Schick, S.: The Percussionist's Art. University of Rochester Press, New York (2006)

KSQuant - Complex Score Manipulation in PWGL through Quantization

Kilian Sprotte[1], Mikael Laurson[2], and Mika Kuuskankare[2]

[1] MKT, TU Berlin
Strasse des 17. Juni 135,
10623 Berlin, Germany
kilian.sprotte@gmail.com
[2] Center for Music and Technology,
Sibelius Academy, P.O.Box 86,
00251 Helsinki, Finland
{laurson,mkuuskan}@siba.fi

Abstract. This paper presents the recent developments dealing with our metrical score representation format and how it can be used to produce and manipulate musical scores in PWGL. The base of these ideas is a special score format, called ENP-score-notation, that allows to describe in textual form various score elements like beats, measures, voices and parts. This basic format can be extended using keywords to represent other score attributes such as pitch, enharmonics, expressions, and so on, resulting in complete scores. A novel PWGL library, KSQuant, uses a similar format: instead of the tree-based representation of the metric structure, KSQuant uses a flat onset-time representation. This format is ideal for many types of score manipulation operations where it is essential to preserve all score attributes.

Keywords: score manipulation, quantization, computer-aided composition.

1 Introduction

Many different text-based formats have been developed for representing the information in a musical score. Some typical examples are CMN, GUIDO, MusiX-TEX [2], GNU LilyPond, and MusicXML [3]. Some Lisp-based representations are also able to preserve only a subset of musical information, such as the rhythm; these include the notation formats of both PatchWork [4] and OpenMusic [5]. Our textual format, ENP-score-notation [7], also provides a way to generate and manipulate rich musical data in PWGL [6]. ENP-score-notation is offered as an intermediate step between the score and the low-level file format. By using ENP-score-notation, a score can be converted into a more readable form that can also easily be converted back to an ENP score. This kind of symmetry is beneficial, as it allows users to view and modify score information without losing information.

S. Ystad, R. Kronland-Martinet, and K. Jensen (Eds.): CMMR 2008, LNCS 5493, pp. 253–261, 2009.
© Springer-Verlag Berlin Heidelberg 2009

The main topic of this paper is a novel PWGL user library, called KSQuant [1], developed by Kilian Sprotte. KSQuant is basically a quantizer, but unlike some of its predecessor libraries found in PatchWork, OpenMusic and PWGL (e.g. OMKant and GRhythm), it is strongly integrated in the PWGL system as it deals not only with rhythmic structures, but also with other score attributes. Thus KSQuant is closely related to ENP-score-notation. The main difference between the systems is that whereas ENP-score-format deals normally with metrical structures, KSQuant is duration/onset-time oriented.This scheme allows KSQuant to be used as a high-level manipulation tool: it can realize besides quantizing tasks also other complex patch-level operations such as splitting and merging scores without loosing the connection to other score parameters.

2 KSQuant Format

KSQuant operates with a format called 'simple-format'. Instead of using a tree-like structure like in ENP, events start at a certain time point and their duration is specified by the time that passes until the next event occurs. The ENP format is more expressive when it comes to the exact description of rhythmical structures – the simple-format can be seen as a possible reduction.

To this purpose, KSQuant provides mainly two conversion functions:

- score2simple transforms a given ENP score into the simple-format. In order to do this, no additional parameters are required.
- simple2score is a much more complex function. It takes a lot of additional arguments to provide for information that is actually missing in the simple-format, such as time-signatures. Other parameters tune the quantization process that might need to be applied (Sect. 3).

As an example, let us consider the score in Fig. 1. It is quite minimal, but demonstrates some important properties of the ENP format. Concerning its rhythmical expressiveness, there is clearly more information inherent in the specific notation of the two triplets, than just a sequence of durations. Without changing them, the second triplet could be re-notated as a sixtuplet, or as two triplets with a tie in between. It also shows the use of some notational attributes. The accent is added to an entire chord, the x-note-head attribute affects individual notes only.

Fig. 1. A simple score using ENP that nevertheless demonstrates its ability to add notational attributes to a skeleton based on rhythm and pitch.

The textual description in ENP-score-notation format of this score is as follows:

```
(((((1 ((1 :notes (67 60) :expressions (:accent))))
    (1 ((1 :notes (60)) (1 :notes (60)) (1 :notes (60))))
    (1 ((1.0 :notes (60))))
    (1 ((-1 :notes (60))))
    :time-signature (4 4))
   ((2
     ((1 :notes ((59 :note-head :x)))
      (1 :notes ((61 :note-head :x)))
      (1 :notes ((60 :note-head :x)))))
    (1 ((1.0 :notes ((60 :note-head :x)))))
    :time-signature
    (3 4)))))
```

The tree-like structure used to represent the rhythmical groupings is clearly visible. When this score is converted using `score2simple`, the structure is translated to the following flatter representation in simple-format:

```
((((0.0 :notes (67 60) :expressions (:accent))
   (1.0 :notes (60))
   (1.333 :notes (60))
   (1.667 :notes (60))
   -3.0
   (4.0 :notes ((59 :note-head :x)))
   (4.667 :notes ((61 :note-head :x)))
   (5.333 :notes ((60 :note-head :x)))
   7.0)))
```

The only rhythmical information that is left is the onset-time of each event (chord[1] or rest), given as the first floating-point number in each list. There is no notion of ties in the simple-format[2], so that tied chords in the ENP-score-notation will be merged to a single event, which is broken up again (possibly under different metrical circumstances) when converting back.

Rests are represented explicitly by giving them a negative onset-time. From this follows that durations are represented implicitly; they are defined to be the inter-onset difference between the onset-time of an event and the onset-time of its successor. For the purpose of defining the last event's duration, an additional time-value is added to the event-list specifying its end-time and exceptionally not representing an event.

On the other hand, all attribute information is exactly preserved as is. This allows the conversion processes to be reversible in the attribute domain, while being subject to change in the rhythmical domain in the case of `simple2score`.

3   KSQuant as a Quantizer

There has been a lot of ongoing research about Rhythm Quantization, especially in the context of Automatic Music Transcription [8][9]. Starting from the naive model of grid quantization, where each onset is quantized to the nearest grid point independent of its neighbours, more elaborate models have been developed

---

[1] Technically, a single note object is always contained in a chord object.
[2] Although this might be added to allow for the representation of partially tied chords.

that take the context into account. On the micro level the goal is then to successfully recognize expressive deviations, whereas tempo extraction on the macro level is performed.

KSQuant takes an intermediate position in this respect. Its quantization algorithm is currently not as sophisticated as it could be. The tempo, for instance, needs to be specified beforehand and can not automatically be extracted from the input. While there is certainly a potential for future work, it should be emphasized that the main goal of KSQuant is not to aid in Automatic Transcription, but to provide means for score transformations that are much more easily conducted on the simple-format representation than on the hierarchical tree representation.

Nevertheless, the quantizer of KSQuant, as present in the function simple2score, features a number of parameters, whose default settings are shown in Fig. 2. Most important is the set of permitted divisions, $PermDivs$ that is for convenience controlled by the parameters $MaxDiv$ and $ForbiddenDivs$:

$$PermDivs = \{d : d \in \{1, 2, ..., MaxDiv\}, d \notin ForbiddenDivs\}$$

Together with the tempo, $PermDivs$ establish a set of possible grids that is evaluated for every group (the group length depending on the time signature) by a simple heuristic employing the mean squared error of onset deviation in that group. The level of control provided by $PermDivs$ often proves to be too limited. Therefore the user can still finetune the result using the argument $ForbiddenPatts$. Fig. 3 shows an example where the first measure is quantized using only $MaxDiv = 8$ (i.e. $ForbiddenPatts$ is nil). The second measure is, however, quantized with $ForbiddenPatts$ set equal to ((1/16 3/32 3/32)) that forces the quantizer to change the second beat.

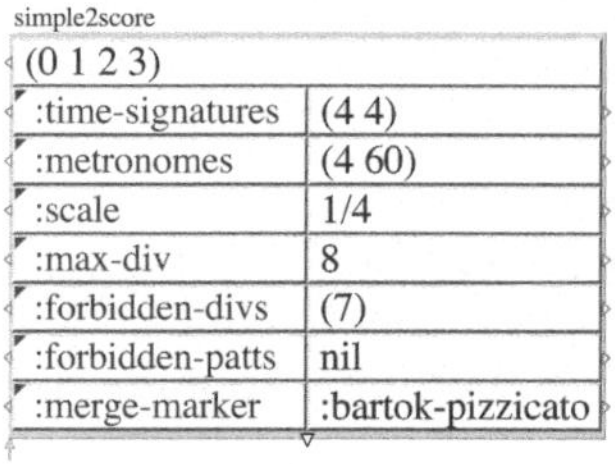

simple2score	
(0 1 2 3)	
:time-signatures	(4 4)
:metronomes	(4 60)
:scale	1/4
:max-div	8
:forbidden-divs	(7)
:forbidden-patts	nil
:merge-marker	:bartok-pizzicato

Fig. 2. The simple2score box with completely opened additional inputs

Fig. 3. The effect of using the $ForbiddenPatts$ argument

4   Score Manipulation

This section enumerates some examples that demonstrate how KSQuant can be used to manipulate and build metrical scores. Often these manipulations would be tedious to perform using the standard ENP-score-notation format or other score building tools provided by PWGL.

Fig. 4 gives a typical quantizing patch example where onset-times and pitch information is given in simple-format to the `simple2score` box. The result is fed in turn to a `Score-Editor` box. Note that the simple-format allows to specify the enharmonic spelling of the sixth note and that this information is preserved in the `simple2score` transformation.

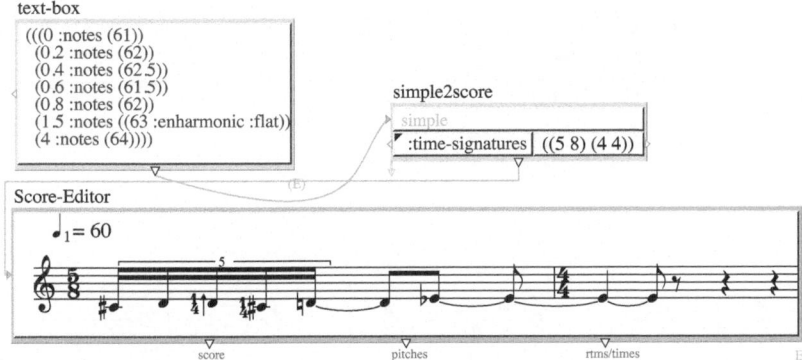

Fig. 4. A patch example that unites pitch information with a quantizing operation

In Fig. 5, in turn, we have two input scores that are first merged to a single voice (to the left), and then appended resulting in a two measure score (to the right). We use here two KSQuant library boxes, `simple-merge` and `simple-append`, that accept as inputs the simple-format.

The append case in this example is trivial due to the fact that the input items are entire bars. This operation could be easily performed in other score editors, e.g. in Sibelius[10]. The more complex case of joining multiple cells of varying duration is shown in Fig. 6. There is no need to mention that for a composer this is quite a fundamental operation. Nevertheless – in the context of n-tuplets – this has not been a well supported feature, e.g. by Sibelius[3].

A similar problem arises, when we need to change the time-signatures of a given passage. Again the presence of n-tuplets poses difficulties when they need to be split across bar lines. Fig. 7 demonstrates this case by changing the time-signature from 4/4 to 3/8. This leads to splitting the first triplet and the second sixtuplet.

---

[3] Typically an error message would appear telling the user that it is not possible to insert a sequence in a metrical position where any n-tuplet of that sequence is divided by a bar line.

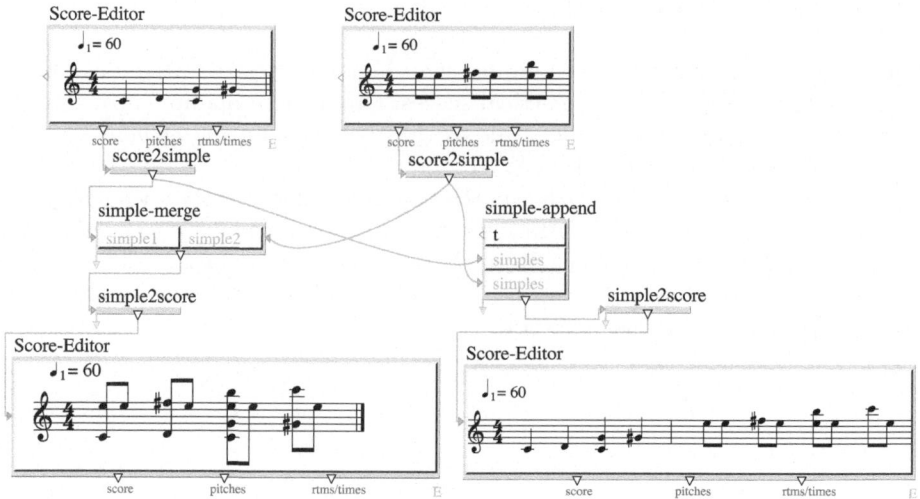

Fig. 5. Simple merging and appending

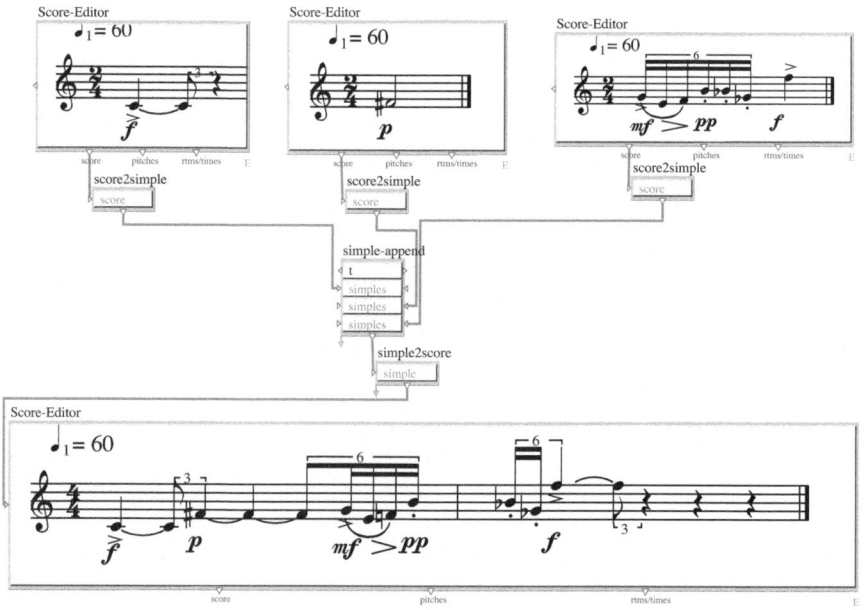

Fig. 6. A more complex case of appending where the joints do not fall on the beat. Again, complex expressions are preserved.

Our final example, shown in Fig. 8, manipulates an input score by scaling all offset-times by 5/8 (see the `scale` input of the `simple2score` box). Note that also here the micro-tonal pitch material is preserved.

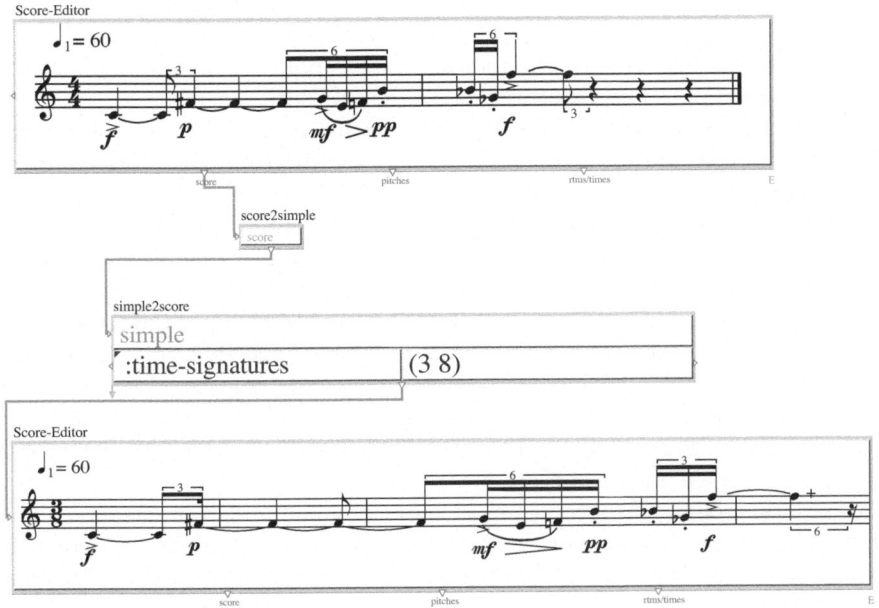

Fig. 7. Changing the time-signature to 3/8. The n-tuplets are clearly affected by the new bar lines.

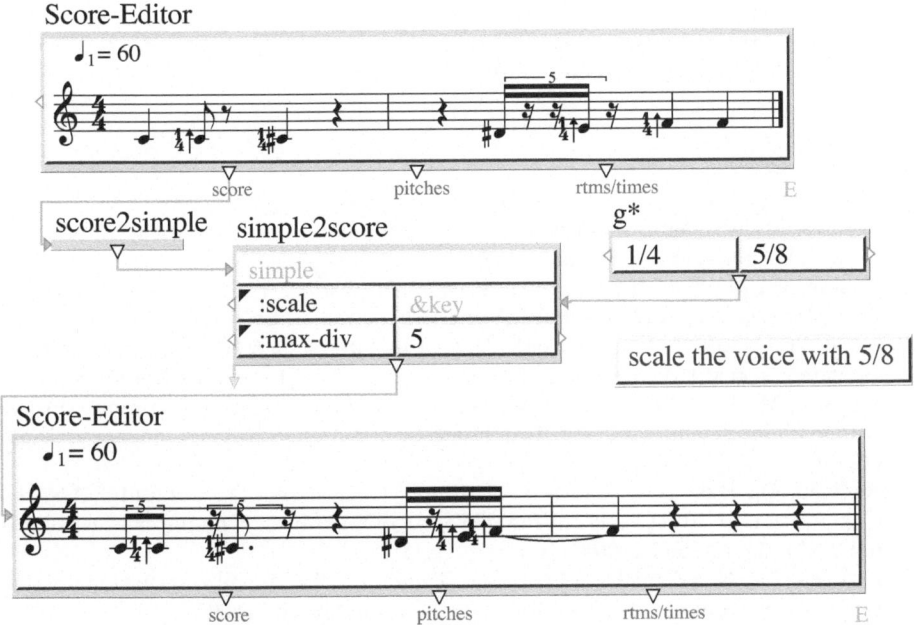

Fig. 8. An input score is scaled by 5/8 resulting in a new score

5   Future Work

It has been shown that quantization allows to manipulate scores with more ease compared to manipulating a hierarchical score structure.

The quantization algorithm of KSQuant potentially modifies the onset-times of the input events (so that they can be notated with given constraints). In the score manipulation examples of this paper, however, no adjustment of onset-times and durations is required – only a rearrangement of n-tuplets and ties is performed. Currently, the user has no influence on how grouping decisons are being made; this would be an interesting addition for the future.

Concerning the quantization part, it would be useful to report the amount of modification to the user. A further step would allow to specify a maximum deviation beforehand, thus allowing the user to control the amount of quantization or even turn it off completely.

Additionally, it would be helpful to be able to specify multiple parameter sets that would be active only in a certain region.

If this parametrization becomes even more detailed and context-dependent, constraint-programming seems to become the appropriate paradigm. Triplet divisions, for instance, could be globally allowed, but not in immediate succession. With this fine-grained control at hand, KSQuant would become an even better suited tool for highly customized manipulations of rhythmical score structures.

Acknowledgement

The work of Mikael Laurson and Mika Kuuskankare has been supported by the Academy of Finland (SA 105557 and SA 114116).

References

1. Sprotte, K.: KSQuant, a library for score manipulation and quantization (2008), http://kiliansprotte.de/ksquant/
2. Taupin, D., Mitchell, R., Egler, A.: MusiXTeX (2003), http://directory.fsf.org/MusiXTex.html
3. Good, M., Actor, G.: Using MusicXML for File Interchange. In: Third International Conference on WEB Delivering of Music, p. 153. IEEE Press, Los Alamitos (2003)
4. Laurson, M.: PATCHWORK: A Visual Programming Language and some Musical Applications. Studia musica no. 6, doctoral dissertation, Sibelius Academy, Helsinki (1996)
5. Assayag, G., Rueda, C., Laurson, M., Agon, C., Delerue, O.: Computer Assisted Composition at IRCAM: From PatchWork to OpenMusic. Computer Music Journal 23(3), 59–72 (Fall 1999)
6. Laurson, M., Kuuskankare, M.: Recent Trends in PWGL. In: International Computer Music Conference, New Orleans, USA, pp. 258–261 (2006)

7. Kuuskankare, M., Laurson, M.: Expressive Notation Package. Computer Music Journal 30(4), 67–79 (2006)
8. Cemgil, A.T., Desain, P., Kappen, B.: Rhythm Quantization for Transcription. In: Proceedings of the AISB 1999 Symposium on Musical Creativity, pp. 64–69 (1999)
9. Agon, C., Assayag, G., Fineberg, J., Rueda, C.: Kant: A critique of pure quantification. In: Proceedings of the International Computer Music Conference, Aarhus, Denmark, pp. 52–59 (1994)
10. Sibelius music notation software, http://www.sibelius.com/

Strategies and Methods for Creating Symbolic Electroacoustic Scores in ENP

Mika Kuuskankare and Mikael Laurson

Sibelius Academy, Centre for Music and Technology,
P.O. Box 86, 00251 Helsinki, Finland
http://www.siba.fi/pwgl

Abstract. In this paper we explore the potential of Expressive Notation Package (ENP) in representing electroacoustic scores. We use the listening score by Rainer Wehinger–originally created for György Ligeti's electronic piece *Articulation*–as reference material. Our objective is to recreate a small excerpt form the score using an ENP tool called Expression Designer (ED). ED allows the user to create new graphical expressions with programmable behavior. In this paper we aim to demonstrate how a collection of specific graphic symbols found in Articulation can be implemented using ED. We also discuss how this information can be later manipulated and accessed for the needs of a sonic realization, for example.

Keywords: Electroacoustic music, Symbolic electroacoustic score, ENP, PWGL, sonification, visual tools.

1 Introduction

The Lisp-based music notation program ENP [1] is among the most recent music-related software packages developed at the Sibelius Academy during the past 20 years. ENP has been developed specifically for the needs of computer-aided composition, music analysis and synthesis control. There is also a strong emphasis on the applications of new music and contemporary notation (for examples see [2] and [3]).

ENP has already been used as a tool in several projects to produce control information for virtual instrument models (see[4], [5], [6], and [7]). ENP offers several attractive features in terms of electroacoustic music, e.g, graphical user-interface (GUI) based on direct manipulation [8], time-based music representation, a rich set of notational attributes called ENP-expressions [9] and the possibility to include user-definable graphical objects as a part of music notation. One interesting aspect in ENP's approach is that, for example, control information can be drawn directly on the score. ENP uses the industry standard OpenGL API [10] for graphics. This provides virtually unlimited possibilities for visualization and user interaction.

In this paper we extend the concept of ENP-expressions to cover the production of electroacoustic scores. To make ENP more extensible in this regard a

S. Ystad, R. Kronland-Martinet, and K. Jensen (Eds.): CMMR 2008, LNCS 5493, pp. 262–271, 2009.

specialized editor was created. ED [11] allows the user to create new customizable expressions using Lisp, a set of graphical tools, or the combination of the two. A set of graphical macros are presented that allow the user to harness the power of OpenGL to create complex and modular graphical objects. We will also shortly discuss how the data in the user-definable graphical scores can be accessed for the needs of sonification.

Our approach can be seen as a continuation of the long tradition of music creation tools, such as, UPIC [12], Hyperscore ([13] and [14]), Acousmographe [15], Pd [16], Animal [17], EMPS [18], and SSSP [19]. The UPIC system was developed by Iannis Xenakis in the mid 70's at the Centre d'Etudes de Mathématique et Automatique Musicales (CEMAMu) in Paris. In UPIC the user designs his music using an electromagnetic pencil. There have been some attempts to recreate the UPIC system using commodity hardware, such as, IanniX [20] and HighC [21]. Pd allows the user to incorporate graphics by using special structures for attaching shapes and colors to the data which the user can then visualize and edit. The data can be entered both manually and algorithmically. Animal and SSSP were among the first to explore the possibilities of combining graphics to synthesis. EMPS is one of the few systems around where the graphic notation is derived from a computer-based sound analysis. Hyperscore, in turn, is a graphical, computer-assisted composition system that allows users to visualize and edit musical structures and Acousmographe inputs FFT information and allows the user to create scores by highlighting important characteristics of the sound.

The remainder of this paper is divided among the following topics. Firstly, we cover the basic concepts behind ED and it's graphical language. Secondly, we use ED to define a small collection of specific graphic symbols found in the listening score created by Rainer Wehinger for György Ligeti's Articulation. Thirdly, we use these expressions to recreate a small score excerpt. Finally, we outline the expression access scheme of ENP which allows the user to access the information contained by the score for the needs of sonification, for example.

2   ED

Modern music–and electroacoustic music in particular–requires special expression markings and new ones are invented all the time. For example, Karkoschka [3] and Risatti [22] list thousands of different notational devices used in contemporary music.

Against this background, it becomes evident that it is an impossible task for a music notation program to make available a comprehensive collection of expression markings. It is more reasonable to provide an interface that lets the user design custom expressions.

ED is a visual tool aimed at rapid expression designing and prototyping in ENP. In this paper we are concentrating on the visual properties of the expressions so the entire work-flow of ED is not covered here. More comprehensive discussion of ED can be found in [11]. One of ED's unique features is that a live preview of the new expression is always shown in the preview score at the bottom of the ED editor window.

There are two fundamental approaches in ED to define new expressions:

1. By using Lisp and a collection of dedicated graphical primitives for drawing lines, polygons, text, etc. Additionally, more experienced users can take the full advantage of the OpenGL graphical language. This approach allows the user to design expressions that can react to their musical context, e.g., to change color, size, or shape dynamically.
2. By using the graphical tools provided by ED. The graphical tools allow the user to enter and edit graphics by using mouse and contextual menus. These objects can also be used alongside of any graphics generated using the former approach. The objects also have the ability–although somewhat limited–to adjust their shape or size dynamically.

One of the most important features of ENP-Expressions is that they can contain user-definable and editable data. The data can be read and written both manually and algorithmically. It can be used to control the visual aspects of the expressions, for example. We will give an example of this feature in Section 2.1.

2.1   Creating Expressions with ED

Next, we demonstrate how to create three specific symbols found in Articulation: (a) the brownish surface representing a spatial effect, (b) comb shapes representing noise, and (c) lines with a square shaped head representing harmonic or subharmonic spectra. (see Figure 1)

We begin with the expression (a). The complete ED definition is given in Fig. 2. Here, we use the algorithmic approach to define the filled, somewhat egg shaped, object. Note that this is a simplified approximation of the original with normalized coordinates.

Let us take a closer look at the definition shown in the code view in Fig. 2. The piece of code is also given below and it should be fairly self-documenting. The three instructions at the top of the code belong to the built-in graphical vocabulary of ED. with-GL-scale, with-GL-color, and with-2D-polygon control the size, color, and the shape of the expression respectively. scaler is a special parameter that contains the value of an individual scaling-factor of the expression. Here, it is used to control the y-dimension (or 'height') of the expression. The width of the expression, in turn, is governed by the duration of the associated musical object (i.e., a note or a chord). The instruction with-2D-polygon creates an OpenGL state for drawing polygons out of a collection of vertices. Inside this context, each vertex of a polygon is added with add-2D-vertex command.

```
(with-gl-scale width scaler
  (with-gl-color :cornsilk3
    (with-2d-polygon
      (iterate (for x in '(0.0  0.1 0.5 0.8 0.96 1.0 1.0 0.96 0.8 0.5 0.1 0.0))
               (for y in '(-0.2 -0.3 -0.3 -0.2 -0.1 0.0 0.0 0.1 0.2 0.3 0.3 0.2))
               (add-2d-vertex x y)))))
```

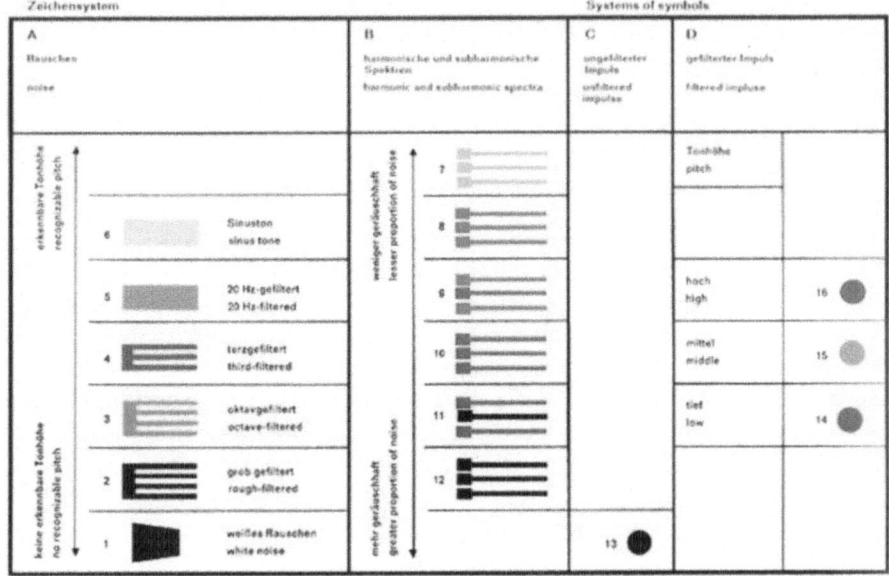

Fig. 1. A table of symbols used in the original score by Wehinger

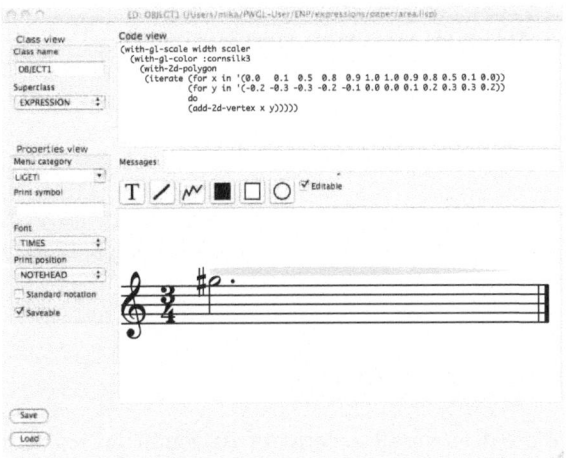

Fig. 2. A filled surface created in ED with the help of a Lisp-algorithm

Our next object (b) demonstrates how user-definable data can be used to control the appearance of the expression. In this case, we access information stored in a special attribute list (see the first line in the code example). The user can manipulate this data either algorithmically or by using the GUI. Here, an attribute called `count` is used to control the number of triangle shaped objects drawn by the code. To save space we give only the code part of the definition below. The resulting graphical object can be seen in Fig. 5.

```
(let ((count (or (get-ENP-property expression :count) 1)))
  (iterate (for y from 0.0 by 1.0 below count)
           (with-GL-translate 0.0 y
             (draw-2d-triangle 0.0 -0.5 0.0 0.5 width 0.0 :filled-p t))))
```

Finally, we define the object (c) by hand with the help of the graphical tools. Fig. 3 gives the relevant part of the ED editor. We use a filled polygon combined with a line shaped object to construct the expression. The end-points of the line are set to 0.0% and 100.0% of the total width of the expression respectively. This allows the line to adjust its length according to the space reserved for the associated score object. The GUI actions cannot be demonstrated here. Instead, the effect can best be seen by studying the final score given in Section 3.

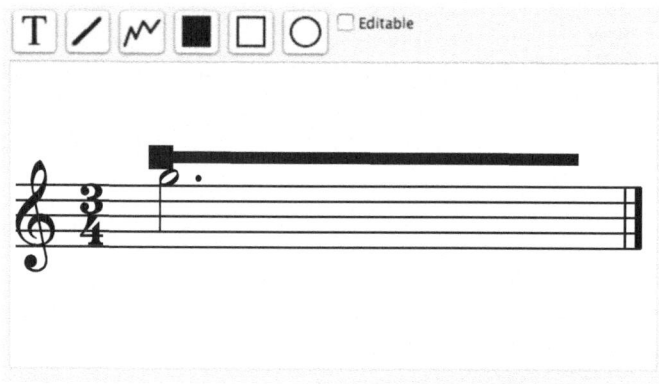

Fig. 3. An expression created manually by using the graphical tools shown at the top of the figure. The expression is a combination of a filled polygon and a connected thick line.

3   (Re)creating Articulations

In this section we create a small excerpt of Articulation using ENP. One of the advantages of ENP is that there is no difference between a traditional instrumental score and an electroacoustic one. In this case, we use a special notation mode called non-mensural notation to realize our score. A non-mensural score is built out of events that have discrete onset and offset times. The events can be freely positioned in a continuous time-line.

In order to realize our final example, a 'raw' score is first created (see Fig. 4) by entering some notes, adjusting their onset times and durations. The final appearance, in turn, is created by attaching the appropriate expressions to the note objects as can be seen in Fig. 5.

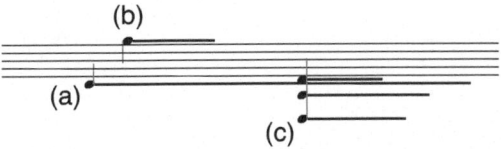

Fig. 4. A non-mensural 'raw' score with some events to attach expressions to

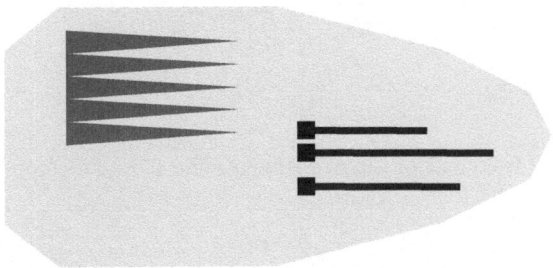

Fig. 5. The final realization of a passage of Ligeti's Articulation containing three symbols found in the original score

In the resulting score the 'surface' expression is attached to the note shown in (a). The duration of the note controls the width of the expression and the height has been adjusted manually. (b) has been associated with the comb shaped expression. The number of comb lines has been entered through the GUI (it is set to 5 here). Finally, each of the three notes found in (c) have been associated with an 'impulse' expression. These notes all have an individual duration, as can be seen in Fig. 4, thus resulting in expressions of different length.

4 Accessing the Expression Information

In this section, we give a concise overview of our scheme for reading expression information form an ENP score. This is typically done using our Scripting language ENP-Script. ENP-Script uses a syntax identical to the PWGLConstraints pattern-matching language. The syntax of the language is not presented here, instead the reader is advised to study [23], [24], and [25].

ENP scripts consist of one or more scripting rules. The scripting rule, in turn, consists of a pattern-matching part and a Lisp-code part (separated by a special symbol ?if). The pattern-matching part contains a set of pattern-matching variables each representing a specific score object (e.g., a note, a chord, or a measure). The pattern matching variables have knowledge about the pitch, the rhythm, the current harmony, etc. This knowledge can be accessed by the scripting rules.

In ENP-Script, e is a special extension to our scripting language that can be used to access information about and contained by ENP-expressions. Below

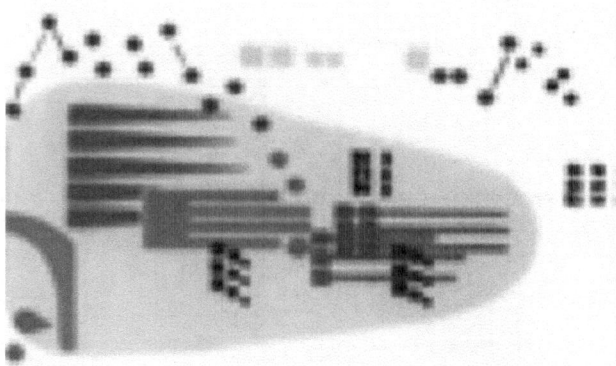

Fig. 6. The original fragment of Ligeti's Articulation (contains more symbols than the ENP version)

we give a few simple script snippets to illustrate the potential of our scripting language in terms of sonification. In the example scripts we use a fairly simple pattern-matching part: the symbol ?1 represents a single note object in the score. Ellipsis points indicates the parts that are typically to be filled in by the user.

4.1   Accessing the Expressions

One of the basic tasks of a script is to check if a score object (i.e., a chord or a note) is associated with any expressions (e.g., articulation, dynamics, or any user-definable one). For example, (e ?1 :object3) or (e ?1 :object3 :all) return the first expression of type *object3* or all of them respectively.

In case of our Ligeti example one of the expressions could be accessed using the piece of code given below. The keyword :object1 in this example is the user-definable name given in Fig. 2 (see entry 'Class name').

```
(* ?1
   (?if (let ((spat (e ?1 :object1)))
         (when spat
           ;; when an object of type :object1 is found
           ;; create some playback information here.
           ....
           ))))
```

4.2   Accessing Time-Varying Information

Let us assume that we want to access some time-varying information contained by an expression (e.g., Score-BPF [9]). Our scripting language allows us to 'sample' an expression at any given time point. This can be accomplished with the combination of two keywords :sample and :at. :sample indicates that we want to access the time varying numeric values. The keyword :at, in turn, defines the point in time that we want to sample. The argument :at can be either absolute time in seconds or, as in this case, a score object. Thus, :at ?1 means that we want to access the value of the expression at exactly the onset-time of the note ?1.

```
(* ?1
   (?if (let ((norm-pitch (e ?1 :object3 :SAMPLE :at ?1)))
          ;; sample the value of the expression at the
          ;; current position and use that to generate
          ;; a new pitch
          (setf (midi ?1) (+ 60 (* norm-pitch 24))))))
```

Here, we are assuming that the score contains an expression named :object3 with time-varying information ranging from 0.0 to 1.0. In the script this value is then scaled inside two octaves (24 semitones). Note, that in this case we physically modify the score data.

4.3   Accessing Other Information Contained by the Expressions

An expression in the score can be made out of smaller graphical units. This could be the case, for example, in our Ligeti example where one of the expressions contains three triangle shaped images. An optional way to realize the object in question is to create a Canvas-expression containing three individual sub-objects. One benefit here would be that the sub-objects can be named which, in turn, allows the user to access them one by one. The following code snippet illustrates how to access this information using the :id keyword. Here we assume that there are two sub-objects named :wedge1 and :wedge2.

```
(* ?1
   (?if (let ((wedge1 (e ?1 :object1 :id :wedge1))
              (wedge2 (e ?1 :object1 :id :wedge2)))
          ;; inspect here the properties of both
          ;; objects and trigger different processes
          ;; depending on the attributes
          ...
          )))
```

The user-definable data can be used to control not only the appearance but also the sonification of the expression. The next script snippet uses the data stored in the expressions attribute list to generate sound. 'spectra' is the comb shaped object (b) created in Section 2.1 where we used a special attribute named :count to control the number of visible cones. In our sonification script this information could again be used to control how the object sounds:

```
(let ((specta (e ?1 :object2)))
  (when spectra
    (let ((count (or (get-ENP-property expression :count) 1)))
      (iterate (for bin from 0 below count)
               ;; generate the components of the sound
               ...))))
```

5   Future Work

As our next step we are planning to do some sonic realizations using PWGLSynth [26] and our macro-note scheme [27]. The combination of these tools could be quite inspiring and powerful. The ENP user-interface facilitates selective and interactive listening process. The user can select an object or any combination thereof and listen to the resulting sound, make modifications and repeat the process as long as needed. PWGLSynth, in turn, can be used to create the synthesis algorithms that realize the individual sonic objects. The idea of macro-notes would also fit in this scheme as it could be used create elaborate algorithmic interpretations of the visual symbols.

Acknowledgment

The work of Mika Kuuskankare and Mikael Laurson has been supported by the Academy of Finland (SA 114116 and SA 105557).

References

1. Kuuskankare, M.: The Expressive Notation Package. Ph.D thesis, Sibelius Academy, DocMus – Department of Doctoral Studies in Musical Performance and Research (2006)
2. Brindle, R.S.: The New Music: The Avant-garde since 1945. Oxford University Press, Oxford (1987)
3. Karkoschka, E.: Das Schriftbild der Neuen Musik. Hermann Moeck Verlag, Celle (1966)
4. Laurson, M., Erkut, C., Välimäki, V., Kuuskankare, M.: Methods for Modeling Realistic Playing in Acoustic Guitar Synthesis. Computer Music Journal 25(3), 38–49 (Fall 2001)
5. Välimäki, V., Penttinen, H., Knif, J., Laurson, M., Erkut, C.: Sound Synthesis of the Harpsichord Using a Computationally Efficient Physical Model. EURASIP Journal on Applied Signal Processing (2004)
6. Penttinen, H., Pakarinen, J., Välimäki, V., Laurson, M., Li, H., Leman, M.: Model-Based Sound Synthesis of the Guqin. Journal of the Acoustical Society of America 120(6), 4052–4063 (2006)
7. Välimäki, V., Laurson, M., Erkut, C.: Commuted Waveguide Synthesis of the Clavichord. Computer Music Journal 27(1), 71–82 (2003)
8. Cooper, A.: About Face. The Essentials of User Interface Design. IDG Books, Foster City (1995)
9. Kuuskankare, M., Laurson, M.: ENP-Expressions, Score-BPF as a Case Study. In: Proceedings of International Computer Music Conference, Singapore, pp. 103–106 (2003)
10. Woo, M., Neider, J., Davis, T., Shreiner, D.: OpenGL Programming Guide, 3rd edn. Addison Wesley, Massachusetts (1999)
11. Kuuskankare, M., Laurson, M.: ENP Expression Designer - a Visual Tool for Creating User Definable Expressions. In: International Computer Music Conference, Barcelona, Spain, pp. 307–310 (2005)
12. Lohner, H.: The UPIC system: A user's report. Computer Music Journal 10(4), 42–49 (Winter 1986)
13. Farbood, M.M., Pasztor, E., Jennings, K.: Hyperscore: A graphical sketchpad for novice composers. IEEE Comput. Graph. Appl. 24(1), 50–54 (2004)

14. Farbood, M., Kaufman, H., Jennings, K.: Composing with hyperscore: An intuitive interface for visualizing musical structure. In: International Computer Music Conference (2007)
15. Geslin, Y., Lefevre, A.: Sound and musical representation: the acousmographe software. In: International Computer Music Conference, Miami, USA (2004)
16. Puckette, M.: Using Pd as a score language. In: Proceedings of International Computer Music Conference, pp. 184–187 (2002)
17. Lindemann, E., de Cecco, M.: Animal–a rapid prototyping environment for computer music systems. Computer Music Journal 15(3), 78–100 (1991)
18. Haus, G.: EMPS: A system for graphic transcription of electronic music scores. Computer Music Journal 7(3), 31–36 (1983)
19. Buxton, W., Sniderman, R., Reeves, W., Patel, S., Baecker, R.: The evolution of the sssp score editing tools. In: Roads, C., Strawn, J. (eds.) Foundations of Computer Music, pp. 376–402. MIT Press, Cambridge (1985)
20. Iannix, http://sourceforge.net/projects/iannix
21. HighC, http://highc.org/
22. Risatti, H.A.: New Music Vocabulary. A Guide to Notational Signs for Contemporary Music. Univ. of Illinois Press, Urbana (1973)
23. Laurson, M.: PATCHWORK: A Visual Programming Language and some Musical Applications. Studia musica no.6, doctoral dissertation, Sibelius Academy, Helsinki (1996)
24. Kuuskankare, M., Laurson, M.: Intelligent Scripting in ENP using PWConstraints. In: Proceedings of International Computer Music Conference, Miami, USA, pp. 684–687 (2004)
25. Laurson, M., Kuuskankare, M.: Extensible Constraint Syntax Through Score Accessors. In: Journées d'Informatique Musicale, Paris, France (2005)
26. Laurson, M., Norilo, V., Kuuskankare, M.: PWGLSynth: A Visual Synthesis Language for Virtual Instrument Design and Control. Computer Music Journal 29(3), 29–41 (Fall 2005)
27. Laurson, M., Kuuskankare, M.: Towards Idiomatic and Flexible Score-based Gestural Control with a Scripting Language. In: Proceedings of NIME 2008 Conference, Genova, Italy, pp. 34–37 (2008)

An IEEE 1599-Based Interface for Score Analysis

Adriano Baratè, Luca A. Ludovico, and Alberto Pinto

Laboratorio di Informatica Musicale (LIM)
Dipartimento di Informatica e Comunicazione
Università degli Studi di Milano
Via Comelico 39/41 – I-20135 Milano, Italy
{barate,ludovico,pinto}@dico.unimi.it

Abstract. This paper deals with a software application to visualize score analysis. Such a tool allows both the enjoyment of music in general, thanks to the synchronized execution of heterogeneous multimedia objects, and the highlighting of the results of score analyses. As a consequence, the user can investigate the compositional process and the relationships among the music objects of a given piece while listening to an audio track and viewing the corresponding score. This is made possible by a new XML-based standard for music representation – namely IEEE 1599 – which will be shortly described.

1 Score Analysis and Its Visual Representation

Musical analysis embraces all those methods aiming at the comprehension of music processes and relationships within a composition. Of course, many different approaches have been employed and are in use to analyze a score, ranging from the traditional methods used in the past centuries to more recent techniques such as the functional analysis by Hans Keller and the Schenkerian analysis by Heinrich Schenker.

A number of ongoing researches are aimed at the analysis of music information through algorithmic processes, in order to obtain automatic segmentation, recognition of recurrent patterns, statistical data, etc. However, the problem of how such results can be obtained, either in a hand-made or computer-based way, is not pertinent to this work.

Rather, we concentrate on the computer-based techniques to produce and enjoy the visual representation of musical analysis. The recipients of this kind of applications include musicologists, music students and untrained people interested in understanding music mechanisms.

Thanks to the application we will introduce in the next sections, we propose a new way to investigate music processes. The results coming from an analysis are presented to the user synchronized with a number of multimedia objects which describe the piece from other points of view. Thus, analysis is not a static description, but it is explained while the score is advancing and the corresponding audio track is playing. As a consequence, an overall comprehension of music can be provided, as regards its symbolic, structural, audio and graphical aspects.

The problem we address has two faces: i) a phase of preparation which includes the encoding of the piece, the recognition of music structures to highlight, the assembly of

S. Ystad, R. Kronland-Martinet, and K. Jensen (Eds.): CMMR 2008, LNCS 5493, pp. 272–282, 2009.

multimedia objects referable to the given piece, and finally the choice of a format to describe all this information within a unique framework; ii) the design and implementation of interfaces to enjoy music according to the key concepts we have introduced.

Even if the choice of a format to represent music and all the related materials is not the main subject of the present work, it should be evident that only a standard with some distinctive characteristics can provide an integrated representation of heterogeneous music contents. Consequently, such *ad hoc* standard is the base for an evolved interface to enjoy music and the corresponding structural information. Needless to say, popular standards for symbolic scores, graphics, audio, video already exist and are commonly used. Nevertheless, their use for a "comprehensive" description of music presents some disadvantages, as follows:

1. Data and metadata can not be synchronised across different formats, as they were not conceived for this purpose. For instance, if TIFF is selected to encode the pages of a score and AIFF is used for the corresponding performances, there is no way to keep information synchronised, unless a third format is used as a wrapper. This problem is even more evident when the user also wants to synchronise structural and musicological analyses, computer-driven performances and textual information such as lyrics.
2. Often music contents are encoded in binary form, unreadable for humans, proprietary and strongly dependent on the current technology.

In our opinion, the new IEEE 1599 standard can solve the above mentioned problems. The general approach and the characteristics of this format are described in the next section.

2   IEEE 1599, a New Standard for Music

IEEE 1599 is a new standard to describe comprehensively heterogeneous music contents. Its development follows the guidelines of IEEE P1599, *Recommended Practice Dealing with Applications and Representations of Symbolic Music Information Using the XML Language* [1].

IEEE 1599, formerly known as MX, is the result of research efforts at the *Laboratorio di Informatica Musicale* (LIM) of the *Università degli Studi di Milano*. The most recent version of its DTD and documentation can be downloaded from http://www.mx.dico.unimi.it.

In a single file, music symbols, printed scores, audio tracks, computer-driven performances, catalogue metadata, text and graphic contents related to a single music piece are linked and mutually synchronised within the same framework. Heterogeneous contents are organised in a multilayered structure that supports different encoding formats and a number of digital objects for each layer [2].

Tools for music visualisation [3], content-based retrieval [4], and automatic segmentation [5] are currently available.

IEEE 1599 is an XML-based format: its name is an acronym which stands for *Musical application using XML*. There are many advantages in choosing XML to describe information in general, and music information in particular. For instance, an XML-based language allows inherent readability, extensibility and durability. It is open, free, easy to read by humans and computers, and can be edited by common software applications. Moreover, it is strongly structured, it can be extended to support new notations and new music symbols, and it can thus become a means of interchange for music with software applications and over the Net. Most of these topics have been treated in [6] and [7].

A comprehensive description of music must support heterogeneous materials. IEEE 1599 employs six different layers to represent information, as explained in [8]:

- *General* – music-related metadata, i.e. catalogue information about the piece;
- *Logic* – the logical description of score symbols;
- *Structural* – identification of music objects and their mutual relationships;
- *Notational* – graphical representations of the score;
- *Performance* – computer-based descriptions and executions of music according to performance languages;
- *Audio* – digital or digitised recordings of the piece.

Not all layers must, or can, be present for a given music piece. For instance, the encoding of a piece does not require to describe all its structural, notational, performance or audio aspects. In some cases, even the symbolic score could not be defined, as it does not exist (such as in jazz improvisation on a harmonic grid) or it is not relevant for the user purposes (as in score following, where only the relationships between the *Notational* and the *Audio* layers must be encoded).

Not only a number of heterogeneous media descriptions is supported, but each layer can also contain many digital instances. For example, the *Notational* layer could link to several notated versions of the score, and the *Structural* layer could provide many different analyses for the same piece. The concept of *multi-layered description* – as many different types of descriptions as possible, all correlated and synchronised – together with the concept of *multi-instance support* – as many different media objects as possible for each layer – provide rich and flexible means for encoding music in all its aspects.

It should be clear that the description provided by such a file is flexible and rich, both in regard to the number and to the type of media involved. In fact, thanks to this approach, a single file can contain one or more descriptions of the same music piece in each layer. For example, in the case of an operatic aria, the IEEE 1599 file could house: the catalogue metadata about the piece, its author(s) and genre; the corresponding portion of the libretto; scans of the original manuscript and of a number of printed scores; several audio files containing different performances; related iconographic contents, such as sketches, stage photographs, and playbills. Thanks to the comprehensive information provided by IEEE 1599, software applications based on such a format allow an integrated enjoyment of music in all its aspects.

The *spine*, the second key concept of the IEEE 1599 format, consists of a sorted list of events. This structure provides both an abstraction level and the glue among layers, thus representing an abstraction level, as the events identified in it do not have to correspond to score symbols, or audio samples, or anything else. It is the author who can decide, from time to time, what goes under the definition of music event, according to the needs: the definition and granularity of events can be chosen by the author of the encoding.

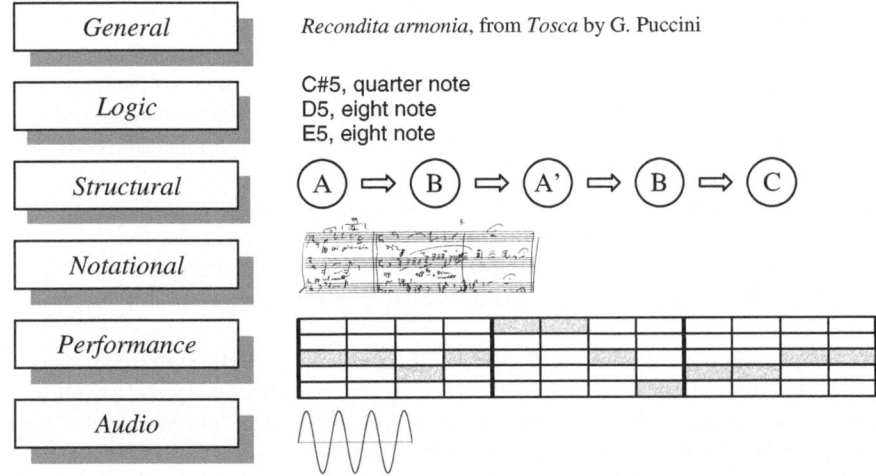

Fig. 1. The characteristic multi-layered structure of IEEE 1599. In the right part of the figure, intuitive graphical examples are provided to illustrate the purpose of the layers.

Since the spine simply lists events to provide a unique label for them, the mere presence of an event in the spine has no semantic meaning. As a consequence, what is listed in the spine structure must have a counterpart in some layer, otherwise the event would not be defined and its presence in the list (and in the file) would be absolutely useless.

For example, in a piece made of *n* music events, the spine would list *n* entries without defining them from any point of view. If each event has a symbolic meaning (e.g. it is a note or a rest), is graphically rendered in many scores and is relevant to a number of analyses, these aspects are treated in the *Logic*, *Notational*, and *Structural* layers respectively.

Music events are not only listed in the spine, but also marked by unique identifiers. These identifiers are referred to by all instances of the corresponding event representations in other layers. Thus, each spine event can be described:

- in 1 to *n* layers; e.g., in the *Logic*, *Notational*, and *Audio* layers;
- in 1 to *n* instances within the same layer; e.g., in three different score versions mapped in the *Notational* layer;
- in 1 to *n* occurrences within the same instance; e.g., the notes in a song refrain that is performed 4 times (thus the same spine events are mapped 4 times in the *Audio* layer, at different timings).

Thanks to the spine, IEEE 1599 is not a simple container for heterogeneous media descriptions related to a unique music piece. It shows instead that those descriptions can also present a number of references to a common structure. This aspect creates synchronisation among instances within a layer (*intra-layer synchronisation*), and – when applied to a complex file – also synchronisation among contents disposed in many layers (*inter-layer synchronisation*).

3 Application Interface and Features

After introducing the concept of visual representations of score analysis (see Section 1) and discussing the layer approach of IEEE 1599 to describe different levels of abstraction in music description (see Section 2), now we present applications that join together these two aspects.

Since the main concept of this work is defining a simple method to represent graphical annotation and to share them, the best choice is using fewer textual annotation and more graphical figures. With this approach, the visual analysis is not dependent by the language and presents also a "visual intuitiveness" even for musicology untrained people.

Before presenting our proposed methodology, a brief digression regarding the IEEE 1599 structural elements involved in our approach is necessary. As presented in Section 2, the layer that houses description of structural considerations is the *Structural* one. In this layer various methods can be used to identify a music object, that is selecting a relevant portion of the music piece. For our purposes we have chosen to use the segmention element, together with its sub-elements, for their simplicity and scalability. In the DTD these elements have the following declaration:

```
<!ELEMENT segmentation (segment+)>
<!ATTLIST segmentation
    id ID #IMPLIED
    description CDATA #IMPLIED
    method CDATA #IMPLIED>

<!ELEMENT segment(segment_event+, feature_object*)>
<!ATTLIST segment
    id ID #REQUIRED>

<!ELEMENT segment_event EMPTY>
<!ATTLIST segment_event
    event_ref IDREF #REQUIRED>
```

Code 1. The fragment of the IEEE 1599 DTD devoted to segmentation element

In the main element, it is possible to define a method for the segmentation process and to add a description in textual form. Within the segmentation element, a number of segments involved in the current analysis must be declared, specifying for each segment all its concerning spine events. The feature_object element is custom implemented for a particular segmentation.

In Code 2 an example is presented to better understand analysis declarations. Only a segmentation is shown, while it is possible to add as many analyses as the like.

```
<segmentation id="segm01" description="Analysis n.1">
  <segment id="s01">
    <segment_event event_ref="p1_meas001_ev01" />
    <segment_event event_ref="p1_meas001_ev03" />
```

```
    <segment_event event_ref="p1_meas011_ev02" />
    <feature_object name="line1">
      <svg width="100mm" height="100mm" version="1.1">
        <rect x="8" y="30" width="30" height="40"
              style="fill:yellow;stroke:red;
              stroke-width:2;opacity:0.6" />
      </svg>
    </feature_object>
</segmentation>

<!ELEMENT feature_object(svg
                         %added_feature_object_classes;)>
<!ATTLIST feature_object
   id ID #IMPLIED
   name CDATA #REQUIRED>
```

Code 2. An example of a segmentation with a visual annotation

The visual analysis annotation process is made by the following steps:

- Definition of one or more score segments to which the annotation is re-lated; this is done by including one or more segment elements in the *Structural* layer;
- Definition of the annotation itself, by inserting symbols and/or drawings such as lines, rectangles, and other figures over a score graphical rendition, i.e. a scan or a computer representation. In IEEE 1599 visual annotations are stored in feature_object, a customizable element that in this ex-ample is declared as an svg (Scalable Vector Graphics) object.

The application developed to edit visual annotations is presented in Figure 2. When the application starts and an IEEE 1599 file is opened, graphical representations of the encoded music piece can be selected; then the application shows the score together with a number of boxes that mark the existing notes, pauses and in general every music symbol described in the *Logic* layer. By a pointing device, the user is allowed to annotate the score iterating the following procedure:

- A visual annotation session is opened;
- The boxes containing the notes involved in the annotation are selected;
- One of the graphic tools is selected;
- The graphical annotations are drawn;
- The current annotation session is closed.

The graphical tools provided for drawing annotations at the moment are: straight lines, curved lines, rectangles, circles and texts, with a personalization of colors, pen widths, and pen types. Clearly this set of tools can be expanded in future releases of

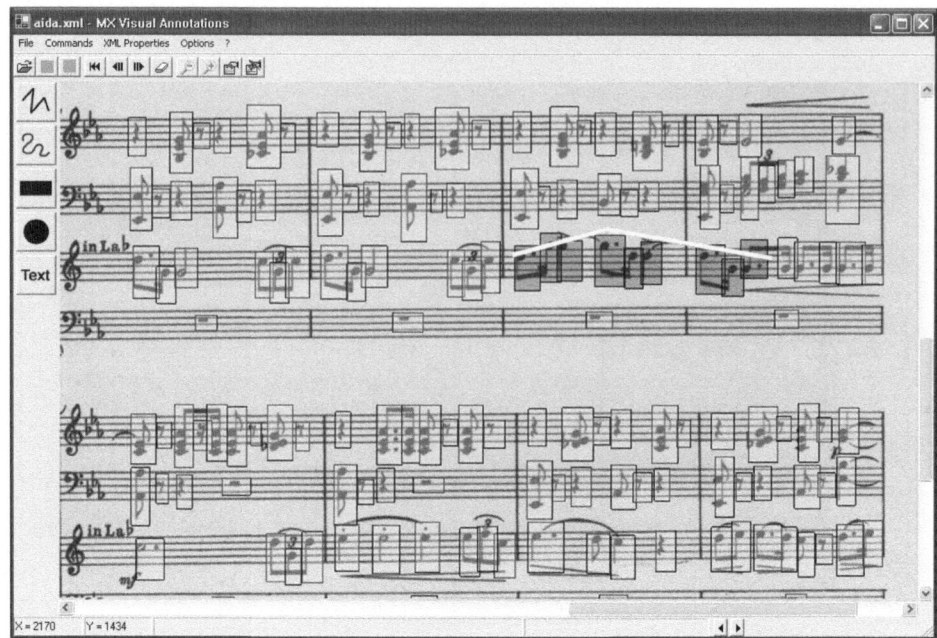

Fig. 2. Visual annotations on an IEEE 1599 score. In the main part of the figure, graphical examples are provided to illustrate the capabilities of the software application.

the software. After inserting the visual annotations, they are added to the IEEE 1599 file using the XML elements previously introduced.

After discussing the editing procedures to create graphical annotations, we now present an example of application that shows analysis in real time, together with the execution of the annotated music piece.

Figure 3 illustrates the interface of the fruition software. The center of the window hosts the graphical score of the music piece, while in the bottom area there is a representation of the corresponding waveform. In the left side of the interface, three examples of visual annotations can be chosen.

The dark rectangle area over the score is the graphical representation of one of the available analyses. During the encoding phase, a macro-segmentation of the piece has been performed, and a number of music objects (in this case, similar phrases) has been described within the *Structural* layer. When the user enables the visualization of this kind of analysis, in the interface dark rectangles remark the occurrence of a music object.

Thanks to the IEEE 1599 format, this application integrates the possibility to view and play various contents from the same layer or from different layers, all in a synchronized way. For example, it is possible to follow two or more score versions, even simultaneously, while a media file is playing, and the current playing note is highlighted in real-time. Besides, musicological analyses can be enjoyed by taking into account their visual and audio counterparts.

Fig. 3. A software application to enjoy intuitively the results of score analysis

4   BWV 636: A Case Study from J.S. Bach's Orgelbüchlein

An analysis is composed of many score segments connected by transition maps, which encode their mutual relationships. For instance, a generic segment B might be the transposition of another segment A by one semitone up.

This kind of analysis is extremely useful in order to understand the compositional process of music pieces and its encoding within a language for music description represents a key feature of every software environment for music analysis.

At a first stage, by exploiting the annotating features of our software, musicologists can encode their own analysis, which is stored into *Structural* layer. Then all the analysis can be made available to other scholars or students for musicological investigation or just music fruition.

As an example of analysis, we considered the choral-prelude "Vater unser im Himmelreich" (Our Father who art in Heaven) BWV 636 for organ by Johann Sebastian Bach. This piece has been chosen because of its shortness (just 12 bars long) and because it is characterized by an extremely dense symbolism.

Baroque music in general, and sacred music in particular, is often characterized by the presence of many "rhetorical figures" which relates for example to the text a piece of music refers to or, more often, to particular moods or "affects" the music wants to induce in the listener's mind and sensibility.

The Theory of Emotions, as it is sometimes referred to, wants to provide a link between music and the world of affects: for example the feeling of joy is often expressed in music by the so called "circulatio", namely a sequence of notes rapidly going up and down by close intervals and drawing in the space of pitches a sort of circles.

Rhetorical references can be even more specific, like in this example, and can involve graphical, and thus musical, representation of concrete objects.

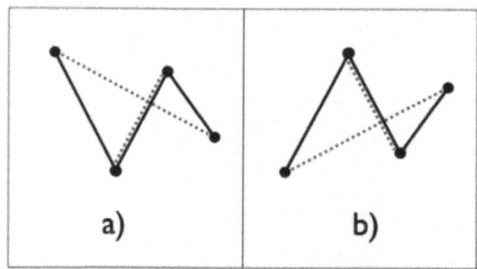

Fig. 4. The scheme of the cross pattern of BWV 636

Figure 4 reports the abstract structure of a cross-shaped recurring pattern whose concrete instances are spread across alto, tenor and bass parts of BWV 636; the first is in the tenor part of the first measure (Figure 5). This is an evident reference to Christ's cross [9] and the understanding of this basic musicological fact is of paramount importance in the comprehension of the whole structure of the piece.

Fig. 5. First cross pattern in the tenor part of BWV 636

Of course, also the main theme of choral "Vater unser im Himmelreich", which is present in the soprano part of BWV 636, is the other fundamental component of the piece.

In our implementation all patterns are stored as feature objects together with other feature vectors related to music information retrieval [10] and linked to each music segment that can be displayed during the playback; the user can mark each specific instance of any kind of musicologically relevant pattern (main themes, peculiar patterns, etc.) within the piece and automatically store it in the *Structural* layer of IEEE 1599.

The advantage is that those instances can be highlighted during the playback of the piece for didactical and study purposes.

Figure 6 shows a representation of BWV 636 analysis with all cross-patterns highlighted. This kind of representation allows for a comprehensive understanding of the overall structure at a glance.

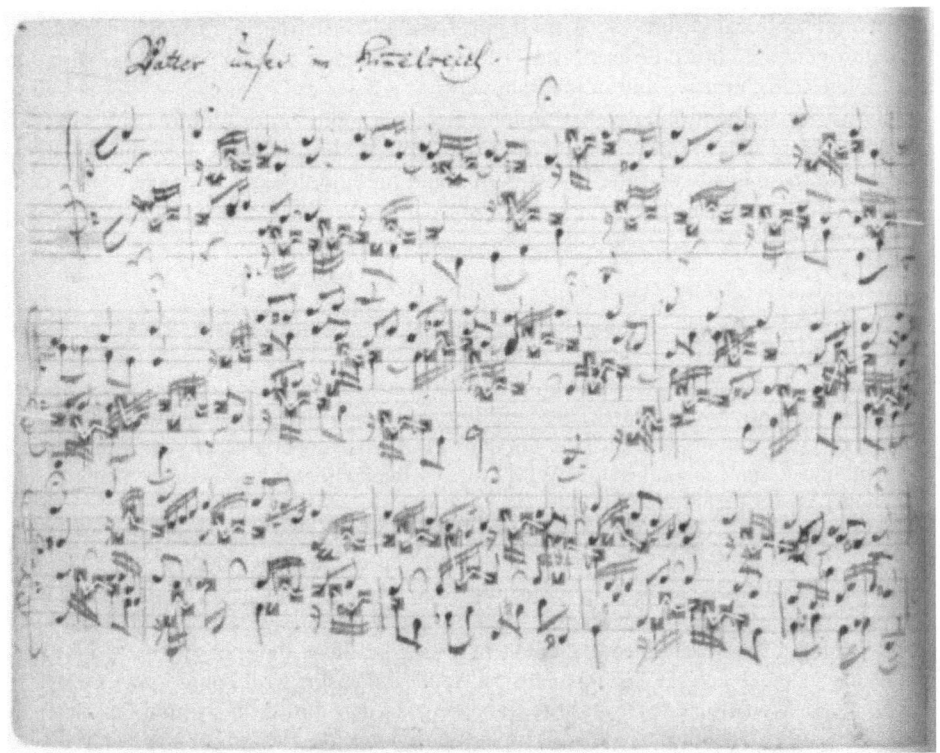

Fig. 6. Representation of the cross pattern on the manuscript of BWV 636

5 Conclusions

In this paper, an advanced application to understand music structures and enjoy music at different degrees of abstraction has been illustrated. This tool allows to follow a music piece in its many complementary aspects: symbolic score, graphical notations, audio, and structure.

The key feature is the ease of showing given characteristics of a music piece, highlighting music symbols or more complex aggregations over one of the possible graphical and audio renderings of a given music sheet. Thanks to our proposal, the results of musical analysis are no more written words that must be referred to a symbolic score to be understood, but they can be enjoyed within an integrated framework where the original score, its revised versions, its many audio descriptions, and much more are easily available. Moreover, the deep integration among multimedia objects strengthens the comprehension of music structures.

The IEEE 1599 standard and its applications present no constraint about music genres, cultural areas, historical periods, or different approaches to composition and musical analysis. As a consequence, the methods and the interfaces described so far can be applied to baroque fugue as well as Indian raga, to operatic arias as well as jazz improvisation. Of course, the kind of analysis and the features to be investigated can change noticeably, but the overall approach – consisting in a unique framework for heterogeneous music descriptions – preserves its capability to convey information in an integrated, intuitive and immediate way.

Interesting applications can be implemented, particularly for cultures and kinds of music far from Common Western Notation, such as those studied by ethnomusicology, where there has been little investigation and methodological research.

References

1. Baggi, D.L.: Technical Committee on Computer-Generated Music. Computer 28(11), 91–92 (1995)
2. Haus, G., Longari, M.: Proceeding of the First International IEEE Conference on Musical Application using XML (MAX 2002). IEEE Computer Society, Los Alamitos (2002)
3. Baggi, D.L., Baratè, A., Haus, G., Ludovico, L.A.: A computer tool to enjoy and understand music. In: Proceedings of EWIMT 2005 – Integration of Knowledge, Semantics and Digital Media Technology, pp. 213–217 (2005)
4. Baratè, A., Haus, G., Ludovico, L.A.: An XML-Based Format for Advanced Music Fruition. In: Proceedings of SMC 2006 – Sound and Music Computing (2006)
5. Haus, G., Ludovico, L.A.: Music Segmentation: An XML-oriented Approach. In: Wiil, U.K. (ed.) CMMR 2004. LNCS, vol. 3310, pp. 330–346. Springer, Heidelberg (2005)
6. Roland, P.: The Music Encoding Initiative (MEI). In: Proceedings of the first IEEE International Conference MAX 2002 – Musical Application using XML, pp. 55–59 (2002)
7. Steyn, J.: Framework for a music markup language. In: Proceeding of the First International IEEE Conference on Musical Application using XML (MAX2002), pp. 22–29. IEEE Computer Society, Los Alamitos (2002)
8. Haus, G., Longari, M.: A Multi-Layered, Time-Based Music Description Approach Based on XML. Computer Music Journal 29(1), 70–85 (2005)
9. Radulescu, M.: Orgelbüchlein, Turris, Cremona (1991)
10. Pinto, A., Haus, G.: A Novel XML Music Information Retrieval Method using Graph Invariants. ACM Transactions on Information Systems 25(4), art. 19 (2007)

New Music in the Atomic Age[*]

Else Marie Pade

Ophus Claussens vej 10, 2920 Charlottenlund, Denmark

In 1948 in France, a new musical language began to be heard: concrete music. "Contemporary music is based on contemporary sound: A perfect universe of sound is working around us," said tone engineer and composer Pierre Schaeffer. He was the one who got the idea and developed the opportunities for realizing it within the framework of the French national radio (RTF).

In that same year, Professor Werner Meyer Eppler in Bonn was working on his first attempts at electronic music (music that uses electro-acoustic apparatus), leading to these "nie erhörte Klänge" ("sounds never heard before" – changes in filtrations of overtones, modulations, speed variations etc).

Karlheinz Stockhausen was quick to seek out Werner Meyer Eppler – having first been to visit Pierre Schaeffer in Paris. Soon after these visits he became an employee at and later the head of the electronic studio that was established at Westdeutscher Rundfunk in Cologne.

In 1952 I heard a program on Radio Denmark (DR) called "Horizon" – an informative program on new trends and the like. On that particular day the program dealt with two musical movements ... I soon felt as if I was experiencing a déjà vu. Shortly afterwards, I contacted Pierre Schaeffer in Paris and later Karlheinz Stockhausen in Cologne. In 1954, I was at it myself.

I was working freelance for DR, doing background music – concrete and electronic mixed with synchronous passages – interviews etc for an experimental film about the amusement park Dyrehavsbakken. It was called A DAY AT THE DEER PARK CARNIVAL. "The experiment" was pretty well received, and some of the technicians – also from DR – stage managers, program people and I subsequently became a small group who received regular instruction at DR's acoustic sound lab by the internationally renowned engineer and researcher Holger Lauridsen (who also cooperated with Professor Eppler in Bonn).

We regularly applied for supplementary equipment so that the lab could be used as an electronic studio (almost) in line with Paris and Cologne. But the interest simply was not there in Denmark at the time (nor in the other Nordic countries, for that matter). It was not until the 1970's that Sweden had a breakthrough with the studio for electronic music in Stockholm (EMS).

---

[*] Translated by Lærke Pade.

S. Ystad, R. Kronland-Martinet, and K. Jensen (Eds.): CMMR 2008, LNCS 5493, pp. 283–284, 2009.

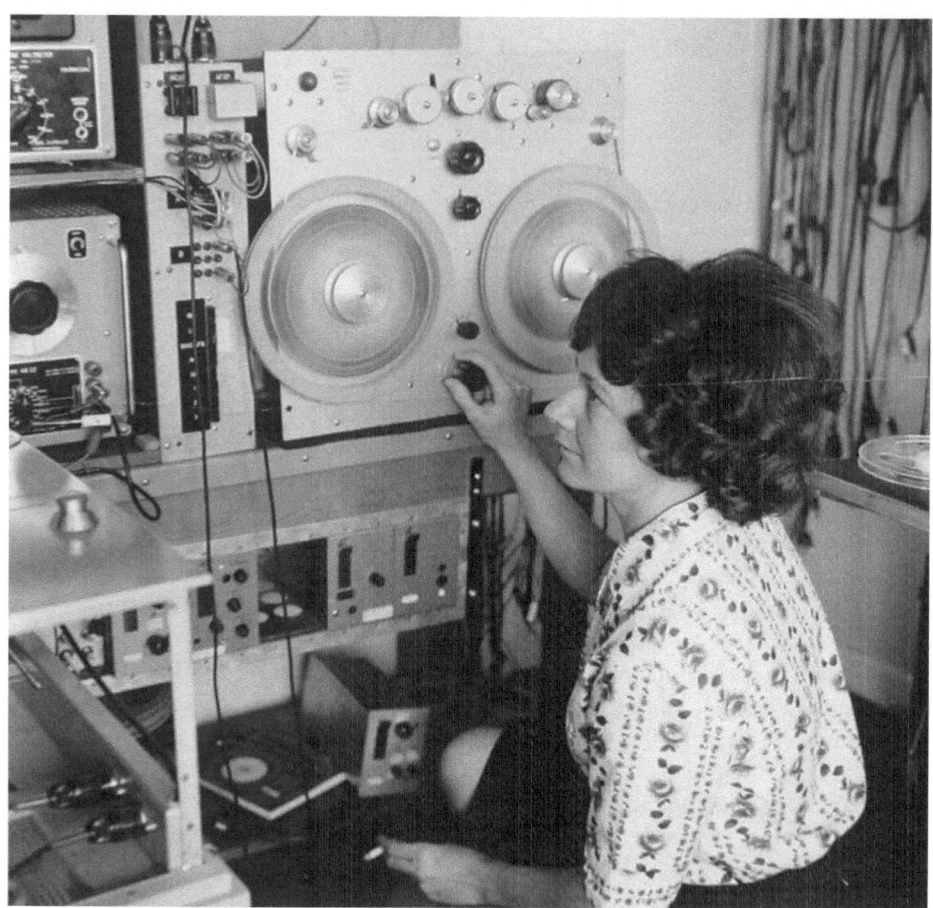

Fig. 1. Else Marie Pade in the DR studio

However, we were still allowed to work in the lab and to seek help from our colleagues abroad when we had difficulties. This permission worked for years and was in itself such a grand and generous gesture on the part of DR that none of the people who were involved will ever forget it.

Author Index